RULING PEACEFULLY

RULING PEACEFULLY

Cardinal Ercole Gonzaga and Patrician
Reform in Sixteenth-Century Italy

PAUL V. MURPHY

The Catholic University of America Press
Washington, D.C.

The paper used in this publication meets the minimum requirements of
American National Standards for Information Science—Permanence
of Paper for Printed Library Materials, ANSI Z39.48-1984.

∞

LIBRARY OF CONGRESS CATALOGING-IN-PUBLICATION DATA
Murphy, Paul V.
Ruling peacefully : Cardinal Ercole Gonzaga and patrician reform in
sixteenth-century Italy / Paul V. Murphy.
p. cm.
Includes bibliographical references and index.
ISBN-13: 978-0-8132-1478-8 (cloth : alk. paper)
ISBN-10: 0-8132-1478-5 (cloth : alk. paper)   1. Gonzaga, Ercole,
1505–1563.   2. Mantua (Italy)—History—16th century.   3. Mantua
(Italy)—Church history—16th century.   4. Cardinals—Italy—
Mantua—Biography.   5. Gonzaga family.   6. Mantua (Italy)—
Biography.   I. Title.
DG975.M32M87 2007
945´.2807092—dc22
2006009570

For Marcia

CONTENTS

ACKNOWLEDGMENTS

In the course of writing this book I have found assistance and support in many quarters. First of all I would like to acknowledge the staffs of the Archivio Segreto Vaticano, the Biblioteca Apostolica Vaticana, the Archivio di Stato, Mantova, and the Archivio Storico Diocesano di Mantova. Their professionalism and courtesy facilitated my work immeasurably. I am also indebted to the libraries of the University of Toronto, Loyola University of Chicago, and the University of San Francisco. Many individuals offered assistance along the way. In Mantua I received hospitality and encouragement from Msgr. Giancarlo Manzoli, Dr. Daniela Ferrari, Anthony Cashman, Stephanie Yuhl, Tony and Paola Durante, Iula Aiello and Sergio Pini, Raffaele Tamalio, and Franco and Sonia Moroni. In Rome the members of the Jesuit Historical Institute, Mark A. Lewis, S.J., Thomas M. McCoog, S.J., and James F. X. Pratt, S.J., in particular, all offered timely support. In Rome, too, John Felice supported my research in his own inimitable fashion.

Over the years various scholars have assisted me in clarifying my thought on the issues concerning Early Modern Catholicism. In particular I wish to recognize John W. O'Malley, S.J., Elisabeth Gleason, Konrad Eisenbichler, Martin Claussen, Thomas F. Mayer, and Megan Armstrong. Fundamental to my growth as a historian has been Paul F. Grendler, who oversaw my first efforts at making sense of Ercole Gonzaga. He remains an example to me of scholarly excellence and generous collegiality. I also acknowledge the many years of support that I have received from my colleagues in the history departments at the University of San Francisco and at John Carroll University. Additionally, Erik Ewen, Peter Togni, S.J., Thomas Lucas, S.J., Ruth McGugan, and Barbara St. Marie all offered more insight and assistance than they might imagine.

My family deserves recognition in a special way. My parents, Richard J. and Elizabeth R. Murphy, were and are my first and best teachers. They provided the foundation for any success I have achieved as a scholar. My children, Daniel, Julia, and Elizabeth, have helped to keep my feet on the ground. For my wife, Marcia Anne Leous, I reserve these final words of recognition. Her willingness to support my work and enter upon the circuitous journey of an academic career has allowed me to accomplish anything here that is of value. Without her this book would not have been written and to her it is dedicated.

Some material in Chapter 2 appeared in different form in "A Worldly Reform: Honor and Pastoral Practice in the Career of Cardinal Ercole Gonzaga (1505–1563)," *Sixteenth Century Journal* 31, no. 2 (Summer 2000): 399–418. Some material in Chapter 3 appeared in "Politics, Piety and Reform: Lay Religiosity in Sixteenth-Century Mantua," in *Confraternities and Catholic Reform in Italy, France and Spain.* © 1999 by Thomas Jefferson University Press. Material in Chapter 4 appeared in different form in "Rumors of Heresy in Sixteenth-Century Mantua," in *Religion and Culture in Early Modern Europe. Sixteenth Century Essays and Studies.* © 2005 by Truman State University. Other material in Chapter 4 appeared in "Between 'Spirituali' and 'Intransigenti': Cardinal Ercole Gonzaga and Patrician Reform in Sixteenth-Century Italy," *Catholic Historical Review* 88, no. 3 (July 2002): 45–54.

ABBREVIATIONS

Manuscript Sources

ASV, AC	Archivio Segreto Vaticano, Acta Camerarii
ASV, AV	Archivio Segreto Vaticano, Acta Vicecancellarii
ASM, AG	Archivio di Stato, Mantova, Archivio Gonzaga
ASM, AN	Archivio di Stato, Mantova, Archivio Notarile
ASM, AP	Archivio di Stato, Mantova, Archivio Portioli
ASDM, MV	Archivio Storico Diocesano di Mantova, *Mensa Vescovile*
BAV, Barb. Lat.	Biblioteca Apostolica Vaticana, fondo Barbariniana Latina
BPP, Affò	Ireneo Affò, *Vita del Cardinale Ercole Gonzaga,* Biblioteca Palatina di Parma, Ms. Affò 1207, ff. 183–257

Printed Sources

Adams	H. M. Adams. *Catalogue of Books Printed on the Continent of Europe, 1501–1600, in Cambridge Libraries.* 2 vols. Cambridge: Cambridge University Press, 1967.
ARSRSP	*Archivio della Reale Società Romana di Storia Patria.*
ASL	*Archivio storico lombardo.*
CT	Societas Goerresiana, editor. *Concilium Tridentinum. Diariorum, actorum, epistolarum, tractatuum, nova collectio.* 13 vols. Freiburg: Societas Goerresiana, 1901–2001.
DBI	*Dizionario biografico degli italiani.* Rome: Istituto della enciclopedia italiana, 1960–.
Dittrich	Franz Dittrich. *Regesten und Briefe des Kardinals Gasparo Contarini (1483–1542).* Braunsberg: Huye, 1885.
Eubel	Conrad Eubel. *Hierarchia catholica medii et recentioris aevi.* Regensburg: Schmitz-Kallenberg, 1923. Vol. 3: *Saeculum XVI ab anno 1503 complectens.*

Friedensburg   Walter Friedensburg. "Der Briefwechsel Gasparo Contarini's mit
Ercole Gonzaga." *Quellen und Forschungen aus italienischen
Archiven und Bibliotheken* 2 (1899), 161–222.

GSLI   *Giornale storico della letteratura italiana.*

Jedin, *History*   Hubert Jedin. *A History of the Council of Trent.* Vols. 1 and 2.
Translated by Ernest Graf, O.S.B. London: Nelson and Sons,
1949.

Jedin, *Storia*   Hubert Jedin. *Storia del Concilio di Trento.* Vols. 2, 3, and 4.
Translated by Giulietta Basso. Revised by Igino Rogger. Brescia:
Morcelliana, 1962, 1973, 1975, 1981.

Pagano   Sergio Pagano. *Il Processo di Endimio Calandra e L'Inquisizione a
Mantova nel 1567–1568.* Studi e Testi, no. 339. Vatican City:
Biblioteca Apostolica Vaticana, 1991.

Pastor   Ludwig von Pastor. *History of the Popes from the Close of the
Middle Ages.* Vols. 7–17. Translated by Ralph Francis Kerr.
London: Kegan, Paul, Trench, Trubner & Co., 1908–28.

RSI   *Rivista storica italiana.*

Scaduto   Mario Scaduto. *Storia della Compagnia di Gesù in Italia.* Vol. 3,
L'Epoca di Giacomo Lainez, 1556–1565. Il governo, vol. 4, *L'Epoca
di Giacomo Lainez, 1556–1565. L'azione.* Rome: Civiltà Cattolica,
1963–74.

STC, German   *Short Title Catalogue of Books Printed in German-Speaking
Countries and German Books Printed in Other Countries from 1455
to 1600, now in the British Museum.* London: Trustees of the
British Museum, 1962.

STC, Italian   *Short Title Catalogue of Books Printed in Italy and of Italian Books
Printed in Other Countries from 1465 to 1600, now in the British
Museum.* London: Trustees of the British Museum, 1958.

INTRODUCTION

Before dawn on March 4, 1563, the funeral procession set out from the city of Trent. Cardinal Ercole Gonzaga (b. 1505), papal legate and president of the Council of Trent, had died two nights earlier. His remains lay in a casket borne on a bier while a servant carried a crucifix before it. The casket was surrounded by twelve lighted torches. The long cortege included more than 150 mounted mourners, among them several bishops and numerous family members. In the view of many, the death of Gonzaga could not have come at a less favorable moment. The council was on the verge of collapse because controversies racked the gathering; this death further shook the assembled prelates.

The testimony of those present about Gonzaga's death and funeral offers a glimpse of the world of late Renaissance social norms and early modern piety. A prolonged decay in health that included increasing deafness and severe gout had preceded his death. During that decline the famed anatomist Gabriello Fallopio was summoned to Trent to care for the cardinal. During the last week of February Gonzaga developed a fever that may have been pneumonia. Physicians in attendance resorted to bleedings on at least two occasions before Gonzaga's life ended.[1] According to those who attended him or witnessed his fi-

---

1. On Gonzaga's final illness and death see Ludovico Nucci to Cardinal Giovanni Morone, March 4, 1563, in *Concilium Tridentinum. Diariorum, actorum, epistolarum, tractatuum, nova collectio* (Freiburg: Societas Goerresiana, 1901–2001), 2/1: 587, n. 2 (hereafter cited as CT); Muzio Calini, *Lettere conciliari (1561–1563),* ed. Alberto Marani (Brescia: Fratelli Geroldi, 1963), 414ff.; Hubert Jedin, *Storia del Concilio di Trento* (Brescia: Morcelliana, 1981), 4/2: 405 (hereafter cited as Jedin, *Storia*). For the description of the cortege see Ludovico Firmano's account in CT, 2/1: 565.

nal days, Gonzaga had prepared himself for death both materially and spiritually. He looked after his family and servants by adding a codicil to his will that outlined generous bequests. The highest ranking members of his household received legacies of as much as 1,000 scudi. These included his court philosopher, his major-domo, and his house physician, the last of whom, according to one observer, had served quite poorly on the occasion of his final illness. Others, such as his valet and master of the stalls, received as much as 500 scudi, including a gift to a chamberlain that one commentator noted because the man had only been in Gonzaga's service for a short time. Gonzaga also left 6,000 scudi to the Monte di Pietà in Mantua and 4,000 scudi to the Society of Jesus for the purpose of establishing a Jesuit college there.[2]

After taking care of these very worldly responsibilities of a great lord, Gonzaga turned to more spiritual matters. He made his confession twice in his final days, received other sacraments of the Church "in a most devoted manner," and celebrated mass on the day before he died. On March 2 he made his last confession to his ordinary confessor, a Carmelite monk, and received *viaticum* from Diego Laínez, superior general of the Jesuits. Later that evening Laínez returned to offer Gonzaga the sacrament of last anointing of the sick.[3] It was said that an hour before his death, as he lay surrounded by clergy, family

---

2. Archivio di Stato, Mantova, Archivio Gonzaga, b. 333, ff. 267–71 (hereafter cited as ASM, AG). See also Ludovico Nucci to Cardinal Giovanni Morone, March 4, 1563, CT, 2/1: 587, n. 2. In the transcriptions that I have done, I have modernized punctuation and accentuation, and expanded abbreviations, but have left spelling as it appears in the documents.

The ducat and the scudo were major units of gold coinage in early modern Europe. The Venetian ducat officially weighted 3.559 grams and, along with the Florentine florin, was the primary international medium of exchange. The scudo was a gold coin worth approximately 93 percent of the ducat. On such currencies see Barbara McClung Hallman, *Italian Cardinals and the Church as Property, 1492–1563* (Berkeley: University of California Press, 1985), 15–16. (Hereafter cited as Hallman.)

3. Juan Polanco to Peter Canisius, March 3, 1563, in Peter Canisius, *Beati Petri Canisii, Societatis Jesu, Epistolae et Acta,* 6 vols., ed. Otto Braunsberger (Freiburg: Herder, 1896–1923), 4: 106–10. See also *Lainii Monumenta,* 6: 702, vol. 51 of *Monumenta Historica Societatis Iesu* (Madrid: Institutum Historicum Societatis Iesu, 1916).

members including his nephew Duke Guglielmo Gonzaga of Mantua, and servants, Gonzaga requested that a theologian in his service read to him the passion narrative from the Gospel of Matthew. When the reader reached the passage where Christ prays, "Lord, if it is possible, take this cup away, but if not, let your will be done," Gonzaga turned to look upon a crucifix and whispered those words under his breath. Death came soon thereafter and the gathered clerics then read the customary prayers for the dead. Gabriele Paleotti, in his diary of events at the council, wrote that "incredible grief seized all on account of Gonzaga's probity, humanity, and virtue."[4] Egidio Foscarari, bishop of Modena, also noted the aura of piety at the cardinal's deathbed, claiming that he had "never seen anyone die so easily and that those who witnessed it were convinced that Gonzaga must have been transported directly to paradise." After the death, he added, "the council was so paralyzed that one would have thought it were Good Friday in Trent."[5] Others were less flattering. An opponent of Cardinal Gonzaga, Tommaso Caselli, O.P., a staunch papalist who had resented the Mantuan's willingness to appease the Spanish and French representatives at the council, wrote that in Gonzaga's death "God had offered the grace to free the council from servitude."[6]

The morning following the death, the master of the Pontifical Chapel, Girolamo Macchabei, celebrated a funeral mass in the cathedral of Trent in the presence of the entire council. Later, the corpse, dressed in full cardinalatial robes, lay in state in the cathedral on a table covered in crimson velvet for a public display of mourning that continued for the remainder of the day. When the cortege finally set out for Mantua and entombment of the cardinal, it presented a regal

4. CT, 3: 587, March 2, 1563.

5. Egidio Foscarari to Cardinal Giovanni Morone, March 4, 1563, Archivio Segreto Vaticano, Acta Vicecancellarii, Conc. 32, fol. 92s (hereafter cited as ASV, AV). As pious as were the descriptions of his death, the cardinals in Rome remembered Gonzaga in consistory in secular and aristocratic terms as *vir nobilissimus magnae virtutis, prudentiae et probitatis.* See Conrad Eubel, *Hierarchia catholica medii et recentioris aevi*, vol. 3, *Saeculum XVI ab anno 1503 complectens* (Regensburg: Schmitz-Kallenberg, 1923), 3:21 (hereafter cited as Eubel).

6. Jedin, *Storia*, 4/1: 407.

spectacle. Duke Guglielmo Gonzaga went ahead to oversee preparations for the burial in Mantua. Another protégé, Duke Cesare Gonzaga of Guastalla, joined the procession on its way. A third relative,
the future Cardinal Scipione Gonzaga, whose education Ercole Gonzaga had supervised and who was then studying at Padua, raced to
the obsequies and joined the procession near Verona. He complained
later that his late arrival caused his share of the cardinal's estate to be
diminished to a mere 6,000 scudi.[7] When Ercole Gonzaga's remains
were finally placed in the sacristy of the cathedral of Mantua, they
rested beside those of his younger brother and confidante, Ferrante,
who had died six years earlier in the Netherlands while in the service
of King Philip II.

The events and commentary surrounding the death of Ercole Gonzaga provide a rich tapestry of detail on the social, political, and religious roles of this prominent figure. His display of patronage and concern for the material well-being of his clients could fairly be said to
have the odor of all those practices that attracted the criticism of reformers, and it occurred almost simultaneously with religious practices
that seemed to raise the curtain on the drama of Counter-Reformation
piety. It is precisely this intermingling of the material and the spiritual,
the patrician and the reformer, that lies at the heart of this study of the
work of Cardinal Ercole Gonzaga.

Despite the magnificence of his funeral and the significance of a
career that included friendships with numerous prominent reformers, both Catholic and Protestant, near-election to the papacy, nearly a quarter of a century of reform activity in the diocese of Mantua,
and a period of stormy activity as the papal legate and president of
the Council of Trent, Cardinal Ercole Gonzaga has not previously attracted much scholarly attention. As long ago as the nineteenth century Ludwig von Pastor lamented the fact that Gonzaga had yet to
find his biographer. Decades later Hubert Jedin reiterated that statement.[8] This lack of due attention resulted partially from Gonzaga's ex-

7. Scipione Gonzaga, *Commentariorum rerum suarum libri tres* (Rome: Salomonium, 1791), 35.
8. Ludwig von Pastor, *The History of the Popes from the Close of the Middle Ages,*

tended residence in Mantua, somewhat removed from the activities of his colleagues in Rome. Until his arrival at Trent in 1561 Gonzaga did not take center stage in the drama of reform in Italy as did his friends Cardinals Gasparo Contarini and Reginald Pole. Historians looking for admirable models of Catholic reforming prelates did not embrace him because his career was seen as too checkered for that role. Finally, his enormous correspondence, the volume of which was due in part precisely to his need to keep informed of the views and activities of friends and enemies who were often quite distant, may have discouraged past scholars from studying it more fully. But this lack of attention to Gonzaga, I must admit, has been an opportunity for which I remain grateful. This book attempts to present Gonzaga as fully and as clearly as his importance requires.

In many respects, Gonzaga was a typical Renaissance prelate from a noble family—wealthy, urbane, worldly. He enjoyed great ecclesiastical wealth, fathered five children, and engaged in Italian and European politics. Nevertheless, in the course of his life he also exhibited a real commitment to reforming the Church and gave serious attention to the theological debates of his day. The seeming paradox in this combination of earnestness in his approach to reform and his own unreformed lifestyle was one of the striking realities of his career. It stands out as a characteristic of his patrician world view. This paradox may be viewed as the intersection of two axes in Gonzaga's life. One axis ran vertically from the top of Italian society to the bottom and remained fairly constant throughout his life. Gonzaga was raised to play a key role as a leading member of the Gonzaga family, the rulers of Mantua. This role placed him at the upper end of a social scale in which he oversaw the lives of those who inhabited Mantua, from the members of the Gonzaga court to the peasants of the Mantuan countryside. His life also may be considered along a horizontal axis that extended from the High Renaissance, before the Sack of Rome, through the final pe-

trans. Ralph Francis Kerr (London: Kegan, Paul, Trench, Trubner, 1908–28), 11: 505 (hereafter cited as Pastor); Hubert Jedin, "Il figlio di Isabella d'Este," in *Chiesa della fede, Chiesa della storia: Saggi scelti* (Brecia: Morcelliana, 1972), 511 (hereafter cited as Jedin, "Il figlio").

riod of the Council of Trent. The Italy in which he lived underwent great religious and political change from the time of his studies in Bologna in the early 1520s, to the establishment of Habsburg hegemony in Italy in the 1530s and 1540s, to the promulgation of the Tridentine decrees in the 1560s. Gonzaga's life reflects those changes.

These axes highlight two important characteristics in the life of Ercole Gonzaga. First, his youth provided him with all of the intellectual and material benefits available to the privileged of Renaissance Italy. Like his near contemporary, Pope Paul III, Ercole Gonzaga grew up to be a Renaissance prince-bishop. It was his fate to carry the burden of that Renaissance formation into the era of the Reformation. In many respects the unquestioned standards of behavior by which he was raised underwent modification in the course of his life and the expectations and possibilities for patricians and prelates changed between the time of his youth and his mature adulthood. But this Renaissance formation, especially in its literary and philosophical aspects, also served him in the exercise of his duties as bishop of Mantua by equipping him with the intellectual tools necessary for the task. Second, Gonzaga reformed his diocese and maintained contacts with other reformers as a patron who approached ecclesiastical questions from the position of a prince-bishop. His sense of his own social superiority, family honor, and civic responsibility contributed greatly to his reform in the diocese of Mantua and to his attitude toward reform in the Church at large. It also bred in him a willingness to hold philosophical and theological discussions with close associates and members of his household that he would never permit among the ordinary inhabitants of Mantua. With this combination of attitudes Gonzaga exhibited an approach to his religious responsibilities that may best be described as one of patrician reform, that is, a reform not unrelated to his role as a great lord of Renaissance Italy.

Gonzaga's life of great personal and public activity stands as a background that is sometimes consonant, sometimes dissonant with the principal theme of this study: Gonzaga's commitment to reform and his close relationships with reformers as an example of late Renaissance religion and culture. Historians have struggled to reconcile

the apparent inconsistencies between Gonzaga's private life and his reform activities. Ludwig von Pastor attributed Gonzaga's children to
the days of his youth when he was yet a "votary" of the Renaissance.
He wanted to see at least a portion of the life and career of Gonzaga
as unsullied enough to place him in the Catholic reform camp. Pastor
claimed that sometime after he became a cardinal, Gonzaga "began to
take life more seriously."[9] But there is no evidence for this chronological distinction. Gonzaga's children and his involvement in the traffic
in ecclesiastical benefices were not youthful indiscretions. They were
significant aspects of the lifestyle of a prince-bishop whose responsibilities required that he maintain family honor and *la bella figura* on
the one hand, and work for ecclesiastical reform on the other. Philip
McNair damns Gonzaga with faint praise by saying that he embodied
the Renaissance ideal of the *mens sana in corpore sano,* but that "from
the standpoint of the Christian Church his *mens* was a shade too *sana,*
and [he] preferred to coast with common sense [rather] than put to
sea with faith."[10]

Each of these attempts to understand him mischaracterizes Gonzaga by trying to fit him into rigid historiographical frameworks that
seek to organize the religious figures of late Renaissance Italy according to clear and unambiguous categories. The life of Ercole Gonzaga
defies such easy categorization. He was a patrician reformer who saw
his responsibilities to the Church and to his family as inextricably in-
tertwined. His role as a member of a ruling house in northern Italy
served as the ground for his understanding of his duties as a bishop as
well as ducal regent. His sense of responsibility to his family's interests
enhanced his willingness to engage in reform of the local Church. Yet
he saw no inconsistency in not living up to the standards he imposed
on his subjects and in this he was typical of his class. This patrician reform model serves as a useful lens for analyzing the work of Gonzaga
at various stages in his career. Moreover, it helps to bring into focus
broader cultural and religious problems on the wider Italian and Eu-

9. Pastor, 11: 506.
10. Philip McNair, *Peter Martyr in Italy: An Anatomy of Apostasy* (Oxford: Claren-
don Press, 1967), 181.

ropean stage. Gonzaga's career exemplifies much of the history of Italy and the Catholic Church in an era of uneasy transition. The process of change that the Church underwent in the sixteenth century only gradually provided theological clarity. This lack of definition exhibited itself not only in theology but also in the lives and works of individuals, including the leaders of the Church. Ercole Gonzaga, who does not fit easily into the categories of spiritual reformer, or intransigent inquisitor, or unreformed noble prelate, may represent the age more fully than any of those ideal types.

Sources for a study of Gonzaga's life and work lie primarily in his letters. Since he spent most of his career in Mantua, Gonzaga stayed in communication with Rome, his friends, and other European courts by means of an enormous correspondence: sixty-nine *buste,* or large file folders, and codices of letters received and written by Ercole Gonzaga. The bulk of these are contained in the Archivio di Stato, Mantova. A good deal of material is also available in the Biblioteca Apostolica Vaticana, fondo Barberiniana Latina. Substantial material, available in the Archivio Storico Diocesano di Mantova, includes records of episcopal visitations as well as the *Mensa Vescovile,* or Gonzaga's household records. Finally, material on Gonzaga is to be found in other Italian and European archives and libraries. Scholars have previously exploited his letters in order to research those with whom Gonzaga corresponded. Indeed, many are familiar with Gonzaga solely through the tangential remarks of scholars looking at these other people. This is the first attempt to study this rich source for the purpose of understanding Gonzaga and his role in the broader spectrum of European events.[11]

This study of the activities and the thought of Ercole Gonzaga brings attention long overdue to an important sixteenth-century cardinal's attitude toward religious reform and society at large. In chapter 1, his family's political and cultural aspirations, his formal education in

---

11. A recent study of Gonzaga that offers a popular presentation of his career but does not employ archival material or recent scholarship is Luigi Pescasio, *Cardinale Ercole Gonzaga: presidente del Concilio di Trento (1505–1563)* (Suzzara: Edizioni Bottazzi, 1999).

Mantua and Bologna, and further studies throughout his life serve to highlight the various cultural and intellectual influences on Cardinal Gonzaga. Chapter 2 addresses Gonzaga's adherence to, and divergence from, contemporary notions of the role of a bishop. Chapter 3 examines his pastoral activity in the diocese of Mantua and provides an example of a vigorous reform program carried out in the years before the Council of Trent that was not merely derivative of reforms elsewhere. In chapter 4, I address Gonzaga's relationships with a variety of individuals involved in reform in Italy, both those who remained within the Church of Rome and some who left it. These relationships and his view of them reveal Gonzaga as a complex man whose conservatism did not overwhelm his considerable open-mindedness. Chapter 5 presents Gonzaga's activities as ducal regent in Mantua from 1540 to 1557, when he directly defended the political interests of the Gonzaga family. In chapter 6, I examine Gonzaga's approach to the broader questions of institutional reform in the Church discussed at the Council of Trent both before his departure for the council and during his period as papal legate. In all of these areas, Gonzaga acted as a patrician reformer whose life reflects the combined influences of sixteenth-century Italian intellectual life, the call for reform in the Church, and the values of a northern Italian ruling family. As he indicated to a colleague, on the authority of Thomas Aquinas, his role as bishop was "to rule peacefully" the diocese in his charge.[12]

12. Biblioteca Apostolica Vaticana, fondo Barberiniana Latina (hereafter cited as BAV, Barb. Lat.), codex 5789, ff. 76r–76v, Ercole Gonzaga to Gian Matteo Giberti, November 13, 1537.

RULING PEACEFULLY

CHAPTER I

THE INTELLECTUAL AND CULTURAL
FORMATION OF A CARDINAL

Ercole Gonzaga's upbringing in the ruling family of Mantua fundamentally shaped his world view. The Gonzaga had ruled there since Luigi Gonzaga took power in a coup d'etat in 1328. At the heart of that state lay the city of Mantua which, in the lifetime of Cardinal Gonzaga, harbored a population of approximately 25,000. The city sits on the banks of the Mincio River, a few miles north of where it joins the Po. In the Middle Ages and the Renaissance, marshes and a canal made an island of the city, protecting it from military incursions until the seventeenth century. The relatively low-lying position of Mantua accounts for its thick fogs in winter and its burdensome humidity in summer. The surrounding countryside spreads out in level and well-watered fields that produced the grain that helped to make Mantua a desirable ally in the sixteenth century.[1]

The Gonzaga had maintained themselves in power during the two centuries prior to Cardinal Gonzaga's life by skillful diplomacy and astute use of their military forces. In 1434 the Holy Roman Emperor Sigismond elevated the lordship of Mantua to the status of a marquisate. As such the Gonzaga further legitimized their hold on Mantua and enhanced their role as feudal vassals of the emperors. As long as

---

1. Leonardo Mazzoldi, Renato Giusti, and Rinaldo Salvadori, eds., *Mantova: La Storia*, vol. 2, *Da Ludovico Secondo Marchese a Francesco Secondo Duca* (Mantua: Istituto Carlo D'Arco per la storia mantovana, 1963), 425–26 (hereafter cited as Mazzoldi, *Mantova: La Storia*).

the emperors were absent from Italy, there were few limits on their independence. Further, their activities as *condottieri* made them useful to other Italian princes and governments and helped them to preserve their own power. Before the French invasion of 1494 such agile diplomacy won for the Gonzaga a relatively secure place in northern Italy. But the Italian Wars (1494–1559) that almost coincided with the life of Cardinal Gonzaga, presented serious challenges to this geopolitical position. The precarious nature of this diplomacy has led to the description of the Gonzaga state as a clay vessel among iron pots.[2]

Ercole Gonzaga was born to one of those *condottieri*, Francesco Gonzaga (1466–1519) and his wife, Isabella d'Este (1474–1539). His birth came at a time of cooperation between his father and King Louis XII of France, so the infant was baptized with the name Luigi in honor of the French king. Nevertheless, Isabella ensured that the child would always be known by the name of her father, Ercole.[3] Ercole's older brother, Federico (1500–40), inherited the marquisate of Mantua upon the death of their father, Francesco, and continued the tradition of Gonzaga art patronage initiated by his predecessors. In particular he employed Giulio Romano, who designed and constructed the Palazzo del Te and portions of the ducal palace. For a time Federico continued the Gonzaga diplomatic tradition of balancing among the French, the Habsburgs, and the popes in the affairs of northern Italy. By his marriage to Margherita Paleologa, the daughter of the marquis of Monferrato, Federico eventually acquired his father-in-law's principality. He also lived a somewhat dissolute life and died at the age of forty.

Ercole's younger brother and close confidante, Ferrante (1507–57), spent his life in service to the Emperor Charles V and King Philip II as viceroy of Sicily and governor of Milan. He eventually established a cadet branch of the Gonzaga family at Guastalla. His close relationship with Charles V enhanced the cooperation between the Gonzaga

2. See Alessandro Luzio, *L'Archivio Gonzaga di Mantova. La corrispondenza familiare, amministrativa, e diplomatica* (Verona: Mondadori, 1922), 2: 225 (hereafter cited as Luzio, *L'Archivio*).

3. Ireneo Affò, *Vita del Cardinale Ercole Gonzaga,* Biblioteca Palatina di Parma, Ms. Affò 1207, f. 1 (hereafter cited as BPP, Affò).

and the Habsburgs until the emperor's death. Ferrante continued to serve the Habsburgs until his own death on campaign in the Netherlands.[4] Ercole's oldest sibling, Eleonora (1494–1570), married Francesco Maria della Rovere, the duke of Urbino. Ercole maintained a close relationship with her and her husband throughout his life. The other two children of Francesco and Isabella were daughters named Ippolita (1501–70), who entered the Dominican convent of San Vincenzo in Mantua, and Livia (1508–69), who took the name Suor Paola when she joined the Poor Clares in the Mantuan convent of Corpus Domini, later known as Santa Paola.

From his infancy, Isabella d'Este planned the ecclesiastical career of her second son. On the day of his birth she claimed that he would make "un bel papono," a fine pope.[5] Isabella's high hopes for his career led her to oversee in great detail his early education in Mantua and later university studies at Bologna from 1522 to 1525. His early schooling drew from the cultural milieu of the court of Mantua in particular. Since the fifteenth century Mantua had been a significant center of Renaissance art and humanism. Marquis Gianfrancesco Gonzaga had brought Vittorino da Feltre to Mantua in 1423 to open his famous humanist school, the Casa Giocosa. Gonzaga's training reflected the humanist reforms of the fifteenth century and Vittorino's ongoing influence. Later, Marquis Ludovico Gonzaga employed Leonbattista Alberti and Andrea Mantegna on building projects and painting in the city. The marriage of Francesco Gonzaga to Isabella d'Este in 1490 was of exceptional importance for further cultural and educational developments in Renaissance Mantua.[6] Isabella was one of

4. On the life of Ferrante see Raffaele Tamalio, *Ferrante Gonzaga alla corte spagnola di Carlo V* (Mantua: Gianluigi Arcari Editore, 1991).

5. ASM, AG, b. 2994, 52r–52v, "Speramo devenirà un bel papono." Cited in Roberto Brunelli, *Diocesi di Mantova*, vol. 8 of *Storia religiosa della Lombardia* (Brescia: Editrice La Scuola, 1986), 101 (hereafter cited as Brunelli).

6. On Isabella d'Este see Julia Cartwright, *Isabella d'Este, Marchioness of Mantua, 1474–1539, a study of the Renaissance* (London: Murray, 1903). See also Clifford Brown, *Isabella d'Este and Lorenzo da Pavia: Documents for the History of Art and Culture in Renaissance Mantua*, Travaux d'humanisme et Renaissance, no. 189 (Geneva: Droz, 1982).

the truly remarkable women of the Renaissance. She came to Mantua from the ducal court of Ferrara where she had won respect for her intelligence, learning, and appreciation for the arts. At Mantua there revolved around her a court whose riches allowed for a flourishing literary and theatrical community. The list of her correspondents reads like an index of the literati of late fifteenth- and early sixteenth-century Italy. This highly cultivated woman took great care in the formation of her second son, Ercole.

A humanist school still operated at the location of the Casa Giocosa throughout Cardinal Gonzaga's life. In his boyhood Francesco Vigilio, the tutor of Federico, operated the school. Vigilio's curriculum combined Latin and Italian studies. Students in his *ginnasio letterario,* as in most other humanist schools, were introduced to Latin by way of an introductory manual known as the "Donatus" and classical texts of Virgil, Ovid, and Livy. Italian studies consisted of the *Canzoniere* of Petrarch and Matteo Maria Boiardo's *Orlando Innamorato.* The curriculum also included recitation of Latin comedies by Plautus and Terence and instruction in *"canto."*[7] Isabella d'Este was accustomed to being present with her court to hear the dramatic recitations. It is quite likely that, apart from his own formal education, young Ercole witnessed these presentations. Specific information on Ercole's primary education is limited. His earliest teacher was Antonio Guarino, of whom little is known. He may have been the grandson of the humanist school master Guarino Guarini of Verona. Battista Guarino (1425–1513), Guarino's son, had been the teacher of Isabella d'Este.[8] Between 1514 and 1522 Antonio Guarino oversaw the education of both Ercole and his younger brother, Ferrante.[9]

7. Stefano Davari, *Notizie storiche intorno allo studio pubblico ed ai maestri del secolo XV e XVI che tennero scuola in Mantova tratte dall'Archivio Storico Gonzaga di Mantova* (Mantua: Segna, 1876), 14, 20.

8. On Antonio and Battista Guarino see Alessandro Luzio and Rodolfo Renier, "La coltura e relazioni letterarie di Isabella d'Este Gonzaga," *Giornale storico della letteratura italiana* 35 (1900): 219 (hereafter cited as GSLI).

9. ASM, AG, libri di mandati 1517–18, ff. 129r and 151r. See also ASM, AG, b. 2126a, unnumbered fascicle of letters from Isabella d'Este to Battista Malatesta, October 9, 1522, for a reference to Guarino.

Pope Leo X made Ercole administrator of the diocese of Mantua when his uncle Cardinal Sigismondo Gonzaga resigned in 1521, and his secondary education soon came to an end. In March of 1522 his mother wrote to her elder son, the Marquis Federico, of her plans for Ercole's university training, noting Ercole's great desire to study *"let-tere,"* and to do so outside of Mantua. She had consulted with Cardinal Sigismondo and had decided not to lose the opportunity. She had determined to send the young man to Bologna, a university that he appeared willing to attend.[10] While the letter continues with a deferential nod to the official dignity of her elder son and his thoughts on the matter, it was clear that Isabella had already made her decision. A woman who would soon brave the Sack of Rome in 1527 in order to acquire the red hat for Ercole was not likely to be put off by any considerations of economy that the marquis might have.

The seventeen-year-old prince left Mantua to take up university studies at Bologna in December of 1522. In addition to the prestige of the university itself, a Mantuan professor attracted Gonzaga. Pietro Pomponazzi (1462–1525) oversaw the education of Ercole during his nearly two and a half years in Bologna and left a profound impact on the young man. Pomponazzi pursued an academic career especially notable for his speculations on the mortality of the soul. An element of these speculations was his separation of the truths of faith from the conclusions of reason. This separation is sometimes referred to, somewhat inaccurately, as the theory of the "double truth." This theory holds that what may be demonstrated by reason may not support and may even contradict Christian revelation. As a practical matter Scholastic philosophers of the late Middle Ages and the Renaissance commonly held to this theory when faith and reason did not coincide. Pomponazzi applied it to his speculations on the soul in his *De immortalitate animae* of 1516. His position that the immortality of the soul could not be demonstrated by reason earned the criticism of conservatives for what they viewed as a rejection of Catholic or-

10. ASM, AG, b. 2126a, unnumbered fascicle of letters from Isabella Gonzaga to Federico Gonzaga, March 20, 1522.

thodoxy. His skepticism was founded on an interpretation of Aristotle in which the soul, the form of the body, does not exist apart from the body. With the death of the body the human soul ceases to have individual existence. As a corollary to that, the human intellect is dependent upon the senses for knowledge. The intellect, therefore, only attains to eternal knowledge, relatively speaking, through individual things. Pomponazzi published retractions of his opinions and dedicated them to Cardinal Sigismondo Gonzaga in 1518.[11] Whatever Pomponazzi believed, his students and the Gonzaga family regarded him highly. These questions about the soul and human knowledge were central to the intellectual milieu in which Ercole lived and studied for a significant portion of his youth. The young prelate maintained great devotion to Pomponazzi. The Mantuan archdeacon who had accompanied Gonzaga to Bologna, Alessandro Gabioneta, wrote that he "does not simply respect, he adores Maestro Peretto."[12]

A second important figure in Ercole's university studies was Lazzaro Bonamico (1477 or 1478–1552). While Pomponazzi saw to Ercole's initiation into Aristotelian philosophy, Bonamico directed his continuing studies in the humanities.[13] Born in Bassano in the Veneto, and a former student of Pomponazzi, he taught successively at Bologna, Rome, and Padua. For a time his preference for literature over philosophy inspired a spirited debate between Reginald Pole, an earlier student of his, and Cardinal Jacopo Sadoleto.[14] On three brief occasions

11. Scholars differ as to Pomponazzi's true religious views. Bruno Nardi holds that Pomponazzi sincerely held the orthodox views of Christianity, yet acknowledged a sharp division between faith and reason. Martin Pine has dissented from this view. He considers Pomponazzi's professions of faith disingenuous, and that in this the philosopher distinguished himself from the rest of the Italian Aristotelian tradition. See Bruno Nardi, *Saggi sull'aristotelismo padovano dal secolo XIV al XVI* (Florence: Sansoni, 1958), 24–26, 95–96; Martin Pine, *Pietro Pomponazzi: Radical Philosopher of the Renaissance* (Padua: Antenore, 1986), 32–33.

12. ASM, AG, b. 1149, f. 239v, Archdeacon Gabioneta to Isabella d'Este, December 12, 1522. ". . . non observa ma adora Maestro Peretto."

13. On Bonamico see R. Avesani, *Dizionario biografico degli italiani* (hereafter cited as DBI), s.v. "Bonamico, Lazzaro."

14. On this debate see Thomas F. Mayer, *Reginald Pole: Prince and Prophet* (Cambridge: Cambridge University Press, 2000), 53–54 (hereafter cited as Mayer, *Reginald Pole*).

he worked in Mantua as a tutor in the service of Cardinal Sigismondo Gonzaga. Bonamico's name does not appear on the lists of university instructors at Bologna. Instead, he acted as an independent master, and prominent families sought his services as a teacher for their sons. The Campeggi family called him to Bologna to act as the tutor for their children.[15]

It was not altogether clear when Ercole arrived in Bologna that Bonamico would agree to supervise the young patrician bishop of Mantua. Money was indeed an object. To Alessandro Gabioneta fell the responsibility of completing the financial agreements between the Gonzaga and the professors of Bologna. It seems that there was some difference between what the Gonzaga originally promised and what their agents in Bologna offered. Soon after Ercole took up residence in Bologna, Gabioneta wrote to Isabella d'Este, informing her that he had had an extensive discussion with Bonamico, who showed great interest in teaching Ercole and being of service to Isabella. The humanist was, however, somewhat unsettled because he claimed to be already receiving a fine salary from the Campeggi. How, Bonamico asked Gabioneta, could he leave that position for one offered by Isabella, and negotiated with the help of Pomponazzi, when the salary now offered by the Gonzaga did not correspond to the promise of three hundred ducats made earlier by another of Isabella's servants. Bonamico promised to respond by the following day.[16]

Perhaps it was the lavish display at Gonzaga's entrance into Bologna on the same day as his negotiation with Gabioneta that led Bonamico to drive a hard bargain. In a letter written on the day of his arrival, December 12, 1522, Ercole gave his mother a report of his progress from Mantua to Bologna. The Benedictines of the abbey of San Benedetto in Polirone had received him and offered hospitality. Count Galeotto II Pico had fired an artillery salute in his honor en route. Upon his approach to Bologna two hundred horsemen rode

---

15. Girolamo Tiraboschi, *Storia della letteratura italiana* (Florence: Molini, Landi, 1824), vol. 7, part 3, 1483 (hereafter cited as Tiraboschi, *Storia*).

16. ASM, AG, b. 1149, f. 239r, Archdeacon Gabioneta to Isabella d'Este, December 12, 1522.

out to meet Gonzaga and accompany him the last few miles. His arrival was met with cheers in the streets and the presence of the local nobility and the governor of the city. Green garlands decorated his door on that winter day. The walls of the house were hung with his own crest as well as those of the pope, the local governor, and those of the city's most influential residents. His apartments were furnished with tapestries and damask bed coverings.[17] Whatever hesitation the archdeacon Gabioneta showed about the price of Ercole's education, there was little skimping on his lifestyle.

Bonamico did not hold out for long. Pomponazzi had also used his influence on Bonamico to accept the offer. He informed Isabella that he and Gabioneta had decided to take advantage of the opportunity, increase their most recent offer, and pay Bonamico one hundred and seventy ducats per annum, a high salary for one in Bonamico's position.[18] The combination of Pomponazzi's influence with the attractiveness of Gonzaga patronage convinced Bonamico to accept the post of teacher to Ercole. On December 17 Bonamico wrote to Isabella in Latin of his satisfaction with the role he was to play in the education of the future cardinal. He also offered the promise, common among educators at all times, of the future success of the son. He complimented Isabella for her wisdom, prudence, and parental love.[19] He commended her for having worked so openhandedly. It was his desire that her son be worthy of the hope that she had placed in him, that he be worthy of that "highest glory" for which he was being educated.[20] But Bonamico also subtly reminded her of the cost of education. His carefully crafted appeal, citing both the past labors and future hopes of Isabella for the career of her son, expresses what was at

17. ASM, AG, b. 1149, f. 244r, Ercole Gonzaga to Isabella d'Este, December 12, 1522.

18. Ibid., ff. 239r–239v, Archdeacon Gabioneta to Isabella d'Este, December 12, 1522.

19. Ibid., f. 457r, Lazzaro Bonamico to Isabella d'Este, December 17, 1522. "Incredibili praeterea veroque illo parentum amore."

20. Ibid., f. 457r, Lazzaro Bonamico to Isabella d'Este, December 17, 1522. "Ut tantae spe filius te dignus, dignus Italiae luce ad Summam gloriam quam innocentissime erudiatur."

stake in his education. Bonamico complimented Isabella as a woman of learning not only by the content of the letter but by composing it in Latin. While Pomponazzi felt no need to do the same when he wrote to Isabella, Bonamico, a humanist, made a point of it. The end of this educational project was to make young Ercole worthy of the work of his mother and of the hopes of Italy. Surely the phrase *"ad Summam gloriam quam innocentissime erudiatur"* points to nothing other than her ambitions, expressed as early as the day of his birth, that Ercole attain the chair of Peter. But education has a cost: *"in primis opus est impense Laboras."* This is a subtle reference to salary. *"Impense"* may simply mean "pressingly." It is at least as likely, if not certain, that in this context it means "at great cost." In other words, Ercole's success would not come cheaply and neither would Bonamico.

Ercole continued his studies in Bologna both in his residence and at public lectures of the university. Although he rarely mentioned studies, letters of others shed light on them. Pomponazzi wrote to Isabella on December 14, 1522, and described the progress of Ercole in the days immediately after his arrival in Bologna. He informed her that Bonamico lectured daily to Gonzaga and spoke very well of him. Pomponazzi described the young bishop as ardent in his studies, thus offering hope that he would have great success in both Greek and Latin.[21] Gabioneta also mentioned his attentiveness to his studies. He informed Isabella that Gonzaga demonstrated a zeal for study that he had never shown in Mantua and interest in becoming acquainted with the bedels and the lecturers.[22]

Ercole's cousin Agostino Gonzaga, a companion at Bologna, wrote to Isabella on the progress of these studies. Bonamico apparently came to Gonzaga's residence to give instruction in the humanities, Cicero in particular. These lectures started sometime after two in the afternoon. Agostino added that this schedule gave Ercole the opportunity to use the morning for the study of philosophy. Pomponazzi came daily at about four in the afternoon in order to accompany Gonzaga to the

---

21. Ibid., f. 182r, Pietro Pomponazzi to Isabella d'Este, December 14, 1522.
22. Ibid., f. 239v, Archdeacon Gabioneta to Isabella d'Este, December 14, 1522.

place where he gave his lectures. At the time of that letter he taught on the *Meteorology* of Aristotle.[23] Agostino Gonzaga revealed Ercole's early attraction to natural philosophy, an interest that continued in later years. Pomponazzi made a strong impression upon him and a bond formed between mentor and disciple.

Ercole's university program included other teachers and subjects in addition to those already mentioned. Vincenzo di Prete, Ercole's secretary, informed Isabella in late February of 1523 that the recess from lectures at Carnival was over and Ercole's academic routine would recommence. This routine included hearing morning lectures in logic by Messer Giovanni Francesco Forno, more Cicero with Bonamico, and ongoing studies under Pomponazzi. The letter states, however, that Pomponazzi's lectures were by that time pro forma. After the time spent with Pomponazzi and a period of recreation, Gonzaga would compose letters, presumably in Latin, for Bonamico.[24] This passage indicates a number of things about Ercole's university studies. His humanistic studies were heavily Ciceronian and still somewhat basic. Bonamico concentrated on the skills learned on the secondary level, including letter writing. There is no specific reference in any of the letters to other authors. Ercole still attended Pomponazzi's lectures, but di Prete's admission that they were only "pro forma" may point to the philosopher's fragile health. Di Prete also mentioned another teacher of Ercole, Giovanni Francesco Forno.

Forno was born at the beginning of the sixteenth century of a Modenese family. He also studied at Bologna under Pomponazzi and may have disputed in his presence during the Dominican chapter meeting in Modena in 1520. Forno subsequently taught natural philosophy in the universities of Pisa and Bologna. In the early 1520s he taught

23. Ibid., f. 455v, Agostino Gonzaga to Isabella d'Este, December 20, 1522. Agostino Gonzaga was later to be the archbishop of Reggio di Calabria from 1537 to 1557. See Eubel, vol. 3, 284. On Pomponazzi's lectures on Aristotle's *Meteorology* see Franco Graiff, "I prodigi e l'astrologia nei commenti di Pietro Pomponazzi al *De Caelo*, alla *Meteora*, e al *De Generatione*," *Medioevo* 2 (1976): 331–61.

24. ASM, AG, b. 1150, f. 175r, Vincenzo di Prete to Isabella d'Este, February 20, 1523.

philosophy at Pisa before becoming Ercole's secretary, companion in studies, and *"ministro dei suoi affari"* no later than 1523. Forno later went to Rome to act as Ercole's agent, remaining there until the sack. The cathedral records of Modena refer to him as Ercole's secretary on the occasion of his death.[25] Forno died at Orvieto on March 13, 1528, when he was with Gonzaga at the court of Pope Clement VII. It seems that Isabella was responsible for providing Forno as a secretary. Gonzaga described him as a learned and well-mannered young man.[26] Ercole may have wanted a secretary who was a peer rather than an elder. With Pomponazzi, Bonamico, and di Prete, Gonzaga may have felt that Isabella had enough adults keeping their eyes on him. Forno also introduced Gonzaga to at least a rudimentary knowledge of Arabic. A letter from Forno to the Marquis Federico indicates that Gonzaga obtained the services of an Arab resident of Bologna for the purposes of translating Arabic books.[27]

Ercole's studies were not solely literary and philosophical. He also attended anatomical dissections directed by the professors of medicine. Such dissections were not frequent, lasted ten or twelve days, and attracted substantial audiences. Vincenzo di Prete informed Isabella that the dissections were seen as useful by all the students of Bologna and that Gonzaga intended to go to them two or three times.[28] This interest in anatomy did not disappear after his departure from Bologna. Twelve years after the conclusion of his studies Gonzaga paid for the binding and covering of at least two medical books, one of them an anatomy text, and at his death his library contained forty books of medicine.[29]

25. Girolamo Tiraboschi, *Biblioteca modenese; o Notizie della vita e delle opere degli scrittori nati negli stati del serenissimo signor duca di Modena* (Modena: Società tipografica, 1781–86), vol. 2, 349 and 351.

26. ASM, AG, b. 1149, f. 253r, Ercole Gonzaga to Isabella d'Este, January 29, 1522.

27. Alessandro Luzio, "Ercole Gonzaga allo studio di Bologna," GSLI 8 (1886): 383.

28. ASM, AG, b. 1150, f. 167r, Vincenzo di Prete to Isabella d'Este, January 10, 1523.

29. Archivio Storico Diocesano di Mantova, Mensa Vescovile, b. 1, f. 61r, 1 June

At times poor health, in particular a recurrent quartan, or malarial type, fever interrupted Ercole's studies. His secretary frequently mentioned Ercole's health in letters to Isabella. Pomponazzi and others advised Gonzaga to take time away from his studies until these fevers abated. According to di Prete, Gonzaga continued to study some in the mornings against doctor's orders.[30] The quartan sometimes kept him in bed for several days when he suffered *"parossismi"* from it. Ercole might not have written to his mother very much about his studies but he often mentioned his health. It is hard to tell how serious it was because he often used it as an explanation for not attending lectures. For example, in one letter di Prete gave Isabella a colorful description of the terrible fevers his master suffered but also mentioned that Ercole had just been at a banquet with about forty of his friends where he protested that he could not go to Mantua because he must first take care of his health. Travel to Mantua may have been too much for him, but travel to a local banquet was not.[31]

Gonzaga's student days at Bologna came to an abrupt conclusion when Pomponazzi died in May of 1525. In a one-sentence letter to his brother Federico, Ercole announced the event.[32] The loss of Pomponazzi must have greatly disturbed the young man. He provided for Pomponazzi's tomb in the Franciscan convent church of San Francesco in Mantua, the traditional burial place of the Gonzaga themselves.[33] For a time he also included the image of Pomponazzi on his

1537 (hereafter cited as ASDM, MV), "La notomia del corpo in 40." ASDM, MV, b. 1, f. 169r, December 29, 1537, mentions "Cornelio Celso": Cornelius Celsus, first-century author of *De medicina*. For the collection of medical books in the library see ASM, Archivio Notarile, Minute, Agostino Ragazzola, pacco 7566, April 1, 1563; 7567 (hereafter cited as ASM, AN).

30. ASM, AG, b. 1149, f. 168v, Vincenzo di Prete to Isabella d'Este, February 20, 1523.

31. Ibid., f. 168r, Vincenzo di Prete to Isabella d'Este, January 31, 1523. Quartan fever seems not to have been his only malady. In a letter to Isabella he referred to a bout with smallpox that he suffered when he had accompanied Cardinal Sigismondo Gonzaga to Rome on the occasion of the conclave that elected Clement VII in 1523. ASM, AG, b. 1150, f. 287r, Ercole Gonzaga to Isabella d'Este, March 17, 1524.

32. ASM, AG, b. 1150, f. 44r, Ercole Gonzaga to Federico Gonzaga, May 18, 1525.

33. Upon the deconsecration of San Francesco in the eighteenth century, the remains of Pomponazzi were transferred to the Basilica of Sant'Andrea. Only a fragment

personal seal.[34] Less than a month after his teacher's death Ercole wrote to his mother of his intention to depart from Bologna and return to Mantua.[35] Gonzaga's departure from Bologna signaled a shift in his academic interests. For a time he continued his education in Mantua under the direction of Romolo Amaseo (1489–1552).[36] Upon leaving Bologna Gonzaga invited the humanist to accompany him and help him continue his studies. This period of study under Amaseo lasted only a few months. It is, however, an early example of Gonzaga's relationship with the circle of Cardinal Pole, of whom Amaseo was a friend.[37] By January 1526 Gonzaga had gone to Venice, where he remained until the spring of 1527. There he continued his literary studies under Federico Malatesta, the brother of the Gonzaga ambassador to Venice. In his letters asking for payment from Ercole's older brother, Federico, who was financially responsible for Ercole, Malatesta revealed the content of Ercole's studies. Malatesta instructed Ercole in Latin, Greek, Hebrew, and possibly in the ancient Semitic Chaldean language as well. In a letter of August 26, 1526, he asked Federico to acquire Chaldean books, perhaps in Rome, so that he might continue his studies in that language.[38] Malatesta expressed repeated satisfaction with Ercole's progress.[39] Years later Bernardo Navagero, the Venetian ambassador to Mantua, attested to Gonzaga's success in these studies by noting that he had "an exact understanding of Greek and Latin, and the knowledge of several sciences."[40]

---

of the life-size statue of the philosopher commissioned by Gonzaga remains at the present tomb.

34. Alessandro Luzio, "Ercole Gonzaga allo Studio di Bologna," GSLI 8 (1886): 386. See also Attilio Portioli, "I sigilli del cardinale Ecole Gonzaga," *Archivio storico lombardo* 8 (1881): 64–67 (hereafter cited as ASL).

35. ASM, AG, b. 1150, f. 52r, Ercole Gonzaga to Isabella d'Este, June 15, 1525.

36. On Amaseo and his association with Gonzaga see Tiraboschi, *Storia*, vol. 7, part 1, 58–60. See also R. Avesani, DBI, s.v. Romolo Amaseo.

37. On Amaseo's relationship with Pole see Mayer, *Reginald Pole*, 188.

38. ASM, AG, b. 1460, ff. 327r–329r, Federico Malatesta to Federico Gonzaga, August 26, 1526.

39. ASM, AG, b. 1460, f. 330r, Federico Malatesta to Federico Gonzaga, September 5, 1526.

40. Eugenio Albèri, *Relazioni degli ambasciatori veneti al Senato*, vol. 2, *Relazioni*

At Mantua and Bologna Gonzaga had pursued a humanistic and philosophical curriculum typical of a well-educated nobleman and university student. He did not take a degree, does not seem to have been enrolled in the university, and employed teachers who were not on the faculty.[41] Under the direction of Pomponazzi he familiarized himself with current issues in Aristotelianism. The subsequent studies in Hebrew and possibly Chaldean that he took up in Venice indicate a turn to theology and scripture. This last period of formal education continued until Ercole was raised to the purple in May of 1527. From then on his cultural and scholarly interests were self-directed and increasingly theological in content. This foundation of humanistic and philosophical studies continued to serve as the basis for the expansion of his personal library and established his outlook on the companionship of learned tutors.

Ecclesiastical Advancement

Ruling the diocese of Mantua had by the sixteenth century become the standard responsibility of younger sons of the Gonzaga dynasty. In 1521 in keeping with this custom, a sixteen-year-old Ercole Gonzaga took possession of the diocese of Mantua as its perpetual administrator and legate *a latere,* an age significantly younger than the canonical minimum age of thirty for bishops. As early as 1523 the family sought the cardinalate for Ercole through the diplomacy of the Mantuan humanist Baldassare Castiglione. Negotiations were protracted and the events leading to the Sack of Rome in May of 1527 complicated Gonzaga's promotion.

Even while Ercole's uncle Cardinal Sigismondo Gonzaga still lived, Isabella d'Este sought to gain the cardinalate for her son. She traveled to Rome for this purpose, arriving on March 2, 1525. Isabella had

---

di mantova dall'anno 1540, series 2 (Florence: Tipographia e Calcographia all'insegna di Clio, 1841), 16 (hereafter cited as Albèri). "La esata intelligenza della lingua greca e latina, e la cognizione di diverse scienze."

41. On university studies in Italy see Paul F. Grendler, *The Universities of the Italian Renaissance* (Baltimore: Johns Hopkins University Press, 2002).

gone there on the pretext of the religious jubilee for that year and remained until after the sack. Her piety notwithstanding, Isabella seems to have devoted as much as or more effort to Ercole's career than she did to her own religious exercises. The death of Cardinal Sigismondo in October of 1525 seemed to open the way for Ercole's elevation. At that time Pope Clement VII promised Isabella viva voce that he would make her son a cardinal. But the close ties between Isabella and the noble Roman Colonna family, in whose palace she was a guest, later caused the pope to hesitate. The Colonna had carried out what amounted to a dress rehearsal for the sack of 1527 when their forces pillaged the Vatican in late September of 1526. Ercole himself came to Rome in October to negotiate with Clement at that delicate moment. The pope finally issued the bull concerning Ercole's promotion on October 4, 1526, but then only secretly: Ercole was neither to wear the cardinal's regalia nor to mention his elevation to anyone. Clement guaranteed, however, that in case of his own death Gonzaga was to enjoy full voting privileges in the conclave.[42]

Ercole Gonzaga was not the only cleric seeking promotion to the sacred college at that troubled time. Clement VII's dire need for financial resources to meet the imperial threat led him to seek a payment of 40,000 ducats from each of the six new cardinals whose elevation he published in May of 1527.[43] Although it is not certain whether Clement ever received payment, Ercole did write years later that he would have been willing to pay 20,000 scudi for the cardinal's hat.[44] In any case, on the evening of May 3, 1527, Clement published Ercole's promotion. His cousin Pirro Gonzaga delivered the red hat to Isabella d'Este at the Palazzo Colonna, where she would weather the storm to come. Only after the violence of the imperial troops had abated was the marquise able to leave Rome for Mantua. Ercole met her at the

---

42. ASM, AG, b. 1903, ff. 16r–19bis, October 4, 1526. This document is a copy maintained by the Gonzaga chancery.

43. The other cardinals elevated at that time were Benedetto Accolti, Niccolò Gaddi, Agostino Spinola, Marino Grimani, and Antoine du Prat. See Eubel, 3: 19–20.

44. Cited in Arturo Segre, *Un registro di lettere del cardinale Ercole Gonzaga (1535–1536), con un'appendice di documenti inedite (1520–1548)* (Turin: Fratelli Bocca, 1912), 25 (hereafter cited as Segre).

town of Stellata and then accompanied her to Mantua. The Marquis Federico met them at the town of Governolo, the site of a suburban villa of the Mantuan bishops, where he himself presented the cardinal's hat to his younger brother.[45]

The boldness with which the Gonzaga family pursued the cardinalate for Ercole was not matched by any concern for the conferral of holy orders. Cardinal Gonzaga did not receive ordination to the priesthood until November of 1556. It is likely that he postponed ordination until it was certain that his nephews would survive him, thus removing the possibility that he himself might become duke. January of 1557 saw the younger of these two, Guglielmo Gonzaga, reach his majority and begin to rule in his own right. Cardinal Gonzaga did not receive episcopal consecration until after he arrived at the Council of Trent in 1561. Thus, he was officially only the episcopal administrator through most of the many years that he ruled the diocese of Mantua.[46]

From early 1528 to the spring of 1537 Cardinal Gonzaga lived mostly in Rome. He maintained a residence for many years at the palazzo adjacent to the Basilica of San Lorenzo in Lucina in the Via Lata, the present day Via del Corso.[47] His responsibilities in Rome included the duties of a cardinal advising the pope. For a time he held the post of papal governor of the town of Tivoli for Clement VII. Most importantly, he acted as the chief representative of the Gonzaga family to the Holy See, a role that included the normal duties of an ambassador. His early correspondence from Rome reveals his inexperience, and he

45. Alessandro Luzio, "Isabella d'Este e il sacco di Roma," ASL 10 (1908): 86.

46. On Gonzaga's ordination to the priesthood see Ippolito Donesmondi, *Dell'Istoria ecclasiastica di Mantova* (Mantova: Aurelio e Ludovico Osanna Fratelli, 1612–16. Reprint Bologna: Forni, 1977), 2: 184. Donesmondi claims that Gonzaga received ordination in order to please his sister, Suor Paola. See also Brunelli, 102. Gonzaga celebrated his first mass on the Feast of Saint Andrew, November 28, 1556. See ASM, Archivio Portioli #6, f. 658r (hereafter cited as ASM, AP). On his episcopal consecration see CT, 2: 356, 549.

47. On his residence, now known as the Palazzo Fiano, at San Lorenzo in Lucina see Massarelli, CT, 2: 171, May 8, 1550. "In palatio card. Portugallensis, quod nunc habet Card. Mantuanus, vulgo detto allo arco di Portugallo." The arco di portugallo was a triumphal arch over the Via del Corso close by San Lorenzo in Lucina.

frequently apologized to his brother for being remiss in his dispatch-es.[48] The cultural and political advantages of being at the center of the Renaissance diplomatic world did not long remain foreign to him, however. During those years he formed friendships with such promi-nent figures as Reginald Pole (1500–1558), Gasparo Contarini (1483–1542), Gian Pietro Carafa (1476–1559), Gian Matteo Giberti (1495–1543), and others. In addition to these personal contacts he gained his earliest governmental experience working for the Gonzaga family in 1536 when he held the office of governor of Monferrato on behalf of his brother Federico. The period from 1528 to 1537 allowed Gonzaga to hone his skills as a courtier, diplomat, and administrator. This pe-riod also witnessed the beginning of the rancorous relationship be-tween Gonzaga and Pope Paul III (1468–1549). The origin of their dif-ficulties lay, at least in part, in Gonzaga's negative reaction, like that of many others in Rome, to the nepotism of the Farnese pope. Further, Gonzaga viewed himself as the representative of an ancient family in comparison to which the Farnese were, in his mind, mere upstarts. As an appointee of Clement VII he was among a group of cardinals not favored by Paul III. A protracted struggle between Cardinal Gonzaga and the pope's grandson, Cardinal Alessandro Farnese, over possession of the Lombard monastery of Santa Maria di Lucedio further compli-cated matters. The relationship worsened during failed negotiations to hold a reform council in Mantua in 1537. Relations between them reached the lowest point when Ercole's brother Ferrante involved him-self in the assassination of the pope's son, Pier Luigi Farnese, in 1547. Gonzaga's decision to leave Rome and return to Mantua in the spring of 1537 was due largely to his falling out with the pope. Their mutual disdain provided Gonzaga with a reason for supporting anyone who had run afoul of Paul III.

48. ASM, AG, b. 883, ff. 246r–249r, Ercole Gonzaga to Federico Gonzaga, Sep-tember 23, 1534.

The Library of Ercole Gonzaga

Ercole Gonzaga became an avid book collector very early in his career. In 1523 he wrote to his brother Federico to seek the acquisition of the library of Prince Alberto Pio da Carpi, who had been expelled from his lordship, claiming that it was the "finest library of Greek and Latin books in Italy, including Rome."[49] Ercole went so far as to send Bonamico to Carpi to make an inventory of the collection.[50] Although this ambitious effort failed when the lordship of Carpi was seized by one of Alberto Pio's relatives, Gonzaga was not overly discouraged. He soon began to build his own sizeable personal library. At his death, the total number of books in the collection was in excess of fifteen hundred titles. An inventory of his possessions completed at Gonzaga's death, while it includes no publishing data, does provide a listing of authors and titles according to subject matter. According to Gonzaga's will of 1557 the library was to be divided between two recipients. He left all his books of philosophy and theology to the Dominicans of Mantua and the works of literature to his younger cousin, Cardinal Scipione Gonzaga. The variety of materials is indicated by the list's subcategories including sacred scripture, theology, philosophy, literature, and medicine. By the standards of the day, this was a notable collection.[51]

49. ASM, AG, b. 1150, f. 8r, Ercole Gonzaga to Federico Gonzaga, January 19, 1523. ". . . la più singulare libraria de libri greci et latini che si trovassi in Italia, non ne cavando Roma." On this library see Ferdinand Gregorovius, *History of the City of Rome in the Middle Ages,* trans. Annie Hamilton (London: George Bell and Sons, 1902), vol. 8, 331, n. 1.

50. ASM, AG, b. 1150, f. 16r, Ercole Gonzaga to Isabella d'Este, March 11, 1523.

51. On the library see the inventory produced at the time of Gonzaga's death in ASM, AN, Minute, Agostino Ragazzola, pacco 7566, April 1, 1563; 7567. There is a further inventory for 1564 in ASM, AN that is a copy made for Ludovico Gonzaga di Nevers. The latter of these two is sixty-two folios in length and was compiled by "messer Henrico Holonio, guardarobbiere et intimo cameriere di Sua Signoria Illustrissima existenti sotto il suo governo." See f. 207 for reference to Gonzaga's secretary. In addition to the inventories themselves see Angelo Cavana, *La Biblioteca del Cardinale Ercole Gonzaga: testimonianza per una nuova sensibilità teologica.* Licentiate thesis, Pontificium Athenaeum Antonianum, Facultas Theologicae. Insititutum de Studiis

While Gonzaga's will and the inventory of his goods offer us the most complete list of titles in the collection at the time of his death, the single most important source of information on his attitude toward the collection is found in forty-three invoices for purchases of books and their binding that are found among his household records.[52] These invoices reveal two major periods of book acquisition. The first was in the year immediately following his return to Mantua from Rome in the spring of 1537, when he acquired more than two hundred and fifty volumes. These purchases represent, therefore, an enlargement of his personal library that coincided with his taking up permanent residence in Mantua and the initiation of his reforms there. The other major period of book purchasing was in 1546 and 1547 when he bought at least another fifty-seven. This period coincided with the opening sessions of the Council of Trent, to which Gonzaga paid close attention. These invoices are bibliographically incomplete and lack precise identifications of the books. Publication dates are absent and in only one case does the publishing information include author, title, publisher, and seller: "bibia in stampa de lion" purchased in Bologna from Bartolomeo Vicino.[53] At other times we are left with only the author or the title: "uno Avicena." Nevertheless, the invoices do offer valuable information about the books that Ercole sought in those two periods. They include the same broad range of disciplines that is in the inventory taken at his death. These periods of intense collecting, therefore, provide a valuable indication of his scholarly interests at two important moments in his career.

The sources of Gonzaga's books were varied. Benedetto Britannico was the only book dealer whose name appears regularly in the invoic-

Oecumenicis, Venice, 1995; Guido Rebecchini, "Libri e letture etterodosse del cardinale Ercole Gonzaga e della sua 'familia,'" *Schifanoia* 22–23 (2002): 199–208; Clifford Malcolm Brown, "Paintings in the Collection of Cardinal Ercole Gonzaga: after Michelangelo's Vittoria Colonna Drawings and by Bronzino, Giulio Romano, Fermo Ghisoni, Parmigianino, Sofonisba Anguissola, Titian and Tintoretto," in *Atti del convegno internazionale di studi su "Giulio Romano e l'espanzione europea del rinascimento,"* October 1–8, 1989 (Mantua: Publi-Paolini, 1991), 206–7.

52. ASDM, MV, Entrate e Uscite, bb. 18 and 19.

53. See the Appendix for all further references to Gonzaga's book purchases.

es. The Britannico family had been involved in the book trade since the fifteenth century in Brescia and, for a time, in Venice.[54] Gonzaga placed a general order for books of all kinds with Britannico.[55] In addition to that source, Mantuan ambassadors purchased books in Venice, Bologna, Rome, and, on occasion, in Germany. Pietro Bertano, for example, purchased some while he attended the Colloquy of Worms in 1540. Periodically there are references to books in the correspondence of Gonzaga. It appears from these indications that Gonzaga sought the best texts available across a wide area of Europe.

The total list of books purchased in 1537 and 1538 contains more than two hundred and ten recognizable titles, including works of sacred scripture, scriptural exegesis, patristic theology, medieval theology, humanist and Protestant works, philosophy, literature, history, geography, as well as others, such as a cook book and a study of the Turks. Despite this interest in a broad range of study, the material available for the period of book buying immediately following his return to Mantua indicates two emphases in Gonzaga's collecting. First, theology: eighty-four of the 1537–38 purchases are in the area of sacred scripture and scriptural exegesis. If Gonzaga showed more interest in philosophy at other moments in his life, his return to Mantua in the spring of 1537 was marked by a manifest interest in biblical studies. Second, acquisitions reflected interests in and tastes for humanists such as Erasmus. A number of purchases provided Gonzaga and those around him with pastoral aids. Very noticeable as well are the works of Protestant reformers. The scripture texts that he purchased included a five-volume Bible published in Paris, an edition of the Pauline epistles in both Greek and Latin, a Septuagint, and the *Glossa ordinaria,*

54. See Paolo Veneziani, *La tipografia a Brescia nel XV secolo. Biblioteca di bibliografia italiana* (Florence: Olschki, 1986), 79–95.

55. Sergio Pagano, *Il Processo di Endimio Calandra e L'Inquisizione a Mantova nel 1567–1568.* Studi e testi, no. 339 (Vatican City: Bibl+ioteca Apostolica Vaticana, 1991), *Secondo Costituto di Endimio Calandra,* March 27, 1568, 261 (hereafter cited as Pagano). Calandra testified that Gonzaga sought the books from a Brescian book dealer. Calandra said: "Ne haveva fatto venire tanti che ne haveva piena una libraria. Al qual libraro Sua Signoria illustrissimo haveva fatto un patente che gliene portasse uno d'ogni sorte."

the standard biblical commentary of the Middle Ages. A letter from the Venetian bookseller Andrea Arrivabene further illustrates his interest in scripture. Arrivabene responded to Gonzaga's inquiry about the best and most beautiful Greek edition of the Bible available in Venice at that time. Of two available Greek Bibles, one was from the press of Aldus Manutius that Arrivabene described as "better, both more beautiful and more expensive."[56] Much later in his career, while he was at the Council of Trent, Cardinal Gonzaga was a target of criticism for his lack of learning in theology. His critics claimed that while he was certainly learned in the humanities and philosophy, he lacked training in theology and canon law.[57] The collection of books that he gathered in 1537 and 1538, therefore, calls this criticism into question.

Examples of biblical exegesis in Cardinal Gonzaga's library represent the work of scholars from the patristic period to the Reformation. These included works by Arnobius, Augustine, John Cassian, John Chrysostom, Fulgentius of Ruspe, Justin Martyr, and others. Early medieval theologians also figure prominently in the lists. In 1537 Gonzaga purchased work by the Venerable Bede and the ninth-century scholars Haimo and Remigius from Auxerre. Psalm commentaries titled *Catena Aurea* appear on two occasions. Only one of these specifically mentions Thomas Aquinas as the author. Commentaries of Thomas on the epistles of Paul appear in a purchase made by Benedetto Agnello in Venice in 1537. That same year Gonzaga purchased five volumes of biblical commentaries by Nicholas of Lyra (ca. 1270–1349). The late medieval author of scriptural commentaries who appears most frequently in Gonzaga's library, however, is Denis the Carthusian (1402–71). This

56. ASM, AG, b. 1474, unnumbered fascicle of letters from *"diversi,"* Andrea Arrivabene to Ercole Gonzaga, January 28, 1540. The only Greek edition of scripture from the Aldine press noted by Antoine Renouard was an Old Testament published in 1518. See Antoine Augustin Renouard, *Annali delle edizioni aldine. Con notizie sulla famiglia dei Giunta e repertorio delle loro edizioni fino al 1550* (1834; reprint, Bologna: Fiammenghi, 1953), 84.

57. Tommaso Caselli, bishop of Cava, said of him that he was "nè leggista, nè theologo, nè ha niuna pratica di queste cose." Camillo Oliva to Francesco Gonzaga, May 22, 1562, cited in Juan de Valdés, *Cartas inéditas de Juan de Valdés al cardinal Gonzaga,* ed. Jose Fernandez Montesinos (Madrid: Aguirre, 1931), liii (hereafter cited as Valdés).

extraordinarily prolific theologian gained the title *"doctor ecstaticus."* Among his works was a thirteen-volume commentary on all the books of the Bible that was published between 1532 and 1540. Twelve of these volumes were available by 1538 and Gonzaga bought six of them. Scriptural commentaries of the humanists and Protestants also hold a prominent place in Gonzaga's library. Of the eighty-four scriptural works purchased in 1537 and 1538, ten are by Protestant authors. These included a commentary on epistles of Paul by Luther that may have been his commentary on Galatians.[58] The library contained Luther's *postills,* or homilies for Sundays and feast days which, according to Luther, pleased even the papists.[59] Gonzaga also purchased works by Philip Melanchthon, Konrad Pellikan, and Johannes Bugenhagen, Luther's assistant at Wittenberg, and Ulrich Zwingli.[60] The centrality of sacred scripture in the methodology of the Reformers made biblical exegesis an important part of all of their works, even those that were essentially controversial or systematic. Thus, even some of the medieval authors in Gonzaga's library must be viewed as products of the Reformation since they were published by Reformation printers.

In addition to these Protestant books Gonzaga purchased works by a number of humanists and reformers who remained within the Roman Catholic Church. These include Jacques Lefèvre d'Étaples's (1455–1536) *Commentarii in Epistolas Catholicas.* The Dutch humanist and Hebrew scholar Jan van Campen wrote a paraphrase of the Psalms, at least three copies of which found their way into the library of Cardinal Gonzaga.[61] Van Campen (1491–1538) lived in Italy from 1534 to 1538. He acted as secretary at various times for Bishop Gian

58. An edition of the Galatians commentary was published at Hagenau in 1535. See H. M. Adams, *Catalogue of Books Printed on the Continent of Europe, 1501–1600 in Cambridge Libraries* (Cambridge: Cambridge University Press, 1967), vol. 1, 679, #1791 (hereafter cited as Adams), for publication data on the Galatians commentary.

59. On the postills see Martin Brecht, *Martin Luther,* vol. 2, *Shaping and Defining the Reformation, 1521–1532,* trans. James L. Schaaf (Minneapolis: Fortress Press, 1990), 16.

60. An invoice indicates a commentary on Job by Bugenhagen but I have not found any other reference to it.

61. Gonzaga also took care that these works were richly bound and covered: "uno Campense coperto di veluto dorato la coperta," see ASDM, MV, b. 1, f. 57r.

Matteo Giberti, Cardinal Reginald Pole, and Cardinal Gasparo Contarini. He lectured on scripture in Verona in the winter of 1535–36. In November of 1536 van Campen arrived in Rome as a part of the household of Contarini. It seems likely that Gonzaga would have met the Dutch humanist there through his friend Contarini.

Noteworthy among the texts in Gonzaga's library are the works of one of the most prominent *spirituali,* the Italian humanist Marcantonio Flaminio (1498–1550), who published his *Paraphrasis in duos et triginta Psalmos* in Venice in 1538. By April of that year Gonzaga had acquired a copy of it. Flaminio is best known as the editor of the *Beneficio di Cristo,* by Benedetto Fontanini da Mantova. Cardinal Gonzaga's secretary, Endimio Calandra, later testified to reading a copy of the *Beneficio di Cristo* in the library of Cardinal Gonzaga.[62] The presence of works by Flaminio indicates the close connection between Gonzaga and that group of reformers. Other humanist works of biblical scholarship in the collection included the *Evangelistiarium* of the Dalmatian humanist Marco Marulo (1450–1524) and the *Interpretatio in Psalmum Miserere mei Deus* by Cardinal Jacopo Sadoleto. Many of the editions that Gonzaga purchased came from the presses of Aldus Manutius of Venice, Johannes Froben of Basel, Johann Schotte of Strasbourg, and others who worked with the humanists of Italy and Germany. These purchases indicate Gonzaga's preference for a humanist method of biblical criticism.

That Cardinal Gonzaga purchased these works is not in itself proof that he read them. Nevertheless, other evidence indicates that he actually did. Gonzaga wrote to Gasparo Contarini on June 6, 1537, and summarized the content of his studies as consisting of Thomas Aquinas and sacred scripture. He added that he was on the verge of beginning his studies of the epistles of Paul under the direction of the lector at the Dominican priory in Mantua, Pietro Bertano (1501–58), who was subsequently bishop of Fano, cardinal legate in Germany, and a

---

62. Pagano, *Confessio di Endimio Calandra,* March 17, 1568, 225. The critical edition of the work is Benedetto Fontanini da Mantova, *Il Beneficio di Cristo con le versioni del secolo XVI. Documenti e testimonianze,* ed. Salvatore Caponetto (DeKalb: Northern Illinois University Press; Chicago: Newberry Library; Florence: Sansoni, 1972).

member of the commission that drafted the 1554 Index of Prohibited Books.[63] Further evidence is found in the testimony of Gonzaga's secretary, Endimio Calandra, who underwent prosecution for heresy a few years after Gonzaga's death. Calandra testified that Gonzaga did in fact read both the Protestant authors and Thomas Aquinas, though he read the former with the supposition that they were in error as demonstrated by the latter.[64] Acquisition of these works in 1537 and 1538 was directly tied to the reading and to the program of studies that Gonzaga undertook upon his return to Mantua.

Reference to Thomas Aquinas is also significant in light of these documents. In 1537–38 there is no indication that Cardinal Gonzaga bought any works by Aquinas other than his scriptural commentaries. There is no record of the purchase of the *Summa Theologiae* until December 1546, just before the Council of Trent formally condemned Lutheran teaching on justification and promulgated a view of justification that was consistent with Aquinas. Until then Gonzaga's purchases focused on biblical rather than systematic theology. The presence of commentaries by Aquinas on the epistles of Paul points to a scriptural focus for his studies even when they were "Thomistic." Endimio Calandra's testimony that Gonzaga read the Protestants with the presumption of their error and always had Thomas read to him on the same topics as those he read in Protestant works also highlights the scriptural character of his studies. Protestant exegetical works heightened the need for Gonzaga to supply himself with corresponding Catholic commentaries on scripture. Gonzaga's desire to apply himself to the study of sacred scripture filled his bookshelves with a wide variety of texts and commentaries.

Most of the books Gonzaga purchased were by authors from late antiquity and the early Middle Ages, or the sixteenth century itself.

---

63. Ercole Gonzaga to Gasparo Contarini, June 6, 1537, in Walter Friedensburg, ed., "Der Briefswechsel Gasparo Contarini's mit Ercole Gonzaga," *Quellen und Forschungen aus italienischen Archiven und Bibliotheken* 2 (1899): 10 (hereafter cited as Friedensburg). On Bertano see G. Rill, DBI, s.v. "Bertano, Pietro." See also Paul F. Grendler, *The Roman Inquisition and the Venetian Press, 1540–1605* (Princeton, NJ: Princeton University Press, 1977), 94.

64. Pagano, *Settimo Costituto di Endimio Calandra*, April 19, 1568, 333.

Relatively few represented the twelfth to the fifteenth centuries. The patristic era is represented in an important way by the purchase of works of Augustine. These include the *City of God*, the homilies, and epitomes of his works. In a letter of November 15, 1539, Gonzaga informed Contarini that he was studying Augustine's homily on the first Epistle of John.[65] At his death, Gonzaga's collection included a ten-volume edition of the works of Augustine published in Basel that must certainly have been the one edited by Erasmus for Froben (1529), thus indicating that the interest in Augustine was not limited only to 1537 and 1538.[66] Other patristic authors in the collection included Gregory the Great, John Chrysostom, Cyprian, Gregory of Nyssa, and the Pseudo-Dionysius.

Patristic titles in Gonzaga's library demonstrate a particular interest in apologetics. Gonzaga's book purchases in 1537 included works by Irenaeus and Justin, both of whom dealt in theological conflict. Irenaeus's *Contra haereses* was the only extant work of the second-century bishop of Lyon during the sixteenth century. Gonzaga's copy must have been Erasmus's edition published in Basel by Froben in 1526 and 1534 because this was the only printed edition of Irenaeus before these purchases. It is not possible to say with certainty which of Justin's works Gonzaga purchased, but all of them have an apologetic tone and at least one is explicitly written against heresies.[67] Further apologetic material is found in the works of Fulgentius of Ruspe (468–533), a North African bishop who worked in the Augustinian theological tradition and opposed the work of both Arians and those known as semi-Pelagians. Again, the records in the diocesan archive do not specifically identify which works Gonzaga purchased. Nevertheless, it is probable that he bought the 1520 edition of Fulgentius's *Opera*, edited and published by the Nuremberg humanist Willibald Pirckheimer.[68] Britannico sold Gonzaga a work by another fifth-century North Af-

65. Ercole Gonzaga to Gasparo Contarini, November 15, 1539, Friedensburg, 38.
66. Augustine, *Opera Omnia*, Erasmus of Rotterdam, ed. (Basel: Froben, 1529).
67. On the Ireneus editions see Adams, vol. 1, 574, ## 150 and 151.
68. The *Opera* of Fulgentius were edited by Pirckheimer and published at Hagenau and Nuremberg in 1520. See *Short Title Catalogue of Books Printed in German-Speaking*

rican bishop, Vigilius, in October of 1537, most likely the *Opus contra Eutychem aliosque haereticos* that he wrote in defense of the dogmatic decrees of the Council of Chalcedon. A final example of patristic apologetics is a work of John Cassian (ca. 365–435), the *De incarnatione Domini* that Gonzaga purchased in September of 1538. In 430, before he became pope, Leo the Great had requested that Cassian write this anti-Nestorian treatise.[69] A 1534 Basel edition, published by Andreas Cratander and edited by Johannes Oecolampadius, was likely the edition that Gonzaga purchased.[70] The homilies of Augustine on the first letter of John that Gonzaga studied also involved the problem of divisions among Christians, since they address the pastoral problem facing Augustine in the Donatist crisis. This apologetic content in the library points to Gonzaga's participation in the doctrinal controversies of his day. Augustine's famous injunction, "compel them to come in," would have come readily to the minds of many in the late 1530s. The presence of patristic apologetics in the collection underlines his interest in using a humanist method of returning to the sources of Christian antiquity in order to address contemporary theological debates. Concerns about Pelagianism had some relevance for the debates over grace and free will, when Protestants frequently accused Catholics of this heresy while Donatism was an early example of schism among Christians. Purchase of these works therefore suggests that Gonzaga associated the Protestants with the "heretics of old."

Gonzaga's purchases of Scholastic authors outside of the field of biblical scholarship were relatively few for the years 1537–38. Among them, Scholastic treatises in systematic theology are remarkably scarce. The most notable Scholastic works that Gonzaga did purchase are examples of *pastoralia* and canon law. Cardinal Gonzaga bought the *Summa angelica* of Angelo Carletti da Chiavasso, the *Summa Tabiena*

Countries and German Books Printed in Other Countries from 1455 to 1600 now in the British Museum (London: Trustees of the British Museum, 1962), 327 (hereafter cited as STC, German).

69. William Smith, ed., *A Dictionary of Christian Biography*, 4 vols. (London: J. Murray, 1900), 1: 415.

70. See STC, German, 454.

of Giovanni Cagnazzo da Taggia, the *Summa Hostiensis* of Henry of
Susa, Cardinal of Ostia, and the *Summa silvestrina* of Silvestro Maz-
zolini da Prierio, O.P.[71] In addition to confessional literature there are
two editions of the canonical work of Pope Innocent IV (1243–54).[72]
These *Summae confessorum*, examples of a genre that sought to bridge
the gulf between the university centers of theological reflection and
the local parish priest who had not benefited from a university education, show Gonzaga's point of reference as he undertook his work
of diocesan reform in the late 1530s. By the time he purchased these
summae he had already begun to carry out the visitation of his diocese through the work of his vicars and suffragan bishops. He called
for a reform of clergy and laity of the diocese of Mantua that included
the type of pastoral care outlined in these treatises on the practice of
the sacrament of penance. In the *Breve ricordo*, a small handbook for
clergy that Gonzaga had published for the diocese of Mantua, he specifically mentioned these *summae*.[73] Limitation of works by Scholastic
writers to scripture commentaries and *pastoralia* points to Gonzaga's
lack of interest in the more purely speculative works of Scholastic theology and philosophy during this period of book buying. The exception that proves the rule is an edition of Durand of Saint-Porçain, a
fourteenth-century commentator on the *Sentences* of Peter Lombard.[74]
Even here, however, Gonzaga's interest in Durand may have been
spurred by the theologian's arguments concerning simony and its implications for reform in the Church. Durand rejected the arguments
of papal canonists who claimed that the pope, as *proprietario* of pre-

71. ASDM, MV, b.1, f. 88r, December 4, 1537; ibid., f. 229v, June 14, 1538;
ibid., f. 229v, August 7, 1538; ibid., f. 229v, August 7, 1538.

72. ASDM, MV, b. 3, f. 36r, undated invoice of 1537 and ASDM, MV, b. 1, f.
78r, November 10, 1537.

73. Ercole Gonzaga, *Breve ricordo di Monsignor illustrissimo et Reverendissimo Monsignor Hercole Gonzaga Cardinale di Mantova delle cose spettanti alla vita dei chierici, al
governo delle chiese, e alla cura delle Anime di questo suo Vescovato di Mantova* (Mantua:
Ruffinelli, 1561), 2v. "Alcuna Summa come sarebbe la summa Angelica, la Tabiena, o
qualunque altra." On the genre of *summae confessorum* see Leonard E. Boyle, "Summae confessorum," in *Les genres littéraires dans les sources théologiques et philosophiques
médiévales* (Louvain-la-Neuve: L'Institut d'Études Médiévales, 1982), 227–37.

74. ASDM, MV, b. 1, f. 169r, December 23, 1537.

bends and benefices, was free to dispense them as he saw fit, so there could be no charge of simony.[75]

Gonzaga's interest in scripture in the late 1530s barely exceeded his passion for humanistic works. He purchased more than forty books in the period 1537–38 written by humanists, both Catholic and Protestant. Some of these have been mentioned above among the purchases in the area of biblical studies. Among the nonscriptural theological works were Erasmus's *Annotationes in leges pontificias et caesareas de haereticis.*[76] The collection also includes a catalogue of the works of Erasmus that was most likely Froben's important *Catalogi duo operum Desiderii Erasmi* of 1537 and an *Apopthegmata* that were purchased together in Brescia. Gonzaga also purchased the works of those who disputed with Erasmus, including Étienne Dolet (1508–46). Gonzaga also bought Jacopo Sanazzaro's (1457/8–1530) *De partu virgini,* a work Erasmus specifically singled out for criticism in his *Ciceronianus.* A work of Fridericus Nausea, a correspondent of Erasmus, also appears. He wrote poetical works, a catechism, and a praise of Erasmus in the years before the purchases listed here. This group of humanist and Protestant books excludes all ancient authors whose works are only vaguely identified in the invoices. Since humanists edited and published many of those works as well, it is clear that Gonzaga's scholarly interests were very consistent with the humanism of his day.

Theological works of the Protestants form a significant group within the library of Ercole Gonzaga. In addition to the scriptural commentaries mentioned above, Gonzaga bought one of Luther's catechisms and five other unidentified works by him. Melanchthon's *Loci communes,* Zwingli's *Opus articulorum,* and an edition of his letters also found a place on the cardinal's bookshelf. Gonzaga's correspondence

---

75. See Jedin, *Storia,* vol. 4, 1, 28.

76. ASDM, MV, b. 1, f. 201r, September 23, 1538. This is not so much a work by Erasmus as one that used some statements of his out of context to lend weight to a Protestant edition of anti-heretical legislation published by Gerard Geldenhouwer (1482–1542). Erasmus was not pleased. See Gilbert Tournoy, s.v. Gerard Geldenhouwer, in Peter G. Bietenholz and Thomas B. Deutscher, eds., *Contemporaries of Erasmus: A Biographical Register of the Renaissance and Reformation* (Toronto: University of Toronto Press, 1985–87).

also indicates purchases of Protestant books not clearly mentioned in the invoices of the episcopal mensa. On July 29, 1545, he wrote to Camillo Capilupi, who was then in Worms, about books that he wanted. Gonzaga wrote to ensure that Capilupi would take advantage of his location to bring the books back to Mantua that were lacking from his library, expressing particular interest in books of a controversial nature.[77] Gonzaga must have expected quite a few since he suggested that if Capilupi could not bring them all by himself he should seek assistance from the archbishops of Augsburg and Trent. In particular he wanted a work by Martin Bucer that he had learned of recently, the *De concilio et legitime iudicandis controversiis religionis*. He wanted it because he found it very strange that one "who seeks every occasion for discord possesses the form and manner of concord. Except that if we only did it his way there would be nothing more to dispute."[78] Gonzaga evidently desired that he and his closer associates might be abreast of theological developments north of the Alps.

During the late 1530s the future papal legate at Trent also showed an interest in conciliar records and theology. In 1537 Pope Paul III intended to convene a reform council at Mantua. Cardinal Gonzaga participated in the negotiations over this failed attempt before his departure from Rome. In November he purchased from Britannico what appears to be a collection of conciliar documents that he termed *"fasciculi conciliorum."* That same month Contarini wrote that he was sending a copy of "that book concerning councils that I wrote for the pope" to Gian Matteo Giberti, who was to forward a copy to Gonzaga. This was most likely the *Conciliorum magis illustrium summa*. In early 1538 Gonzaga wrote again to Contarini requesting that he send a copy of one of his works on the councils.[79] Although by the date of

77. ASM, AG, Copialettere di Ercole Gonzaga, codex 6497, letter #78, ff. 28v–29r, Ercole Gonzaga to Camillo Capilupi, July 29, 1545. On Camillo Capilupi, nephew of Ippolito Capilupi see G. De Caro, DBI, s.v. "Capilupi, Camillo."

78. ASM, AG, Copialettere di Ercole Gonzaga, codex 6497, letter #78, ff. 28v–29r, Ercole Gonzaga to Camillo Capilupi, July 29, 1545. "A me pare molto strano che da chi cerca ogni occasione di discordia possidarsi forma et maniera di concordia ecceto se non . . . che facciamo a modo suo et così non vi sia più che disputare."

79. Gasparo Contarini to Ercole Gonzaga, November 22, 1537, in Edmondo

that letter it was clear that the council was not to meet in Mantua as
Paul III had originally intended, it does not seem that Gonzaga or
others believed that it was to be delayed as long as in fact it was and he
continued to purchase conciliar literature.[80] Gonzaga did not neglect
the treatises by Contarini from the 1530s as the years passed. In December of 1544 Ercole mentioned to the Duke of Ferrara that he had
found among his books "a summary of councils that Cardinal Contarini made for the pope that is very brief and beautiful and that sheds
light also on many beautiful things."[81] Although Gonzaga did not attend the Council of Trent until its final period, he purchased books
on conciliar theology and conciliar canons in order to prepare himself
for the issues that would arise. Gonzaga's attention to scripture, theology, and conciliar issues came to be known outside of his own diocese.
Pier Paolo Vergerio (1498–1565) had informed Cardinal Pietro Bembo
of them. In May of 1539 Bembo praised Gonzaga for his studies, judging them to be entirely in the service of God, a significant assessment
from a contemporary humanist prelate.[82]

Solmi, "Lettere inedite del cardinale Gasparo Contarini nel carteggio del Cardinale Ercole Gonzaga," *Nuovo archivio veneto*, n.s., vol. 4, part 2 (1904), 255. "Quel libro de
conciliis, lo quale scrissi al papa." Ercole Gonzaga to Gasparo Contarini, January 2,
1538, Friedensburg, 26. In a letter of November 19, 1541, Contarini also responded to
requests for the works of Juan de Torquemada (1388–1468). See Gasparo Contarini to
Ercole Gonzaga, November 19, 1541, Friedensburg, 58.

    80. Francesco Chierigati purchased two recently printed volumes of conciliar doc-
uments for Gonzaga in December of 1538. Gonzaga's agent in Rome, Bernardino de
Plotis, informed him in February of 1539 of the acquisition of another recently published conciliar collection. ASM, AG, b. 1909, f. 12v, Bernardino de Plotis to Ercole
Gonzaga, February 3, 1539. "Un libro di concilio stampato nuovamente." Finally in
1541 the Venetian printer Antonio Putelleto dedicated to Gonzaga an edition of the
canons of the Provincial Council of Cologne with an *Enchiridion Christianae Institu-
tionis* of Johann Gropper. See Adriano Prosperi, *Tra evangelismo e controriforma. G. M.
Giberti (1495–1543)* (Rome: Edizioni di storia e letteratura, 1969), 254 (hereafter cited
as Prosperi).

    81. BAV, Barb. Lat. codex 5792, ff. 120r–121r, Ercole Gonzaga to Ercole d'Este,
December 4, 1544. "Un sommario de concilii che fece il Cardinal Contarini al Papa
molto brieve et bello che da luce di pure belle cose." Gonzaga sent the copy to Ferrara with a letter to the same on December 8, 1544, in BAV, Barb. Lat. codex 5792, ff.
125v–126r.

    82. Pietro Bembo, *Opere del cardinale Pietro Bembo*, 4 vols. (Venice: Hertzhauser,
1729. Anastatic reproduction, Ridgewood, NJ: Gregg Press, 1965), vol. 3, *Le Lettere*

A large number of the books purchased in 1537–38 are literary texts: there are no less than forty-six volumes of classical and Italian literature. At Gonzaga's death the inventory of his goods included 471 works of *"humanità."* The collection is unremarkable in its conformity to standard humanist interests.[83] Most of the authors represent Latin antiquity. Among the few literary figures in the list that are not ancient were Giovanni Boccaccio and Lorenzo Valla. Nevertheless, there is a noteworthy presence of Greek literature, an unsurprising element since Gonzaga knew Greek well. In the spring of 1538 he purchased a Greek and Latin dictionary as well as Greek editions of the *Iliad* and the *Odyssey* and an edition of Didymus Alexandrinus's commentary on Homer.[84] There is also a work of the Greek grammarian Theodore of Gaza (1400–ca. 1476), the *De mensibus.*[85] Theodore had worked with Vittorino da Feltre in Mantua in the 1440s. Erasmus valued him as the best of the Greek grammarians. Gonzaga's books of history included Herodotus, Thucydides, the *Commentaries* of Caesar, and an unspecified work by Tacitus. Gonzaga also bought a Latin translation by Janus Lascaris (1445–1534) of a work of military history

volgare, Pietro Bembo to Ercole Gonzaga, May 6, 1539, 25 (hereafter cited as Bembo, *Opere*).

83. Twelve of the volumes are either by Cicero or commentaries on his works. Quintilian also figures prominently with purchases of the *Institutio Oratoria* and the *Declamationes.* ASDM, MV, b. 1, f. 57r, October 10, 1537, and f. 169v, April 13, 1538. ASDM, MV, b. 1, f. 56r, October 8, 1537. "Quintiliano con li annotationi declamationi." Gonzaga also purchased books by other Latin authors, such as Virgil, Terence, Plautus, and Varro. We know that Gonzaga read Virgil with a good deal of interest since there is a sixteenth-century Aldine edition of the ancient Mantuan in the British Library that contains the cardinal's annotations. On this edition see John Dreyfus et al., eds., *Printing and the Mind of Man: An Exhibition of Fine Printing in the King's Library of the British Museum* (London: British Museum, 1963), #47, Pl. 5b. Cited by Harry George Fletcher in *New Aldine Studies: Documentary Essays on the Life and Work of Aldus Manutius* (San Francisco: Rosenthal, 1988), 96.

84. Didymus Alexandrinus's commentary on Homer was published in Venice by Aldus Manutius in 1521 and 1528. There was also an edition published in Rome in 1517. See Adams, vol. 1, 350, #440, #441, and #443.

85. Italian editions of his grammar appeared repeatedly between 1495 and 1545. See Adams, vol. 2, 270, #530 and #532; Charles Schmitt, s.v. Theodorus Gaza in Peter G. Bietenholz and Thomas B. Deutscher, *Contemporaries of Erasmus;* Nigel Guy Wilson, *From Byzantium to Italy: Greek Studies in the Italian Renaissance* (Baltimore: Johns Hopkins University Press, 1992), 35.

by Polybius titled *Liber ex Polybii historiis excerptus de militia Romanorum et castrorum metatione.* The ecclesiastical history of Eusebius also found a place in Gonzaga's library. The invoices make clear that not all of these books were for Gonzaga himself. The Greek-Latin vocabulary, for example, was intended for a friend. The Herodotus was purchased for those studying in the house of Cardinal Gonzaga. In addition to his role as bishop of Mantua, Gonzaga oversaw the education of a number of young men at court. A shadowy figure in the invoices of the diocesan archive is someone simply referred to as *"lo Episcopino,"* i.e., the "little bishop."[86] On a number of occasions Gonzaga bought books specifically for this person: two volumes of the works of Cicero and Greek works including those of Herodotus, Plutarch, Thucydides, Sophocles, Euripides, and Suidas.[87] It is difficult to speculate on who this person was. It is likely, however, that the "little bishop" was a relative or ward of Cardinal Gonzaga whose education he provided for with great care. Thus, just as his own scholarly activities influenced the purchases of theological works, so too did Gonzaga's activities as a guardian influence his purchase of literature.

Even when Gonzaga's intellectual interests turned to theology, he did not lose his early love of philosophy and natural science. From his days as a student at Bologna, Gonzaga always maintained a keen interest in the writings of Aristotle. He may have begun to collect philosophical texts before his return to Mantua in 1537, but he did not buy many after returning there. There are only eleven recognizable titles in philosophy among his purchases. These include an Avicenna, commentaries on the *Ethics* of Aristotle by Jacques LeFèvre d'Étaples and Donato Acciaiuoli, as well as philosophical works of Cicero, Philo of Alexandria, Bede, and Diogenes Laertius. Rounding out his collection, Gonzaga purchased scientific works including an edition of Pliny, anatomy texts, and Cornelius Celsus' *De medicina.* Francesco Zorzi's *De harmonia mundi* also entered the library in 1537.[88] On the borders of science Gonzaga pur-

86. ASDM, AV, b. 1, f. 230r, October 12, 1538.
87. The *Suidas,* of whose author little is known, was composed ca. 1000. For an Aldine edition of 1514 see Adams, vol. 2, 245, #2062. For a 1527 Bologna edition see STC, Italy, 651.
88. This was published in Venice in 1525. See Adams, v. 1, 479, #467.

chased a work by Alexander Achillinus called *De chyromantia principis et physionomia,* and an unidentified work by the Arab astronomer and astrologer Albumasar. Among the modern writers in the field of Aristotelian physics there is the name of the sixteenth-century Italian philosopher Lodovico Boccadiferro (1482–1545). In September of 1545 Gonzaga wrote to his ambassador in Bologna, Francesco dalle Arme, requesting a work by Boccadiferro "that is on Aristotle on natural fibers because I intend to study that this winter."[89] As the ducal regent from 1540 to 1557 Ercole Gonzaga oversaw government intervention in the local economy. An example of this intervention was an edict of 1545 by which the regents protected the status of Jewish merchants who worked in the silk industry.[90] The realities of the Mantuan economy and silk as a source of revenue were no doubt the origin of his interest in Aristotle's writings on natural fibers.

After 1538 the next major period of book acquisition documented in the diocesan archive took place from late 1546 to late 1547. Invoices for the purchase and covering of books from this period continue to reflect Gonzaga's role as educator of his nephews and other youthful courtiers, since most of the books purchased in that year were intended for the use of these young men and others. Many are literary texts that indicate a young audience still studying on the secondary level. They also reflect the changing religious conditions in Italy and an important change in emphasis in theology. The purchase of a *Summa Theologiae* in December of 1546 indicates a shift toward a more Thomistic basis for his theology in keeping with the decrees of the Council of Trent. Earlier records mention only the biblical commentaries of Thomas Aquinas. Further, invoices of 1547 show that another edition of this work was purchased for others. Also among these later purchases is *"uno istrutione del principe Christiano"* that may be Erasmus's treatise *Institutio principis christiani,* a fitting work in the hands

---

89. ASM, AG, Copialettere di Ercole Gonzaga, codex 6497, letter #196, ff. 70r–70v, Ercole Gonzaga to Francesco dalle Arme, September 13, 1545. "Che è sopra i panni naturali di Aristotele perche disegno di fare quello studio questa invernata." See also letter #203, f. 72r, where Boccadiferro is referred to as a recently deceased beneficiary in Bozzolo. Gonzaga may have met Boccadiferro at Bologna when he was a student.

90. Giuseppe Coniglio, *I Gonzaga* (Milan: Dall'Oglio, 1967), 299–300.

of the school master of a Gonzaga duke. Dedication of the first Italian edition of this treatise to one of Cardinal Gonzaga's nephews is supporting evidence that this purchase is the work of Erasmus.[91] In these invoices the name of Messer Rodrico appears repeatedly as one for whom the books were intended. But almost always it is specified that he is to have the book "per il signore Francesco," the young duke, or some other individual.[92] This Rodrico was also known as Rodrigo or Henrico da Hollonia or di Liegi. His signature is found on many of the invoices for book purchases. During the 1540s he may have acted as a school master whom Gonzaga hired to oversee the studies of the young prince and his fellow students. In the 1550s he became the caretaker of Gonzaga's library and was a *conclavista* or assistant to Gonzaga during the papal conclave of 1555. In 1568 he underwent trial for heresy and abjured.[93] It is not possible to identify all of the students at the ducal court. It seems, however, that Cardinal Gonzaga provided humanistic and religious education on a rather elevated scale for young men at court and in his cathedral school, including the future dukes, Francesco (1533–50) and Guglielmo (1538–87).[94]

Apart from those books specifically purchased for these others, earlier acquisition patterns remain. Gonzaga continued to buy scripture and theology. He paid for a luxuriously bound New Testament.

91. On the dedication of the Italian edition see Silvana Seidel-Menchi, *Erasmo in Italia: 1520–1580* (Turin: Boringhieri, 1987), 166.

92. ASDM, MV, b. 1, f. 331r, December 7 to January 5, 1547.

93. On Rodrigo see Pagano, *Primo Costituto di Endimio Calandra,* March 25, 1568, 260, and 243, n. #6. Rodrigo worked for Gonzaga until his death. Gonzaga allocated to Rodrigo the sum of 500 scudi in his will to cover the expenses of dowering his daughter. See the will of Cardinal Gonzaga in ASM, AG, D, VI, no. 3, f. 267v.

94. ASDM, MV, b. 1, f. 331r, January 19, 1547. "Doi volumi della Suma de Santo Tomaso, cioe la seconda parte et la seconda seconde alla romana, have Cesaro paggio di sua sinoria." See also ibid., January 21, 1547. "Per haver ligato altri doi volumi dela Suma de Santo tomaso." During the 1550s Gonzaga employed Antonio Possevino as tutor for the future cardinals Francesco Gonzaga and Scipione Gonzaga. Possevino wrote of his duties: "In 4 anni lessi varii auttori di humanità, greci et latini, et Xenofonte dell'Institutione di Ciro in greco, i dieci libri delli Morali di Aristotele in greco, et tutta la Rettorica di Aristotele in greco." See Giuseppe Castellani, S.J., "La vocazione alla compagnia di Gesù del P. Antonio Possevino da una relazione inedita del medesimo," *Archivum historicum Societatis Iesu* 14 (1945): 103.

He continued to buy Protestant books, including "twenty-two Lutheran books sent from Germany." The activity of the Council of Trent continued to attract his attention. In April of 1547 he purchased two books on the council's decree on justification. Gonzaga's intellectual interests in the mid-1540s also emerge from the correspondence that he maintained with Cardinal Reginald Pole. On July 4, 1545, Gonzaga wrote to Pole and thanked him for a book that the English cardinal had written and sent to him. He wished to make Pole certain that he holds it "more dear than any other thing that I have and yet your lordship by his natural modesty values it less than he should."[95] Even taking account of sixteenth-century epistolary flourish, this suggests a closeness to the English cardinal on an intellectual level. The book in question is certainly Pole's *De Concilio liber*, which he wrote in the spring of 1545. The English cardinal composed this treatise in order to prepare for his duties as papal legate to the Council of Trent and to outline the operations and purposes of the council. It is an example of the interests of the Italian *spirituali* in reconciliation with the Protestants insofar as possible and reform of the Church.[96] That Gonzaga valued it highly is borne out by the fact that in 1562 he supplied two hundred copies of the work in an Aldine edition to the members of the Council of Trent when he himself was papal legate there.[97]

Sometime in the summer of 1545 Pole received a small devotional work by Gonzaga, an exposition on the Lord's Prayer, from Pier Paolo Vergerio the Younger. Gonzaga was unaware that Vergerio, who was largely under his protection at the time, had sent the work. In a letter

95. ASM, AG, Copialettere di Ercole Gonzaga, codex 6497, letter #12, f. 6v, Ercole Gonzaga to Reginald Pole, July 4, 1545. "Più che si voglia altra cosaccia ch'io habbia et anchora che vostra signoria per sua naturale modestia lo stimi meno di quel che sia di stimar." On this letter see also Thomas F. Mayer, ed., *The Correspondence of Reginald Pole*, St. Andrews Studies in Reformation History, 2 vols. to date (Aldershot, England, and Burlington, VT: Ashgate, 2002), 1: 333 (hereafter cited as Mayer, *The Correspondence*).

96. Reginald Pole, *De Concilio liber* (Rome: Paolo Manuzio, 1562). On this work see Mayer, *Reginald Pole*, 143–74; see also Dermot Fenlon, *Heresy and Obedience in Tridentine Italy: Cardinal Pole and the Counter Reformation* (Cambridge: Cambridge University Press, 1972), 100–115.

97. CT, 8, 534, n. 2

of September 7, 1545, Gonzaga expressed to Pole his embarrassment over this. He wrote that on the one hand he considered it charming that Vergerio had sent it because the bishop of Capodistria knew that Gonzaga considered Pole to be an alter ego. On the other hand, he continued, he was displeased that this unworthy item had come into the hands of the English cardinal.[98] This letter makes an intriguing reference to what is the only known religious tract from the pen of Ercole Gonzaga. The exposition is now lost. That it was available to Vergerio is an indication of the trust between the two men even as Vergerio struggled with ecclesiastical authorities. Further, the fact that Vergerio sent it to Pole may say something about its content. It seems likely that Vergerio thought Gonzaga's treatise would not be out of place among the works read by the group that gathered around Pole. During the 1540s that group had been highly influenced by the *Beneficio di Cristo*, a theological work associated with the circle of Juan de Valdés and the Italian *spirituali*.

This small work by Gonzaga may actually be connected with the catechism that he commissioned from the Dominican Leonardo de Marini, for the diocese of Mantua and was published in 1555. A first edition is in the Biblioteca Comunale di Mantova. In that copy, immediately before the section of the catechism that is a conventional discourse on the Lord's Prayer, Marini wrote in his own hand that he was not the author of anything that follows:

Here ends the catechism composed by me, bishop Don Leonardo de Marini, which I have left unfinished for reason of my departure from Mantua to go to Spain as nuncio of His Holiness, in such manner that the following declaration on the Lord's Prayer is not mine.[99]

98. ASM, AG, Copialettere di Ercole Gonzaga, codex 6497, letter #165, f. 62r, Ercole Gonzaga to Reginald Pole, September 7, 1545. "...una altro mi stesso." On this letter see also Mayer, *The Correspondence*, 1: 336.

99. Leonardo de Marini, *Catecismo overo istruttione delle cose pertinenti alla salute delle anime, di commissione del Rmo. et Illmo. S. Cardinale di Mantova composto et pubblicato per la città e Diocesi sua da Monsignore Leonardo de Marini Vescovo di Laodicea suo Soffraganeo* (Mantua: Ruffinelli, 1555), 163. "Qui finisse il cathecismo *[sic]* composto da me il vescovo don Leonardo de Marini, il quale lassai imperfetto per causa che mi parti di Mantova per andare in Spagna nontio di sua santità, in modo che la dichiarizione seguente sopra il pater noster non è mia."

Given the existence of such a treatise by Gonzaga, it is quite plausible that Gonzaga would include it in the published catechism, despite his modest reference to it as a mere trifle.[100]

Gonzaga as an Intellectual and Cultural Patron

Gonzaga's lifelong interest in studies involved him in periodic searches for tutors and lecturers. His choices of teachers are as indicative of his intellectual preferences as are his book purchases. Gonzaga assigned to his agents in Bologna and Rome the responsibility of finding scholars to study with him and explained the kind of philosopher he sought. In a letter of September 22, 1550, to his agent in Bologna, Francesco dalle Arme, Cardinal Gonzaga made himself clear. Of the two most obvious candidates for Gonzaga's companion in studies, the most likely was a Dottore Locatello, probably Gian Antonio Locatelli (d. 1571), who taught at Bologna between 1545 and 1553. The ability to interpret Aristotle in Greek was most important in this selection. Gonzaga specifically instructed his agent that what he wanted to know was not which of the two had better Latin. While he considered that a fine accomplishment, it was not necessary for philosophical studies. He wanted to know which of the two knew more Greek in order to read Aristotle and his commentaries in that language, and which was most ready for disputation: "Because it appears to me that knowledge of Greek is necessary in a philosopher."[101] He also wanted a philosopher with a pleasant personality who was able to carry on a conversation at

---

100. ASM, AG, Copialettere di Ercole Gonzaga, codex 6497, letter #165, f. 62r, Ercole Gonzaga to Reginald Pole, September 7, 1545. On the authorship of this section see also Roberto Rezzaghi, *Il "Catecismo" di Leonardo de Marini nel contesto della riforma pastorale del Cardinale Ercole Gonzaga*, Biblioteca di Scienze Religiose, no. 73 (Rome: Libreria Ateneo Salesiano, 1986), 130 (hereafter cited as Rezzaghi, *Il "Catecismo"*).

101. ASM, AG, Copialettere di Ercole Gonzaga, codex 6498, ff. 46r–46v, Ercole Gonzaga to Francesco dalle Arme, September 22, 1550. "Mi pare necessaria in un Filosofo la intelligentia della lingua greca." On Locatelli see Giovanni Fantuzzi, *Notizie degli scrittori Bolognesi*, vol. 5 (Bologna: Stamperia di S. Tommaso d'Aquino, 1786), 71–72. Locatelli received a degree in philosophy from Bologna in 1545 and taught there until 1553.

court.[102] This description carries not only a professional message but a social one. Ercole Gonzaga was well-trained in the classical languages. But his interests were not primarily literary. Rather, he wanted to study the Greek commentaries then available. In addition, dalle Arme was to ensure that the chosen tutor be presentable both intellectually and socially. In this directive Gonzaga continued his mother Isabella's tradition of bringing to Mantua outstanding scholars who would also be ornaments at court. Emphasis on Greek also points to the humanistic element in his philosophical studies. He seems to have exceeded even his teacher Pomponazzi, who knew little Greek and relied upon Latin editions of Aristotle's works. By the time Gonzaga sought tutors in philosophy who were accomplished in Greek, editions of Aristotle and his commentaries in the original language were not uncommon.[103] Although Locatelli never actually served as Gonzaga's tutor, this incident illustrates Gonzaga's intellectual preferences very well.[104] In the fall and winter of 1551 and 1552 Gonzaga continued his search for a suitable tutor in philosophy. On October 28 he wrote to Capilupi and asked for information on a scholar named Girolamo da Imola who was then in Rome. He wanted to know about the nature of his learning, character, and conversation.[105] He was also interested not only in a single philosopher but a whole team including men of varied backgrounds: "I don't want to have only one, but several, and not only of high social standing but also of middling and lower origin, and not only a person of good

---

102. ASM, AG, Copialettere di Ercole Gonzaga, codex 6498, ff. 46r–46v, Ercole Gonzaga to Francesco dalle Arme, September 22, 1550.

103. On Greek texts of Aristotle published in the sixteenth century see Charles B. Schmitt, *Aristotle and the Renaissance* (Cambridge, MA: Harvard University Press, 1983), 34–63; and his "Aristotle's Ethics in the Sixteenth Century: Some Preliminary Considerations," in *Ethik im Humanismus,* ed. W. Ruegg and D. Wuttke, Beitrage zur Humanismusforschung 5 (Boppard: Harald Boldt, 1979), 91–93. Reprinted in Charles B. Schmitt, *The Aristotelian Tradition and Renaissance Universities* (London: Variorum Reprints, 1984).

104. On the efforts to draw Locatelli to Mantua, ASM, AG, Copialettere di Ercole Gonzaga, codex 6498, f. 134r, Ercole Gonzaga to Francesco dalle Arme, March 31, 1551, and ASM, AG, Copialettere di Ercole Gonzaga, codex 6498, letter #340, ff. 129v–130r, Ercole Gonzaga to Marcantonio Genova, March 21, 1551.

105. ASM, AG, Copialettere di Ercole Gonzaga, b. 1945, libro 1, ff. 54v–55r, Ercole Gonzaga to Camillo Capilupi, October 28, 1551. "Della dottrina, della natura, et della conversazione."

doctrine but of good manners and conversation as well."[106] Gonzaga's desire to study philosophy endured throughout his life.

For many years after 1538 Gonzaga relied upon the services of a tutor in both theology and philosophy who appears frequently in his correspondence as Messer or Maestro Angelo. He seems to have taken the post of tutor as the replacement for Pietro Bertano, who had taken up his duties as bishop of Fano in 1537. His importance is manifested by the material rewards he received from Cardinal Gonzaga. A Maestro Angelo is mentioned in the records of Gonzaga's parish visitations as the absentee holder of a rural benefice.[107] A more specific example of the value Gonzaga placed on this individual's contribution to his studies appears in a letter of 1550 in which Gonzaga stated the terms of his employment: "one hundred and fifty scudi per annum of salary and the expenses for him and for a servant and the use of a horse if he wanted it."[108] Maestro Angelo's duties involved lecturing on or explaining both philosophy and theology to the cardinal. Gonzaga stated in a letter to Contarini in January of 1538 that he had read through all of the second book of the *De anima* of Aristotle since the beginning of November and was in the process of going through it a second time. He was making annotations on many things that he thought *"belle et nove"* from the lectures of Messer Angelo.[109] Lessons learned from Pomponazzi on the immortality of the soul would have come back to Gonzaga at that time. In another letter to Contarini of November 15, 1539, Gonzaga stated that he had made little progress in philosophy because of the illness of Messer Angelo and added that he hoped to finish the section on the intellect within the next few days.[110]

106. Ibid., Copialettere di Ercole Gonzaga, b. 1945, libro 1, ff. 54v–55r, Ercole Gonzaga to Camillo Capilupi, December 20, 1550. "Non desidero d'haverla solamente di uno ma di più, et non solo da persone grandi ma da medio et da basse ancora, et non pur della dottrina sua ma delli costumi et della conversatione." 54v.

107. See G. Zagni, "Le visite pastorali e inquisitoriali alla diocesi di Mantova (1534–1560)," 2 vols. (Laurea thesis, Università di Bologna, 1976–77) (hereafter cited as Zagni).

108. ASM, AG, Copialettere di Ercole Gonzaga, codex 6498, ff. 43r–44r, letter #114, Ercole Gonzaga to Francesco dalle Arme, September 21, 1550.

109. Ercole Gonzaga to Gasparo Contarini, January 2, 1538, Friedensburg, 25.

110. Ercole Gonzaga to Gasparo Contarini, November 15, 1539, Friedensburg,

The most significant moment in Messer Angelo's work with Gonzaga came during negotiations between Catholics and Lutherans at Regensburg in 1541 over the doctrine of justification. While Cardinal Contarini was in Regensburg for those negotiations, he sent Gonzaga a confidential advance copy of the agreement reached there. Contarini urged him to show it to only two people, Maestro Angelo and Gregorio Cortese, abbot of San Benedetto in Polirone.[111] Maestro Angelo exercised an important advisory role for Gonzaga at a critical moment in Catholic-Protestant relations, and more particularly, in Italian religious history.[112] The salary Angelo had received, the trust he enjoyed, and the regularity of his intellectual contact with Gonzaga all point to the seriousness of the cardinal's purpose and his desire for scholarly companionship. The Aristotelian intellectual foundation laid down by Pomponazzi in the 1520s served as the basis for Gonzaga's ongoing studies into the 1550s.

In Mantua Ercole Gonzaga not only looked to his library and his own continuing education, but also played an active role as a patron of the arts. He continued the patronage displayed by his parents. After the death of his brother Federico, Ercole continued to employ Giulio Romano as his chief architect. Their most noteworthy accomplishment was renovation of the cathedral of San Pietro in Mantua. Its interior, modeled on ancient Christian basilicas of Rome such as Santa Maria Maggiore and the old Basilica of San Pietro in the Vatican, served as an appropriate forum and symbolic focus for the higher standards that Gonzaga demanded of his cathedral clergy and diocesan priests. Cardinal Gonzaga also employed Romano on smaller devotional objects, such as portraits of Saints Peter and Paul and the decoration of his personal apartment in the episcopal palace in Mantua that included

---

38. "Per segno di ciò io non ho anchora finita la parte del intelleto, benchè fra dui o tre giorni pensi di spedirmene." Angelo's involvement also extended to book purchases. See ASDM. MV, b. 1, f. 201v, September 23, 1538. "pella permissione di infrascritto Agnolo philosopho."

111. Gasparo Contarini to Ercole Gonzaga, May 3, 1541, in Franz Dittrich, ed., *Regesten un Briefe des Kardinals Gasparo Contarini (1483–1542)* (Braunsberg: Huye, 1881), 324.

112. On these negotiations see Chapter 4, below.

twelve sets of tapestries. Clifford M. Brown's research on the material possessions of the cardinal has led him to describe Gonzaga as displaying a "positive obsession with fabric, tooled leather and figurative wall hangings." Gonzaga and Romano together commissioned a drawing of Michelangelo's fresco of the *Last Judgment* in the Sistine Chapel. When Romano died in 1546, Gonzaga said that he felt as if he had lost his right arm. Gonzaga also involved himself directly in the process of developing some other local projects. In a letter of March 10, 1535, Gonzaga reprimanded an agent of his in Mantua for not carrying out the paintings in the church at Felonica according to his design, but producing instead a work that was "too common."[113] Gonzaga complemented his active patronage of the arts by avidly collecting works of art. His painting collection included works by Sofonisba Anguissola, Bronzino, Parmigianino, Tintoretto, and Titian. Benvenuto Cellini designed a seal for Gonzaga in 1528.[114] Gonzaga even seems to have sought the services of Michelangelo on an architectural project for his palace in Rome.[115] Giorgio Vasari noted Gonzaga's admiration for Michelangelo's work by including his positive judgment of the *Moses* for Julius II's tomb in his *Lives of the Artists*.[116] Gonzaga also employed the composer Jacquet of Mantua, who spent many years producing polyphonic works for cathedral liturgies.[117] Clerical students of Gonzaga's cathedral school learned music under Jacquet's direction.

113. ASDM, MV, b. 1, f. 7r, Ercole Gonzaga to his Fattore, March 10, 1535. ". . . troppo volgare."

114. On the portraits see ASM, AG, b. 885, f. 313v, Erole Gonzaga to Giovanni Giacomo Calandra, July 29, 1535. Gonzaga also attempted to purchase a portrait of Christ by Romano that was in the possession of Cardinal Reginald Pole. See BAV, Barb. Lat. codex 5793, ff. 135r–135v, Ercole Gonzaga to Pietro Bertano, May 21, 1546. On Gonzaga's wall hangings see Clifford M. Brown, "Paintings . . . ," 203–26. On the collaboration between Gonzaga and Romano see Paolo Piva, *L'"Altro" Giulio Romano. Il Duomo di Mantova, la chiesa di Polirone, e la dialettica col medioevo* (Quistello: Officina Grafica CESCHI, 1988), 99–120.

115. ASM, AG, b. 1910, f. 104r, Pietro Ghinucci to Ercole Gonzaga, June 12, 1540. "M. Curtio si risolverà con Michelangelo della moda et fra un mese mi ha permesso il mastro finirla."

116. See Giorgio Vasari, *Lives of the Artists,* 10 vols., trans. Gaston C. de Vere (London: Macmillan, 1912–15), 9: 54.

117. Iain Fenlon, *Music and Patronage in Sixteenth-Century Mantua* (Cambridge: Cambridge University Press, 1980), 45–78.

Cardinal Gonzaga received a good deal of criticism when he was papal legate at the Council of Trent, and even posthumously, for his lack of training in theology and canon law. This lack has been partially blamed for the storminess of those sessions of the council. An opponent, Tommaso Caselli, the bishop of Cava, referred to him as *"il vecchio pro forma,"* saying that Gonzaga had to hold himself back from actively participating in the discussions at the council for lack of training, and that he had to leave much of his work to *periti*. It is true that Gonzaga was not as theologically prepared as the members of the religious orders who were present at the council. That was no doubt true of many bishops at Trent. But it would underestimate his education to say that he was merely in possession of *"lettere di cavaliere."* Cardinal Seripando, in fact, gave evidence of Gonzaga's familiarity with scripture by indicating to Gonzaga's secretary that:

what amazed me above all was that in that discussion he used many appropriate quotations from scripture that I, who have preached for so many years, would not have been able to recall without thinking hard about it.[118]

The contrasting praise for Gonzaga's knowledge of scripture and the criticism for his purported lack of training in theology and canon law reflect the tensions in the council more than the level of his learning.

Ercole Gonzaga's early passion for Aristotelian philosophy never cooled. When he did turn from philosophy to theological studies he followed the norms of the circle of Italian reformers that included Contarini and Pole. His reading reflected a humanist approach to theology. He applied himself to scripture, patristic writers, and contemporaries who adopted the patristic manner. Scholastic systematic theology played only a small role in his reading, but he did turn to Thomas, Nicholas of Lyra, and Denis the Carthusian on scriptural and pastoral matters. He never departed from traditionally orthodox positions. Yet Gonzaga, the conservative and aristocratic churchman, used his considerable gifts to develop himself as a striking representative of many streams of sixteenth-century thought and culture.

118. Valdés, liii–liv.

CHAPTER 2

GONZAGA, REFORM, AND THE OFFICE OF BISHOP

In 1537 Ercole Gonzaga wrote with twofold advice to his cousin Agostino Gonzaga, who was then assuming the post of Archbishop of Reggio di Calabria:

When you reach your archbishopric look first to the cult and the honor of God with that diligence and with that sincerity of heart that you have promised me out of your great goodness. Then assign to Don Giacomo Severino, my chaplain, that part of the fruits that will suffice to pay the pensions.[1]

This dual advice contains in an abbreviated form much of what Ercole Gonzaga considered to be his own role as a cardinal and bishop. A combination of patrician and ecclesiastical influences contributed to Gonzaga's outlook on his own duties. He did carry out a reform of his own diocese and his works did focus on the quality of public worship as well as the quality of the participation of the clergy and the laity in it. But he also made certain that he fulfilled his responsibilities as a patron toward his family and his servants. On one occasion, for example, Gonzaga suffered a severe illness that made him think of his own death and salvation. Consequently he felt that he should look to

---

1. BAV, Barb. Lat., codex 5789, f. 180r. Ercole Gonzaga to Agostino Gonzaga, November 8, 1537. "Giunta ch'ella sarà al suo Arcivescovato, d'attendere principalmente al culto et honore divino con quella diligentia et con quella sincerità di cuore che sempre mi sono repromesso della molta bontà di lei. Et dapoi farà consegnare a Don Jacomo Severino mio capellano quella parte de frutti che sarà bastante a pagare le pensione."

pious works. These "pious works," however, included helping in temporal ways his many nephews who were deserving on account of family ties and his many servants on account of their merits.[2] The religious demands of reform and the social requirements of his role in Mantua dwelt together in the mind of Ercole Gonzaga.

Concern for the pastoral responsibilities of bishops led Gonzaga to consider seriously the qualities necessary for his successor in the diocese of Fano, which he held as a perpetual regress, that is, the diocese reverted to him at the death or transfer of its incumbent, an arrangement that allowed him to appoint the Dominican Pietro Bertano to the diocese. Another assistant of Gonzaga, Reginaldo Nerli, also a Dominican and one who had worked for Gian Matteo Giberti, disagreed with the choice and made his opinion known to Giberti. Nerli harshly considered Bertano to "have no more religion than a Jew and no more conscience than the dog belonging to my [servant] Guido."[3] Giberti became concerned enough to contact Gonzaga himself, eliciting an explanation of the choice. Bertano possessed two qualities of importance to Gonzaga: an abundance of religion without superstition and solid learning. Gonzaga described the first of these in comparison to a "bella festa" that Nerli had created when he had preached in Verona and worked the people into such a frenzy that they took to the streets, apparently with little or no clerical supervision. With crosses in their hands they cried out *"Christo, Christo,"* and then began to discuss predestination. Evidently Gonzaga considered Bertano to be more discreet. He admitted that Bertano did not possess as much charity as might be desired but thought it more important that he have good judgment. As an authority on this preference Gonzaga cited Thomas Aquinas in the *Summa Theologiae,* who had argued that to choose the best candidate for the office of bishop does not mean choosing the one who is greater in charity. Rather, Thomas held, the best candidate is the one capable of instructing, defending, and ruling

2. Ibid., ff. 30v–31v, Ercole Gonzaga to Nino Sernini, July 30, 1542.

3. Ibid., ff. 75r–78v, Ercole Gonzaga to Gian Matteo Giberti, November 13, 1537. "Et quanto alle ragione ch'egli adduce ch'l Lettore non habbia più religione che un Giudeo ne piu conscientia che un cane ch'a Guido mio nella camera."

peacefully the church that he is to govern.[4] This principle of episcopal election appealed to Gonzaga and he projected his own values onto it. In his discussion of the duties of a bishop he noted that the office required good judgment and learning. Charity may in fact have been problematic if the results of Nerli's preaching in Verona were taken as an example. Ercole Gonzaga, the ecclesiastical representative of a ruling house, saw no value in stirring the people to emotional displays of faith if that led to questionable behavior and discussion. Intelligent, sober teaching and good government stood at the heart of his perception of a bishop's duties. Bertano, a trusted advisor and learned theologian, met those qualifications.

This attitude reflected Gonzaga's general view of society. However aristocratic his mentality was, it did not result in neglect. As the brother of the duke of Mantua, and later as regent for his nephews, Cardinal Gonzaga enjoyed an authority that was not available to many other Italian bishops. Unlike his colleague Gian Matteo Giberti, for example, who had to negotiate continually with the Venetian Senate over his reforms in Verona, or Carlo Borromeo, who struggled with the government of Philip II over ecclesiastical policy in Milan, Gonzaga's influence as a member of the ruling house of Mantua allowed him to act with great effectiveness in the reform of his diocese.[5] Gonzaga's patrician outlook is the most significant motivating factor in his reform. His understanding of how the sacred and temporal in-

4. Ibid., ff. 76r–76v, Ercole Gonzaga to Gian Matteo Giberti, November 13, 1537. See Thomas Aquinas, *Summa Theologiae*, vol. 47, *The Pastoral and Religious Lives* (IIa IIae. 183–9), Jordan Aumann, O.P., ed. (London: Blackfriars, 1973), 70. "Ille qui debet aliquem eligere in episcopum, vel de eo providere, non tenetur assumere meliorem simpliciter, quod est secundum caritatem, sed meliorem quoad regimen ecclesiae, qui scilicet possit ecclesiam et instruere et defendere et pacifice gubernare."

5. For the experience of Giberti see Prosperi, 149–79. For Borromeo see Agostino Borromeo, "Archbishop Carlo Borromeo and the Ecclesiastical Policy of Philip II in the State of Milan," in *San Carlo Borromeo: Catholic Reform and Ecclesiastical Politics in the Second Half of the Sixteenth Century*, ed. John M. Headley and John B. Tomaro (Washington, DC: Folger Books, 1988), 85–111. On the experience of Gonzaga's contemporary Bishop Egidio Foscarari see Michelle M. Fontaine, "For the Good of the City: The Bishop and the Ruling Elite in Sixteenth-Century Modena," *Sixteenth Century Journal* 27 (1997): 27–41.

tertwined encouraged him to take action in the Mantuan context in a way not unlike that undertaken by ruling elites in other Italian states. But the combination of spiritual and temporal power that he retained for much of his career allowed him to reconcile, at least temporarily, the stresses inherent in the relationship of church and state in early modern Europe.[6] This is most evident in his correspondence with his family and his ecclesiastical subordinates and reveals how his self-awareness as a patrician figure and his need to maintain honor formed his way of proceeding.

In addition to the patrician matrix of his views of episcopal office, Gonzaga drew upon other contemporary sources. The most immediate influence was that of Gian Matteo Giberti, with whom his work has long been associated. Giberti pursued a reform of the diocese of Verona that served as an important model for others until it was overshadowed in the later sixteenth and seventeenth centuries by the example of Carlo Borromeo. This learned papal administrator went to Verona after the Sack of Rome in 1527. Giberti's work there is noted primarily for his residence in his see and the supervision of the clergy. Testimony of Gonzaga's reliance on Giberti appeared during his own lifetime. Gregorio Cortese, abbot of San Benedetto in Polirone in the duchy of Mantua and one who was soon to be a cardinal himself, likened the relationship of Giberti to Gonzaga to that of a rider putting the spur to a willing horse.[7] In the only sixteenth-century biography of Gonzaga, Giulio Castellani began his description of the pastoral work of Gonzaga by linking it directly with the reforms of Giberti,[8] whose relationship to the diocese and duchy of Mantua antedates the work of Ercole Gonzaga. Giberti had corresponded with Duke Federico Gonzaga about areas of the diocese of Verona that lay within Man-

6. See Lorenzo Polizzotto, "The Medici and the Youth Confraternity of the Purification of the Virgin, 1434–1506," in *The Politics of Ritual Kinship: Confraternities and Social Order in Early Modern Italy,* ed. Nicholas Terpstra (Cambridge: Cambridge University Press, 2000), 98–113.

7. Cited in Pastor, 11: 505, n. #4. "Addens calcaria sponte currenti."

8. Giulio Castellani, *Vita di Monsignore Hercole Gonzaga Cardinale di Mantova* in *Opuscoli volgari di Mes. Giulio Castellani, editi e inediti* (Faenza: Conti, 1847), 12 (hereafter cited as Castellani, *Vita*).

tuan territory.[9] For example, when Federico sought the suspension of two priests of the diocese of Verona living in his duchy, Giberti complied.[10] When Giberti carried out his own visitations within the duchy of Mantua he needed the permission of Federico, who gave it readily.[11] The spiritual and temporal arms cooperated in the administration of churches in the duchy of Mantua even before Ercole undertook his own reforms. The nearly complete lack of other Italian bishops who resided in and reformed their dioceses in the 1530s and 1540s makes the examples of Giberti and Gonzaga rather unique.

In addition to Giberti, Gonzaga drew from others who sought reform. For example, he did not depart from Rome to return to Mantua until after the presentation of the *Consilium de emendanda ecclesia* to Pope Paul III on March 9, 1537. A commission of prominent reformers and curial officials including Gasparo Contarini, Gian Pietro Carafa, Jacopo Sadoleto, Reginald Pole, Federigo Fregoso, Girolamo Aleandro, Gregorio Cortese, Tommaso Badia, as well as Giberti drew up this document. These prelates presented to the pope a candid assessment of the abuses in the Roman curia and the Datary and the problems that befell the church as a result. Absenteeism by bishops, sale of ecclesiastical office, and lack of suitable preparation for those who were to be ordained are only the most noteworthy of its points. Members of the commission hoped to move the pope to take action to correct these abuses and thereby initiate reform. It is frequently noted that this report had little real effect. For purposes of understanding Gonzaga's reform, however, it is important to keep in mind that all the cardinals were provided with a copy of this document prior to its publication. Thus Gonzaga returned to Mantua the following month with an example of this reform plan in hand. The criticism and the advice that it contained were fresh in his mind when he began to personally supervise his own reform in Mantua. The correlation between

9. ASM, AG, b. 1462, Gian Matteo Giberti to Federico Gonzaga, February 3, February 7, April 25, April 29, 1528.

10. Ibid., b. 1468, ff. 561r–561v, Gian Matteo Giberti to Federico Gonzaga, August 29, 1534.

11. Ibid., b. 1469, f. 472r, Gian Matteo Giberti to Federico Gonzaga, April 19, 1535.

the advice in the *Consilium* and Gonzaga's own activities in Mantua indicates that this was one of the few instances in which that document had any measurable effect after its publication.[12]

Finally, Gonzaga's contact with figures such as Contarini and Pole had a significant impact on him. The ideas that Contarini proposed in his treatise on preaching, *Modus concionandi,* and his treatise on the duties of bishops, *De officio episcopi,* as well as Pole's views on preaching echo in the work of Gonzaga in Mantua, showing both where he conformed to and where he diverged from these ideals. Pole wrote of the need for a *"vivum exemplum"* in a bishop.[13] Contarini's views also emphasized the place of exemplary leadership in a bishop even more than a bishop's regulations for church life. The bishop must be, in the words of Contarini, a living book that could teach his flock through his own behavior. The bishop should be learned and spend part of his day in studies. The foundation for this example is ethical behavior and the ability to act with prudence.[14] One scholar has identified this emphasis on prudence to reveal a secular and quite Venetian attitude toward a bishop's duties. Contarini's view on the relationship between church and state also reflects his Venetian origins, especially his advice that the temporal power be called upon to enforce reforms called for by religious authorities. In other words, Contarini's views themselves are substantially patrician.[15] Gonzaga's efforts in Mantua correspond to these views.

Upon establishing his residence in Mantua, Gonzaga arranged for lectures in theology to be given in his own chambers. As early as six weeks after his arrival he had Pietro Bertano, then the lector at the Dominican convent in Mantua, begin to explain the letters of Paul.

---

12. On the *Consilium* see Elisabeth Gleason, *Gasparo Contarini: Venice, Rome, and Reform* (Berkeley: University of California Press, 1993), 143–49 (hereafter cited as Gleason, *Gasparo Contarini*); Hubert Jedin, *A History of the Council of Trent,* trans. Ernest Graf, O.S.B. (London: Nelson and Sons, 1949), 1: 424–26. (Hereafter cited as Jedin, *History.*)

13. Pole, *Epistolarum Reginaldi Poli S.R.E Cardinalis et aliorum ad ipsum Pars III* (Brescia: Rizzardi, 1748), II: 38. Cited in Prosperi, 216–17.

14. Gasparo Contarini, *The Office of a Bishop,* ed. and trans. John Patrick Donnelly, S.J. (Milwaukee, WI: Marquette University Press, 2002).

15. Gleason, *Gasparo Contarini,* 94–97.

Gonzaga's intention, so he claimed, was not primarily his own edification, although he hoped to learn something from the lessons. More importantly, he wanted to provide a forum where priests and others of his city could learn more theology. He further hoped that his example of listening to these lectures might spur others to serious study. His claim is perhaps not completely candid. Gonzaga's ongoing interest in study, his purchase of large numbers of books during the very period in which he arranged these lectures, and his continuing desire for the intellectual companionship of learned tutors make the claim seem disingenuous. Nevertheless, his concern for providing both opportunity and example to others appears authentic. It is also in keeping with the views of Contarini as expressed in the *De officio episcopi*.[16]

After Bertano's lectures had proceeded for a time, Gonzaga told Contarini about the gatherings in his apartments. He described them as almost daily occurrences. The participants were members of his own household and a "good number of priests and many gentlemen of this city." They came for his company and to hear the Dominican lector.[17] Gonzaga's position as a high-ranking member of the Gonzaga family allowed him to use the influence of the ducal house in the reform of his diocese. Priests and nobles would have come to pay court to him regardless of the activity that he provided. Gonzaga used the deference of the subjects of Mantua and his role as a patron to the advantage of reform and to cultivate the leadership of his diocese and city. Thus, Gonzaga himself attempted, at least in a limited fashion, to reform through example. Contarini returned to this theme and praised Gonzaga for it: "there can be no greater doctrine for the people, given by a pastor, than the good example which I see that Your Lordship has taken, and I rejoice in it, both for the good of your people as well as for yourself."[18] Gonzaga viewed his own efforts in much the same terms but with lower expectations.

16. Ercole Gonzaga to Gasparo Contarini, June 6, 1537, Friedensburg, 10. For Contarini's views see *Gasparis Contareni Cardinalis Opera* (Paris: Sebastianum Nivellium, 1571), 401–31.

17. Ercole Gonzaga to Gasparo Contarini, June 16, 1537, Friedensburg, 11.

18. Gasparo Contarini to Ercole Gonzaga, January 19, 1538, Friedensburg, 27.

I strive to be less of a bad example, by this way teaching my priests part of the Christian life, because I cannot teach with tongue and doctrine, which it has not pleased God to grant me.[19]

In this, Gonzaga was realistic about his status as a role model. His views on his own inability to teach point to his own lack of preaching in Mantua. In this his reform departed significantly from the reforms of Giberti in Verona and Borromeo in Milan, since both of them gave preaching by the bishop a central place.[20] Gonzaga should be viewed, therefore, as a reformer inspired by a patrician mentality, as well as one who was by the late 1530s quite conversant with the debates over reform and the examples of reform offered by other prelates.

Gonzaga and Ecclesiastical Wealth

As cognizant as he was of calls for reform and the restoration of the episcopal office, Gonzaga was certainly not the model bishop. With good reason, no one has ever written a hagiographical version of his life. His own limitations and inconsistencies when it came to reform offer a contrast not only with the proposals for reform offered by his colleagues such as Contarini and Pole but, as we shall see, with the ideals set out in his numerous publications, decrees, and calls for reform of the diocese of Mantua. These inconsistencies, therefore, further illustrate the contours and limits of Gonzaga's patrician reform; they also show both the extent to which reform ideals could influence

"Non puole essere melgio [sic] doctrina di un populo data dal pastore, che il buon exemplo, la quale vegio che V. S. ha preso et molto me ne ralegro, sì per il bene del populo suo, come per quello di lei istesa." For the role of example in Contarini's concept of the episcopal office see Gleason, *Gasparo Contarini,* 94.

19. Ercole Gonzaga to Gasparo Contarini, January 2, 1538, Friedensburg, 24. "Io mi sforzo ad essere manco cattivo essempio, insegnando per questa via alli miei diocesani parte del vivere christiano, perche non posso con l'opera dello insegnare colla lingua et dottrina, qual non è piaciuto a Dio di darmi."

20. On preaching in Giberti's reform program see Prosperi, 235–61. On Borromeo's preaching see John W. O'Malley, S.J., "Saint Charles Borromeo and the *Praecipuum Episcoporum Munus:* His Place in the History of Preaching," in Headley and Tomaro, eds., *San Carlo Borromeo,* 139–57.

as worldly a cardinal as Ercole Gonzaga and the extent to which ingrained habit and custom limited his ability to live according to those ideals. This is especially true in terms of ecclesiastical wealth and his relationship to his family.

In Gonzaga's letters there are repeated references to honor, an important matter for Italian Renaissance elites that had a direct impact on his involvement in this problematic area of Renaissance Church life. Renaissance humanists addressed the issue of honor and saw it as a means of maintaining all of the other valued possessions of one's life as well as personal dignity. The Florentine historian Francesco Guicciardini emphasized the need to use wealth for this purpose:

Honor and reputation are more to be desired than riches. But since a reputation nowadays can scarcely be gained or maintained without riches, virtuous men should seek them—not immoderately, but just enough to acquire or preserve reputation and authority.[21]

Ercole Gonzaga would have agreed with Guicciardini. Repeatedly he explained and defended himself on the basis of honor. His possession of benefices and pensions served to maintain his honor and reputation as a lord and cardinal as well as the fortunes of his family. It was at the core of Gonzaga's inability to refrain from seeking pensions or benefices either for himself or his servants; his pursuit of honor limited his willingness to implement ecclesiastical reform as it had been portrayed by friends such as Contarini, Pole, and Giberti. They identified absenteeism and pluralism by bishops as root causes of many of the Church's problems, but Gonzaga did not fully embrace the program of the *Consilium* when it would have limited his access to ecclesiastical wealth, even if the views expressed in it informed some of his other pastoral activities.

Like all other ecclesiastical figures of his rank, Ercole Gonzaga trafficked in benefices and used that wealth to exercise political, in-

---

21. Francesco Guicciardini, *Maxims and Reflections of a Renaissance Statesman (Ricordi),* trans. Mario Domandi, intro. Nicolai Rubinstein (New York: Harper, 1965), 102.

tellectual, and artistic patronage. He received a base annual income of 3,000 ducats from his father, Francesco.[22] His income from ecclesiastical sources included 8,000 ducats per annum as administrator of the cathedral. He also earned, according to his own estimate, 700 scudi per annum from the see of Fano from 1528 to 1530.[23] Possession of the Mantuan abbey of Santa Maria in Felonica enhanced his annual income by 1,200 ducats, while the abbey of San Tommaso in Acquanegra brought in approximately 2,000 scudi more. For a number of years prior to 1537 Gonzaga held the French abbey of St. Pierre in Lezat, which may have had an income of 3,000 scudi, as a gift from King Francis I.[24] He collected as much as 9,000 ducats per annum from Spanish benefices including the diocese of Tarazona. Gonzaga acted as "protector of Castile" early in his career and by 1546 held the title of "protector of Spain" in recognition of his services to the Emperor Charles V. Cardinal protectors enjoyed the privilege of nominating candidates for benefices granted by the pope in the kingdoms for which they held their title. The *propina,* or service charge, for this privilege was equivalent to 15 percent of the annual income of the benefice for the cardinal and an additional 5 percent for his chamberlains. It has been estimated that cardinal protectors received up to 5,000 ducats per annum by this means.[25] Gonzaga did not disdain less

22. Mazzoldi, *Mantova: La Storia,* 2: 320. The Venetian ambassador, Bernardo Navagero, indicated that Ercole received 8,000 scudi from his father, of which he was to return 5,000 scudi of his patrimony upon taking control of the diocese of Mantua. See Albèri, 2: 14.

23. BAV, Barb. Lat., codex 5789, ff. 75r–78v, Ercole Gonzaga to Gian Matteo Giberti, November 13, 1537. Gonzaga received Fano in the consistory on February 17, 1528. See ASV, AV, vol. 4, f. 13v. Gonzaga was also the administrator of the diocese of Sovana starting in 1529. I have located no information on the income of that see. See ASV, AV, vol. 4, f. 31v, July 5, 1529.

24. Ercole Gonzaga to Federico Gonzaga, October 2, 1531, in Pietro Aretino, *Un Pronostico satirico di Pietro Aretino (MDXXXIIII),* ed. Alessandro Luzio (Bergamo: Istituto italiano d'arti grafiche, 1900), 88 (hereafter cited as Aretino, *Un Pronostico*). On Gonzaga's possession of the monastery see Denis Sainte-Marthe and Paul Piolin, eds., *Gallia christiana in provincias ecclesiasticas distributa qua series et historia archiepiscoporum, episcoporum, et abbatum Franciae vicinorumque ditionum,* vol. 13 (Paris: Victor Palmé, 1865–70), column 215, B.

25. The Mantuan orator in Rome, Fabrizio Pellegrino, reported this estimate to

lucrative benefices; his sources of income also included 70 ducats per annum for chaplaincies that he held in the church of Santo Stefano in Mantua and 35 ducats as the rector of the church of San Giovanni Evangelista. This diversified portfolio of benefices and other sources of ecclesiastical revenue provided Gonzaga with an annual income of about 35,000 ducats. He also used his influence to gain pensions for his servants from other dioceses, thus reducing his expenditures.[26] By way of comparison, in 1510 the Roman humanist Paolo Cortesi generously suggested in his treatise on the office of cardinal, *De Cardinalatu*, that an appropriate annual income for a cardinal would be 12,000 ducats.[27] Cardinal Gonzaga would have been comfortably well off.[28]

In addition to the material benefits of using the system of ecclesiastical offices, Gonzaga employed it to diplomatic advantage. The perpetual regress to the diocese of Fano allowed him to possess it on three occasions and to confer it on Pietro Bertano, in 1537. Bertano continued to serve Cardinal Gonzaga as an informant, especially during the first sessions of the Council of Trent, which he did not attend. In 1560 Gonzaga bestowed Fano upon another servant, Ippolito Capilupi.[29] Thus this wealth supported a large number of servants and family members. For Gonzaga, this was of the greatest importance since it helped to ensure that others would see him as a "gentleman and a sincere and faithful person," as he explained to Capilupi, in 1550.[30] Cardinal Gonzaga's possession of multiple benefices and pensions was an

---

Marquis Francesco Gonzaga in 1531. See D. S. Chambers, "The Economic Predicament of Renaissance Cardinals," in *Studies in Medieval and Renaissance History* (Lincoln: University of Nebraska Press, 1966), 3: 302.

26. On one servant's income see BAV, Barb. Lat., codex 5789, ff. 180r–181r, Ercole Gonzaga to Agostino Gonzaga, November 8, 1537.

27. See John F. D'Amico, *Renaissance Humanism in Papal Rome: Humanists and Churchmen on the Eve of the Reformation* (Baltimore: Johns Hopkins University Press, 1983), 230.

28. On Gonzaga's benefices see also Zagni, 1: 45–46.

29. On the see of Fano see Eubel, vol. 3, 194. On Ippolito Capilupi's career see G. De Caro, DBI, s.v. "Capilupi, Ippolito," and G. B. Intra, "Di Ippolito Capilupi e del suo tempo," ASL 20 (1893): 76–142.

30. ASM, AG, b. 1945, codex 1, ff. 23v–26v, Ercole Gonzaga to Ippolito Capilupi, August 3, 1550. This letter is also cited in Hallman, 122–23.

element in his and his family's ability to play a role in the ecclesiastical and international politics of his day.

Those moments in his life when Gonzaga came into conflict with friends or enemies often resulted from a perception that they had impugned his honor. In the late 1530s and 1540s Cardinal Gonzaga's efforts to reform the Lateran Canons, of whose congregation he was the cardinal protector, led to conflict with the vice-protector, Gasparo Contarini, who proceeded to take action without consulting Gonzaga as fully as the Mantuan would have preferred.[31] Contarini's action, Gonzaga wrote, was taken "without any regard for my honor." The result, he feared, would be a loss of reputation among the Lateran Canons.[32] Even in his relationship with as trusted a mentor and colleague as Contarini, Gonzaga jealously defended his dignity. The same was true in his relations with his bitter foes the Farnese. Gonzaga interpreted their virtues and vices as the inverse of his own. He preserved real honor while they only sought to maintain their "black honor."[33] Gonzaga's relationships with other ecclesiastical figures were dependent, at least to some degree, upon care for his own honor.

The pursuit of honor not only placed limits on Gonzaga's willingness to carry out reform, but paradoxically, it could also motivate him to a degree of reform consistent with those reform-minded friends of his. In letters describing his attitude toward religious governance, Gonzaga frequently mentions honor. In his correspondence with Isabella d'Este on the matter of a simoniacal priest, Cardinal Gonzaga had begged his mother to consider more the honor of God and that of Gonzaga himself than what he considered the unjust demands of the priest.[34] This combination of personal honor and the call for reform is best seen in all its ambiguity in Gonzaga's attitude toward a benefice

31. See Chapter 4 below.

32. Ercole Gonzaga to Gasparo Contarini, April 2, 1540, Friedensburg, 41–42.

33. ASM, AG, b. 1908, unnumbered fascicle, copy of a letter from Ercole Gonzaga without indication of the addressee, December 1, 1539. "Si vede chiaramente che Farnese disse che ne pigliarebbe di pensioni 4 mille scudi con li quali il loro negro honor si vederebbe."

34. ASM, AG, b. 883, f. 280r, Ercole Gonzaga to Isabella d'Este, November 19, 1534.

he held in Spain. In addition to his role as protector of Castile, and later as protector of Spain, Gonzaga also enjoyed revenue from a number of benefices there, primarily the diocese of Tarazona, which he received from Charles V in January of 1537.[35] The diocese was located in Aragon near the borders of Castile and Navarre. During the years he held that benefice he never visited it. Tarazona did not always provide Gonzaga with the income that he had expected, however. Valued at 7,200 ducats, it was burdened with pensions worth 3,000 ducats for other servants of the emperor.[36] Further, Gonzaga made his own revenue from the diocese available to Charles in 1542 in order to support his military campaigns.[37]

The status of Spanish benefices had become a point of contention between Paul III and Charles V by the mid-1530s. In a letter written in 1535 to Giovanni Agnello, a Gonzaga ambassador at the imperial court, Cardinal Gonzaga related the substance of a conversation with Paul III over pensions to laymen and nonresident clerics from the income of certain churches in Spain. Gonzaga was at that time already the protector of Castile and reaped for himself a substantial income on that basis. The pope and the cardinal discussed how and where to start reforms in the holding of benefices. In that conversation Paul III tended to focus on Spain. Gonzaga justified his activities and those of the emperor in the churches of Spain by arguing that those benefices were so rich that they could handle the burden of pensions for laymen and nonresident clerics, as well as supporting resident clergymen. The pope, at least publicly, wanted to avoid even this misuse of benefices. Gonzaga, however, viewed the pope's attitude as a clever and convenient way to place obstacles before the emperor and do it in the name of reform. Gonzaga told Agnello that Paul III wanted to force

35. Ibid., b. 887, ff. 174r–175r, Ercole Gonzaga to Federico Gonzaga, January 27, 1537. The see of Tarazona was granted in consistory on January 26, 1537. ASV, AC, vol. 2, f. 68r.

36. ASM, AG, b. 887, f. 160r, Francisco de los Cobos to Ercole Gonzaga, December 7, 1537. "El obispado esta agora arendado en 7,200 ducados. Es la pension passada y present 3,000. Quedaran 4,200."

37. BAV, Barb. Lat., codex 5791, ff. 39v–40r, Ercole Gonzaga to Cardinal Antoine Perrenot de Granvelle, August 13, 1542.

Charles V to begin reforming the churches for which he was responsible before the pope had carried out his own reform of the Roman curia. Cardinal Gonzaga implied this in the conversation and admitted to Agnello that he did not use all the tact that he should have with the pope. Paul III responded by asking: "So, these imperial supporters hold me in suspicion?"[38] Gonzaga's experience reveals the complexity, pragmatism, and messiness of the problems and personalities involved in an important area of reform.

These debates touched upon Cardinal Gonzaga's own wealth and influence. With the passage of time Gonzaga grew increasingly uncomfortable with both his absenteeism and his lack of profit from Tarazona. By August of 1544 he had begun to consider seriously how he could extricate himself from that benefice without losing out entirely on its material benefits. In a letter to his brother Ferrante, Ercole had expressed the hope that in a recent distribution of Spanish ecclesiastical posts Charles V would reward him more richly, that is, with a diocese that would be of "greater usefulness and less effort." Tarazona was located in a "very terrible country," he added. Disappointed in this hope, Gonzaga subsequently came to believe that the emperor considered him no more than a humble servant. But, he claimed, he would rather be a servant without remuneration than have to suffer the burden of that diocese. Up to that point, Cardinal Gonzaga had revealed no more pastoral concern for the diocese of Tarazona than would be the case for any other income-seeking prelate. Before concluding the letter, however, he also indicated to Ferrante that he felt incapable of doing the things in that church that he should do in good conscience because of the opposition that he expected to meet from the canons of the diocese as well as the people. This bothered him, he added, because "all of my other affairs concerning the Church, thanks be to God, are in good condition."[39] Gonzaga was caught in a bind because

38. Ibid., codex 5788, ff. 86r–89v, Ercole Gonzaga to Giovanni Agnello, January 19, 1535. "Donque questi Imperiali m'hanno per sospetto?" f. 87r.

39. Ibid., codex 5792, ff. 102v–103v, Ercole Gonzaga to Ferrante Gonzaga, August 19, 1544. "Cosa di maggior utile et di manco carrico. Poi il detto vescovato si truova in una natione molto terribile et abbraccia di tre Regni Catalogna Aragon et

of responsibilities to his servants, his family, and the Church. He did
not lack concern for his responsibilities as a bishop. But it did not preclude his involvement in pluralism and absenteeism. Gonzaga had expressed similar sentiments in a letter two days earlier to Camillo Capilupi, but perhaps in an even more mercenary fashion. If the emperor
wouldn't bestow upon Gonzaga another more profitable diocese, he
would rather have done with Tarazona and receive a dependable pension.[40]

When Gonzaga began to negotiate his renunciation of Tarazona,
he initiated a correspondence with the emperor's confessor, Pedro de
Soto, that extended over more than a year.[41] Gonzaga wrote the first of
these letters to the confessor in July of 1544 in a formal Latin style that
was unusual in his correspondence.[42] He explained what for him were
the problems in his continued possession of the diocese, the difficulty
of retaining a pension from it, and the need to do so. In November of
1545 he explained that when he had accepted the see of Tarazona eight
years earlier he took it in much the same spirit that anyone else might.
That is, he took control of the diocese like those "who do not know
well what they need to know, but truly with the intention of visiting
it and carrying out those things that I ought to have done, discharging
my own responsibilities and those toward His Majesty who gave me
it."[43] Gonzaga, therefore, took possession of the diocese of Tarazona
for much the same reason as any other seeker after benefices, though
with perhaps some concern for his pastoral responsibilities.[44] It was

---

Navarra." f. 102r. "Tutte l'altre cose mie di chiesa a Dio gratia stano assai bene." f.
103v.

40. Ibid., codex 5792, ff. 87v–88v, Ercole Gonzaga to Camillo Capilupi, July 17,
1544.

41. The letters themselves are addressed simply to the "confessore dell'Imperatore."
The salutations read "Reverendo Padre." The recipient must be Soto (1500–1563)
who served as Charles V's confessor from 1542 to 1548 and later as a theologian for
Pius IV at Trent.

42. BAV, Barb. Lat., codex 5792, ff. 87r–87v, Ercole Gonzaga to Pedro de Soto,
Confessore dell'Imperatore, July 18, 1544 (XV calendas Augusti 1544).

43. BAV, Barb. Lat., codex 5793, f. 37v, Ercole Gonzaga to Pedro de Soto, Confessore dell'Imperatore, November 10, 1545.

44. In his correspondence with Contarini Gonzaga had expressed a commitment

not until later, he wrote to the confessor, that he began to realize the gravity of his responsibilities as a cardinal and as regent of Mantua. His role in Italy precluded any visit to Spain so, within two or three years, he began to consider renouncing Tarazona rather than holding it with so "little satisfaction to my soul and responsibility."[45] He added that he had not renounced the benefice up to that point out of fear that others might take it as sign of disdain for Charles V. Recently, however, he had received a pension from the diocese of Badajoz from Charles and could therefore do so without that fear. Further, since he was much preoccupied with his role as tutor for his nephews he was certain that he would be unable to go to Spain. The condition of the diocese of Tarazona, astride the borders of the three Iberian kingdoms of Catalonia, Aragon, and Navarre, required a resident bishop who could provide the cure of souls.[46]

By late 1545 Gonzaga found himself near the conclusion of the delicate negotiations over the resignation of the diocese of Tarazona that had involved matters of conscience, finance, and family responsibility. He could report to his brother Ferrante on the happy outcome:

It has pleased the goodness of God to place together my desire to be unburdened of this weight in such manner that His Majesty may compensate me with something which will be of equal utility, no burden on my conscience, and will also turn out well for our Francesco.[47]

---

to govern well other benefices from which he was absent. Gonzaga specifically mentioned visiting the monastery of Acquanegra in the summer of 1537. See Ercole Gonzaga to Gasparo Contarini, September 1, 1537, Friedensburg, 14. He also assured Contarini of his intention to govern the abbey of Lucedio according to the views of Contarini. See Ercole Gonzaga to Gasparo Contarini, June 16, 1537, Friedensburg, 12.

45. BAV, Barb. Lat., codex 5793, f. 37v, Ercole Gonzaga to Pedro de Soto, Confessore dell'Imperatore, November 10, 1545.

46. Ibid., f. 38v, Ercole Gonzaga to Pedro de Soto, Confessore dell'Imperatore, November 10, 1545.

47. Ibid., ff. 56r–57r, Ercole Gonzaga to Ferrante Gonzaga, November 14, 1545. "È piaciuto mo alla bontà di Dio di mettere insieme il disiderio mio di sgravarmi di tale peso col modo che tiene Sua Maestà di ricompensarmi d'una cosa la quale a mi sarà d'eguale utilità di niun carico di conscientia et ancho a Francesco nostro tornerà meglio." f. 56v.

This quotation illustrates the varied interests of Gonzaga as he approached issues that were debated throughout the Church. How he proceeded and what he thought about ecclesiastical wealth in the midst of the struggles to reform the Church in the years between 1533 and his departure for Trent in 1561 reveal much about efforts for reform and their limits. His views on the reform of the Church and his own rights and privileges as a bishop and cardinal came to the fore in his dealings with the emperor and the pope over these benefices. On the one hand, Gonzaga appears to have seen the need to preserve the income of these benefices for those clergy who were actually in residence. But he also expressed the concerns of a patron who had grown accustomed to using them for his own purposes. Gonzaga burdened churches with pensions for *"gentilhuomini,"* that is, laymen of some social stature, but only, he claimed, in cases he judged necessary. He never specified exactly what constituted a necessity, however, and left himself room to maneuver. While committed to reform on many levels, the degree to which he committed himself to it in terms of ecclesiastical revenues was determined by those worldly issues themselves.

By March of 1546 Gonzaga had successfully concluded negotiations for the resignation of Tarazona and acquired the pension from Badajoz. The amount of his pension was 4,500 ducats, of which 500 ducats were reserved for the prelate who would be in residence and carry out the visitation of the diocese of Tarazona.[48] Gonzaga expressed his satisfaction with this arrangement to the imperial confessor, explaining that he was unable to carry out the necessary visitations of the diocese. He added that in this negotiation two important interests were at stake: the unburdening of his soul and the honor of this world. He recognized that the latter was not to be preferred to the former, but he hoped that the imperial confessor would be able to find a way to reconcile the two. But if that is not possible "the prudence of the flesh should cede to the prudence of the spirit such that the hon-

48. Ibid., ff. 107r–108v, Ercole Gonzaga to Pedro de Soto, Confessore di Sua Maestà, March 4, 1546. In an earlier letter to Paul III Gonzaga estimated the value of the pension at 3,000 scudi. See ibid., ff. 36v–37r, Ercole Gonzaga to Paul III, November 10, 1545.

or of the world in this case would cede to that of Our Lord God."[49] These sentiments of ecclesiastical duty appear again in a letter to Cardinal Pole, who had already gone to Trent. Gonzaga wrote to the English cardinal of his decision to dispossess himself of Tarazona. He asked Pole to inform the cardinals at Trent of this decision, "which I have made only for reason of the reproof I have for myself in conscience and not because I wish to burden others or play the school master."[50] He added the request that Pole pray God to forgive him for past failings in Tarazona and give him the strength to administer "this diocese of Mantua alone to the glory of his Divine Majesty and the benefit of so many souls."[51] Pole responded positively to this decision of Gonzaga but not without chiding him for having delayed so long in carrying it out.[52]

If letters to Soto and Pole were the only evidence available, it would be reasonable to conclude that these are the words of one who rationalized his activity for the sole purpose of impressing an influential member of the imperial court and the assembled prelates at Trent. The letter to Pole is difficult to read as anything other than an advertisement of Gonzaga's purported newfound virtue. He was certainly engaging in public relations by contacting Pole at Trent about this decision. However, Gonzaga repeated the same sentiments in other confidential letters to members of his own family. In December of 1545 Gonzaga wrote to his cousin, the duke of Ferrara, on the same issue. Again the cardinal reveals mixed motives. He admits that in exchange for the diocese he has received from the emperor the pension worth

49. Ibid., ff. 107r–108v. Ercole Gonzaga to Pedro de Soto, Confessore dell' Imperatore, March 4, 1546. "La prudentia della carne deve cedere alla prudentia dello spirito, così l'honore del mondo in questo caso ceda a quel di Nostro Signore Dio." f. 108v.

50. BAV, Barb. Lat., codex 5793, ff. 35v–36r, Ercole Gonzaga to Reginald Pole, December 14, 1545. "Cio che ho fatto, l'ho fatto solamente per la riprensione ch'io n'havevo dalla conscientia mia non per tassare altri, ne per fare del maestro di scola o per qual'si voglia altro rispetto del mondo." f. 36r.

51. Ibid., f. 36r.

52. ASM, AG, b. 1915, ff. 575r–575v, Reginald Pole to Ercole Gonzaga, January 11, 1546.

4,000 scudi to him, benefiting both his family and their state, then explains his motive as the desire to unburden his conscience. He believed that it would be impossible for him as a distant foreigner, obligated with many other temporal and spiritual cares, to visit Tarazona and uphold his responsibilities there.[53] In a further letter to the confessor, Gonzaga said that he was then able to enjoy quietly the generosity of the emperor and "with a tranquil soul attend to the things I ought to in service to God and His Majesty."[54] Rarely is Gonzaga more expressive of the combination of motives in his attitude toward benefices and pastoral obligation.

On the surface, Gonzaga's manifestation of pastoral concern for the well-being of the diocese of Tarazona can be read as an empty excuse for extricating himself from a troublesome benefice. He was, indeed, looking to profit from all of these negotiations, but if he was not truly concerned about his own pastoral responsibilities and the limits of his ability to fulfill them, there would have been no reason for him to repeat those concerns privately to his brother Ferrante or his cousin the duke of Ferrara. Gonzaga continued to employ the old system of providing benefices to prelates for political and economic advantage. But in addition, he does seem to have shown greater recognition than he had in previous years of the problems with that absenteeism. Within two days of his original request to the imperial confessor that he be relieved of Tarazona and acquire a pension in its place, he wrote again with the further request that he be allowed to transfer all or part of the pension to his nephew. He even gave advice on how Charles could do this with a clean conscience. Gonzaga argued that pensions are drawn upon the temporal revenues of a diocese and may be bestowed upon anyone of any age as long as that person is able to receive the tonsure. His nephew Francesco Gonzaga, who was then preparing for what

53. BAV, Barb. Lat., codex 5793, ff. 53r–53v, Ercole Gonzaga to Ercole d'Este, December 13, 1545.

54. Ibid., ff. 54v–55r, Ercole Gonzaga to Pedro de Soto, Confessore dell' Imperatore, December 13, 1545. "Accio che Io possa quietamente godere della mercede di Sua Maestà et attendere coll'animo tranquillo a quel che devo per servigio di Nostro Signore Dio et di lei." f. 55r.

was to be his own career as a cardinal, was such a person. The authority he cited was Cardinal Gasparo Contarini, author of a short treatise on the subject that Gonzaga forwarded to the confessor.[55]

In his letter to Ferrante near the conclusion of the negotiations, Cardinal Gonzaga admitted that he had been in a difficult position because he could not dispense with Tarazona without some reasonable financial compensation from the emperor. In a last letter to Ferrante on this topic, Cardinal Gonzaga pursued a more evangelical line by likening his previous delay to that of the guests in the Gospel who were invited to a wedding banquet, delayed in coming, and were therefore replaced by those who would come. He also cited Augustine, who in the *Confessions* described his own delay of conversion: *"cras Domine Deus meus numquam inveniebat"* ["tomorrow, my lord God, never came"].[56] He preferred not to act like the individuals in the Gospel story or as the young Augustine had. But he followed that evangelical and patristic explanation with the more mundane fact that he could not let the opportunity for a pension worth 4,000 scudi to slip past, especially when it could go to Francesco.[57]

In these two letters to Ferrante, Cardinal Gonzaga expressed the nub of the issue. He hoped to confer the pensions on his own nephew, Francesco, who was himself later to attain the rank of cardinal. Dynas-

55. Ibid., ff. 60r–60v, Ercole Gonzaga to Pedro de Soto, Confessore dell'Imperatore, December 17, 1545. The treatise on pensions by Contarini is mentioned in a letter from Gonzaga to Contarini in which Gonzaga describes it as a response to a treatise on the same subject by Cardinal Antonio Pucci. See Ercole Gonzaga to Gasparo Contarini, September 1, 1537, Friedensburg, 14.

56. There are two examples of the parable that he cited: Mt 22:1–4 and Lk 14:15–24. Gonzaga's quotation of Augustine is not accurate. He may have been referring to Augustine's description of being without answers to his religious questions at the age of thirty yet still trying to convince himself that "cras inveniebam; ecce manifestum apparebit." *St. Augustine's Confessions* (Cambridge, MA: Harvard University Press, 1912), vol. 1, bk. 6, ch. 11, 310. Or Gonzaga may have also referred to Augustine's description of his delay in coming to the faith in bk. 8, ch. 5, "'modo,' 'ecce modo,' 'sine paululum.' sed 'modo et modo' non habebat modum et 'sine paululum' in longum ibat." Ibid, vol. 1, 426.

57. BAV, Barb. Lat., codex 5793, ff. 88v–89v, Ercole Gonzaga to Ferrante Gonzaga, February 6, 1546. The appointment of Gonzaga's successor in Tarazona took place on December 3, 1546. See ASV, AC, vol. 6, f. 64r.

tic concerns placed limits on the degree to which Gonzaga conceived of reform but did not prevent him entirely from addressing reform issues with a degree of sincerity, inconsistent as he may have been. Between 1537, when he acquired the diocese of Tarazona, and 1545, when he gave it up, Cardinal Gonzaga seems to have become somewhat more sensitive to absenteeism and to his own participation in it.[58] In the years before Gonzaga went to the Council of Trent, therefore, his thoughts on benefices and reform underwent a noticeable degree of development. His experiences illuminate the career of one who was far from heroic. As the scion of a prominent ruling house he exhibited an understandable ambivalence toward the requirements of reform. Nevertheless, he did grow increasingly uncomfortable with his own pluralism and absenteeism. Gonzaga struggled to balance the need to implement reform with the needs of his family. He continued to seek those elusive benefices that would bring wealth and honor to the Gonzaga and their clients but would not burden his conscience. A few years later the combination of honor and the management of ecclesiastical office again appeared when, in 1551, a banker in Rome offered to provide a long line of credit to Gonzaga for obtaining a benefice. Gonzaga responded with complete disdain for this offer that bordered on simony, saying that he would never accept such a benefice or any other thing without knowing beforehand

whether I could take it up with my honor and without a burden on my conscience, because God did not have me born so poor nor of so vile a soul that I would not serve the soul and my reputation more than possessions.[59]

This conflict between family honor and the requirements of reform is representative of much of his career and influenced much of his activity. Honor and reputation, therefore, were a two-edged sword. At times they spurred Gonzaga to manage better his dioceses and his own

58. Paul III did not forbid cardinals to hold more than one episcopal benefice until February of 1547. In this, at least, Gonzaga was ahead of some of his contemporaries. See Hallman, 32.

59. ASM, AG, b. 1945, ff. 69–71v, Ercole Gonzaga to Ippolito Capilupi, January 20, 1551. "Io non farei mai quello falso latino d'accetare, o benficio o altero in persona

benefices. At others times they inhibited his willingness to implement fundamental reforms of ecclesiastical office. In general, his possession and use of ecclesiastical wealth are indistinguishable from the practices of other high-ranking Italian clergy of the sixteenth century.[60]

Gonzaga and His Children

In his family and personal relationships, Cardinal Gonzaga also demonstrated a paradoxical outlook typical of a Renaissance prelate. He did not uphold the standards of clerical celibacy that he, publicly at least, insisted upon for his clergy and that the Church as a whole would increasingly insist upon in the years following the Council of Trent. For example, in a letter to his mother, Ercole candidly thanked her for a set of bed linens that he promised to use with as much chastity as possible so as not to make her a participant in his sin.[61] As a young man he attended lavish banquets in Rome and on at least one occasion may have been present at a dinner in the company of the famed Roman courtesan Tulia d'Aragona.[62] Over the course of the years he fathered five children: Anna, Eleonora, Camillo, Elisabetta, and Giulio Cesare. The identity of the mother or mothers of the first four is uncertain. Anna and Eleonora became nuns in the Dominican convent of San Vincenzo in Mantua. His correspondence with them reveals a lifelong attention to their needs, both material and spiritual.[63] Camillo lived for a time in the household of Ercole's friend Cardinal Benedetto Accolti. After Accolti's death the young man moved into the household of Cardinal Giovanni Salviati, the archbishop of Ferrara.[64] Gonzaga provided Elisa-

---

mia senza sapere prima che cosa fosse et se potesse pigliarlo con honore mio et senza carico di conscienza, perche Dio per sua grazia non mi ha fatto nascere così povero ne d'animo così vile che non habbia da servare molto di più l'anima et la riputatione mia cha la robba."

60. Gonzaga's practice is consistent with that of the ecclesiastics Hallman has studied.

61. Ercole Gonzaga to Isabella d'Este, January 28, 1536, in Segre, 343.

62. Aretino, *Un Pronostico*, 62.

63. See ASM, AG, b. 1941, f. 503r, Suor Anna to Ercole Gonzaga, May 29, 1562.

64. Ibid., b. 1920, unnumbered fascicle, the Duke of Tuscany to Ferrante Gonzaga, March 27, 1550.

betta with an honorable place at the Mantuan court and saw her married to Count Federico Maffei, a Mantuan noble.

The one exception to this paternal attentiveness concerned his youngest child and reveals both Gonzaga's capacity for callousness and something about the advance of reform efforts in the 1540s and 1550s. Giulio Cesare was born in 1557 of Isabella Petrozzani, a member of a prominent Mantuan noble family. This was long after Gonzaga had begun to reform his own diocese and participate in discussions on reform of the universal Church. In 1575, more than twelve years after Cardinal Gonzaga's death, Petrozzani filed a suit on behalf of her son Giulio Cesare in order to gain recognition of Ercole's paternity. The following year the court ruled in her favor. Cardinal Gonzaga had never formally acknowledged this child as his own and left nothing to him in his will. Yet, according to the testimony of his daughters, Suor Anna and Suor Eleonora, Gonzaga had openly referred to the boy as his son.[65] This reveals both an openness and a deceptiveness in Gonzaga's attitude to his family and others. It is quite striking to think of the papal legate to the Council of Trent arriving at his post in 1561 while at home he left an unrecognized four-year-old child. If the changing climate of reform in the Church in the 1550s did not lead Gonzaga to remain chaste, perhaps it is the cause of his hesitancy about, and possibly his embarrassment at, acknowledging that last child as he had the earlier four. Indeed, Giulio Cesare was the only one of Gonzaga's children born after his ordination to the priesthood. The lateness of this birth in the career of a man who in 1557 still entertained hopes of being elected pope may be the cause of such unwonted negligence.

Gonzaga may not have changed his way of life but he seems to have judged that candidacy for papal office was beginning to demand greater probity, or at least a reputation for such probity. Gonzaga's apparent, but most likely feigned, dismay at his own capacity to produce natural children was expressed in the testimony of a servant in the pa-

<hr />

65. On four of Gonzaga's children see Luzio, *L'Archivio*, vol. 2, 272, n. #1. For the records of the paternity suit see ASM, AG, b. 418, D, XIV, document #5. The only reference I have found to Cardinal Gonzaga's daughter Eleonora is also contained in this court record.

ternity suit who quoted the cardinal as saying: "I am ever carrying this disgrace, that when I love a woman, I immediately get her pregnant. May God's will be done. He who sows, reaps."[66] Another example of this concern about public knowledge of his indiscretions is evident in a letter of 1546 from Camillo Capilupi, who wrote from Ratisbon recounting a conversation he had had with Emperor Charles V's advisor, Antoine Perrenot de Granvelle. Granvelle joked of the good time Gonzaga must have been having in Mantua, "especially concerning the ladies." Capilupi assured Gonzaga that he had informed Granvelle of the great change in life that Gonzaga had effected six years earlier, partially for reasons of greater maturity, partially for other reasons. Granvelle responded, still jesting, that it was Capilupi's special mandate to deny such things and defend Gonzaga.[67] Thus, while Gonzaga's private life was not noticeably different from that of many other prelates of his generation, he seems to have taken increasing care, though it seems not very successfully, to keep it private.

Ercole Gonzaga presents a useful counterpoint to other figures of his generation. He was personally acquainted with Contarini, Pole, Giberti, Carafa, and, late in his career, Carlo Borromeo. His presence in his diocese, his attention to scripture studies, and his desire to be, in at least a limited fashion, an example to others are all consistent with models for bishops proposed by his contemporaries, Contarini in particular. Yet he does not truly presage changes in episcopal leadership after the Council of Trent. His control and use of ecclesiastical wealth and his attitude toward his children demonstrate no significant differences from most of his contemporaries. This paradoxical combination of characteristics both reformed and worldly, as well as his capacity to deceive himself and others, may not be entirely explicable. It is, however, at least partially understandable as a result of social values that could simultaneously encourage and impede the programs of reform of his generation. In this paradoxical behavior he was a creature very much of his own day.

66. ASM, AG, b. 418, D. XIV, document #5, f. 11.
67. Ibid., b. 1915, f. 323r–324r, Camillo Capilupi to Ercole Gonzaga, May 30, 1546.

CHAPTER 3

REFORM IN THE DIOCESE
OF MANTUA

❧

During the lifetime of Ercole Gonzaga there rose within the city of Mantua twenty-seven churches including the cathedral of San Pietro. The largest of these was the basilica of Sant'Andrea that by tradition housed the blood of Christ preserved by Saint Longinus. Sant'Andrea had benefited in the fifteenth century from the patronage of the Marquis Ludovico Gonzaga and the Marquise Barbara of Brandenburg, who had commissioned Leonbattista Alberti to reconstruct the church according to his own design. Outside the city Cardinal Gonzaga had responsibility for churches and chapels in one hundred eleven towns and villages. Religious orders active in Mantua included Dominicans, Friars Minor Observant, Capuchins, Benedictines, Carmelites, Servites, Augustinians, and Lateran Canons. The last of these groups had Gonzaga as their cardinal protector. In addition, the Cassinese Congregation of Benedictines held the monastery of San Benedetto in Polirone, located in the Mantuan *contado*.

By taking up residence in his diocese in the spring of 1537, even if initially out of little more than the desire to distance himself from Paul III, Ercole Gonzaga responded to one of the standard complaints of reformers: absenteeism among bishops. This period of residence lasted for twenty-four years and did not conclude until he went to the Council of Trent in 1561. Over this period Gonzaga ordered the visitation of the parishes of Mantua, saw to the publication of several pastoral and theological guides for his priests, revitalized the training of priests at his cathedral school, reformed the convents of Mantua, and worked toward a renewal of spiritual life among the laity. Moreover, as ducal regent for his nephews, Cardinal Gonzaga exercised his office in such a way that the secular arm acted in matters that were almost purely religious. This conscientiousness has been noted subsequently. Pastor wrote, with the intention of praising Gonzaga and with a good deal of overstatement, that he ruled his diocese with a "rod of iron."[1] Sixteenth-century writers were also aware of his pastoral work. The Venetian ambassador Bernardo Navagero observed:

He governs the clergy of Mantua in such manner that in all of them in so far as it touches upon the clerical habit and as much as one can see of their life, it appears to be the true image of the true religion. In granting benefices and choosing priests he is very diligent, nor does he admit any one to the cult of God, whose life is not thoroughly tested and without stain.[2]

Though no doubt exaggerated, this description indicates that contemporaries viewed his efforts as effective and worthy of note. In his own work as the bishop of Mantua, Gonzaga sought to instruct, defend, and rule peacefully the diocese placed in his care.

Episcopal Visitations

Gonzaga began to put his diocese in order as early as 1533. The first instrument of reform that he employed was a series of visitations of the parishes of the diocese. Visitations became a major vehicle for reform in the latter half of the sixteenth century. The work of Carlo Borromeo is only the best example of this tool for renewal and reorganization of a diocese. Unlike Borromeo, Gonzaga assigned this duty to his episcopal vicars and suffragan bishops, who carried out visitations on his behalf. This delegation was in itself not unusual. In the diocese

1. Pastor, 11: 506.
2. Albèri, *Relazioni,* 16. "Governa il clero di Mantova con tal maniera, che in tutti loro, e in quanto aspetta all'abito, e in quanto si può intendere della vita, appare la vera immagine della vera relgione. Nel concedere i benefizi ed eleggere i sacerdoti è molto diligente, nè ammette alcuno al culto di Dio, la vita del quale non sia probatissima e senza alcuna macchia."

of Salerno the absentee bishops for much of the sixteenth century assigned the work to their own assistants. Even after he took up residence there, Gonzaga's future colleague at Trent, Girolamo Seripando, left the work of the visitations to his vicar.[3] The arc of time covered in Gonzaga's visitations included the period 1534 to 1560, or more than twenty-six years. Of these, records are extant in the Mantuan diocesan archive for visitations that took place in nineteen of those years. The most complete examination of the diocese took place in 1553, when Gonzaga's officials visited all one hundred eleven towns in the *contado* and twenty-five of the twenty-seven city churches.[4]

Visitations were of two types. The first were "inquisitorial visitations," bearing the name "inquisitorial" as they involved inquiry among the nobles of the parishes as to the learning, pastoral care, and probity of life of their pastors.[5] Urban parishes received this type of visitation more frequently than the rural churches. Gonzaga also ordered "pastoral visitations" that focused on the physical and material state of church buildings and the level of piety of the parishioners. Records of both types of visitations are not always precise or consistent in their descriptions. In the case of the inquisitorial visitations, for example, a different group of nobles judged each cleric. The visitors did not always ask the same questions in each visitation or word their questions precisely. Nor did the suffragans and vicars who carried out this work always visit the same churches in each visitation. In spite of the large number of visitations that Gonzaga's assistants conducted over the years, therefore, it is difficult to make judgments about changes or improvements in standards of clerical life and practice based on visitation records alone. In general, however, Gonzaga

3. On visitations in Salerno and the work of Seripando in particular see Francesco Cesareo, *A Shepard in Their Midst: The Episcopacy of Girolamo Seripando (1554–1563)* (Villanova, PA: Augustinian Press, 1999), 141–43.

4. Zagni, 1: 36.

5. Such involvement of the laity was not without precedent. In the diocese of Città di Castello there were "alcuni informatori scelti fra il popolo" in 1215. See Mario Sensi, "Sinodi e visite pastorali in Umbria nel '200, '300, e '400," in *Vescovi e diocesi in Italia dal XIV all metà del XVI secolo,* Italia Sacra, No. 43, Studi e documenti di storia ecclesiastica (Rome: Herder, 1990), 343.

was rather pleased with the results of his work. In a letter to Gasparo Contarini in June of 1537, Gonzaga wrote of the visitations he "had done continuously for three or four years." He added that he was satisfied with the outcome even if not everything he had ordered had been completely enacted.[6]

Despite these imprecise assessments, all the priests of the city seem to have been literate, and most of them seem to have had some learning beyond bare literacy. Of the nineteen priests that Gonzaga's visitors examined in 1534 the most negative cultural assessment was of seven priests who were *"mediocriter litterati,"* or moderately literate. Their colleagues included at least one individual with a master's degree in theology, three who were held to be *"pollet litteris,"* two who were *"competenter litterati,"* three *"litterati,"* one *"satis competenter litterati,"* and two individuals who *"non caret litteris,"* that is, were not lacking letters. Beyond these generalizations little may be asserted about the learning of the urban clergy. The rural clergy, however, did not measure up to their urban colleagues in the area of education. In 1538 in the *contado* of Mantua, those priests whom the visitors considered to have *"poche lettere,"* that is, little education, or those whom they characterized as *"nihil scientes,"* or knew nothing, outnumbered those of superior education by a margin of two to one.[7]

In the areas of pastoral care and probity of life the parishioners held varying opinions about the lives and work of their clergy. In 1534 the parishioners judged only 55 percent of the city clergy to be leading lives of sufficient personal virtue. They considered 85 percent, however, superior in their pastoral care. This difference in opinion was nearly matched in rural communities in 1538, where 75 percent of the clergy received good marks for pastoral care but only 50 percent were considered to be living well.[8] Many of the laity of Mantua, apparently, did not include probity of life as an essential element in adequate pastoral care by a clergyman. When they did judge a priest severely

6. Ercole Gonzaga to Gasparo Contarini, June 16, 1537, Friedensburg, 10–12.
7. Zagni, 1: 71–72, 164.
8. Ibid., 69–70, 150.

for his manner of life it was often because of an irregular relationship with a woman, or the suspicion of one.[9] The visitations demonstrated the needs not only of the clergy, but of the laity as well. Visitors reported lax religious practice, lack of knowledge of basic Christian doctrine, and negligence of the needs of the local parish churches and their pastors among the laity of the diocese. The visitations really had two functions. On the one hand they served to supervise and to improve the tenor of religious life in the diocese. On the other, they provided Gonzaga with information on the state of his church so that he might respond more adequately.

Gonzaga began this work of pastoral supervision while living in Rome, and until 1537 he managed his diocese through correspondence. As early as August of 1534 Giberti complimented him on his work. It pleased him that Gonzaga was proceeding with the reform of his diocese and fulfilling promises to do so that he had made to Giberti. Gonzaga had apparently sought further advice from his friend in Verona, but Giberti would not venture to offer any since he believed that the Mantuan cardinal was proceeding quite well on his own. He thought that "not even Solomon could offer better counsel" than that which Gonzaga had already received, that is, that he look to nothing other than being a Christian and "one who loves the well-being of God's Church."[10] A few weeks later he repeated his encouragement of Gonzaga's undertaking in Mantua. He was pleased that this work was bearing fruit and he hoped that it would abound all the more. Giberti added that if things continued as they had thus far he would consider it a miracle and could not help but rejoice with Gonzaga over the success.[11] The view of a neighboring and conscientious bishop such as Giberti provides strong testimony about the commitment of Gonzaga to reform in Mantua. In time, Gonzaga decided to return to Man-

9. Ibid., 148–49.

10. ASM, AG, b. 1903, f. 242r, Gian Matteo Giberti to Ercole Gonzaga, August 27, 1534. "Parendomi ch'Salomone non si potessi dar miglior consiglio"; "amatore del bene dela santa chiesa sua."

11. Ibid., b. 1904, f. 264r, Gian Matteo Giberti to Ercole Gonzaga, January 7, 1535.

tua and personally direct his diocese. While a major reason for leaving Rome was his unpleasant relationship with Paul III, by 1536 Gonzaga was also planning to return to Mantua for pastoral reasons. In October of that year he wrote to his brother Ferrante that he intended to live in his diocese and put his own church in order.[12]

News of this work of reform circulated among other prominent Italians. Gasparo Contarini commended Gonzaga for his attention to religious duty carried out "for the cause of Christ and for the right living of his clergy."[13] Even earlier Giberti had expressed astonishment at the good favor Gonzaga had earned with Gian Pietro Carafa, whom he considered hard and severe, but who had spoken with such approval of Gonzaga that Giberti wanted to have the "recipe" used to achieve it.[14] Gonzaga's ambassador in Rome informed him in 1539 that the poet Vittoria Colonna expressed her approval of his work. She hoped that he would persevere in it, because "here and everywhere news of his work resounds."[15]

Among Gonzaga's concerns for the parishes of Mantua was maintenance of basics: buildings, income, and good order. In 1537 his assistants drew up a collection of eighteen chapters on the reform and good administration of the diocese.[16] These chapters refer either to the financial management of the diocese or to the maintenance of proper order in the churches. The document calls for a more rational distribution of incomes from benefices and includes the necessity of both raising further funds from parishioners to support their priests and transferring funds from wealthier benefices to poorer ones. The thir-

12. Ercole Gonzaga to Ferrante Gonzaga, October 10, 1536, Segre, 391.

13. Gasparo Contarini to Ercole Gonzaga, August 21, 1535, Friedensburg, 7.

14. ASM, AG, b. 1903, f. 250r, Gian Matteo Giberti to Ercole Gonzaga, December 2, 1534. "Ho voglio dire a vostra signoria quanto habbi trovato Monsignore di Chieti innamorato di vostra signoria che certo mi son stupito con quanta tenereza quel prelato cussi tenuto duro et severo mi habbi parlato di lei. Et quanto mostra haverla in mezzo et core. Ch'essen'si posto in questo proposito non poteva partire sene haro charo un di saper la ricetta ch'quella li ha usata."

15. Ibid., b. 1909, ff. 424r–424v, Ottaviano de' Lotti to Ercole Gonzaga, February 4, 1539.

16. Ibid., b. 1906, ff. 640r–641v. The document is untitled. It begins with the words "Inveniuntur nonullas [sic] parrochiales."

teenth chapter sets forth a principle of pastoral service as the raison d'être of the clerical life. Benefices are not inherent in the churches. Rather, they exist so that clerics may carry out the services for which they have been rewarded.[17] The document invokes that principle in order to transfer income to support those student clerics who studied and served in the cathedral. While this plan called for this support for young clerics still in their studies, it also sought guarantees for the elderly. The fifteenth chapter calls for the assignment of assistants to rectors who have grown weak with age, to ensure that the income of their churches does not suffer.[18] Salaries for rural clergy, always below the levels of pay for urban clergy in Mantua, do seem to have improved during Gonzaga's lifetime. In two towns, Cardinal Gonzaga himself intervened to raise the pay of those clergy who acted as substitutes so that their salaries were more in accord with the income of the benefices.[19] Attention to clerical salaries continued throughout Gonzaga's career. In 1562 he received from his episcopal vicar, Francesco Galvagno, an accounting of salaries for substitute clergy working in parishes of the diocese of Mantua. Galvagno had composed lists that indicated where rural pastors were themselves in residence and lists of what substitutes received elsewhere. These lists enabled Gonzaga to see who was "contented and who was discontented."[20] Galvagno included a total of ninety-three parishes of which forty-four were cared for by their pastors who, presumably, were satisfied with their income. Of the remainder, thirty-nine were sufficiently paid and ten "grieved" over their condition. Those who were paid monetarily, as opposed to receiving supplies in kind, received between fifteen ducats and thirty

17. Ibid., ff. 641r. "Quoniam presummendum est clericatus non ab re institutos esse in ecclesiis sed potius ut illos obtinentes serviunt ut deserviri faciant in dictis ecclesiis quod tam minime fit, expediens videretur ut illos erigere in beneficia sacerdotalia ut illos supprimere et transferre ad ecclesiam Cathedralem Mantuanam pro decentiori sustentione Clericorum inibi servientium ac musicae bonisque litteris et moribus operam navantium."

18. Ibid., b. 1906, ff. 641r.

19. Zagni, 1: 141–42.

20. ASM, AG, b. 1940, ff. 390r–391v, Francesco Galvagno to Ercole Gonzaga, August 9, 1562.

scudi. Of these, Galvagno stated, none was dissatisfied and one was contented. The substitutes who did consider themselves underpaid received between twelve and fifteen ducats annually. Galvagno added at the end of these lists that the curates of the pastors in the city of Mantua itself offered no complaints.

The document also reflects Gonzaga's concern with emphasizing a more public or universal application of ecclesiastical law. He subordinated the personal idiosyncrasies of individual clergymen and the prerogatives of families to more standard norms of conduct. For example, priests who were bearded and not dressed in clerical habit were forbidden to carry out liturgical functions. Gonzaga sought a more rational distribution of priests between the city and the *contado*. As for the laity, the priests were to announce publicly the names of those who had been excommunicated. The document canceled the privileges granted to wealthy families of burying their dead in the churches. Rectors were ordered to exhume such cadavers and rebury them in the cemeteries. Gonzaga limited the rights of families to have masses said in their own homes to circumstances when members of the family and their domestic servants were legitimately and necessarily impeded from attending public services. This regularization of conduct is also evident in the call for the church bells in all churches to be rung at noon for the Angelus prayers, for the "extinction of heresy and for the defense and propagation of the orthodox faith and the defeat of her enemies."[21]

These acts of supervision stand against the background of a society in which ducal authorities increasingly employed both civic and religious rituals to enhance the status of the ruling house. As bishop, Gonzaga circumscribed the locus of worship to include only public places supervised by Gonzaga. Curtailing the privilege of private liturgical celebrations by the local nobility was consistent with a tendency toward exaltation of the Gonzaga family in public liturgies that reached its zenith in the ducal chapel of Santa Barbara only after the death of Cardinal Gonzaga.[22] Visitations of the parishes of the diocese

21. Ibid., b. 1906, ff. 640r–641v.
22. On the chapel of Santa Barbara see Brunelli, 121–22.

and this early working document on reform served as a foundation for more specific attempts to raise and direct the level of religious belief and practice. Gonzaga focused on three significant areas of concern: renewal of the clergy, restoration of convent life, and reform of the laity. Each of these areas offers glimpses of the complex personality of Gonzaga and the cultural and ecclesiastical conditions of Italy on the eve of the Council of Trent.

Reform of the Clergy

From the spring of 1537, when he took up residence in Mantua, until his departure for Trent in 1561, Gonzaga directly administered his diocese. Soon after arriving, he wrote to Contarini of his satisfaction with the state of the church in Mantua and his hope for success in his future work.[23] He fully admitted, however, that conditions there were not without need of improvement.[24] One of the first issues that Gonzaga addressed was the education of his clergy. His involvement in this reform may be considered on three levels: first, his personal involvement as a man of letters; second, the encouragement he gave to the formation of young clerics in his cathedral school; and third, his use of the printing press to provide manuals for his clergy.

Upon his return to Mantua Gonzaga arranged for lectures in theology to be given in his own chambers. He sponsored these lectures and attended them in a way that reflects the desire of Contarini that the bishop be an example to others. They also illustrated his ability to use the resource of his place in the Mantuan ruling house to further reform. Even though aware of his own scholarly limitations, Gonzaga saw this program of lectures as a means of reforming his clergy. If Gonzaga did not consider himself sufficiently learned in theology to offer much instruction himself, he sought to give the opportunity for it to young men who would follow him. His sixteenth-century biographer, Giulio Castellani, emphasized the financial assistance that Gon-

---

23. Ercole Gonzaga to Gasparo Contarini, May 15, 1537, Friedensburg, 7–8.
24. Ercole Gonzaga to Gasparo Contarini, June 6, 1537, Friedensburg, 9–10.

zaga provided for clerical students to attend universities. He also high-lighted the arrangements that Gonzaga made for the education and maintenance of student clerics at the cathedral.[25] At least as early as the 1520s a cathedral school operated for the education of boys who would one day serve as clergy of the diocese of Mantua.[26] The can-ons of the cathedral and Cardinal Gonzaga shared the expenses of the school.[27] This institution has a significance that reaches far beyond its place in Mantuan history and represents broader currents in Europe-an culture and religion. It looked back to the cathedral schools of the Middle Ages in its origins. Gonzaga was also no doubt influenced by the "schola Accholythorum" that Giberti operated in Verona.[28] The rules, while brief, outline a life that was regulated by the liturgical cal-endar and its exigencies.[29]

The school offered admission to boys of at least twelve years of age who were sound in body, had been tonsured or were free to re-ceive it, knew how to read and write, and knew the *"Dottrina Chris-tiana,"* or catechism, at least in a literal sense. In addition, they were to carry with them letters of recommendation from their parish priest and from their previous school master. This threshold of twelve must have been somewhat flexible, since younger boys of six to eight years of age also studied there. The enrollment fluctuated between eighteen

25. Castellani, *Vita*, 13.

26. Rezzaghi, *Il "Catecismo,"* 42.

27. ASDM, Fondo Capitolo Cattedrale, Miscellanea 2D, n. 4, Chierici della Cat-tedrale e Chiericati, 1560. "Memoria che il vescovo concorre à vestire li chierici per 2 terzi, et il Capitolo per un terzo di spesa."

28. Prosperi, *Tra evangelismo*, 233–34. For an analysis of clerical education throughout Europe in the early modern period see Kathleen M. Comerford, "Cler-ical Education, Catechesis, and Catholic Confessionalism: Teaching Religion in the Sixteenth and Seventeenth Centuries," in Kathleen M. Comerford and Hilmar Pabel, *Early Modern Catholicism: Essays in Honor of John W. O'Malley, S.J.* (Toronto: Univer-sity of Toronto Press, 2001), 241–65.

29. The rules for the clerics of the cathedral are conserved in the ASDM, Fon-do Capitolo Cattedrale. These were published in *Atti del Sinodo Diocesano di Arrigoni 1718*. See also Roberto Rezzaghi, "L'Origine del seminario a Mantova ed il capitolo XVIII della XIII sesione del Concilio di Trento," in *L'Impegno dell'educare. Studi in onore di Pietro Braido* (Rome: Facoltà di Scienze dell'Educazione dell'Università Ponti-ficia Salesiana, 1991), 135–49 (hereafter cited as Rezzaghi, "L'Origine del seminario").

and thirty-five students.[30] Once admitted they were to live as clerics, including wearing a black clerical habit. The school does not seem to have offered boarding facilities to students, since the rules refer to times when students are at their homes and what prayers they are to say when they arrive at school.

The education provided to these young clerics consisted of two parts, religion and letters. Religious formation prepared them for the liturgical life of the Church by having them serve as acolytes and choristers at the cathedral liturgies. Repeated experience of the liturgical year accustomed the clerics to the requirements of the Church's worship. They were also to go to confession once a month and on feast days to an assigned confessor who then gave them license to take communion. The daily order included specified prayers to be recited upon rising, in school, and before going to bed at night. These included the Pater Noster, Ave Maria, and Credo. Gonzaga arranged for the student clerics of the cathedral to be exempt from the obligation of reciting the Divine Office, or *"offitio grande."* Instead they prayed with the *Officium Beatae Mariae Virginis,* or Little Office of Our Lady, a scaled-down cycle of psalms, prayers, scripture readings, and hymns that was commonly used by both secular clergy and laity in the Middle Ages and the Renaissance.[31] On their way to classes the clerics were to walk silently, two by two, according to age and were to be silent in class and in the church. Prohibited activities included swearing and playing in the streets, the school courtyard, or the bishop's residence. This elementary training, carried on over a period of years, prepared them for serving in the liturgical and social roles required of the clergy. The literary formation of these youths included "Latin grammar, singing, writing, and other studies."[32] Teachers were to give recognition to the varying gifts of the students: each was to learn according to his capac-

---

30. For details on the enrollment see Rezzaghi, *Il "Catecismo,"* 42–44.

31. An indult exempted seven *"clericis mantuanis"* from the obligation to say the Divine Office, permitting them to say the "officium beatae Mariae Virginis"; see ASM, AG, b. 1909, f. 505. On the Little Office of Our Lady see Paul F. Grendler, *Schooling in Renaissance Italy: Literacy and Learning, 1300–1600* (Baltimore: Johns Hopkins University Press, 1989), 353–54.

32. Rezzaghi, "L'Origine del seminario," 147.

ity. All students studied the *"Dottrina Christiana."* The rules called for the students to use only suitable books, that is, only those books "necessary to studies, and that are not prohibited in the Index, or are lascivious, or of bad example, Latin or vernacular, whether in school or at home."[33] On Saturdays the teachers arranged disputations among the students on the material they had learned.

These rules found concrete expression in the actual practice of the school. Francesco Galvagno, the episcopal vicar, wrote to Gonzaga in 1562 and described the Latin studies and requirements for boys of various ages at that moment. He had given the examinations for all of the students held before the school vacation. The assessment of the students that accompanied the letter offers a glimpse of the day-to-day studies of twenty-seven students between the ages of six and fifteen whom he divided into lower and upper "forms." Ten of these, age six to nine, were reported to conjugate verbs, decline nouns, and begin to make concordances, that is, they did agreement exercises. Five boys age nine to eleven *"latinano per li activi,"* or began to formulate some Latin phrases using active verbs and listened to Virgil's *Bucolics*. The most promising of the scholars in the lower form was a fifteen-year-old named Alessandro Fretada who wrote letters well on his own and listened to all the lessons. Three thirteen-year-olds also formed Latin phrases using active verbs and listened to the *Bucolics* as well. Three students thirteen to fifteen underwent examinations on the rules of grammar and listened to lessons on Virgil and Cicero. Four more advanced fifteen-year-olds composed Latin letters from vernacular models and heard lectures on Virgil, Terence, and Horace, and on Cicero's letters and his *De officiis*. The most outstanding of the students in the upper form appears to have been a fifteen-year-old named Carolo Ghiselo, who composed letters by himself and was able to follow easily all of the lessons.[34]

33. Ibid., 148. "Niuno tenghi libri se non necessarii a'studii, et che non sieno prohibiti nell'Indice, ò lascivi, ò di mal essempio, latini, ò volgari, così in Scuola, come in casa." It is not clear which index is indicated here. It is possible that the eighteenth-century edition of the rules makes reference to an edition of the index subsequent to the lifetime of Ercole Gonzaga.

34. ASM, AG, b. 1940, ff. 416–417, Francesco Galvagno to Ercole Gonzaga, Sep-

As the boys advanced in studies, the school required those who were capable of learning Latin well to refrain from speaking anything else. Galvagno also indicated in his assessment which students were able to sing in the cathedral choir. Of the twenty-seven, twelve mostly older were listed as in the choir. The references to singing mean something more than simply being able to read Gregorian chant notation. Gonzaga employed the composer Jacquet of Mantua (ca. 1495–1559) as his *maestro di capella*. In Jacquet, who also taught music to the clerics at the cathedral, the young clerics had as their music instructor one of the most prolific composers of polyphonic music in sixteenth-century Italy.[35]

If the plan of studies outlined in the rules was carried out, then Gonzaga himself took at least some part in the training of these future priests. Primary responsibility for good order fell on the teachers, who were to see that the students acted in conformity with the rules. But every fifteen days two of the canons of the cathedral were to visit the school. On those occasions all of the students were to come before the bishop to show him what they had learned. Those who were negligent in their studies were to be punished, while those who did well were to be rewarded. Gonzaga not only supervised the students closely while they were in studies, but it is also clear that he was directly involved in granting permission for ordination or determining the timing of ordinations.[36]

Little is known of the teaching staff of the school. Antonio Cerutti, episcopal vicar of Gonzaga, described an unnamed master in 1550, who may have been Fra Pietro d'Hostillia, as very religious, so-

---

tember 12, 1562. Also cited in Laura Bertazzi Nizzola, "Infiltrazioni protestanti nel ducato di Mantova (1530–1563)," *Bollettino storico mantovano* 7 (1957): 218.

35. Jacquet of Mantua, or Jacquet Colebault, was born in Brittany and had worked in Ferrara before his work in Mantua. Iain Fenlon, 45–78. See also George Nugent, *The Jacquet Motets and their Authors* (Ann Arbor, MI: University Microfilms, 1973), and *The New Grove Dictionary of Music and Musicians*, s.v. "Jacquet of Mantua" (London: Macmillan Publishers, 1980), 456–58.

36. ASM, AG, b. 1940, ff. 593r–594r, Francesco Galvagno to Ercole Gonzaga, September 10, 1562, and b. 1940, f. 463r, Francesco Galvagno to Ercole Gonzaga, November 19, 1562.

licitous, and concerned that the boys not become discouraged in their studies. The vicar admitted that the man was not very accomplished in letters but believed that this shortcoming could be tolerated since he made up for it with those other virtues.[37] Subsequent school masters demonstrated greater competency. In 1562 a priest named Don Nicolò Vilmercato left his teaching post at the cathedral to take up residence in his benefice. Galvagno wrote to Gonzaga with the assumption that the cardinal would not mind because the man "had served for many years in this enterprise."[38] In discussing a possible replacement for Don Nicolò, Galvagno subsequently described him by comparison. He did not judge the candidate "equal to Don Nicolò because he does not know Greek, though he does have enough Latin for these clerics."[39] In time, therefore, Gonzaga was able to supply the student clerics of Mantua with highly trained instructors whose studies had formed them in the traditions of Renaissance humanism. A cathedral canon named Battista Negrisuoli appears in the correspondence of Cardinal Gonzaga as one of the officers responsible for the school, although not its school master. His responsibilities as a canon were admission of candidates, their examinations, and the financial operations of the school, as called for in the rules. He wrote in February of 1550 about the fitness of three candidates for the school, that is, whether they knew music, were well behaved, and had good voices. He himself was able to attest only to their aptitude in music, which he judged to be sufficient. He did add that they were able to understand literally what they read in the breviary and missal.[40]

---

37. Ibid., b. 1920, unnumbered fascicle, Antonio Cerutti to Ercole Gonzaga, February 7, 1550. On Pietro d'Hostillia see also ibid., unnumbered fascicle, Antonio Cerutti to Ercole Gonzaga, January 18, 1550.

38. Ibid., b. 1940, f. 348r, Francesco Galvagno to Ercole Gonzaga, April 22, 1562. "Per molti anni ha servito in questa impresa."

39. Ibid., f. 355r, Francesco Galvagno to Ercole Gonzaga, May 1, 1562. "Ma non gia pari di Don Nicolo perche non ha lettere greche ne ha pero di latine a bastanza per quelli chierici." In the end a man named Girolamo da Sorlo was selected for this post; ibid., f. 373r, Francesco Galvagno to Ercole Gonzaga, June 19, 1562.

40. Ibid., b. 1920, unnumbered fascicle, Battista Negrisuoli to Ercole Gonzaga, February 1, 1550.

These three boys might have one day undergone an ordination examination such as that mentioned by Gonzaga's vicar Cerutti. On one occasion he informed Gonzaga that he intended to be present when the suffragan bishop went for the ordinations at the cathedral school. Cerutti would accompany him with the school master in order to carry out the customary examinations, "so that they will turn out to be priests worthy of this most holy order and that they will understand what they read."[41] With time, many of these students must have attained a high degree of classical culture. During the carnival season of 1542 the students of the school recited Plautus's comedy *Captivi* in Latin before an audience of Mantuan nobles and merchants. Cardinal Gonzaga himself paid for the costumes, which were designed by Giulio Romano. Apparently he used a certain amount of discretion when applying the severe rules of behavior for the clerics when it was carnival season.[42]

Gonzaga's school for young clerics was one of his most successful endeavors. Some of the students went on to distinguished academic careers and served beyond the boundaries of the diocese of Mantua. In 1545 Gonzaga recommended one alumnus, Don Francesco Felonico, to Cardinal Marino Grimani. Gonzaga described the young man as one whom he had trained in letters and music in his school and had intended to take on as one of his own clergy when he reached the appropriate age.[43] A young cleric enrolled in the school in 1539, Federico Pendasio (d. 1603), continued with his studies and taught at Bologna, Padua, and Pavia, held a post as a canon of the cathedral of

41. Ibid., unnumbered fascicle, Antonio Cerutti to Ercole Gonzaga, February 16, 1550.

42. Emilio Faccioli, ed., *Mantova: Le Lettere* (Mantua: Istituto Carlo D'Arco per la Storia di Mantova, 1962), 2: 565. On the play itself see Sir Robert Allison's introduction and translation in *The Complete Roman Drama: All the Extant Comedies of Plautus and Terence and the Tragedies of Seneca, in a Variety of Translations,* ed. George E. Duckworth (New York: Random House, 1942), vol. 2, 223–73. *Captivi* is unique among the works of Plautus in its restraint and serious tone. Even when they performed Plautus, Gonzaga maintained decorum among his students.

43. ASM, AG, Copialettere di Ercole Gonzaga, codex 6497, letter #55, ff. 22v–23r, Ercole Gonzaga to Marino Grimani, July 20, 1545.

Mantua, and acted as theologian for Cardinal Gonzaga in Trent from 1561 to 1563.[44] The most noteworthy alumnus was Settimio Borsieri, who later became a colleague of both Carlo Borromeo and Niccolò Sfondrato, later Pope Gregory XIV. Borsieri eventually became bishop of Casale.[45] The Mantuan cathedral school was an early example of the reform of clerical education that was soon to be mandated by the Council of Trent. Unlike many Tridentine seminaries, it formed not only simple priests of modest ability but some individuals outstanding in academic training as well. Given the size of its enrollment and the quality of the education it provided, it is likely that these younger clerics came to have an increasingly significant impact on the character of religious life in Mantua.

While Cardinal Gonzaga directed his efforts with the students at his cathedral school toward cultivating a well-trained body of clergy who could appreciate classical literature and would be capable of serious study in theology, he also sought to improve the religious knowledge and pastoral practice of those priests who already served the diocese of Mantua but had not necessarily benefited from such an education. In another way reminiscent of Gian Matteo Giberti, Gonzaga worked in the area of publishing to that end. In 1543 he helped the Venetian printer Venturino Ruffinelli establish a press in Mantua. He offered the printer and his employees full immunity from taxes, buildings for the printing house itself as well as for residences, and a monopoly on all printing in Mantua.[46] By means of this press, Gonzaga provided handbooks and pastoral aids to his clergy. These include the *Breve ricordo di Monsignore Illustrissimo et Reverendissimo Monsignor Hercole Gonzaga Cardinale di Mantova spettanti alla vita dei chierici,*

44. See *Enciclopedia Cattolica* (Vatican City: Ente per l'Enciclopedia Cattolica e per il Libro Cattolico, 1949–54), s.v. Pendasio, Federico; Girolamo Seripando, Seripandi Commentarii, CT, II: 483, n. 1. On his presence at the cathedral school ASM, AG, b. 1909, f. 505r, "Dispensio dell'officio grande per alunni chierici," June 7, 1539.

45. ASDM, Fondo Capitolo della Cattedrale, Miscellanea 2D, #4, Chierici della Cattedrale e Chiericati, March 1, 1554. See also Eubel, 3: 103, 155.

46. ASM, *Decretorum Mantuae de Anno 1542 usque ad Annum 1547,* F. II. 10, ff. 44v–45r. On Ruffinelli see Fernanda Ascarelli, *La Tipographia cinquecentina italiana* (Florence: Sansoni, 1953), 88.

the *Constitutioni per la Chiesa Cathedrale di Mantova,* the *Ordo baptizandis secundum ritum Romane Ecclesiae ad usum civitatis mantuae,* and the *Catecismo overo instruttione* of Leonardo de Marini. Gonzaga published these for provision to the churches of his diocese in order to enhance the quality of pastoral care offered by the clergy who were already ordained. The *Breve ricordo* is in fact a republication under Gonzaga's name of a book that Giberti had published for the clergy of Verona. Giberti's work probably circulated in the diocese of Mantua even before it was reissued under Gonzaga's name. Gonzaga had it published in the same volume as an Italian edition of a work then thought to be by Thomas Aquinas, the *De officio sacerdotis.* The purpose of this document was to remind the priests, first of Verona, later of Mantua, of their duty. It is associated, in the mind of Gonzaga, with the visitations that were an occasion for reemphasizing the responsibilities of the priest. Near the beginning of the book the hope is expressed that lay people "of good will and lovers of the things of God" who see this book will urge it upon their priests and help them.[47] This hope recalls the practice of the inquisitorial visitations, during which the opinions of local nobles were sought in the matter of their priest's education and pastoral care. Gonzaga intended to avail himself of the desires, and perhaps the resentment, of the laity in order to reform the clergy.

Within this description of clerical practice in the *Breve ricordo* is a list of books that the priests of Mantua were to use in order to prepare themselves. It is as revealing for what Gonzaga and his associates left off the list as for what they included. The reading material included the Bible and commentaries on it, such as that of Nicholas of Lyra, or a *Catena aurea,* a commentary on the Gospels and the Psalms. The priests should also have a book of homilies for the year and on the saints. In addition, they ought to have some *summa* or manual for confessors such as the fifteenth-century *Summa angelica* of Angelo Carletti da Chiavasso or the *Summa Tabiena* of Giovanni Cagnazzo da Taggia. Gonzaga also added the works of Antonino Pierozzi, the

47. Ercole Gonzaga, *Breve ricordo* (Mantua: Ruffinelli, 1561), 2r.

fifteenth-century bishop of Florence, such as the *Manipulus curatorum* and the *Defecerunt*.[48] The *Defecerunt* is a commonly used title for a work also known as the *Summa confessionalis*, a handbook for confessors. Priests were also to possess a *Manuale* or a book of sacraments "that is usually called the baptismal."[49] These handbooks, sometimes referred to as *Cerimoniali*, outlined the rituals of the Church. Finally it is suggested that priests study the *opusculi* of Thomas Aquinas and Antonino Pierozzi that "were given by His Most Reverend Lordship for the assistance of ignorant priests."[50] The minimum required of priests was that they grasp the basics of liturgy, homiletics, and cases of conscience. In order to assist them Gonzaga arranged for the lecturer in the Dominican convent of San Domenico to instruct any in need. It is far from certain, and perhaps doubtful, that many priests bought some or all of these books. The only church where a complete collection was ever found during the course of the visitations was that held by the *vicar foranea,* or episcopal vicar for the *contado*.[51]

This reading list presents both continuity and contrast with the book purchases Gonzaga made from the 1530s to the 1550s. The suggested reading material was orthodox, but even among these Catholic books, there is a distinct difference in emphasis from Gonzaga's personal collection. Whereas Gonzaga himself displayed great interest in the works of patristic writers and a wide array of biblical commentaries, the advice to the clergy of Mantua is far more modest. The Bible, however, is still at the heart of the reading list and the first scripture scholar whose name is mentioned is Nicholas of Lyra, whose works Gonzaga

48. Ibid., 2v–3r. On these late medieval *summae* see Pierre Michaud-Quantin, *Sommes de casuistique et manuels de confessions au moyen âge (XII–XVI siècles)* (Louvain: Nauwelaerts, 1962); Boyle, "Summae confessorum," 227–37. On Antonino see A. D'Addario, DBI, s.v. "Antonino Pierozzi."

49. Gonzaga, *Breve ricordo*, 5r. In September of 1538 Gonzaga bought "una cassa de libri da batezare da venetia." Such a supply was probably intended for distribution to the priests of Mantua. See ASDM, MV, b. 1, f. 258r, September 4, 1538.

50. Gonzaga, *Breve ricordo*, 14r. "E di più vuole e ordina espressamente che si studino i libretti di San Thommaso, e San Antonino Arcivescovo Fiorentino quali sono stati da Sua Reverendissima Signoria dati per soccorso dell'ignoranza delli sacerdoti idioti."

51. Zagni, 1: 174.

had purchased. The clergy are told to equip themselves with Thomas, *summae* of cases, and the works of Antonino. Theological reading for the priests of Mantua was more limited than that of Gonzaga and his closer associates and less noticeably humanist in character.

The *Ordo baptizandi* is a short book of rituals published in 1558. The preface indicates that Gonzaga had it published "lest those things which concerned the worship of God and the good of souls be neglected."[52] He ordered that all the clergy of Mantua with responsibility for the care of souls, whether archpriests or chaplains, acquire a copy.[53] The book covers baptism, catechumens, care of the sick and dying, and sacramentals such as the blessing of holy water, of various foods, of candles, and of pilgrims. The theological reflection used in it included a good deal of allegorical interpretation of ritual, a good example being the instructions given for baptism. The priests are to use ordinary water for the sacrament "because pure water flowed from the side of Christ."[54] They are forbidden to use rose water, other liquors, or wine. Gonzaga ordered the priests to memorize the words used in baptism and urged them to ensure that midwives also knew them.[55] In general the book addresses the priest as one who needs education himself yet who will be called upon to educate his parishioners, in this case the parents and godparents of infants. That instruction consisted of simple prayers including the Angelus, the Apostles' Creed, the Pater Noster, and the Ave Maria.

The *Ordo baptizandi* is not well organized. In the midst of the directions that priests are to give to the parents and godparents, there is a list of warnings that priests were to announce frequently at mass. These included warnings against women who acted as wet nurses for Jews, against the practice of abortion, and against parents' bringing

---

52. Ercole Gonzaga, *Ordo baptizandi secundum ritum Romane Ecclesiae ad usum civitatis mantue* (Mantua: Ruffinelli, 1558), 2r. "Ne quid quod ad ipsius Dei cultum salutemque animarum spectet pretermittatur librum hunc cathecuminorum . . . imprimendum curavit."

53. Gonzaga, *Ordo baptizandi,* 2r. "Omnibus Archipresbyteris, Prioribius, Prepositis, Ecclesiarum Rectoribus seu capellanis animarum curam gerentibus."

54. Ibid., 2v. "Quia fluxit de latere Christi aqua pura."

55. Ibid., 2v.

small children to bed with them lest they be smothered either through negligence or deliberately. Those who learned about such transgressions should inform their pastor or his vicar. Priests were to take care that a fit atmosphere in church be maintained during the sacrament of the Eucharist: no laughing or noise. Priests as well as those who assisted them were to be devout and use caution lest the Eucharist be stolen from the church. They were warned not to baptize anyone from outside of the parish.[56] Only when the editors finished with this list of warnings did they return to the principal matter of the book, the rituals of the Church. The emphasis is on practical matters and surprisingly, given the environment in which Gonzaga worked, did not address issues of heresy. The abrupt inclusion of these warnings points to intentions that go beyond care for liturgical rubrics. In this publication the reform of the clergy and the reform of the laity meet. Priests are to control their parishes and parishioners according to the regulations established by the universal Church and their lord, Ercole Gonzaga.

The relationship between reform of clergy and reform of the laity is also evident in the *Constitutioni per la Chiesa Cathedrale di Mantova*. This handbook for the cathedral clergy was published in its definitive form in 1558. The introduction indicates that most of it had already appeared many times before.[57] Already in 1538 Gonzaga had expressed exasperation at the conduct of his cathedral canons. In a letter to Contarini he explained that he had made his secretary a canon with precedence over the others in order to be sure that even in Gonzaga's absence his orders would be obeyed. His problems at the cathedral stemmed from the fact that many of the canonries were in the hands of "little boys who think of everything but residing" at the cathedral.[58]

Although Gonzaga directed the *Constitutioni* toward the comport-

56. Ibid., 5v–7v.

57. Ercole Gonzaga, *Constitutioni per la Chiesa Cathedrale di Mantova* (Mantua: Ruffinelli, 1558), 3r.

58. Ercole Gonzaga to Gasparo Contarini, January 16, 1539, Friedensburg, 36. "Essendo tutte le dignitati di essa chiesa in mano di putti, li quali pensano ad ogni altra cosa che a fare residenza."

ment of those clergy who served as canons of the cathedral, the document emphasizes the apostolic importance of the lives of all clergy. Gonzaga called for clergy to engage in the kind of exemplary reform that he himself sought to offer. If it is possible to speak of an attempt on the local level to reform the Church in "head and members," then Gonzaga seems to have tried to do this in Mantua. The *Constitutioni* describe the highest duty of the bishop as that of ensuring that the manner of life of the clergy is such as to attract others to the love and worship of God.[59] The purpose of the *Constitutioni* is to begin this task with his cathedral chapter. Gonzaga wanted his canons to obtain their posts legitimately; he imposed on them the obligation to wear appropriate clerical garb and insisted that they appropriately participate in the Divine Office. Gonzaga also encouraged them to go to the sacrament of penance on a weekly basis.

Striking in this rather dry litany of unsurprising liturgical duties is the list of authorities that are used to defend and promote appropriate behavior by the canons. The *Constitutioni* make no reference to canon law to articulate the duties of the cathedral clergy. There are several references to sacred scripture, the fathers of the Church, and canons of Church councils and synods. These include the Book of Exodus, the Psalms, Jeremiah, Augustine, Basil, Jerome, the Pseudo-Dionysius, the Councils of Carthage and Toledo, and local synods in France and Germany. The names of two popes, those of Anacletus and Innocent III, appear in the pages of the book to lend weight. There is one general reference to the "Apostles and the Holy Fathers."[60] With the exception of Innocent III, the appeal is to the authority of the early Church, those authorities most highly esteemed by reformers imbued with humanistic literary and religious preferences. The Bible and the patristic writers form the core of Gonzaga's understanding and defense of the importance of the liturgical duties of his cathedral clergy.

The use of Augustine is revealing when taken in the context of

59. Gonzaga, *Constitutioni*, 2r.

60. Ibid., 3r, 4r, 5r, 6r, 6v, 12r, 17v, 18r, 19r. It is not clear from the text whether Gonzaga distinguished between the Denis who was the reputed first bishop of Paris and the Pseudo-Dionysius whose works he had purchased for his library.

Mantuan religious life, illuminated by the heresy trial of Gonzaga's secretary, Endimio Calandra, in 1568. Calandra testified to the widespread currency of heretical thought in the preaching of Mantuan clerics.[61] Perhaps some of them had enlisted these arguments in defense of their own lack of attention to their other liturgical responsibilities. The clergy of Verona had used an evangelical and Pauline argument themselves when resisting the reforms of Gian Matteo Giberti, arguing that Christ had freed them from the law.[62] In this regard Gonzaga's use of Augustine's letter to Januarius on liturgical matters in the *Constitutioni* takes on a particular significance:

Those things that are not against the faith and good morals that have been established in any place, provided that they have some edification of a better life, are always to be praised and imitated; therefore, we order that you always enter the choir in procession with the cross and the candles in front, and having arrived there, before kneeling, say a Pater Noster and an Ave Maria, then the Office begins and in the Office they should act in a manner that is fitting, and when one is to sit, all sit and when one is to stand all stand; and similarly they are to kneel at the required times.[63]

Augustine's purpose in the letter to Januarius was to affirm that customs differ and that no single liturgical practice applies universally. It is a counsel to freedom. But in this context Gonzaga used Augustine to mandate particular behavior and to defend the practices that he required of his canons. This affirmation of practices that are not against the faith and which may in fact serve to edify others sounds, paradoxically, not unlike Martin Luther's defense of the temporary use of some Catholic practices in the face of more radical followers such as Andreas Karlstadt, who sought rapid and radical liturgical reform

61. Pagano, *Secondo Costituto di Endimio Calandra,* March 27, 1568, 251.

62. Prosperi, *Tra evangelismo,* 176.

63. Gonzaga, *Constitutioni,* 6r. "Come dice Santo Agostino scrivendo a Ianuario quelle cose che non sono contra la fede e buon costumi le quali sono state instituite in qual si voglia luogo purche habbiano qualche edificatione di miglio vita sono sempre da lodar e imitar, percio ordinamo che s'entri in Choro pocessionalménte col la croce & li cerosti innanzi." For the letter to Januarius see *Sancti Aurelii Augustini Hipponensis episcopi Opera omnia,* vol. 2, ed. J.-P. Migne (Paris: Garnier Fratres et Mignes Successores, 1902), letter #54, columns 199–204.

founded on the requirement of explicit affirmation of liturgical practice in the scriptures. Gonzaga similarly defended conservative liturgical practice in terms of the *adiaphora,* or indifferent matters. In the
Mantuan case, however, Gonzaga's purpose was to correct his own cathedral clergy. It is also consistent with the attitude of Gasparo Contarini and Reginald Pole that clergy ought to be very careful about what
they communicate to ordinary people about the faith.[64]

Gonzaga's commitment to the liturgical reform of his cathedral is
borne out by evidence of financial support that he gave to composers
and musicians. He granted benefices to singers and instrumentalists in
order to provide them with income. In particular he may have permanently set aside the benefice of the church in Cerea for this purpose.
After the death of a Fra Francesco, who sang bass in the cathedral
choir, Gonzaga granted the benefice to another Francesco who served
as his organist.[65] The most notable of these musicians was Jacquet of
Mantua, who worked for Gonzaga from about 1527 until his death in
1559. His compositions are almost exclusively liturgical in character,
including at least twelve masses. One musicologist has seen in this collaboration between Gonzaga and Jacquet an early attempt to carry out
a liturgical reform that integrated the arts, such as the one later enacted by Carlo Borromeo.[66]

In addition to reform in Mantua, the *Constitutioni* reflect Gonzaga's ongoing candidacy for the papal tiara. For many generations those
concerned about reform in the Church had called for it to begin *in ca-
pite,* at the papal curia. Earlier popes resisted calls for a general council by pointing to their own putative reforms at Rome. The failure of
popes to carry out such reform in any meaningful way scandalized
Catholics as well as Protestants. It may be that Gonzaga used the reform of his cathedral in part to position himself for election in a future conclave. Having reformed the canons of Mantua, he could present himself as the candidate who would reform the curia at Rome. It

64. See Gleason, *Gasparo Contarini,* 266–69.

65. ASM, AG, b. 876, ff. 358r–358v, Ercole Gonzaga to Federico Gonzaga, April
28, 1528.

66. Iain Fenlon, 45–78.

is an indication of the advance of reform in Italy that a figure such as Gonzaga viewed active engagement in local reform as part of the calculation necessary to attain the papacy.

Among his assistants, Gonzaga enjoyed the collaboration of the Dominican bishop Leonardo de Marini (1509–73), who served as his suffragan bishop from 1550 to 1553. Along with other of Gonzaga's assistants, Marini carried out the visitations that Gonzaga ordered for the diocese. Subsequently he served on papal commissions that were to compose the new missal and breviary and collaborated on the new Roman Catechism. Marini gained experience in this area during his years in Mantua by writing, at the request of Gonzaga, a catechism for the diocese that was published in 1555. In the preface Marini states that Cardinal Gonzaga charged him to write it to educate ignorant people in the things they need to know about the salvation of their souls.[67] What is significant to note, however, is that Gonzaga provided such a work for his diocese. In conjunction with the other publications that he authorized for the clergy and the laity of Mantua, it gives evidence of the seriousness with which he ruled his diocese.

These handbooks for priests describe the duties of clerics in limited terms. The clergy of Mantua were to wear the cassock, attend to the sacraments, and rule their parishes in accordance with the norms of the Church. More positive encouragement to virtue must have been reserved for those personal encounters between bishop and priests during the visitations or other meetings. Gonzaga's vicar Cerutti wrote of one such meeting that took place in January of 1550 while Gonzaga was in Rome for the conclave that elected Julius III. By order of Duchess Margherita Paleologa, Cerutti had gathered all the clergy of the city for a convocation for the purpose of determining provisions for the "truly poor."[68] Cerutti chose not to miss the opportunity to exhort the clergy to a more fervent practice of pastoral care. He offered "many words," asking them to be solicitous for the good

67. Rezzaghi, Il "Catecismo," 123.
68. ASM, AG, b. 1920, unnumbered fascicle, Antonio Cerutti to Ercole Gonzaga, January 18, 1550.

of their souls, vigilant, and above all to remember charity. He asked them to be loving toward their parishioners and to carry out all of the things that had been ordered on the last visitation by his predecessor. Cerutti's letters are filled with protestations of loyalty to Gonzaga, as he expressed his desire to avoid anything displeasing his bishop. It is hard not to see more than a touch of the sycophant in him. For this very reason his description of his lecture to the clergy of Mantua is significant. Cerutti does not seem to be the kind of man who would tell Gonzaga anything other than what he wanted to hear already. Thus, it is reasonable to see in this general description of the exhortation a reflection of the desires of Gonzaga for the clergy of his diocese.[69]

Reform of Monasteries of Nuns

Cardinal Gonzaga's work of reforming monasteries began, as had visitations of parishes, while he was still resident in Rome. As early as 1531 Duke Federico reported to his brother about problems in monasteries of nuns in the Mantovano. On more than one occasion he reported that nuns had attempted to flee the monastery of the Annunciata in Borgo di San Giorgio. Federico assured Cardinal Gonzaga that he would take all necessary measures to preserve order. He also encouraged Gonzaga to order the friars who were in charge of that monastery to be more vigilant.[70] The earliest known response from Cardinal Gonzaga to this sort of appeal is from October of 1536. At that time he simply expressed his satisfaction that Federico displayed such interest in the reform of the monasteries.[71] By January of 1537, how-

69. Cerutti came under suspicion of heresy by the Inquisition and was the subject of a bitter struggle over jurisdiction in 1567 between Duke Guglielmo Gonzaga and the Mantuan inquisitor, Cammillo Campeggi. The inquisitor overcame the duke and Cerutti was extradited to Rome where he eventually abjured. Endimio Calandra identified him in his testimony not simply as a heretic but as an atheist. See Pagano, 244, n. 28 and passim.

70. Federico Gonzaga to Ercole Gonzaga, February 28, 1531, cited in Bertazzi Nizzola 7 (1957), 205–6.

71. Ercole Gonzaga to Federico Gonzaga, 26 October 1536, cited in Bertazzi Nizzola 7 (1957), 206.

ever, Gonzaga had turned his attention more fully to this reform project. Fra Reginaldo Nerli assisted him in it as in others. He had written to Gonzaga to express what must have been his discouragement at the prospects for success. Gonzaga admitted that some of "ours" who have daughters and relatives in the monasteries are dissatisfied with what they hear and see of the reform. Nevertheless, he urged Nerli not to lose heart because he would soon return to Mantua and carry out his intentions. Already, he added, the nuns of the monastery of Santa Marta were engaged in reform. He assisted them by assigning a benefice for a priest to act as their chaplain.[72] Gonzaga did not, in fact, consider conditions in the convents to be excessively problematic. He further described his intentions in a letter to Contarini in June of 1537, stating then that he was about to turn his attention to the reformation of monasteries of nuns. This was not, he claimed, because they lived dishonorably or scandalously. The concern he expressed to his friend was that they had gone without visitations for so long that certain "innovations" had crept into their practice of religious life, which in time might cause some disorder. His proposed reformation would demonstrate itself to be "useful, good and holy."[73]

Gonzaga's views on the matter reflected sixteenth-century clerical approaches to women in religious orders and they anticipated later reforms.[74] In large measure Gonzaga tried to regain authority over these

72. BAV, Barb. Lat., codex 5789, 26v–27r, Ercole Gonzaga to Reginaldo da Nerli, February 24, 1537.

73. Ercole Gonzaga to Gasparo Contarini, June 16, 1537, Friedensburg, 11–12. "A questo attendo hora et alla riformatione de monasterii delle monache, quali benchè non fossero incorse in maniere di vivere men che honeste nè scandalose, nondimeno per essere state tanto senza visitatione, s'erano pure innovate delle cosette che in processo di tempo havriano potuto causare qualche disordine, sichè tale riformatione non può essere se non utile, buona et santa." More than two years later Contarini sent to Gonzaga an "instructione breve il [sic] la vita monastica" that he had written for his own sister who was a nun. He thought it might be of some use to Gonzaga, since his sister Livia Gonzaga was also a nun. The document is no longer extant. See Solmi, "Lettere inedite," 257–58.

74. On the reform of female monastic communities see Pio Paschini, "I monasteri femminili in Italia nel '500," in *Problemi di vita religiosa in Italia nel cinquecento, Atti del convegno di storia della Chiesa in Italia* (Padua: Antenore, 1960), 31–60; Raimondo Creytens, "La riforma dei monasteri femminili dopo i Decreti Tridentini," in *Il Con-*

institutions. By March of 1537 he had established a set of rules with this move in mind.[75] These *Capituli per la reformatione de monasterii de sore* formed a rough draft of Gonzaga's intended reforms.[76] He had impaneled a board of nine men to oversee the reform that included three members of the Gonzaga family: an Archbishop Gonzaga, who was most likely Agostino Gonzaga, Archbishop of Reggio di Calabria, plus Alvisio Gonzaga and Giacomo Gonzaga. The other six included nobles and physicians. In addition, Reginaldo Nerli wrote at least some sections of the document.[77]

The sixteen chapters focus on increased control over the nuns by the bishop and their religious superiors. The document emphasized strict enclosure, limiting membership in the communities to financially manageable levels, and demands for guaranteed support from the families of nuns. It also called for regular oversight by the bishop or his vicar and official protectors that each monastery would elect. The *Capituli* called for these protectors to be men of exemplary life who had concern for the monastery and would be drawn from both the noble and middle classes. Their responsibilities looked to the good ordering of the monastery and making provision for its needs. Further controls on monastery life included the requirement that monasteries receive the approval of the bishop or his vicar in order to accept novices, for the protectors to enter the monastery, for a priest to stay overnight because of the imminent death of a nun, for the entry of a religious superior or confessor to make a visit, and for receipt of any basket or package that had been left for a nun. Protectors were to meet with the bishop on the first day of every month to inform him of the state of the monasteries. These *Capituli* underline the conservative character of Gonzaga's reforms. The document is not a plan

---

cilio di Trento e la riforma tridentina, atti del convegno storico (Rome: Herder, 1965), 1: 45–79.

75. ASM, AG, b. 1906, ff. 656r–658r, Simone Andreasino to Ercole Gonzaga, March 23, 1537.

76. Ibid., 634r–636r, undated. All other documents in this fascicle are from the summer of 1537, including the responses to the plan.

77. Ibid., ff. 632r–632v, Gian Lodovico Gonzaga to Ercole Gonzaga, July 5, 1537.

for a monastery. It does not attempt to prescribe the life or purpose of these communities or offer any novel remedies. Rather, these rules reflect concern for limiting contact between nuns and their families and friends. Thirteen of the sixteen chapters regulate contact between nuns and the outside world. Even when fathers came to visit daughters a "listener" was always to be present. In this respect Gonzaga acted as a gatekeeper.

These measures encountered a combination of resistance and doubt. Early in this effort Gonzaga's vicar at the time, Simone Andreasino, informed him that the prior of the Augustinian priory of Sant'Agnese had acknowledged receipt of Gonzaga's instructions and that the confessor of a particular unnamed monastery would no longer spend time with the nuns other than when he needed to dispense the sacraments, nor would he sleep there as he had done in the past. On the other hand, the nuns did not want to be governed by the *Capituli* or have the protectors of the convent interfere in their affairs.[78] Other observers doubted that these measures would succeed. Another relative of the cardinal, Gian Lodovico Gonzaga, advised him that the *Capituli* were not strong enough and that nothing would prevent the nuns from living as freely as they did before, if not more so. Only those chapters that Nerli had written seemed sufficiently firm to him.[79] Above all, Gian Lodovico Gonzaga wanted the cardinal to ensure that the nuns observe the constitutions of their monastic communities.

Gonzaga does seem to have effected a stricter interpretation of cloister in the convents of Mantua. More than ten years later he received a letter from his cousin Suor Angelica Gonzaga, abbess of the convent of Corpo di Cristo. Marquise Paola Malatesta had founded this house in 1416 and it became a frequent choice for women of the Gonzaga family who took the veil.[80] Angelica wrote to the cardinal requesting that he seek a dispensation from the pope from the strict rules of the cloister. It seems that she and some of the other sisters had

78. Ibid., f. 657r, Simone Andreasino to Ercole Gonzaga, March 23, 1537.
79. Ibid., ff. 632r–632v, Gian Lodovico Gonzaga to Ercole Gonzaga, July 5, 1537.
80. Ibid., b. 1920, unnumbered fascicle, Suor Angelica Gonzaga to Ercole Gonzaga, February 12, 1550. On the role of the Gonzaga in this convent see Jeryldene M.

scruples about what they viewed as the corrupting influence of too many women of the court inevitably entering the house when members of the Gonzaga family, such as the cardinal's brother Ferrante or the children of the duchess, would visit. She suggested that one woman in the entourage of the duchess be chosen as the regular companion of whoever made a visit. She further added that it would not always be necessary that the woman be present, but only when those members of court forced such visits upon them. That the community would seek papal dispensation in order to limit the individuals who might visit along with members of the most privileged family in the duchy demonstrates a high degree of discipline. Since they could hardly prevent the ducal family from coming to their community, they sought a papal brief to regulate the visits and to limit the number of guests. By the time that letter was written in 1550, the superior of the house at least was interested in reducing contact with the outside world.

Mantuan families, like those in other cities of northern Italy, did not always offer sufficient financial support to daughters and sisters in the convents. Many fathers consigned young women to convents because they were not financially capable of providing them with dowries substantial enough to allow them to marry according to their social position. The numbers of nuns swelled, straining the resources of the monasteries themselves.[81] Often the families did not provide any financial support for these women. This problem seems to have genuinely bothered Cardinal Gonzaga. In 1550 he sought a papal brief that would allow him to send nuns back home if their families did not support them. His experience showed that only when he forced families to support their daughters and sisters did they do so, and then only unwillingly. In fact, they thought he was strange for insisting on support. He felt certain that conditions would have become far worse had

---

Wood, *Women, Art, and Spirituality: The Poor Clares of Early Modern Italy* (Cambridge: Cambridge University Press, 1996), 89–96.

81. On the financial problems of monasteries of nuns see Kathryn Norberg, "The Counter Reformation and Women: Religious and Lay," in *Catholicism in Early Modern Europe: A Guide to Research,* ed. John W. O'Malley, S.J. (St. Louis: Center for Reformation Research, 1988), 133–46. See also Jutta Gisela Sperling, *Convents and the Body Politic in Late Renaissance Venice* (Chicago: University of Chicago Press, 1999).

he not taken his responsibilities seriously and had he not held temporal authority in the duchy, given how little concern some families had "for their own flesh and blood and how little fear they had of divine justice."[82] It was this situation that led him to seek authority from the Holy See to send nuns back to their families. His purpose was not in fact to send nuns home and thereby unburden the nuns who remained. Rather, Gonzaga wanted to use the papal brief as a stick with which to threaten families who failed in their duties of support. He was confident that such a weapon in his hand would have effect because, as he put it, these families would rather have their daughters in the monasteries than in their own homes, where there would be no doubt that the family was responsible for them and their presence would be the source of "infinite discomfort and discontent."[83] He further sought to prohibit the entrance of girls under fifteen, because he well knew that they often left home not knowing where they were going, or against their will if they did. Furthermore, Gonzaga wanted to guarantee that no nun be admitted to a monastery without having been examined by his suffragan, vicar, or other person assigned by him in order to ensure that novices entered willingly.[84] Reform by restricting the admission of candidates may have been too successful for some convents. In 1562 Gonzaga received a request from the nuns of the Servite monastery of San Barnaba to allow them to admit two sisters aged fifteen and ten as nuns in the convent. The community at that time was in difficult financial straits and saw the admission of the two with dowries as a means to alleviate the situation. By 1562 they could not be admitted without the license of Cardinal Gonzaga.[85]

Gonzaga published his final statement on monasteries of nuns in 1560, twenty-four years after he first began to address their situation.[86] By means of a *grida,* or edict, he stated once again the importance of

82. ASM, AG, b. 1945, ff. 60v–61r, Ercole Gonzaga to Ippolito Capilupi, December 27, 1550.

83. Ibid., f. 61v, Ercole Gonzaga to Ippolito Capilupi, December 27, 1550. ". . . incommodo et discontentezza infinita."

84. Ibid., f. 62r, Ercole Gonzaga to Ippolito Capilupi, December 27, 1550.

85. Ibid., b. 1941, ff. 511r–511v, Il Primicerio to Ercole Gonzaga, June 12, 1562.

86. Ibid., b. 2047, f. 110r–113v, October 12, 1560.

strictly maintaining the rules of cloister. Unlike the earlier *Capituli,* this *grida* made no reference to lay protectors. Perhaps by 1560 the role of protectors was taken for granted. More significantly, Gonzaga intended this public edict for the population at large even more than for the nuns. The cardinal helped the monasteries maintain standards that he had established by threatening laymen with sanctions for disobeying him. Pope Pius IV enhanced Gonzaga's authority with a special brief covering monasteries. Duke Guglielmo had apparently been consulted, since he added to the document an appendix that contained his own threats. Gonzaga's interest in the reform of monasteries of nuns is not unusual, because many in the mid-sixteenth century had particular concern for the reform of religious orders of both men and women. It is noteworthy, however, for taking place before the Council of Trent. The Church brought into effect a more universal application of the rules of cloister for nuns in the years following the Council of Trent. Gonzaga, to a certain extent, anticipated this reform and shared in these desires. He also recognized how interrelated were the issues of cloister and financial support. He wanted to maintain a strict rule of cloister but he also realized how important it would be to keep these *"poverelle"* from starvation if they were not to be allowed out to beg for alms as freely as before. Furthermore, his own understanding of his work in the Church was inextricably bound up with personal and family honor. That fathers and brothers would abandon their daughters and sisters struck him as dishonorable. As in so many other times in his career, motivations that arose from his role for many years as governor of the duchy and head of the ruling family shaped Gonzaga's attitude toward reform of convents.

Reform of the Laity

Gonzaga carried out a reform of the laity by means of both correction and instruction. The more negative correction can be observed in Gonzaga's temporal rule of the duchy and in an instrument of that authority over which Gonzaga had complete control after 1540: the *grida,* or edict. Rulers of Mantua frequently used these *gride* in order to remind their subjects of duties and prohibitions already published, but perhaps not well observed, and also to make known new laws. Gonzaga used this temporal instrument to condemn unacceptable belief and practice. In a more constructive vein, Gonzaga provided for the laity of the diocese of Mantua a renewed program of confraternal organization and an attempt at religious education in the Schools of Christian Doctrine.

The government of Ercole Gonzaga increased both the total number of *gride* and the number of those proclamations that dealt with matters of religion. Between 1531 and 1540, the nine-year period immediately before Cardinal Gonzaga assumed authority in the duchy, the government of Mantua published only five religious *gride.* In the sixteen years of Cardinal Gonzaga's regency of the duchy, forty-five separate *gride* that can be considered religious in nature appeared.[87] Ten of these dealt with specifically theological questions such as heresy and correct understandings of the sacraments. Fifteen addressed issues that may be termed liturgical, including the observation of feasts and reverence for the churches of the city. Another twenty concerned practical or moral issues such as usury, prostitution, and treatment of the poor. Cardinal Gonzaga took full advantage of his position as regent to institute reforms on a broad scale among the laity of Mantua. Theological questions that the *gride* addressed involved heresy, a problem similar to that in other Italian cities in the mid-sixteenth century. In March of 1541 Gonzaga condemned any open speech against the Catholic faith, particularly in the town of Viadana. He had learned that people there had disputed publicly on matters of religion, including the powers of the pope, pictures of saints, fasting, confession, free will, predestination, purgatory, and other things that, as the *grida* reads, "they have no business discussing."[88] Punishment for these acts, as well as other forms of inappropriate behavior such as blasphemy, was based on a scale of relative severity: how public the discussion was, whether it was the first offense or a recurring

---

87. Ibid., bb. 2038–41.
88. Ibid., b. 2038–9, fascicle 16, ff. 7v–8r, March 24, 1541.

problem, and whether the individual in question was a man, woman, adult, or child. Punishments could include fines, lashings, having one's tongue cut out, and even death. Ultimate decisions on the severity of the punishment lay with Cardinal Gonzaga and the Duchess Margherita. In addressing the challenge of Protestantism in the duchy of Mantua, Gonzaga seemed not to hesitate when it became a matter of public record among ordinary people. In one recorded instance of blasphemy, the regents Ercole and Margherita ordered two men to have their tongues perforated in public and remain on display for an hour during the Saturday market in the town of Revere.[89] It does not appear, however, that anyone was ever executed for heresy in Mantua during Gonzaga's lifetime.[90]

One religious *grida* that addresses annual confession and communion at Easter was published in the spring of 1550.[91] The bulk of this *grida* is a defense of the sacrament of penance. It describes the sacrament in remarkable detail in order to argue in favor of individual confession to a priest. Gonzaga used the *grida* to express an orthodox Catholic position on sin and forgiveness. He used the Gospel of John, the first epistle of John, Paul's letter to the Corinthians, and Augustine as authorities. The document rejects in particular the view that an individual may repent individually to God alone. It also argues for the utility of receiving advice from a confessor in order to distinguish more serious sins from lesser ones. Promoting this type of discernment was an important goal of the confessional manuals that Gonzaga urged upon his priests. Those who still refused to receive the sacrament of penance and receive communion were to be excommunicated, fined by civil authority and, if they persisted in their resistance, banished from the duchy. If they were government officials and professionals such as notaries, procurators, teachers, and judges they were to be stripped of their offices. This *grida* indicates both the degree

89. Bertazzi Nizzola, 7 (1957), 213. For an illustration of this form of punishment see Salvatore Caponetto, *La Riforma protestante nell'Italia del Cinquecento* (Turin: Claudiana editrice, 1992), 270.

90. Bertazzi Nizzola, 6 (1956), 121.

91. ASM, AG, b. 2040–41, fascicle 18, ff. 13v–15r, May 13, 1550.

to which unorthodox views had spread among the Mantuan population and the resolve of Cardinal Gonzaga to control and inhibit unorthodoxy. In certain respects issuing this *grida* resembles the efforts
of other reformers of the practice of penance to link personal confession with issues of social conformity. Carlo Borromeo's work in Milan
is only the most outstanding example of this practice. Gonzaga's effort to instill a practice of annual confession and communion, nevertheless, was a modest proposal in comparison to confessional practice
later in the century, when there is no discussion of effecting substantial change of life. The references to popular attitudes toward confession among Protestants indicate that Gonzaga was more concerned
with eliminating deviant religious practice than with the much more
daunting task of changing hearts and minds.[92]

These concerns for social practice also appear in a *grida* of March
1542 that prohibited clandestine marriages. This document addresses a fundamental problem in marriage practice in early modern Europe, the oftentimes conflicting needs of families and spouses. The
Church had included marriage as one of the seven sacraments at the
Fourth Lateran Council in 1215, but precisely how individuals con-
tracted matrimony was not specified until the Council of Trent. Family interests often conflicted with the opinions of theologians. Families wished to control the fates of their children as a matter of family
wealth and honor. In contrast theologians tended to hold to the belief
that the freely given consent of two adults was sufficient to validate a
marriage, the desires of parents and relatives notwithstanding.

Gonzaga's decree on clandestine marriages reflects the ongoing tension between these two views. He staked out a position approaching
that of Trent but, on balance, he favored the prerogatives of families
more. In Gonzaga's decree, a marriage was considered clandestine if
it did not take place in the home of the father, mother, or relatives
of the bride, or in a church, or with sufficient witnesses, that is, four

92. On the efforts to transform penitential practice in Milan see Wietse de Boer,
*The Conquest of the Soul: Confession, Discipline, and Public Order in Counter-Reforma-
tion Milan* (Leiden: Brill, 2001).

people other than the father, mother, or closest relative of the bride. If the bride lacked a family, the parish priest of the bride should be present. Gonzaga was defending what he termed *"honestà politica,"* or civic honesty.[93] He attempted to solve the problem of clandestine marriages by civil rather than ecclesiastical means. The church building still appears as a secondary venue for the marriage after the home of the bride. The priest is the last mentioned witness after parents and close relatives. The decree suggests that it is always appropriate for a priest to be present, but it does not mandate his presence except when there are no family members. Gonzaga's decree on marriage attempted to balance both theological and social interests. Enforcement of this sacramental edict was a prerogative of police officials of the duchy who were to act against those who disobeyed the civil regulations.[94] As the leader of a large clan of relatives he acted as much on behalf of families and their social interests as he did on behalf of the dignity of the sacramental life of the church. The Council of Trent resolved the problem somewhat differently through the compromise of asserting the doctrinal position of the theologians while guaranteeing that the Church would not recognize as sacramentally valid any marriage that it did not announce in advance and that a priest did not bless in a public ceremony.[95]

The decorum Gonzaga sought from his cathedral chapter is echoed in his statement of liturgical concerns for the laity. The liturgical *gride* have two primary purposes. They repeatedly call for reverence for

93. ASM, AG, b. 2038–9, fascicle 16, f. 16r, March 20, 1542.

94. Ibid., f. 16v, March 20, 1542. Gonzaga also intervened in more personal ways in the marriages of his subjects. Three times from December of 1543 to April of 1544 he wrote to a man named Cabrio who held the post of "Horlogio," perhaps the clock maker, to insist that he end an adulterous relationship with a married woman. Gonzaga threatened the man with the loss of his favor if he did not act. Thus, not only did Gonzaga threaten civil penalties but also the loss of patronage. See BAV, Barb. Lat., codex 5791, f. 167r, Ercole Gonzaga to Horlogio, December 14, 1543; codex 5792, ff. 4r, January 7, 1544, and 32v–33r, April 20, 1544.

95. On the changes in marriage regulations in the sixteenth century see John Bossy, *Christianity in the West, 1400–1700* (Oxford: Oxford University Press, 1985), 21–25. For the decrees of Trent on marriage see Norman P. Tanner, S.J., ed., *Decrees of the Ecumenical Councils*, 2 vols. (Washington, DC: Georgetown University Press, 1990), 2: 755–57 (hereafter cited as Tanner).

churches, because Mantuans were accustomed to walk through the churches for reasons of convenience, particularly when they carried loads of goods; they had made the houses of God *"vie publiche,"* or public streets. In March of 1542, in order to stop this behavior, Gonzaga forbade anyone from entering a church for reasons other than the worship of God.[96] These *gride* also emphasize the need for participation in the liturgies of the Church on feast days and walking in the principal processions. Gonzaga found it difficult to get people to do so in a manner that he considered fitting. In June of 1555 he issued a *grida* reminding people to participate in processions for honorable reasons. Therefore men were to remain separate from women, walking before them; laity of both sexes were to remain separate from the clergy who led the processions.[97] These pronouncements reveal a focus on clarity and order. Indiscriminate mixing of sacred and profane, male and female, clergy and laity in processions and in the use of churches was increasingly curtailed. In these edicts Gonzaga was not unique. His attitude was consistent with broader currents in Italian society that are also exemplified in the attitudes of Carlo Borromeo in Milan.[98]

The combination of religious and civic concerns in this patrician reform program is clearly revealed in Gonzaga's reform of the diocesan liturgical calendar. This reform anticipated both liturgical reforms mandated by Rome in the decades following the Council of Trent and ongoing concentration of political power in the hands of the Gonzaga family.[99] Gonzaga reduced the number of obligatory feasts celebrated in Mantua to those of the universal Church and only three local feasts. After July 1, 1541, the local celebrations included, on March 18, the feast of Sant'Anselmo, a Lombard bishop during the Gregorian

96. ASM, AG, b. 2038–9, fascicle 16, f. 15v, March 21, 1542.

97. Ibid., b. 2040–41, fascicle 20, f. 7v, June 12, 1555.

98. On Borromeo's attitude to the laity see Adriano Prosperi, "Clerics and Laymen in the Work of Carlo Borromeo," in Headley and Tomaro, eds., *San Carlo Borromeo,* 112–38.

99. *The Roman Breviary,* published by Pius V in 1568, contained a greatly reduced number of feasts. See Pastor, 17: 195. On the liturgy in Mantua prior to Ercole Gonzaga's reforms see Giuse Pastore and Giancarlo Manzoli, *Il Messale di Barbara* (Mantua: Editrice Sintesi, 1991).

Reform and collaborator with Gregory VII. Gonzaga further emphasized the cult of Sant'Anselmo by transferring his remains to the high
alter of the cathedral of in 1545. Gonzaga also retained, on August 16,
the feast of San Leonardo, one that coincided with the anniversary of
the coup d'etat that had brought the Gonzaga to power in 1328 and
had long been used as a means of reinforcing Gonzaga supremacy in
Mantua. Finally the feast of Osanna Andreasi on June 18 remained
on the calendar. Andreasi was a Mantuan noblewoman and third order Dominican who had been a confidant of Cardinal Gonzaga's parents and who was beatified in 1515 by Leo X.[100] These three local feasts
focused the liturgical attention of the Mantuan church firmly on the
ruling house of the duchy. On the feast of San Leonardo people were
required to celebrate the Gonzaga family's accession to power. On that
of Blessed Osanna Andreasi, the diocese highlighted the example of
one who served both the spiritual and political interests of the Gonzaga. When one takes into consideration that for all but seventeen years
between 1466 and 1620 a member of the Gonzaga family was the bishop of Mantua, veneration of the remains of the bishop Sant'Anselmo
itself can be viewed as a Gonzaga feast. In terms of both the liturgical
calendar and liturgical practice, Cardinal Gonzaga presided over a reform that on one hand exalted the ruling house of the duchy and pre-
saged the role of court chapels in the seventeenth century, and on the
other conformed to the reform of liturgical practice mandated by the
Tridentine Church that also reduced the total number of feasts in the
Church calendar.

Gonzaga's efforts to reform the laity were not limited to the correction of inappropriate behavior through civil means. He also sought
to reorganize their activities in a more positive way. No more promi-

100. ASM, AG, b. 2038–9, fascicle 16, f. 10v, July 1, 1541. On Sant'Anselmo
see Brunelli, 32–35. On Osanna Andreasi see A. L. Redigonda, DBI, s.v. "Andreasi,
Osanna." See Stefano Gionta, *Il Fioretto delle cronache di Mantova,* ed. Antonio Mai-
nardi (Mantua: Negretti, 1844), 122. For an analysis of the rituals on the feast of San
Leonardo see Anthony B. Cashman, III, "The Problem of Audience in Mantua: Understanding Ritual Efficacy in an Italian Renaissance Princely State," *Renaissance Quarterly* 16, no. 3 (2002): 355–65.

nent locus of lay piety existed in late medieval and Renaissance Europe than lay confraternities, organizations that became institutions with substantial religious and social influence. After the Reformation began, their relative autonomy from the authority of local bishops caused concern in the Catholic hierarchy. Gonzaga had direct experience of these organizations while he was still living in Rome and had enrolled as a member of the confraternity of San Girolamo della Carità.[101] Experience of this Roman organization that sought to encourage charitable activities by both clergy and laity influenced his thinking about confraternal organizations in Mantua.

The Mantuan laity had organized a number of confraternities before the sixteenth century. Among these were the Dominican-sponsored confraternity dedicated to San Pietro Martire, established in 1444, and the *Preziosissimio Sangue* operating from the basilica of Sant'Andrea that by tradition housed a relic said to be the blood of Christ.[102] In 1538 Gonzaga began to reorganize these lay associations by bringing them more fully under his control. The instrument for this action was *Compagnia del Corpo Santissimo del Signore,* or *Compagnia del Santissimo Sacramento,* which he ordered established in all of the parishes of the diocese. The responsibilities of this confraternity included visiting the sick, giving aid to the indigent, providing dowries for young women, burying those who died in poverty, and caring for travelers in need. The religious commitment of the members consisted of daily prayers, joint reception of the Eucharist three times a year (at Christmas, Easter, and Corpus Christi), participation in the processions of Holy Thursday and Good Friday, and prayers for those of the *Compagnia* when they died. Gonzaga had negotiated with Paul III for an indulgence for all of those who participated in the organization that allowed for absolution from any and all ecclesiastical censures and penalties, excommunications, suspensions, or interdicts.[103] The *Breve ricordo* called on the pastors to emphasize this organization and to ensure that it become the dominant confrater-

101. Pastor, 10: 394.
102. On Mantuan confraternities see Brunelli, 81–82.
103. ASM, AG, b. 3362, ff. 3r–5r.

nity in their parishes. The institutional method of attaining his goal of control was insistence that the officers of the *Compagnia del Corpo Santissimo* in any parish be the officers of all of the other confraternities. He also ensured that the pastor be one of them.[104] Gonzaga's action resembled that of a number of other bishops in sixteenth-century Italy. Giberti in Verona sought the same control. Use of Blessed Sacrament confraternities in this way was also consistent with the actions of Paul III in Rome and later with those of Gabriele Paleolotti in Bologna. Thus Gonzaga's activity is consonant with that of many other bishops who progressively subordinated lay confraternities to the rule of the clergy.[105]

In addition to encouraging participation in one large and semi-official confraternity, Gonzaga attempted to reform the laity by establishing a School of Christian Doctrine in 1542. Such schools emerged in the mid-sixteenth century in a number of Italian cities as a means of teaching the catechism to poor children who in other ways received only a rudimentary education.[106] Although little documentation on the Mantuan schools survives, they do not seem to have prospered. As late as 1562 Gonzaga's episcopal vicar, Francesco Galvagno, was still trying to implement an effective means for accomplishing this catechetical task. He had conferred with one of Gonzaga's collaborators, Reginaldo Nerli (1494–after 1566), a Mantuan-born Dominican who served in the household of Gian Matteo Giberti before working with Gonzaga. His preaching on the letters of Paul in Verona in 1537 did not impress Gonzaga, as we have seen. Yet, Gonzaga did value his advice enough to involve him in the reform of monasteries in Mantua.

---

104. Ercole Gonzaga, *Breve ricordo,* 20r.

105. See Christopher F. Black, *Italian Confraternities in the Sixteenth Century* (Cambridge: Cambridge University Press, 1989). On the relationship of confraternities and parishes in general see Christopher F. Black, "Confraternities and the Parish in the Context of Italian Catholic Reform," in *Confraternities and Catholic Reform in Italy, France, and Spain,* ed. John Patrick Donnelly, S.J., and Michael W. Maher, S.J., vol. 44 of *Sixteenth-Century Essays and Studies* (Kirksville, MO: Thomas Jefferson University Press, 1999), 26. On the example of Paleotti see Nicholas Terpstra, *Lay Confraternities and Civic Religion in Renaissance Bologna* (Cambridge: Cambridge University Press, 1995), 222–25.

106. See Grendler, *Schooling,* 333–62.

In 1539 Nerli went to Bologna where he acted as *"magister studentium"* in the Dominican school.[107] He acted as inquisitor in Mantuan territory in 1543 and 1544, and was also the author of a catechism published at Pavia called *Utile e breve istruttione christiana dal padre fra Reginaldo dell'ordine di predicatori ampliata.*[108] For a time Cardinal Giovanni Morone employed Nerli to carry out the visitation of his diocese of Modena.[109] From 1552 to 1554 he was the inquisitor in Bologna and also testified in Cardinal Giovanni Morone's heresy trial between 1553 and 1559.[110] Galvagno's description of Nerli's advice closely follows the content of the *Sommario,* or primer, used by the Schools of Christian Doctrine. The schools were to provide the students with the Christian's basic knowledge of the love and grace of God, how to make the sign of the cross, definitions of faith and vows made at baptism, the Creed, the Lord's Prayer, the Ave Maria, and the two commandments of natural law: do not do to others what you do not wish them to do to you, and do unto others as you would have them do unto you. The list continues with the seven sacraments, works of mercy, seven mortal sins, seven gifts of the Holy Spirit, the sin against the Holy Spirit, three theological virtues, four cardinal virtues, five senses of the body, three powers of the soul, seven beatitudes, what one must possess in order to be baptized, and who may baptize.[111] In short, this was a traditional catechetical curriculum. The vicar had chosen officers to carry out this work of catechesis on feast days and had ordered announcements of the school's activities to be read in the churches.

107. Massimo Firpo and Dario Marcatto, *Il Processo inquisitoriale del cardinale Giovanni Morone,* 4 vols. (Rome: Istituto storico italiano per l'età moderna e contemporanea, 1981–95), 1: 250–51, n. #18 (hereafter cited as Firpo and Marcatto, *Il Processo*). A list of Italian inquisitors refers to him as "Il P.M. fra Reginaldo da Mantova inquisitore di Bologna, raro di dottrina et di santa vita, sotto Paolo Quarto." See Paolo Simoncelli, "Inquisizione romana e riforma in Italia," RSI 100 (1988): 118.

108. On this catechism and Nerli see Giambattista Castiglione, *Istoria delle scuole della dottrina cristiana* (Milan: Cesare Orena, 1800), 66–69.

109. Firpo and Marcatto, *Il Processo,* 2/1: 299–300, n. #10.

110. Nerli's testimony is contained in Firpo and Marcatto, *Il Processo,* 2/1: 254–55; 2/1: 296–311; 2/2: 784–802.

111. Matilde Mazzocchi, "Aspetti di vita religiosa a Mantova nel carteggio fra il cardinale Ercole Gonzaga e il vescovo ausiliare (1561–1563)," *Aevum* 33 (1959): 398–99.

The operations of the schools did not run smoothly. The difficulty lay partially in the resistance of artisan parents to sending their children to the school rather than keeping them in their shops, and also in wealthy parents' practice of hiring their own teachers. It seems that only the students of school masters who were also teachers of the catechism participated with regularity.[112]

The failure of these attempts led to the introduction to Mantua of one of the most significant educational endeavors of the late Renaissance. As early as 1559 Gonzaga had corresponded with the Jesuit superior general, Diego Laínez, about the possibility of opening a college. In this new religious order he saw a solution to his problem of providing religious education in his diocese. He had already met Antonino Gaietano, S.J., along with a group of youths who were on their way to Rome to enter the Society of Jesus. It appears that Gaietano had explained the basics of the Jesuit order and the works that it had undertaken. Gonzaga was sufficiently impressed that he asked Gaietano to initiate discussions with Laínez about bringing Jesuits to Mantua.[113] In 1561, writing from Trent, Gonzaga asked his suffragan and his vicar for their opinions on bringing to Mantua this new organization of well-trained priests. Their initial response was negative. The vicar and the suffragan did not know anything about "those Jesuit priests." They stated that while they hoped the good things Gonzaga had heard at Trent were true, they themselves had heard otherwise and did not want the cardinal to be fooled. By 1563 this opinion had changed and Gonzaga and his associates continued plans to establish the Jesuits in Mantua. Laínez, who was a papal theologian at Trent, visited Mantua in February of 1563 to investigate the possibility of opening a school there. By the time of his death Gonzaga had gained such confidence in the Jesuits that he asked to receive the last sacraments of the Church from Laínez and left 4,000 scudi to them for

112. Mazzocchi, 400.

113. Ercole Gonzaga to Diego Laínez, April, 16, 1559, *Monumenta Historica Societatis Iesu, Epistolae Hieronymi Nadal,* II, 592 (Madrid: Typis Augustini Avrial, 1899). See also Mario Scaduto, *Storia della Compagnia di Gesù in Italia,* vol. 4, *L'Epoca di Giacomo Lainez, 1556–1565. L'Azione* (Rome: Civiltà Cattolica, 1963–74), 204–5.

the founding of a school.[114] Hesitancy on the part of Duke Guglielmo Gonzaga, however, delayed the opening of the school until 1584.

Gonzaga's efforts at reformation of the laity reflect broader changes in Italian religious life. His use of confraternities speaks of both traditionalism in form and novelty in management. Gonzaga established the confraternities of the *Santissimo Sacramento* on the foundations of earlier confraternal organizations. But the role he assigned to the clergy reflects new uses for such organizations. The clerical direction of the *Compagnia* and its establishment throughout Mantua reveal it as consistent with the growing uniformity of Tridentine Catholicism, in which one form of institution can be placed on top of, or entirely replace, earlier forms of community or institutional life. The variety of medieval religious experience began to be replaced with the increasing standardization of the early modern world. The problems of religious formation of youth also reflect this transitional character in the work of Gonzaga. Like other Renaissance prelates he welcomed the presence of the Schools of Christian Doctrine. The teaching in these schools was traditional in content. But their failure to win the favor of Mantuan parents, thereby failing in their mission of broad religious education, led him to investigate another innovative aspect of late-sixteenth-century Italy, the schools of the Society of Jesus. Gonzaga's efforts to reform the laity of Mantua illustrate one facet of the transition from a somewhat experimental stage of early modern Catholicism to one of more certain institutional responses and commitments.

Administration of the Diocese

Gonzaga managed the day-to-day affairs of his diocese in addition to laying out large-scale plans for it. His daily activity provides a clearer picture of his thought and action than the official documents and delegated work of his assistants. Publication of regulations and texts and establishment of schools and confraternities presented a model of

114. Mazzocchi, 400–401. On Laínez's relationship to Gonzaga at Trent and Mantua see Pastor, 15: 310–11. For the bequest in the will see ASM, AG, b. 333, ff. 267–71.

religious behavior for clergy, laity, and nuns. But this model did not meet with immediate and universal acceptance. Serious problems of simony, absenteeism, violence, and concubinage still existed.

On September 1, 1534, while Gonzaga was still in Rome, a diocesan official named Bergondio wrote to inform him of the situation at home and on how he had fulfilled Gonzaga's directives. These included visitations as he had ordered, provision of books for the clerics of the cathedral, and settling a case of simony involving a local priest. On the same day the Dominican provincial, Frate Angelo da Faenza, wrote to Gonzaga in response to the cardinal's request for two preachers for the coming Lent. Thus, despite the distance between Rome and Mantua, Gonzaga paid attention to the details of administering his church. By July of 1535 he could report to his brother Federico on the visitations that he had ordered for the reformation of the churches of Mantua. He expressed his belief that he would not have been faithful to his responsibilities as bishop had he not carried out this work "to the praise and honor of God."[115] Gonzaga's place in the ruling family, moreover, added force to that emphasis. Gonzaga called for the assistance of Duke Federico in the administration of the diocese. At that time Gonzaga commissioned his episcopal vicar and visitor to carry out all that he had ordered for the reformation of the churches of his diocese and for that purpose requested the assistance and cooperation of Federico.[116] In the fall of 1536 he again asked Federico to assist the episcopal vicar, Simone Andreasino, in any way possible. He further specified this assistance as anything licit and reasonable concerning Andreasino's office, "especially for the reformation of priests and the carrying out of my orders to the honor of Our Lord God and the adornment of the Church."[117] Unlike his friend Giberti in Verona, Gonzaga could address the problems of his diocese as the ultimate insider who worked with the full cooperation of the government. After 1540, with Gonzaga himself as the ducal regent, that co-

115. ASM, AG, b. 885, f. 137r, Ercole Gonzaga to Federico Gonzaga, July 13, 1535.
116. Ibid.
117. Cited in Bertazzi Nizzola, 7 (1957), 208.

ordination of ecclesiastical and civil authority was enhanced. Reliance on civil authority did not, however, blind Gonzaga to what he considered unacceptable requests from his family to provide benefices to their servants. It is often in these refusals that his commitment to a higher standard of pastoral care demonstrated itself.

In 1534 Gonzaga intervened in a judicial process involving a charge of simony against a priest named Don Ugolino Gastaldoni, who held the benefice of San Biagio di Bagnolo in the town of Formigosa. The local officials handled the details of the problem for Gonzaga while he was in Rome, including sequestering the income of the benefice. Don Ugolino retained a lawyer who produced a bull of absolution for simony that he had obtained from the papal penitentiary.[118] The assistance that Don Ugolino received from no less a figure than Gonzaga's mother, Isabella d'Este, complicated the matter further. Despite this well-placed support, Cardinal Gonzaga did not overlook the priest's actions. He explained to Isabella that she had been misinformed about Don Ugolino: the man was manifestly guilty of simony. The Church could not accept such a crime; it would be the ruin of his diocese if he were to allow him to continue to hold the benefice. Gonzaga did not deny that there were plenty of other examples of such individuals, but if he pardoned this man he would have to pardon all the rest. He refused to do so and asked Isabella to consider more the honor of both God and Ercole than the unjust demands of this "wicked priest."[119] Duke Federico had also sought the benefice for one of his servants. Gonzaga did not respond favorably to that familial request either, explaining that he had already made other commitments.[120] The responsibilities of Cardinal Gonzaga at times required responses conforming to the needs of the Church as he saw them, even if he had to deny requests from his family.

In some cases Gonzaga stated his concerns and intentions as bish-

118. ASM, AG, b. 1903, f. 242r, Bergondio to Ercole Gonzaga, September 1, 1534.

119. Ibid., b. 883, f. 280r, Ercole Gonzaga to Isabella d'Este, November 19, 1534. ". . . trito prete."

120. Ibid., f. 272r, Ercole Gonzaga to Giovanni Giacomo Calandra, November 11, 1534.

op in response to his family's appeals for ecclesiastical favors. In December of 1535 he was able to assent to a request of his mother that he grant the benefice of Santa Maria di Betlemme to her chaplain, a certain Don Antonio. He hoped that he had at the same time satisfied the service of God and his own conscience. His only request to Isabella was that she permit the man to go to his benefice, because he had not granted the request for any other end than that the man be present in his parish and officiate himself.[121] Gonzaga made similar remarks to his brother Federico on another occasion. He had provided a benefice to a non-Mantuan who later became a servant of Gonzaga's nephew Francesco, heir to the duchy. But the priest wanted to be able to send a substitute, so that he could remain at the ducal court. Cardinal Gonzaga responded that his purpose in conferring benefices upon foreigners was nothing other than to act in conscience and to provide resident priests according to the needs of the parish. He reminded his brother that one of his own servants had previously held the benefice and had used a substitute in order to be able to remain with Ercole. The man had had to give up the benefice precisely on account of his absenteeism. Cardinal Gonzaga did not want to see another such example. Furthermore, he added, the income of the parish was so limited that it could only support one individual. Therefore, he asked that Federico ensure that the priest do one of two things: either go to the parish and remain there or give it up so that one who would stay there could have the benefice.[122] Ironically, Gonzaga wrote this letter from Rome where he was living, absent from his diocese.

The more human failings of his clergy did not escape Gonzaga's attention, since his assistants repeatedly informed him of problems concerning the orthodoxy and the lives of his priests. He could show both severity and pragmatism in his decisions. It was not uncommon for him to call upon local police officials to arrest a priest accused of civil crimes.[123] An arrest by civil authority did not involve civil punishment, however. In one instance Duke Federico was prepared to send

121. Ibid., b. 885, f. 339r, Ercole Gonzaga to Isabella d'Este, December 22, 1535.
122. Ibid., f. 341r, Ercole Gonzaga to Federico Gonzaga, December 22, 1535.
123. See Bertazzi Nizzola, 7 (1957), 209–11.

a priest to the galleys of the Genoese admiral Andrea Doria. Cardinal Gonzaga responded that such punishment was not permitted under canon law. He admitted that the "rogue priest" probably deserved that punishment or worse. Given the differences between ecclesiastical and civil law, however, he would not permit any punishment greater than that permissible in his diocesan tribunal, that is, banishment from the diocese.[124]

Among the more common failings of Gonzaga's clergy were concubinage and other examples of sexual activity. If it came to his attention that a given priest was living with a woman he would order the man to separate from her. The approach of Gonzaga and his assistants is well illustrated in a case described by Francesco Marno in September of 1549. A Don Giulio, the chaplain in the church in the Mantuan town of Quingentole, was publicly accused of having "impregnated a woman and led her astray." The relationship between the injury and the issue of public scandal quickly becomes clear in the letter. Marno adds that he was particularly sorry both for the "offense to God and by the public scandal." Initially, while the relationship with the woman was still secret, Marno was confidentially informed of the case as well as of the fact that the woman was going to flee for fear of her life. His initial solution was to have Don Giulio offer the woman a dowry, something the priest was ready to do. Marno would then have had Don Giulio beg the forgiveness of Gonzaga, who would also give him a strong warning in secret and transfer him to another town "because otherwise he is a good man and very adequate as far I know." However, the woman had fled to the home of a relative and the matter had become public. Marno wrote for advice and with the hope that Gonzaga could act in a way that showed whatever mercy was possible without neglecting justice.[125] Much of Marno's assessment revolves around issues of confidentiality and secrecy. While it is probable that Marno's efforts to maintain secrecy were at least partially on account of his

124. ASM, AG, b. 887, ff. 174r–175r, Ercole Gonzaga to Federico Gonzaga, January 27, 1537.
125. Ibid., b. 1919, f. 51r, Francesco Marno to Ercole Gonzaga, September 18, 1549.

concern to maintain the reputation of the woman, he expressed greater concern for the priest and the interests of the Mantuan church. He sought to find a solution that hid the imperfections of the clergy and would allow Don Giulio to continue his priestly activity elsewhere. The reality of ecclesiastical life in Mantua often contrasted with the ideals expressed in Gonzaga's handbooks for his priests.

Over the years Cardinal Gonzaga clearly outlined his intentions for the diocese of Mantua. This is not to say that some did not find ways to evade his decrees, publications, and personal correspondence. Nevertheless, by 1550 the episcopal vicar, Antonio Cerutti, was able to inform him that, in general, conditions were improving. He noted that the priests were happily complying with his ordinances, adding, "I can assure you that at present, among the priests there is the peace of Octavian," making reference to the peace in the Roman Empire under Caesar Augustus.[126] This must have been overstatement: Cerutti's letters tend to read like victory proclamations. But he does not hesitate to mention particular problems, so the descriptions of good order may be fairly accurate. Regular visitations and clear pastoral direction had taken effect.

Ercole Gonzaga understood his duties and those of his clergy in terms of concern both for the worship of God and responsibility to one's temporal lords. His role in Mantua and in the larger Church required that he exercise a patronage both civic and ecclesiastical. His understanding of family honor colored this patronage and the offices of the Church provided a means to accomplish his purpose. Gonzaga did not, however, function simply as a secular prince using the Church as a formal opportunity for patronage. He displayed authentic episcopal concern within the constraints of his own upbringing and his role as the head of the Gonzaga clan. His servants functioned as extensions of his own authority and their disgraces brought dishonor upon him. For this reason the comportment of the clergy had great importance for him in his role as bishop. In the Mantua of Ercole Gonzaga,

126. Ibid., b. 1920, unnumbered fascicle, Antonio Cerutti to Ercole Gonzaga, January 4, 1550.

the bishop was the patron par excellence, preserving the honor of the Church and the Gonzaga family.

Ercole Gonzaga's reform of the diocese of Mantua between 1534 and 1561 looked in two directions, to both tradition and innovation.[127] His desires for the clergy, laity, and religious of Mantua were traditional. His regulations reflected a belief that he was restoring a traditional order that had declined over time. Such an outlook fits well with someone who spent much of his career defending the interests of his family. Ercole Gonzaga was a conservative man. But some of his reforms were consonant with many of the formulations that would be adopted by the Council of Trent and its later interpreters. A more rational organization of clerical formation, insistence on a higher standard of *cura animarum,* stricter and more universal claustration of women religious, and an active laity more firmly directed by the clergy all became recognizable elements in early modern Catholicism. Gonzaga's patrician reform program reflected the changes that European religion underwent in the sixteenth century as well as the interests of a ruling family whose well-being he guarded for much of his career. Gonzaga began his work as a typical aristocratic bishop of the Renaissance, but in time he enacted policies that in retrospect can be viewed as a part of broader tendencies in early modern Catholicism.

127. Jedin wrote that Gonzaga "ci appare come una testa di Giano," looking in both directions, in "Il Figlio," 511.

CHAPTER 4

GONZAGA AND THE *SPIRITUALI*

In May of 1549 Reginaldo Nerli questioned the orthodoxy of Ercole Gonzaga based on another person's doubts and wrote to the cardinal about them. Gonzaga responded in his own hand to clarify the matter, saying that he did not know if it was simplicity or charity that made the Dominican so credulous. He defended his orthodoxy in the following terms:

> I am a Catholic and a good one and I have in my house someone who knows and wants to teach me what I ought to say and think as a Catholic; if I am not a member of the Company of the Rosary or of the Sisters of Ravenna, have patience. It is enough that I am of the Company of Christ and I sense the need that I have for him, because I confess myself to be a sinner, and so I am.[1]

This is a firm yet ambiguous statement of loyalty to the Catholic Church. Gonzaga was committed to the Church, but admitted that he

---

1. ASM, AG, b. 1918, f. 318r, Ercole Gonzaga to Reginaldo Nerli, May 7, 1549. Also transcribed in Gottfried Buschbell, *Reformation und Inquisition in Italien um die Mitte des XVI Jahrhunderts*, Quellen und Forschungen aus dem Gebiete der Geschichte, no. 13 (Paderborn: Ferdinand Schoningh, 1910), 282–83. "Sono catholico così fussi buono et ho in casa persona che sa et mi vuol insegnar quello che debbo dir et sentir catholicamente; si non sono mo [i.e., modo] della compagnia del rosaro o delle Suore di Ravenna, ha patienza, basta che sono di quella di Christo et sento il bisogno che ho di lui, perchè mi confesso peccatore et così sono." The "Suore di Ravenna" may refer to "beate da Ravenna," who were the patronesses of a confraternity at the Ospedale Maggiore in Mantua. See ASM, AG, b. 3358, unnumbered fascicle, no signature, May 27, 1535. See also ibid., b. 887, f. 407r, Cardinal Jacopo Simonetta to Federico Gonzaga, August 27, 1537, about the beatification of two women from Ravenna.

needed someone to show him what that meant in specific terms. His reference to his membership in the "Company of Christ" indicates the use of a rather inclusive standard for membership in the Church. His statement also demonstrates that even in his own lifetime Gonzaga's work and relationships with others led some to wonder where he stood on the religious issues of the day.

Four centuries have not lessened the difficulty of understanding Ercole Gonzaga. In the landscape of sixteenth-century Italian religious history, he stands as a well-recognized but not well-understood figure. His enormous correspondence and the diversity of his relationships to others have made him a familiar source for historians seeking witnesses to the political and ecclesiastical history of his day. Yet the caution with which he operated and the lack of any extant theological or religious works from his pen have made it difficult for scholars to understand Gonzaga clearly or to place him in any prominent religious faction of his generation. The difficulty is not that he held himself above the fray, however. During Gonzaga's years in Mantua he was no stranger to the many and conflicting currents of reform thought in Italy. Through his correspondence and his relationships with others he involved himself in debates over the nature and implementation of reform in the Church. His friendships with and support of people who eventually chose to become Protestants led to questions such as Nerli's. Yet, he finished his life presiding at the Council of Trent.

Just as the patrician character of his world view informed Gonzaga's education and reform activities, it also influenced his relationships with other significant religious figures of his day. This complexity resists categorization that would encapsulate the religious realities of this period. For example, recent scholarship on sixteenth-century Italy has given attention to opposing groups among Italian reformers like the *spirituali,* who are said to have embraced a humanist, Bible-based theology and sought an irenic solution to the religious conflict of their day, and the *intransigenti,* who are described as holding to a Scholastic theological method and sternly opposing religious deviance. Gonzaga has figured in this literature largely because of his friendships with a number of *spirituali.* Yet he does not easily fit either of the categories because he manifested characteristics of both groups. Gonzaga participated in the community of interest that the *spirituali* formed while rejecting some of their more notable views. He cannot be included in their number if holding to some form of the doctrine of justification by faith alone is one of the principal characteristics of the *spirituali*. But he fits no more easily into the category of *intransigenti*. He engaged in discussion, at least among close associates, of matters that raised questions about Catholic orthodoxy. To some extent he shared with the *intransigenti* their concerns about the threat of heretical activities in Italy, but he generally responded to such activities with less harsh means than one such as Gian Pietro Carafa. This leniency brought suspicion upon him both during his lifetime and in the years after his death, when zealous inquisitors scrutinized his activities.[2] Analysis of these relationships demonstrates on a more inti-

2. Debates among historians over appropriate labels for religious figures of sixteenth-century Italy are extensive and subtle. I have benefitted from historians whose scholarship represents opposing views. Those historians who understand Catholicism in sixteenth-century Italy in terms of an increasing degree of inquisitorial activity that eliminated the more open theological milieu of the Renaissance, the progressive marginalization of the *spirituali* by the *intransigenti,* and replacement of an aristocratic ecclesiastical elite with one directed by theological commitments have provided an impressive array of studies. Most noteworthy among these are Massimo Firpo and Dario Marcatto's *Il Processo Morone,* and *I Processi inquisitoriali di Pietro Carnesecchi (1557–1567),* 3 vols. (Vatican City: Archivio Segreto Vaticano, 1998–2000). For an allied view see Paolo Simoncelli, *Evangelismo italiano del Cinquecento. Questione religiosa e nicodemismo politico* (Rome: Istituto storico italiano per l'età moderna e contemporanea, 1979). For a valuable assessment of the historiography see Anne Jacobson Schutte, "Periodization of Sixteenth-Century Italian Religious History: The Post-Cantimori Paradigm Shift," *Journal of Modern History* 61 (1989): 269–84. The passing of control of the Italian Church from aristocratic elites to those committed to theological ideals is well illustrated in Dario Marcatto, *"Questo passo dell'heresia": Pietrantonio di Capua Tra valdesiani, "spirituali" e inquisizione* (Napoli: Bibliopolis, 2003). Other historians have tended to see a less sharp distinction between the *instransigenti* and the *spirituali* and have focused on matters that go beyond the issues of heresy and inquisitorial activity, including a broad interest in biblical scholarship and a genuine desire to restore the Church to its ancient traditions. Among these see Silvana Seidel Menchi, "Inquisizione come repressione o inquisizione come mediazione? Una proposta di periodizzazione," *Annuario dell'istituto storico italiano per l'età moderna e contemporanea* 35–36 (1983–84): 53–57; William V. Hudon, *Marcello Cervini and Ecclesiastical Government in Tridentine Italy* (DeKalb: Northern Illinois University Press, 1992), and his "Religion and Society in Early Modern Italy: Old Questions, New Insights," *American Historical Re-*

mate level the characteristics of a patrician reformer that Gonzaga evidenced in his reform efforts in the diocese of Mantua.

Gonzaga's Relationship with the Spirituali

Gonzaga found supporters and confidants in two of the most significant ecclesiastical figures of his generation, prelates considered to have been the leaders of the *spirituali:* Gasparo Contarini and Reginald Pole. Gonzaga and Contarini met in the spring of 1528 at Viterbo, where the papal court resided after the Sack of Rome. Contarini, then a Venetian diplomat, wrote to the Venetian Senate that Gonzaga esteemed him far more than he deserved.[3] The extant correspondence of Gonzaga with Contarini extended from the spring of 1535 until the latter's death in the late summer of 1542. The two were in regular contact during Gonzaga's years in Rome. Contarini professed that all of his thoughts, both public and private, would always be known to Gonzaga.[4] After his return to Mantua in 1537, Gonzaga communicated with Contarini as both friend and disciple on religious and political matters, especially his reform activity in Mantua. Contarini, in turn, shared with Gonzaga his own writings and negotiations for reform. Contarini and Pole made a joint visit to Gonzaga in Mantua in the spring or summer of 1538.[5] The closeness of the two was made evident in 1541 when Contarini sent Gonzaga a confidential advance copy of the understanding reached by the theologians at Regensburg about justification and sought his opinion.[6] Gonzaga's theologian, Messer Angelo, responded to Contarini with some doubts as to the formula. Contarini then wrote a defense of the Regensburg formula in his *Epis-*

---

view 101, no. 3 (June 1996): 783–804; Elisabeth G. Gleason, *Gasparo Contarini*; Mayer, *Reginald Pole;* and John W. O'Malley, *Trent and All That: Renaming Catholicism in the Early Modern Era* (Cambridge, MA: Harvard University Press, 2000).

   3. Gasparo Contarini to the Venetian Senate, April 2, 1529, in Dittrich, 50.

   4. Gasparo Contarini to Ercole Gonzaga, August 21, 1535, Friedensburg, 7.

   5. ASDM, MV, Serie Entrate e Uscite, b. 1, f. 184r, June–July 1538, indicates purchases in preparation for the visit "delli reverendissimi cardinali Contarino e Inghilterra."

   6. Gasparo Contarini to Ercole Gonzaga, May 3, 1541, Dittrich, 324–25.

tola de iustificatione of May 25, 1541, which he sent with an accompanying letter to Gonzaga on June 9.[7] Beyond the doubts of his theologian, it is not clear what Gonzaga thought about the theory of double justification. In a following letter Contarini, who had not yet received a response from the Mantuan cardinal, suggested that perhaps Gonzaga had been scandalized by his formula.[8] Scandalized or not, Gonzaga cited favorably Contarini's other writings in giving advice on the future direction of the Church even after the Venetian cardinal's death.[9] For example, Gonzaga requested that Contarini send him a treatise on the sacraments that the Venetian had written, a request Contarini was willing to fulfill.[10]

The friendship between Contarini and Gonzaga was not without moments of tension. One of Gonzaga's duties was that of cardinal protector of the Congregation of Lateran Canons.[11] These Augustinian clerks regular came to prominence in the fifteenth century as a part of Pope Eugenius IV's attempt to reform his own cathedral chapter at the basilica of Saint John Lateran. In Mantua they had enjoyed the patronage of Ludovico Gonzaga, who commissioned Leonbattista Alberti to design their church of San Sebastiano, a well-known example of *quattrocento* architecture. The history of the congregation in the sixteenth century was stormy. Its most prominent member during Gonzaga's lifetime was Pietro Martire Vermigli who, like Bernardino Ochino, gained renown as a preacher and then fled to Geneva. In the late 1530s two canons gained such great and, in Gonzaga's view, negative influence in the congregation that the cardinal referred to them as the "two tyrants." These were Don Giovanni Francesco Gaddi da Mi-

7. Gaspari Contarini to Ercole Gonzaga, June 9, 1541, ibid., 195. The defense of the article on justification is found in CT, 12: 314. See also Gleason, *Gasparo Contarini*, 229–35.

8. Gasparo Contarini to Ercole Gonzaga, July 19, 1541, Friedensburg, 58.

9. BAV, Barb. Lat., codex 5792, f. 121v, Ercole Gonzaga to Ercole d'Este, December 4, 1544.

10. Ercole Gonzaga to Gasparo Contarini, April 18, 1540, Friedensburg, 46; Gasparo Contarini to Ercole Gonzaga, July 13, 1540, ibid., 54; Gasparo Contarini to Ercole Gonzaga, December 13, 1540, ibid., 56.

11. On this congregation see C. Egger, *Dizionario degli istituti di perfezione,* s.v. "Canonici regolari della Congregazione del Salvatore Lateranense."

lano and Don Francesco da Vicenza.[12] Forces within the congregation seeking reform did not passively accept the power of these two and they became the focus of an effort to reform the congregation led by Gonzaga and Contarini. Gonzaga's relationship to Contarini was tested during this effort at reform.

The reformers sought to establish themselves at an annual chapter general of the congregation. Gonzaga's absence from Rome presented a practical difficulty in planning and carrying out the reform. On February 8, 1540, Gonzaga wrote to his agent in Rome, Nino Sernini, with specific advice on who should meet to plan the reform of the congregation. These included Cardinals Girolamo Ghinucci (d. 1541), Francisco Quiñones (1475–1540), and Gian Pietro Carafa. In addition, he told Sernini to include Contarini as the "fourth evangelist." He added that if Gonzaga's own views on how to manage the reform did not seem appropriate to the cardinals in Rome they should feel free to proceed with their own plans.[13] Contarini and the other cardinals in Rome had the ear of Paul III, an advantage that Gonzaga lacked.

In late winter of 1540, the pope appointed Contarini as vice-protector of the congregation with virtually full authority over the upcoming chapter.[14] It seems that Contarini took Gonzaga at his word that the prelates in Rome should act as they saw fit. Contarini consulted with a number of people, including Gian Matteo Giberti in Verona, but reached conclusions on what action to take without further involving Gonzaga. Contarini's way of proceeding was not what Gonzaga had in mind. Contarini outlined his plans to Gonzaga in a letter of March 20, 1540. It was Contarini's intention to name the *definitori,* or supervisory board for the chapter general, on his own and to iden-

12. BAV, Barb. Lat., codex 5789, ff. 170v–172r, Ercole Gonzaga to Gasparo Contarini, April 17, 1540.

13. Ibid., ff. 148r–152r, Ercole Gonzaga to Nino Sernini, February 8, 1540. "Quando mo il mio parere non fosse conforme a quelli d'essi Reverendissimi in tutto o in parte, senza alcuna eccettione voglio che si faccia quanto per loro Signorie Reverendissime sara commesso et ordinato et che i brevi siano spediti conformi alle loro openione et non alla seda quelle si troviere essere diversa." f. 151v.

14. Gasparo Contarini to Ercole Gonzaga, March 20, 1540, Friedensburg, 38–41. Ordinarily the cardinal protector would have appointed the vice-protector.

tify those canons who would be willing to participate in the reform.[15] Gonzaga must have been surprised that the Venetian cardinal acted with that much independence. He felt slighted and, in a heated response, Gonzaga claimed that Contarini had shown no regard for his honor at all. "If I were not certain, as I am, of the good nature of your reverend lordship and of the love that you have for me, I would be the most confused man in the world." Further, he added, Contarini's consultation with the outgoing rector general, Gabriele Arborio da Gattinara, had led to a rumor spreading throughout the congregation that the pope had deprived Gonzaga of his protectorship, "with little good to my reputation." He concluded by saying that if these friars saw this loss of authority they would have no respect for him.[16] Gonzaga followed that angry letter with a milder one giving a calmer explanation of his opposition to Contarini's plans and another that continued to plan, in accord with Contarini, the reform of the Lateran Canons.[17]

This correspondence of Gonzaga and Contarini reflects their common desire to seek reform and the limits of that desire when it conflicted with personal honor. Gonzaga took it as an insult when Contarini left him out of the process of investigating the canons. Gonzaga's sincere interest in the reform of the Lateran Canons did not lead him to overlook his status and reputation, and this conflict has relevance for Gonzaga's relationship to the *spirituali*. Philip McNair has argued that the episode demonstrates that Gonzaga was not fully trusted by the "reform party" led by Contarini.[18] Misunderstanding between the two cardinals was more likely the issue at stake. Gonzaga may have delegated a great deal of responsibility to Contarini and his associates in Rome, but he probably did not expect to be left entirely out of the planning of the reform. Sensitivity about his relationship to the pope

---

15. Gasparo Contarini to Ercole Gonzaga, March 20, 1540, ibid., 38–41.

16. Ercole Gonzaga to Gasparo Contarini, April 2, 1540, ibid., 41–42.

17. BAV, Barb. Lat., codex 5789, ff. 169r–171v, Ercole Gonzaga to Gasparo Contarini, April 17, 1540. Ercole Gonzaga to Gasparo Contarini, April 18, 1540, Friedensburg, 45–48.

18. McNair, 189. McNair seems to have been unaware of Gonzaga's letters to Nino Sernini specifically calling for Contarini's involvement and sanctioning the independent judgment of the prelates in Rome.

would have further increased Gonzaga's anxiety. Clearly, this conflict in the relations between the two cardinals was personal, political, and transitory rather than religious and permanent. The following spring Contarini manifested his ongoing trust of Gonzaga by sending to him the confidential copy of the formula of Regensburg.

The relationship of Ercole Gonzaga to Reginald Pole dated from at least early 1537. At that time Pole mentioned Ercole in a letter to Federico Gonzaga acknowledging the duke's best wishes at the time of his elevation to the cardinalate.[19] At the start their relations may not have been cordial. The pope's granting of the diocese of Tarazona to Gonzaga inspired some of the cardinals in the consistory, including Pole, to oppose the grant because they wanted to see a beginning of reforms in the provision of benefices to cardinals.[20] Nine years later, when Pole was at Trent, Gonzaga wrote to inform him, as we have seen, that he had given up that diocese. In a postscript to his response, Pole expressed satisfaction at Gonzaga's decision and at the same time gently chided him for having taken so long to come to that conclusion. He rejoiced that the "divine seed planted in Gonzaga's heart was now bearing fruit."[21]

Any animosity that may have resulted from that conflict does not seem to have endured very long. Pole visited Mantua in late spring or summer of 1538. Throughout the 1540s and in the 1550s Pole appears in the correspondence of Gonzaga as a colleague and an authority in religious matters. On the eve of his departure for the Council of Trent, Pole sent to Gonzaga a copy of his *De concilio liber,* which outlined his understanding of how the council should proceed and what its intentions should be. He placed heavy emphasis on the need for

19. ASM, AG, b. 887, ff. 162r–162v, Reginald Pole to Federico Gonzaga, January 18, 1537.

20. See the letter of Lorenzo Bragadino to the Venetian Senate, January 27, 1537, Dittrich, 94. "Ieri fece [the Pope] concistoro, nel qual fu data la chiesa di Terranuova [*sic*] al Reverendissimo di Mantova; non passò senza grandissima contradizione di alcuni reverendi Cardinali, li quali voriano far dar qualche principio a mutar quel che si osserva hora in quel corte circa li vescovati de Cardinali." Pole acknowledged that he was one of those cardinals in a letter to Gonzaga on January 11, 1546. See ASM, AG, b. 1915, ff. 575r–575v.

21. Ibid., Reginald Pole to Ercole Gonzaga, January 11, 1546.

humility on the part of the cardinals and bishops at the council for their part in causing the division among Christians. Gonzaga thanked the English cardinal for the book and expressed high praise for it.[22] Gonzaga's praise was not merely out of courtesy. In 1562, when he was himself papal legate at Trent, Gonzaga ordered two hundred copies of the work from the press of Paolo Manuzio that he then distributed to the members of the council.[23] Gonzaga's connection to Pole is further borne out by his relationship to others in the English cardinal's circle such as the poet Vittoria Colonna (1490–1546) and Marcantonio Flaminio. Gonzaga carried on correspondence with Colonna, a confidante of Pole and Michelangelo, about the preaching of Bernardino Ochino.[24] After Flaminio left Naples when suspicions surfaced there about Ochino's preaching, he was a guest in the palace of Ercole Gonzaga in Rome.[25] Later Flaminio visited Gonzaga in Mantua in the company of Pole, not long after Ochino's flight to Geneva in 1542.[26]

Gonzaga's work of diocesan reform reflects the theological and religious influences of Cardinals Contarini and Pole. He took their advice on theological matters seriously, especially in the supervision of preaching. In 1537 Contarini became involved in a debate over preaching at Siena and expressed his thoughts on the matter in a letter to the Sienese nobleman Lattanzio Tolomei. The controversy centered around the preaching of justification and predestination by Agostino Museo, who held an Augustinian doctrine of justification by faith and was imprisoned for heresy. Contarini later presented his views for the benefit of priests in his first treatise on preaching, the *Modus conciona-ndi*.[27] Contarini encouraged preachers to proclaim the Gospel but not without caution in matters of dispute such as justification and pre-

22. ASM, AG, Copialettere di Ercole Gonzaga, codex 6497, letter #12, f. 6v, Ercole Gonzaga to Reginald Pole, July 4, 1545. On this work see Mayer, *Reginald Pole*, 143–47; Dermot Fenlon, 100–115.

23. CT, 8: 534, n. 2.

24. Vittoria Colonna to Ercole Gonzaga, January 16, 1539, in Alessandro Luzio, "Vittoria Colonna," *Rivista storica mantovana* 1 (1885): 34, n. 1.

25. Massimo Firpo, *Tra alumbrados e "spirituali." Studi su Juan de Valdés e il valdesianesimo nella crisi religiosa del '500 italiano* (Florence: Olschki, 1990), 177–78.

26. Pagano, *Quarto Costituto di Endimio Calandra*, April 2, 1568, 298.

27. The text of the *Modus concionandi* is found in Dittrich, 305–9.

destination. Preachers were not to underemphasize or disparage good works in the process of salvation. Contarini even admitted in the text that justification by faith alone, when properly understood, was an accurate view of human redemption. This work reflected the preoccupation of Contarini that the Gospel be preached authentically, but not in such a manner that simple and uneducated people would consider themselves exempt from the necessity of doing good works.[28] This distinction between the capacities of the educated elite and the ordinary people remained a central feature of Contarini's attitude to reform and the Church.[29] The treatise exhibits the tension in the mind of a Venetian noble who valued the traditional ordering of society and also held to a belief in justification by faith.

At the same time that the controversy over preaching in Siena surfaced, Gonzaga kept Contarini abreast of his studies, informing him as early as mid-June 1537, that lectures on the epistles of Paul by Pietro Bertano had become a daily event.[30] Six months later he wrote to Contarini that they had continued, though with some irregularity. He claimed to have examined Paul's letter to the Romans up to the eleventh chapter and felt that he understood less of it with every passing day. Chapter eleven itself declared of the experience of God: "How unsearchable are his judgments and how inscrutable his ways."[31] Gonzaga admitted that it was difficult to understand and that "in so many Christian centuries every saint has written on it and labored over it and only penetrated a small part." Indeed, he went on to claim that he had never seen anything more difficult to understand than the letter to the Romans and that even Aristotle is but "prattle" in comparison. Nevertheless, Bertano was wearing himself out in trying to overcome his "incapacity."[32]

28. Ibid., 308–9.

29. See Gleason, *Gasparo Contarini*, 261–76.

30. Ercole Gonzaga to Gasparo Contarini, June 16, 1537, in Friedensburg, 11.

31. Romans 11: 33, *New Oxford Annotated Bible with the Apocrypha. Expanded Edition. Revised Standard Version* (hereafter cited as RSV).

32. Ercole Gonzaga to Gasparo Contarini, January 2, 1538, Friedensburg, 25. "In tanti centinara christiani ogni santo vi ha scritto sopra et a faticha con tutto ciò se ne penetra una particella."

Admission of the difficulty of interpreting Paul reveals Gonzaga's personal frustrations as well as his awareness of how pervasive were the commentaries on Paul, many of which he then owned. It also reflects the confusion that could be produced in an atmosphere charged with conflicting interpretations of Paul in print and discussion. The theological environment of Mantua in the 1530s was similar to that in other Italian cities such as Modena and Florence. Many publicly held to some form of the doctrine of justification by faith alone and Bertano may have been one of them.[33] The expression in correspondence with Contarini of Gonzaga's inability to understand Paul's description of grace has been employed as evidence of his lack of theological training.[34] These admissions of incomprehension are not, however, simply a reflection of his inability to understand Paul. Rather, they signal his acceptance at that time of the tendency among the circle of Contarini and Pole to de-emphasize the rational aspects of faith in the face of what they viewed as its exceeding mystery. This emphasis on the incomprehensibility of grace is not inconsistent with the attitudes of many *spirituali,* who emphasized faith over reason in the matter of salvation.[35] In short, by admitting that he did not understand Romans 11, Gonzaga essentially indicated that he had gotten the point, that this matter was beyond human understanding. Thus Gonzaga did not simply confess to Contarini his lack of understanding or his intellectual limitations. His statement on the incomprehensibility of God was a statement about his experience of faith and concurrence with the theological views of Contarini.[36]

Gonzaga learned of the controversy over Museo's preaching in Siena as a result of this correspondence. It was after reading Gonzaga's descriptions of his studies of Paul that Contarini sent him a copy of his letter to Tolomei. Contarini commended him for his studies and

---

33. Pagano, *Primo Costituto di Endimio Calandra,* March 25, 1568, 238. On Bertano's position on justification at Trent see Giuseppe Alberigo, *I vescovi italiani al Concilio di Trento (1545–1547)* (Florence: Sansoni, 1959), 374, n. 2.

34. Valdés, intro. Montesinos, xlvi.

35. See Mayer, *Reginald Pole,* 122.

36. On this aspect of the *spirituali* see Mayer, *Reginald Pole.*

gave encouragement. Contarini noted of the letter to the Romans that the meaning is *"altissima,"* a phrase similar to the one that he had quoted from the eleventh chapter of Romans in the letter to Tolomei when the mysteries of justification lay just beyond his ability to describe and that Gonzaga had cited to him: *"O altitudo divitiarum sapientie Dei, quae incomprehensibilia sunt iuditia eius et quam investigabiles vie eius!"*[37] Contarini sent the copy of the letter to Tolomei to assist Gonzaga in his studies, "because it is not unrelated to the reading of St. Paul to the Romans."[38] Thus, Gonzaga's correspondence with Contarini should be seen as an expression of his immersion in the spirituality and theology of Contarini, Pole, and others, not an example of his incapacity to understand it.

A year later, in January of 1539, Gonzaga acknowledged receipt of Contarini's handbook on preaching, the *Modus concionandi,* and informed the Venetian cardinal that it would serve to instruct the preachers of his own diocese.[39] It is not surprising, given Gonzaga's social position, that he would find attractive Contarini's advice to preachers to use caution when dealing with justification and predestination. It was consonant with Gonzaga's role as the religious governor of the duchy of Mantua. No area of Christian ministry received greater attention in the sixteenth century than preaching. The Council of Trent referred to it as the *praecipuum episcoporum munus,* or chief task of bishops.[40] Ercole Gonzaga also emphasized the need for sound preaching in his publications for the diocese of Mantua and in correspondence. In addition to the work of Contarini, he suggested that his priests use manuals such as the biblical commentaries of Nicholas of Lyra and collections of homilies for saints' days and Sundays. These suggestions indicate that he wished his priests to follow a traditional

---

37. Gasparo Contarini to Lattanzio Tolomei, transcribed in Aldo Stella, "La lettera del Cardinale Contarini sulla predestinazione," *Rivista di storia della Chiesa in Italia* 15 (1961): 431.

38. Gasparo Contarini to Ercole Gonzaga, January 19, 1538, Friedensburg, 27. "Perchè non è aliena dalla lectione di san Paulo ad Romanos: sed de hoc satis." The letter is also printed in Stella, "La lettera," 420–21.

39. Ercole Gonzaga to Gasparo Contarini, January 16, 1539, Friedensburg, 36.

40. Tanner, 2: 669.

style of preaching and to emphasize virtues and vices. In his letter to Gian Matteo Giberti in November of 1537 about the qualities necessary in a bishop, Gonzaga had identified Reginaldo Nerli as one who preached on predestination without prudence. His preaching caused the common people to take to the streets in spontaneous displays of piety and discuss predestination on their own. That, for Gonzaga, was an example of the effect of bad preaching and matches the concern of Contarini as expressed in the *Modus concionandi*.[41] It seems clear, therefore, that in the years prior to the Council of Trent's definition of justification, Gonzaga held a view similar to that of Contarini, at least in terms of preaching cautiously. Prudence in the preaching of difficult doctrines and emphasis on virtues and vices was the model for Gonzaga's preachers.

Notwithstanding this concern about preaching, there is also evidence that he exhibited a broad-mindedness when it came to licensing visiting preachers and disciplining those preachers who departed from the norms of Catholic orthodoxy. Endimio Calandra, Gonzaga's secretary, noted this "negligence," but he credited the presence of many who preached reformed doctrine to the widespread practice of Protestant preaching throughout Italy, even in Rome. This was so, Calandra testified, because "in those days things were not so strict."[42] This openness resulted in the presence of a series of preachers who came to Mantua or lived there and preached, as Calandra put it, "bad doctrine." Most of these, Calandra said, were Dominicans from the Mantuan convent of San Domenico.[43] Calandra's characterization of Gonzaga's attention to preaching as negligent must be judged in the more heated context of the inquisitorial investigations of 1567 and 1568. What appeared to be negligence in years following the Council of Trent may not have been regarded as such in the 1530s and 1540s.

Among numerous preachers whom Gonzaga welcomed to Mantua were the Capuchins. As early as 1530 he wrote to his brother Federi-

41. BAV, Barb. Lat., codex 5789, ff. 75r–78v, Ercole Gonzaga to Gian Matteo Giberti, November 13, 1537.
42. Pagano, *Settimo Costituto di Endimio Calandra,* April 19, 1568, 333.
43. Pagano, *Secondo Costituto di Endimio Calandra,* March 27, 1568, 251.

co asking him to make them welcome.[44] Among these Capuchins was Bernardino Ochino, whose sermons he had heard in Rome. Ochino entered the recently founded Capuchin Order in 1534 and served as its vicar general from 1538 until his apostasy in 1542. Calandra testified that Gonzaga was present when Ochino preached in Rome in 1534 in the basilica of San Lorenzo in Damaso. On that occasion the Capuchin spoke openly about reserved cases, those penitential matters that could be handled only by a local ordinary or the pope.[45] Ochino came to Mantua in 1538 to give a series of Advent sermons. The Florentine cardinal, Niccolò Gaddi, praised Gonzaga in May of 1539 for having provided for the preaching of Ochino. Gaddi was confident that Gonzaga would be confirmed in the good opinion that he already had of the preacher.[46] Vittoria Colonna further encouraged Gonzaga in this support for Ochino, expressing her admiration for the friar several times. Colonna also informed him that he had gained the respect of Ochino who, after his stay in Mantua during Advent of 1538, informed her of Gonzaga's "solid and real virtue."[47] Following this visit Ochino wrote to Duke Federico to thank him for the kindness shown him there. After a return trip to Mantua in April of 1539, Ochino wrote to the duke again, then in Monferrato, about the kind reception he received from Ercole.[48] Cardinal Gonzaga's sister-in-law, Margherita Paleologa, wrote a few days later to express her pleasure that Ochino had spent three days with Gonzaga.[49] Such was Gonzaga's esteem for the Capuchin that even in the very days of Ochino's flight to Switzerland

44. ASM, AG, b. 1153, f. 295r, Ercole Gonzaga to Federico Gonzaga, January 29, 1530.

45. Pagano, *Secondo Costituto di Endimio Calandra,* March 27, 1568, 250.

46. ASM, AG, b. 1908, unnumbered busta. Fascicle identified as "1539. dal 180 Febraio al 12 Xbre. Paese vari. Diversi." Niccolò Gaddi to Ercole Gonzaga, May 11, 1539.

47. Vittoria Colonna to Ercole Gonzaga, January 16, 1539, in Luzio, "Vittoria Colonna," 34, n. 1.

48. Bernardino Ochino to Federico Gonzaga, April 26, 1539, in Benedetto Nicolini, *Bernardino Ochino e la Riforma in Italia* (Naples: Ricciardi, 1935), 62.

49. ASM, AG, b. 1908, unnumbered fascicle, Margherita Paleologa to Ercole Gonzaga, May 1, 1539. "Me stato molto caro per la litera di Vostra Reverendissima Signoria che per tre di l'abia avuto seco a Mantua el padre fra bernardino."

he negotiated through his ambassador in Rome to have Ochino return to preach at Mantua. On August 7, 1542, as questions about his orthodoxy were raised more seriously in Rome, Ochino wrote to Cardinal Gonzaga from Verona indicating that he might not make it back to Mantua as requested. He added: "Wherever I will be, I will always be most devoted to you."[50]

In the weeks after Ochino avoided Paul III's summons to Rome and fled Italy in August of 1542, Cardinal Gonzaga publicly expressed surprise at the Capuchin's decision. But his knowledge of it must have been more intimate than he let on for, by his own account, Gonzaga met the fleeing Ochino by chance along a road in the Mantovano. On September 22, 1542, he wrote to the Duke of Ferrara: "I saw with my own eyes Fra Bernardino dressed in secular clothing between le Grazie and Mantua going all alone to Germany, but then I did not know that." He added that he learned only later of Ochino's destination by a letter from Gian Matteo Giberti, who informed him of Ochino's arrival in Switzerland.[51] In November, Gonzaga wrote two further letters on Ochino's flight. On November 6 he wrote to his brother Ferrante to inform him that it was true that Ochino had gone among the "Lutherans." He expressed astonishment that such a friar, and at his age, would do such a thing.[52] The same day he wrote to Girolamo Vida,

50. Ibid., b. 1475, unnumbered fascicle labeled "paesi dello Stato," Bernardino Ochino to Ercole Gonzaga, August 7, 1542. "Ma dove sarò, li sarò sempre affetionatissimo."

51. Ercole Gonzaga to Ercole D'Este, September 22, 1542, in Luzio, "Vittoria Colonna," 42. "Io con questi occhi proprii vidi fra Bernardino travestito in habito di secolare fra le Gratie e Mantova, che andava tutto solo alla volta di Alemagna, ma allhora non seppi già questo particolare, ma poco dapoi per una di lui al Vescovo di Verona intesi che di già era arrivato in Terra di Grisoni." In a letter dated August 28, 1542, Giberti wrote of the fate of the *spirituali* and suggested to Gonzaga that "sara bene lassare la loro compagnia." ASM, AG, b. 1912, f. 849, Gian Matteo Giberti to Ercole Gonzaga, August 28, 1542.

52. BAV, Barb Lat, codex 5791, ff. 71v–79r, Ercole Gonzaga to Ferrante Gonzaga, November 6, 1542. "Fu vero che Fra Bernardino andò tra Lutherani dove si sta di presente. Et chi potra giammai credere in huomo che viva poi che un tale religioso et nel l'età ch'egli si truova ha rotta la capezza: quello che sia di lui più oltra, non lo so, senon che si dice essere in Gineva Terra di suiceri et ivi predicare come se fosse il vescovo." ff. 76r–76v.

bishop of Alba, in response to a request for information about the Capuchin's flight along with that of Pietro Martire Vermigli. Gonzaga volunteered that, from what he had heard, Ochino had been called to Rome for a "very good and holy purpose." He acknowledged that Ochino passed through the Mantovano dressed as a soldier and forwarded to Vida a copy of the letter that he had received from Giberti on the subject.[53] With these letters Gonzaga may have been protecting himself in the tense religious climate in Italy in the months following the departure of Ochino.

The sixteenth-century Capuchin historian Bernardino Croli da Colpetrazzo also left an account of the meeting between Gonzaga and Ochino. This version conflicts somewhat with Gonzaga's account and raises questions as to Gonzaga's candor. The Capuchin historian recorded that while Ochino was on his way to Geneva "he went to a *palazzo* outside of Mantua where Cardinal Gonzaga and Ascanio Colonna were staying," and Gonzaga recognized him.[54] Ochino, according to the Capuchin account, asked Gonzaga not to be scandalized by his being dressed without a habit, because he was escaping for his life. He requested that Gonzaga not ask for any further information.[55]

As Gigliola Fragnito has argued, this account seems far less suspect than Gonzaga's.[56] It is unlikely that Gonzaga and Ochino would have encountered one another in a chance meeting on the road, as Gonzaga's version indicated. Nor does it seem credible that Gonzaga's suspicions would not have been aroused by the friar's secular clothing. It is more likely that Ochino had intentionally gone to Gonzaga at one of his residences, displaying both confidence in approaching Gonzaga

53. Ibid., ff. 71v–78r, Ercole Gonzaga to Girolamo Vida, November 6, 1542.

54. Bernardinus A. Croli da Colpetrazzo, *Historia ordinis fratrum minores capiccinorum (1525–1593). Liber primus praecipui nascentis ordinis eventus,* ed. Melchior Pobladura, O.F.M. Cap., vol. 2 of *Monumenta historica ordinis minorum cappucinorum* (Assisi: Collegio S. Lorenzo da Brindisi, 1939), 437. "Se n'andò a un palazzo fuor di Mantova dove stava l'Illustrissimo Cardinale Consaga [*sic*] e il Signor Ascanio Colonna."

55. Ibid. "Vostra Signoria non si scandalize di questo, perchè io fo per scampare la vita; et se contenti de non saper'altro."

56. Gigliola Fragnito, "Gli 'spirituali' e la fuga di Bernardino Ochino," *Rivista storica italiana* 84 (1972): 784–85.

and concern for the cardinal's well-being. The relationship between the two must have been sufficiently secure for Ochino to be sure that the cardinal would not interfere with his escape. By withholding complete information on his intentions, Ochino provided Gonzaga with the basis of plausible denial that he knew what the Capuchin intended.

Gonzaga's circumspection about Ochino came to light several years after Gonzaga's death in the testimony of Endimio Calandra. During his trial, Gonzaga's former secretary recounted the events following Ochino's flight. The inquisitors asked him if he knew Marcantonio Flaminio and Calandra admitted knowing him somewhat. He indicated Flaminio had visited Mantua once with Pole at the time that Paul III had appointed the English cardinal legate to the Council of Trent in October of 1542, shortly after the flight of Ochino and Vermigli. Calandra elaborated: "When we were at table in the house of my cardinal Ercole, Flaminio said publicly that the apostles of Italy had departed, meaning the above mentioned friars."[57] The inquisitors further asked if Flaminio had made it clear of whom he was speaking and whether Cardinals Gonzaga and Pole had understood him. He responded: "Sir, Marcantonio Flaminio specifically named Fra Bernardino and Don Pietro Martire and spoke strongly, so that whoever was at table understood. And the cardinals also understood if they wanted to understand, and they made no reply at all nor did any one else make a reply to Flaminio."[58]

Both Croli and Calandra present a portrait of a cardinal who avoided interfering in the flight of an apostate or of criticizing him afterwards. Gonzaga offered no resistance in the face of Ochino's flight nor to his defense by others at his very table. Although Gonzaga never publicly approved the open preaching of heretical doctrines among the people of Mantua, this episode illustrates that he seems to have

57. Pagano, *Quarto Costituto di Endimio Calandra,* April 2, 1568, 298. "Et essendo a tavola il detto Flaminio in casa del cardinale mio Hercole, disse publicamente ch'erano partiti gli apostoli d'Italia, intendendo delli sopradetti frati."

58. Ibid., 298. "Signor, Marc'Antonio Flaminio nominò in specie fra Bernardino et don Pietro Martire et disse forte, che ogniuno ch'era a tavola intese: et intesero anco i cardinali se volsero intendere, et non replicarono cosa alcuna nè vi fu altra persona che replicasse o dicesse cosa alcuna al Flaminio."

avoided, when possible, disciplining those who did so. Further, in the late 1530s and early 1540s Gonzaga did not view Ochino's preaching as so much in conflict with his own vision of the Church in Mantua that he needed to take punitive action. That it was Paul III who had summoned Ochino would have also inclined Gonzaga to step aside when the Capuchin took flight.

Gonzaga's relationship with Pier Paolo Vergerio similarly underlines this willingness to deal with the learned or those of high social rank in a lenient fashion, so long as they exercised discretion in discussing religious issues. As papal nuncio in Germany in the 1530s, Vergerio had worked for the convocation of a general council to solve the religious division of Christendom. In 1535 he became the bishop of Capodistria, then a province of the Venetian empire. Only later did he become a Protestant himself, ending his days in Germany writing Protestant polemics. Gonzaga and Vergerio had come to know one another at least by the summer of 1535 when the Mantuan cardinal supported Vergerio's candidacy as bishop of Capodistria.[59] Vergerio first visited Mantua in November of 1537,[60] returning there in the spring of 1539. In May of 1539 Cardinal Pietro Bembo reported to Gonzaga about the favorable impression he had left upon Vergerio. The Venetian cardinal said that Vergerio had spoken well of Gonzaga's studies and of his piety, adding that Vergerio felt he had left Mantua a better person than when he had arrived.[61] Anne Schutte has argued that Gonzaga was the source of his first encounter with Evangelism.[62] This seems quite likely, given the scholarly interests of Gonzaga in the years immediately following his return to Mantua and the fact that

59. On Vergerio in Italy see Anne Jacobson Schutte, *Pier Paolo Vergerio: The Making of an Italian Reformer* (Geneva: Droz, 1977) (hereafter cited as Schutte, *Vergerio*). On Vergerio's work in Germany see Robert A. Pierce, *Pier Paolo Vergerio the Propagandist* (Rome: Edizioni di storia e letteratura, 2003). On Gonzaga's roll in his promotion to bishop see BAV, Barb. Lat., codex 5793, f. 87r, Ercole Gonzaga to Cristoforo Madruzzo, January 30, 1546. "Fui in questi anni passati in buona parte cagione di fare Monsignore Capodistria vescovo della Patria sua."

60. Schutte, *Vergerio*, 121–22.

61. Pietro Bembo to Ercole Gonzaga, May 6, 1539, in Bembo, *Opere*, vol. 3, 25.

62. Schutte, *Vergerio*, 121.

Vergerio would have had access to the many books that Gonzaga had purchased in the previous two years. Vergerio's association with Evangelism deepened during a trip to France in the entourage of Cardinal Gonzaga's cousin Cardinal Ippolito d'Este. His commitment to a reform consonant with the ideals of the *spirituali* became more pronounced during his four years of residence in Capodistria, from 1541 to 1545. He left there after accusations against him of heresy surfaced in late 1544. Vergerio's participation in the spreading of scandalous rumors about the pope's son, Pier Luigi Farnese, further complicated his difficulties.[63]

As his conflict with Roman authorities intensified, Vergerio grew more dependent upon the protection of Ercole Gonzaga. Their common dislike of the Farnese prepared the ground for their friendship. Vergerio avoided a summons to appear in Rome in 1545 by traveling to Ferrara and then Mantua when, with the protection of Gonzaga, he refused to present himself to the Inquisition in Venice. For many months in 1545 and 1546 Vergerio found a haven in Mantua itself and in the Mantovano at the Benedictine monastery of San Benedetto in Polirone. He used Gonzaga's residence as his mailing address during that time.[64] Gonzaga spent time at the monastery with Vergerio in August of 1545.[65] During this period Vergerio had easy access to the theological and humanist works in Gonzaga's library and the two had many opportunities to discuss religious matters. Gonzaga displayed his trust in Vergerio by seeking his advice on chaplains for nuns and by permitting him to ordain some of his clergy in December of 1545.[66]

63. Vergerio repeated a common rumor that Paul III's son, Pier Luigi Farnese, had raped Cosimo Gheri, the bishop of Fano. According to the rumor, Gheri then committed suicide out of shame. See Gigliola Fragnito, "Gli 'spirituali,'" 788. Pio Paschini claimed that the earliest reference to the rumor is found in a letter of Ercole Gonzaga to the duke of Ferrara dated November 25, 1537. See Pio Paschini, *Pier Paolo Vergerio il giovane e la sua apostasia: un episodio delle lotte religiose nel Cinquecento* (Rome: Scuola tipograficha Pio X, 1925), 56. An extract of Gonzaga's letter is found in Segre, 444–45.

64. In January of 1546 Vergerio wrote to Girolamo Muzio that he should write to him in care of Gonzaga's residence. See Schutte, *Vergerio,* 207, n. 62.

65. See Piva, 119, n. 92.

66. BAV, Barb. Lat., codex 5793, ff. 32r–33r, Ercole Gonzaga to Pier Paolo Verge-

That same year Gonzaga wrote to Cardinal Pole of Vergerio's having sent a copy of the Mantuan cardinal's treatise on the Lord's Prayer to the English cardinal without his knowledge. Vergerio characterized the work as "full of doctrine and spirit."[67]

Gonzaga and Vergerio also collaborated on a work to assist the dying called *Il modo di consolar gli infermi et condannati alla morte.* Gonzaga mentioned the work in a letter to Vergerio of October 22, 1545, in which he said that the inquisitor was examining it. It received two readings by the inquisitors before it was officially held up. This obstruction disturbed Gonzaga, who expressed his concern about it in a letter to the Dominican Reginaldo Nerli.[68] Vergerio also began to write a paraphrase of the seven penitential Psalms while in the Mantovano.[69] Gonzaga had access to that work but chose not to express his opinion on it in print. He preferred to withhold his views until they could meet in person, a reservation common in the correspondence of the *spirituali* during this period of rising theological tensions.[70] Neither the work on dying nor the paraphrase survives. Not long before his departure from Mantua in January of 1546, Vergerio wrote of Gonzaga: "This lord cardinal is headed in a good direction, completely intent on sacred studies and on the governance of souls."[71]

During this period Gonzaga offered diplomatic support to Verge-

rio, October 22, 1545. On the ordinations see the letter of Giovanni Pietro Ferretto to Giovanni della Casa, December 17, 1545, in Buschbell, 283.

67. Pier Paolo Vergerio to Ercole d'Este, January 13, 1546, in Walter Friedensburg, "Vergeriana 1534–1550," *Archiv für Reformationsgeschichte* 10 (1913): 93.

68. BAV, Barb. Lat., codex 5793, ff. 32r–33r, Ercole Gonzaga to Pier Paolo Vergerio, October 22, 1545. Published in Rodolfo Renier, "Vergeriana: notizie sul Vergerio e due lettere inedite indirizzate al medesimo cardinale Ercole Gonzaga," GSLI 24 (1894): 454. BAV, Barb. Lat., codex 5793, f. 124, Ercole Gonzaga to Reginaldo Nerli, April 15, 1546. Schutte noted that in 1549 Vergerio took credit for the work but later credited Gonzaga for most of it. See Schutte, *Vergerio,* 192–93. On this work see also J. M. De Bujanda, *Index de Rome 1557, 1559. Les premiers index romains et l'index du Concile de Trente,* vol. 8 of *Index des livres interdits* (Sherbrooke: Centres d'Études de la Renaissance, and Geneva: Librairie Droz, 1990), 623.

69. Schutte, *Vergerio,* 193, n. 22.

70. BAV, Barb. Lat., codex 5793, ff. 32r–33r, Ercole Gonzaga to Pier Paolo Vergerio, October 22, 1545. Also published in Renier, "Vergeriana," 454.

71. Pier Paolo Vergerio to Ercole d'Este, January 13, 1546, in Walter Friedensburg, "Vergeriana," 93.

rio in his struggle with ecclesiastical authorities. On July 1, 1545, he instructed his agent in Rome, Ippolito Capilupi, to fulfill any requests made by Vergerio.[72] Later he specified that support by directing Capilupi to speak to the pope on Vergerio's behalf.[73] Gonzaga assisted Vergerio in attempting to arrange meetings with sympathetic ecclesiastical officials. In August of 1545 Gonzaga wrote to Cardinal Marino Grimani, the brother of the patriarch of Aquileia, Vergerio's immediate ecclesiastical superior and one whose duty it might have been to judge him. Gonzaga informed Grimani that he had asked Vergerio to present himself to him in order to make his case more effectively.[74] Vergerio eventually left Mantuan territory in January of 1546 to place himself under the judgment of the Council of Trent. Gonzaga then wrote to Cardinal Cristoforo Madruzzo, bishop of Trent, in order to ensure that Vergerio would be given a fair hearing. Gonzaga volunteered that he himself had had a hand in Vergerio's promotion to the see of Capodistria and considered the effort well spent. This was especially so, he added, considering Vergerio's work while in residence there, a telling affirmation from a resident bishop who had been carrying out his own reform for over ten years. Gonzaga explained to Madruzzo that he had offered Vergerio his support as he would to any friend in order to see that justice was done. He hoped that it would be done in the council, as had been the case for previous prelates accused of various sins. Gonzaga proceeded to warn Madruzzo of the alternative, noting the choice made by others such as Ochino and Vermigli: "He may hasten as others of ours have done, or keeping himself on his feet he will go from here to there shrieking desperately, and so, wanting to prohibit his speaking we will make him furious, both in words and deeds."[75] Gonzaga concluded his appeal with a quotation from Paul's first letter to the Corinthians that "God has chosen the weak of

72. ASM, AG, Copialettere di Ercole Gonzaga, codex 6497, Ercole Gonzaga to Ippolito Capilupi, July 1, 1545.

73. Ibid., Copialettere di Ercole Gonzaga, codex 6497, f. 62r, Ercole Gonzaga to Ippolito Capilupi, August 7, 1545.

74. BAV, Barb. Lat., codex 5793, ff. 8r–8v, Ercole Gonzaga to Marino Grimani, August 29, 1545.

75. Ibid., ff. 87r–88r, Ercole Gonzaga to Cristoforo Madruzzo, January 30, 1546.

the world [to shame the strong]," an admission that Vergerio was not
a theological or ecclesiastical heavyweight but one who might be an
instrument of God nevertheless. He encouraged patience on the part
of the bishops in Trent toward his "friend and brother."[76]

Gonzaga's appeal on Vergerio's behalf illustrates his loyalty to a
friend and protégé. The Mantuan cardinal may never have agreed with
the direction that Vergerio was taking on fundamental theological
questions, or perhaps he did not fully appreciate the significance of
Vergerio's ideas. But he must have viewed him as a positive pastoral
influence and therefore allowed the Istrian bishop to engage in writing
and discussions with Mantuan clergy on, as it turned out, some questionable topics. Gonzaga also sought for him the benefit of a fair hearing. He saw this not only as the right thing to do but as most practical. In essence, Gonzaga urged the Council of Trent not to encourage
further apostasies from the Roman Church. The fact that Vergerio's
opponents were the Farnese did nothing to lessen Gonzaga's interest
in protecting him.

Even Ercole Gonzaga had his limits, however, and by August of
1546 his patience with Vergerio had run out. The immediate cause
for the break in relations was that Vergerio had made public a letter from a Mantuan subject named Giulio Cipada that erroneously
claimed that Bishop Pietro Bertano had apostatized and gone to Germany. In a letter of August 13, 1546, Gonzaga expressed his resentment
and asked Vergerio to stop writing to him because he had become too
much trouble and had caused him much displeasure. Although he expressed his love and desire to be of service to Vergerio, Gonzaga wanted it to be at a distance and without intimacy, because Vergerio had
shown himself to be "more loving than prudent" in risking damage to

---

"Come sono state terminate tante altre di vescovi accusati di varii peccati." "Si precipi-
terà come hanno fatto degli altri nostri, o, tenendosi pure in piedi andrà di qua o di la
stridendo come un disperato e così volendogli prohibir il parlare il faremo furiare e con
parole e con fatti." f. 87v.

76. Ibid., Ercole Gonzaga to Cristoforo Madruzzo, January 30, 1546. The scriptural citation is 1 Corinthians 1: 27 RSV: "God chose what is weak in the world to
shame the strong."

the reputation of another bishop by showing the letter from Mantua about Bertano. Gonzaga took umbrage at the suspicions at the Council of Trent and among officials in Rome concerning his own work in Mantua and his relationship with Vergerio. He therefore ordered Vergerio to stay away from him and his priests. Gonzaga concluded, with a comment on the Istrian's prodigious capacity to publish his thoughts, by expressing the hope that God would give Vergerio as much prudence as he had words.[77] Vergerio tried to explain himself by claiming a misunderstanding on the part of Mantuans with whom he had spoken of his problems, but to no avail.[78]

Any likelihood that the relationship might have been reestablished disappeared the following month precisely as a result of Vergerio's relationships with Gonzaga's subjects. In the course of a visitation, Gonzaga's vicar, Francesco Marno, found that one of the priests of Mantua was preaching heretical doctrines and possessed forbidden books. Testimony was taken that the priest had spoken against sacramental confession, vows, the intercession of the saints, fasting, prayers for the dead, satisfaction for sins, and purgatory. He was found to be in possession of works by Luther, Melanchthon, Calvin, Bucer, and others. The priest denied all of the accusations and excused his possession of the books by saying that Vergerio had suggested them.[79] In this episode the limit that Gonzaga set for theological discussion shows up clearly. Vergerio had gone beyond it and fell out of the good graces of Gonzaga.

Gonzaga appears to have felt aggrieved on a number of counts. First, Vergerio had impugned Gonzaga's honor as the ruler of Mantua. Gonzaga had risked his reputation to provide cover for Vergerio in difficult times. Vergerio's activities in Mantua and Trent did not reflect an awareness that the bishop of Capodistria might show some grati-

77. Ibid., ff. 156v–157r, Ercole Gonzaga to Pier Paolo Vergerio, August 13, 1546.
78. ASM, AG, b. 1915, unnumbered fascicle, Pier Paolo Vergerio to Ercole Gonzaga, August 29, 1546.
79. Francesco Marno to Ercole Gonzaga, September 6, 1546, Buschbell, 279. The other authors included Bartholomäus Westheimer, Erasmus Sarcerius, and Otto Brunfels. On the works of these authors see De Bujanda, *Index des livres interdit,* passim.

tude by staying out of trouble. In giving heretical advice to Mantuan priests he had crossed a social as well as a theological boundary. The concession of theologically questionable discourse among members of the cardinal's entourage did not extend to ordinary priests. Second, Vergerio had been imprudent. Prudence was the quality that Gonzaga used to describe Bertano when he had chosen him to be bishop of Fano and it was an element in his appraisal of other preachers. Gonzaga, the ruler of Mantua, demanded greater circumspection from his associates. Vergerio had left him no recourse other than to hold him at arm's length. Although Gonzaga separated himself from Vergerio, he did not forget him. Fifteen years later he attempted to draw him back to the Roman Catholic Church when he himself went to Trent as papal legate.[80] Gonzaga's actions may be understood as those of one responsible for both religious and civic life in Mantua. His defense was against activities that threatened to overturn the society and social norms he understood to be valid. Therefore he offered a degree of tolerance to those in the upper levels of society as long as they operated within prudent limits. Strict orthodoxy, however, was required of people of more modest social status. This distinction highlights again his role as an aristocratic guardian of religious and social order.

This pattern of offering comfort to those in difficult circumstances with inquisitorial officials is further evident in Gonzaga's relationships with Cardinal Giovanni Morone (1509–80) and Archbishop Pietrantonio di Capua (d. 1578). Morone underwent what is probably the most celebrated heresy trial of sixteenth-century Italy.[81] He had served as bishop of Modena and Novara and had been papal legate in Germany and Bologna. His work had brought him into contact with a number of Italian Protestants and *spirituali* over the years. These contacts moved Pope Paul IV, a man naturally inclined to suspicions of heresy in others, to arrest Morone in the spring of 1557. The charges

80. On the negotiations for Vergerio's attendance at the council in 1561 see Frederic C. Church, *The Italian Reformers 1534–1564* (1932; reprint, New York: Octagon Books, 1974), 328–30.

81. The fundamental source for the trial of Morone is Firpo and Marcatto, *Il Processo Morone.*

against him included reading forbidden books, error in the matter of justification, association with individuals suspected of heresy, and circulating copies of the *Beneficio di Cristo*. Morone defended himself by noting that he had held papal permissions to read heretical literature; that since the Council of Trent had passed its decree on justification in 1547 he had taken it to heart; that those suspected of heresy with whom he had associated included Cardinal Pole and Marcantonio Flaminio, whom he held to be good Catholics; and that at the time he had distributed the *Beneficio di Cristo* it had not yet been banned. Proceedings against Morone dragged on until the death of Paul IV in 1559 put an end to them. Morone then recovered his reputation and influence. Pope Pius IV signaled his rehabilitation when he named Morone papal legate to the Council of Trent in its closing sessions of 1563.

Gonzaga assisted Morone in his defense against the Inquisition. In this aid he was not alone; imperial cardinals and others came to the aid of Morone as best they could under the circumstances of Carafa's Rome. Gonzaga sought information on a regular basis from his agent in Rome, Bernardino Pia.[82] In October of 1557, Gonzaga wrote to Pietro Bertano about the Morone trial, characterizing the charges as harsh and mad. He added that until convinced by greater testimony he would maintain his previous good opinion of the cardinal.[83] Throughout the legal proceedings, Gonzaga was one of Morone's staunchest defenders.[84] He wrote directly to Morone on June 22, 1559,

82. Ercole Gonzaga to Bernardino Pia, October 19, 1558, in Firpo and Marcatto, *Il Processo Morone*, vol. 5, 393.

83. ASM, AG, b. 1945, codex #4, ff. 34r–34v, Copialettere di Ercole Gonzaga, Ercole Gonzaga to Pietro Bertano, October 16, 1557. Also in Firpo and Marcatto, *Il Processo Morone*, vol. 5, 307. Paolo Simoncelli has suggested that Gonzaga's knowledge of the accusations against Morone came from Bertano, who may have sent a copy of them to Mantua and that Gonzaga may have sent the accusations to Pier Paolo Vergerio, who published them in Germany with a preface of his own. Such a sequence of events is unlikely given the decisiveness with which Gonzaga broke off contact with Vergerio in 1546. That the copy of the accusations that Vergerio received came from Mantua, however, is quite possible since Henrico da Hollonia had access to his papers. On Henrico's role in book purchasing see ASDM, MV, b. 1, ff. 57r, 60r, 62r. On his relationship with Endimio Calandra and role as a conclavista see Pagano, 235, 243, note 6.

84. Firpo says that Gonzaga was the most energetic of Morone's colleagues in giv-

to give encouragement and to express his own assurance that his colleague would soon be out of this difficulty.[85] Morone responded with thanks for the "many evident signs" of Gonzaga's concern.[86] Gonzaga had a brief drawn up giving the opinion of three lawyers on the right of Morone to participate in a conclave should Paul IV die before the trial concluded.[87] As the point in the legal process approached when Morone had the opportunity to defend himself, in 1559, he and his associates attempted to draw out the proceedings. The Mantuan agent, Bernardino Pia, had apparently informed Morone of Gonzaga's opinion that the longer the judicial procedure could be stretched out, the better it would be for Morone, who agreed, Pia informed Gonzaga, believing that if he outlived the pope, he would be set free. Morone, however, also believed that the inquisitors would obstruct such an attempt.[88] In any case, Morone's difficulties came to an end with the death of Paul IV on August 18, 1559. In March of 1560 the Inquisition formally dismissed the charges against him. In April he wrote again to Gonzaga to reiterate his thanks for the assistance he had received from the Mantuan cardinal. "I remain very much obliged on account of the perseverance, love, and good opinion that your lordship has had for me in my difficulties."[89] Gonzaga involved himself in the defense of Morone for both political and religious reasons. Morone and Gonzaga were both members of the imperial faction in the college of cardinals. He no doubt hoped for Morone's support in a future conclave. Gonzaga defended Habsburg interests and his own when he defended Morone, but his expression of trust in the future legate to Trent demonstrates genuine belief in his innocence as well. As in the case of Vergerio, Gonzaga provided shelter for one whom he believed to be unfairly accused by authorities in Rome.

---

ing him assistance. See Massimo Firpo, *Inquisizione romana e controriforma: studi sul cardinal Giovanni Morone e il suo processo d'eresia* (Bologna: Il Mulino, 1992), 279.

85. Ercole Gonzaga to Giovanni Morone, June 22, 1559, in Firpo and Marcatto, *Il Processo Morone,* vol. 5, 463.

86. Giovanni Morone to Ercole Gonzaga, June 30, 1559, in ibid., 472.

87. See ibid., 482.

88. Bernardino Pia to Ercole Gonzaga, July 28, 1559, in ibid., 487–88.

89. Giovanni Morone to Ercole Gonzaga, April 6, 1560, in ibid., 616.

Gonzaga found himself the unsuccessful defender of another prelate in the imperial camp, Pietrantonio di Capua. The Gonzaga family and di Capua were linked by the marriage of Ferrante Gonzaga to Pietrantonio's sister, Isabella di Capua. Pietrantonio had enjoyed early success in his career through the favor of the Farnese and became archbishop of Otranto. By 1551 Charles V pressed Pope Julius III to name him a cardinal. Nevertheless, officials of the Holy Office became interested in di Capua on account of his friendships with many in the circle of Juan de Valdés and, subsequently, with Reginald Pole. He became the focus of inquisitorial investigations that might have led to a trial were it not for the pressure of the imperial party and the resistance of Julius III. Ercole and Ferrante Gonzaga were among di Capua's staunchest defenders. Cardinal Gonzaga considered the charge against di Capua baseless and blamed much of the problem on his own difficult relationship with Cardinal Marcello Cervini, one of the officers of the Holy Office. In the end, di Capua was exonerated by means of a canonical purgation without trial. Julius III ordered that he not be investigated further. The taint of his earlier associations was, however, such that he could not hope for further advancement. This episode demonstrates that Gonzaga's support arose for political reasons as well as theological ones. Ercole and Ferrante served the interests of Charles V in their defense of di Capua. Further, had they succeeded, di Capua would certainly have been in Gonzaga's debt at a future conclave, when the Mantuan would be a prominent candidate for papal office.[90]

Gonzaga and the Heterodox in Mantua

Destruction of the Mantuan Inquisition records in the eighteenth century renders analysis of heresy and its prosecution there somewhat difficult, but the correspondence of Cardinal Gonzaga and his associates demonstrates how his understanding of his roles as bishop, ruler, and patron informed his way of proceeding against those accused of

90. On di Capua's unsuccessful attempt to be named cardinal and Gonzaga's support for him see Marcatto, *"Questo passo dell'heresia."*

heresy. Along with this correspondence, there is nothing so important as the story of Endimio Calandra (d. 1576?), Gonzaga's secretary for twenty years. He was born of a prominent Mantuan family that had served in the Gonzaga chancery. His father, Giovanni Giacomo Calandra, was *castellano,* or major-domo, for Ercole's brother Federico, and was succeeded in this post by Endimio's brother Sabino. During the many years of his association with Gonzaga, Endimio had complete access to the cardinal's books and papers. Only he and Gonzaga's other principal secretary, Camillo Olivo, had the privilege of deciphering Gonzaga's most private correspondence when it arrived in code. The two secretaries also shared their thoughts on theological issues. Following the death of Pope Paul III in December of 1549, Calandra accompanied Gonzaga to Rome for the conclave to serve as one of the cardinal's *conclavisti.*

Soon after their return to Mantua in late February of 1550, Calandra lost the confidence of Gonzaga and left the post of secretary. Reasons for this rupture remain somewhat unclear. It was partially due to the distrust of Cardinal Gonzaga's brother Ferrante, who claimed that Endimio had spoken too freely on matters of faith.[91] Criticism from Cardinal Marcello Cervini may also have played a role. Calandra testified that Cervini "held certain things against me for which he would have proceeded against me were it not for regard for Cardinal Gonzaga."[92] Calandra added that it was then that Gonzaga informed him that he no longer considered him worthy of his favor.[93] Calandra no longer had access to the cardinal's library and within a year he left Mantua. Gonzaga steadfastly refused to allow him back into the good graces of the family. Not until after the death of the cardinal did Calandra return to the Gonzaga court.[94]

91. Pagano, *Nono Costituto di Endimio Calandra,* May 3, 1568, 350. "Una riprensione dal signor don Ferrante perch'io parlassi troppo liberamente in queste cose della fede."

92. Ibid. "Haveva delle cose contra di me, che haverebbe potuto procedere conto della religione et che restava per amor di Sua Signoria illustrissima."

93. Ibid. "Et allhora il cardinal mi disse che, poichè ci era questa opinione di me, non mi reputava più degno della gracia sua."

94. Pagano, 132, for citation of a letter from Luigi Rogna to an anonymous corre-

Four years after the death of Ercole Gonzaga, the Mantuan inquisitor, Camillo Campeggi, initiated a stern prosecution of heresy there. In 1567 and 1568 Calandra, along with many other Mantuan notables, became a prisoner of the Inquisition. He cooperated with his judges by giving extensive testimony on many religious figures of sixteenth-century Mantua. In particular he described conditions in the 1530s and 1540s, painting a picture of a city where discussion of unorthodox religious views was widespread. He did not hesitate to point the finger at those who held heretical views. According to Calandra many of Gonzaga's closest associates as well as highly placed Mantuan nobles held beliefs that contradicted the teachings of the Catholic Church. He also spoke of his own previous heretical beliefs, admitting to holding the doctrine of justification by faith alone, albeit in a form that Martin Luther would not accept. Calandra believed that works do not merit salvation. But he did believe that works might merit a higher place in heaven. He also held that in the Eucharist there was not truly the body and blood of Christ, but a symbolic presence. His conversion to this view, he claimed, was the result of his discussions with Pietro Bertano, Gonzaga's tutor.[95]

Calandra's testimony also contains the clearest available statements available on Gonzaga's explicit refusal to share in heretical beliefs. When officers of the Inquisition specifically queried Calandra about the orthodoxy of his late employer, Calandra testified: "I never knew the cardinal to be a heretic."[96] He also stated that while it was common to speak openly about these matters of religion, even then he did not often speak about them with Gonzaga. Apparently such issues came up only in a controlled manner. Gonzaga assigned Calandra the duty of reading the prohibited books in his library and reporting to him what he thought of them. Of one such interchange Calandra testified:

---

spondent, July 30, 1563. On Endimio's assuming the post of Castellano see L. Bertani Argetini, DBI, s.v. "Sabino Calandra."

95. Pagano, *Primo Costituto di Endimio Calandra,* March 25, 1568, 237–38.

96. Pagano, *Settimo Costituto di Endimio Calandra,* April 19, 1568, 333. "Per me non ho mai conosciuto il cardinal per heretico."

In the reporting that I made I once said to the cardinal that the arguments
that those Lutheran authors made moved me, and he replied to me that they
did not move him at all because he read them with this opinion: that they
were false. And at the same time that he had these Lutheran opinions reported to him, he had Thomas read to him on the same issues.[97]

After attesting to the orthodoxy of Gonzaga, Calandra admitted that
the Mantuan cardinal had been negligent in supervising preachers. He
attributed this negligence to the general openness of the period: "I
knew him to be negligent concerning preachers: but perhaps this was
because even in Rome preachers were heard who preached Lutheran doctrine, just as they preached here too in Mantua, because then
things were not so strict."[98] Calandra's testimony demonstrates that
Gonzaga employed men whom he knew to be of questionable orthodoxy as late as the 1550s. Indeed, Gonzaga does not seem to have been
very strict. The degree to which such discipline was civically useful significantly influenced his willingness to impose orthodoxy.

In the 1540s the changing religious climate of Italy is evident in the
limits of Gonzaga's openness to preachers who expressed unorthodox
ideas but who did not enjoy the ecclesiastical rank of some of Gonzaga's other associates. His views on preaching continued to correspond
to those of Contarini and Pole, as is evident in Gonzaga's reaction to
the preaching of the Augustinian Observant, Frate Andrea Ghetti da
Volterra (d. 1599), who came to Mantua in Lent of 1542.[99] Ghetti had
a long career as a preacher in many cities of Italy. He attended the

97. Ibid., 333. "Lui mi replicava che lui non movevano niente perchè le leggeva
con questa opinione: che fussero false. Et nel medemo tempo che lui si faceva referire
queste opinioni lutherane, si faceva legger san Tomaso sopra le medesime."

98. Pagaon, *Settimo Costituto di Endimio Calandra,* April 19, 1568, 333. "L'ho ben
conosciuto per negligente nelle cose delli predicatori: ma forse anco questo poteva procedere perché in Roma s'erano anco sentiti delli predicatori che predicavano pure alla
lutherana, come so predicava anco qui in Mantova, perche allhora le cose non andavano così strette."

99. On Ghetti see Mario Battistini, *Fra Andrea Ghetti da Volterra, O.S.A., teologo,
oratore, pedagogista* (Florence: Libreria editrice fiorentina, 1928); Hubert Jedin, *Papal
Legate at the Council of Trent: Cardinal Seripando,* trans. Frederic C. Eckhoff (St. Louis
and London: Herder, 1947), 227–30; Firpo and Marcatto, *Il Processo Morone,* 1: 254,
n. 27.

Council of Trent on two occasions and enjoyed the favor of Cardinals Madruzzo, Gonzaga, and Seripando. He wrote, among other things, a theological worked titled *Trattato utile della grazia e delle opere* that emerged from sermons he gave in Florence in 1544. Endimio Calandra testified that Ghetti brought with him to Mantua a catechism by the Lutheran Justus Jonas.[100] He was accused of heresy by two ardent opponents of Protestantism, Dionigi Zannettini, bishop of Chironia in Crete, known as *Grechetto,* and Ambrogio Catarino Politi, O.P., bishop of Minori. Periodically during Ghetti's career he came under investigation by the Roman Inquisition, but he avoided imprisonment until 1555 when Paul IV had him incarcerated. Ghetti did not regain his liberty until the death of the pope. He then went to Trent in the company of Cardinal Seripando, Gonzaga's colleague as legate.

At the beginning of January 1543 Cardinal Giovanni Salviati's secretary wrote to Calandra seeking information on Ghetti. Cardinal Salviati (1490–1553), the archbishop of Ferrara, came from a noble Florentine family and was an old friend of Gonzaga. He considered bringing the friar to preach in Ferrara but wanted Gonzaga's opinion before extending the invitation, since he was aware of the rumors concerning Ghetti's theology. Calandra later testified that the man did indeed hold Protestant views. In particular Gonzaga had specifically asked Frate Andrea to preach on purgatory when he had been in Mantua. Concerning that doctrine Calandra cited Gonzaga as saying: "there was a purgatory and woe to us if there is not." Ghetti nevertheless managed to avoid the topic.[101] He did, however, manage to preach at Ferrara.

100. Pagano, *Primo Costituto di Endimio Calandra,* March 25, 1568, 235. Justus Jonas (1493–1555), a collaborator with Luther at Wittenberg. I have found no reference to such a catechism by Jonas. Jonas did write introductions for catechisms by Johann Spangemburg. See Pagano, 230, n. 19. Calandra said that he did a translation of the work and passed it on to Leonardo de Marini to assist in the composition of the Mantuan catechism.

101. ASM, AG, b. 1913, unnumbered fascicle, secretary of Cardinal Salviati to Endimio Calandra, January 2, 1543. See also Pagano, *Secondo Costituto di Endimio Calandra,* March 27, 1568, 253. According to Calandra, Gonzaga said of purgatory, "vi era il purgatorio et guai a noi se non vi fusse stato purgatorio."

Several years later Gonzaga, Salviati, and Ghetti corresponded again on the question of the preacher's orthodoxy. A controversy, the basis of which remains unknown, had arisen between Gonzaga's secretary Camillo Olivo and Ghetti. This second discussion of Ghetti's views took place after the Council of Trent had issued its decree on justification and therefore in a changed theological milieu. The Augustinian wrote to Gonzaga to clear his name of the charge of heresy, reminding the cardinal that he had preached in his presence.[102] But the friar had held to justification by faith alone and denied the existence of purgatory.[103] Gonzaga responded a week later by saying that at the time Ghetti had preached at Mantua he had considered investigating him on account of the scandalous things he had said. But since then he had not heard anything bad about him. Gonzaga did criticize him, however, for not taking his advice. His letter indicates that on that previous occasion both he and Cardinal Pole had counseled the man to study further and to exert himself in avoiding giving scandal to his friends.[104] In Gonzaga's mind Ghetti had not done that. This incident provides evidence of a concern for preaching very close to that of the *spirituali* such as Contarini and Pole. When a preacher spoke in a manner that raised problems about justification, predestination, or purgatory, the *spirituali* would counsel the preacher to study more in order to avoid the scandal that might ensue when ordinary people heard controversial theology. In his letter to Lattanzio Tolomei, Contarini had criticized preachers who learned a smattering of St. Augustine and then presumed to preach on difficult matters before the people.[105]

Both Ghetti and Salviati wrote to Gonzaga of the friar's intention to speak in an orthodox manner. Salviati affirmed that Ghetti

102. Ibid., b. 1917, unnumbered fascicle labeled "Paesi vari dal 10 Gen. al 10 Decembre, Diversi," Andrea Ghetti to Ercole Gonzaga, January 1, 1548.

103. Pagano, *Secondo Costituto di Endimio Calandra,* March 27, 1568, 258.

104. ASM, AG, b. 1917, unnumbered fascicle, Ercole Gonzaga to Andrea Ghetti da Volterra, January 8, 1548.

105. Gasparo Contarini to Lattanzio Tolomei. The letter exists as an enclosure in a letter to Gonzaga dated January 19, 1538, in Stella, 428.

had promised to "preach as a Christian and a Catholic and to edify the people and not scandalize them." He added that Ghetti had in fact carried out that promise the previous year at Naples.[106] Ghetti also wrote to Gonzaga, obsequiously noting the reconciliation that had taken place between himself and Olivo. He stated that as a result of the controversy he had become aware again of Gonzaga's "zeal" for him and the cardinal's desire that he "exercise the gifts that God has given me to his honor and for the public well-being, and without scandal, which I was forced to do after I left Mantua where the precepts and documents and loving encouragement of Your Reverend Lordship were inviolable to me."[107] Ghetti insisted that he did remember the advice of Gonzaga.

Gonzaga had proceeded in such a way that Ghetti had to restrain himself from preaching as openly or as "scandalously" as he might have. Gonzaga did not prosecute the man, but he did attempt to influence his preaching. Gonzaga, Salviati, and Ghetti used negotiation to achieve the desired end of preaching that did not upset any social or religious conventions even in a period of stricter theological definitions. This negotiation stands in sharp contrast to the attitude of Gian Pietro Carafa, whose dealings with Ghetti were far more severe.[108] In an era of increasingly stern proceedings against those suspected of heresy, Gonzaga pursued less harsh means of maintaining order in his diocese and duchy.

The relationship of the political and the religious emerges in Gonzaga's way of dealing with the questionably orthodox preaching of Don Costantino da Carrara, a Lateran Canon. Don Costantino had gained election as prior of his congregation's houses at Lucca, Mantua, Cremona, and Ravenna. At one time he had close ties to Piet-

---

106. ASM, AG, b. 1917, unnumbered fascicle, Giovanni Salviati to Ercole Gonzaga, January 11, 1548.

107. Ibid., unnumbered fascicle, Andrea Ghetti to Ercole Gonzaga, January 11, 1548. "Sempre desiderando ch'io eserciti i doni che mi ha dati Iddio in honore suo e pubblica salute, e senza scandolo. Cosa che io mi son forzato di fare poi ch'io uscii di Mantova, dove sempre mi sono stati inviolabili precetti e documenti, et amorevoli accorgimenti di vostra signoria reverendissima."

108. Firpo and Marcatto, *Il Processo Morone*, vol. 1, 255.

ro Martire Vermigli.[109] According to the testimony of Endimio Calandra, while Costantino was in Mantua he preached justification by
faith alone, that there was no difference between bishop and priest,
and that confession was unnecessary. During that period he preached
at least one sermon in Gonzaga's presence for which the cardinal reprimanded him.[110] This incident did not end his career, and Don Costantino's reputation extended to Ferrara. The duchess of Ferrara, Renée
of France (1510–76), was a daughter of King Louis XII and a Protestant. In 1545 she requested that Gonzaga send Costantino to Ferrara.[111] Cardinal Gonzaga first consulted with her husband, his cousin
Ercole d'Este. Gonzaga described the man to the duke of Ferrara as
"not very learned, but much given to these new doctrines."[112] He also
informed the duke of the occasion less than two years earlier when
Don Costantino preached in Mantua in his presence. He made him
retract "some things that he had not said well, and were it not for the
reputation of his religious congregation I would have imprisoned him,
and I still hold that view."[113] Again, Gonzaga found a way to restrain
unorthodox preaching without having to go so far as to imprison the
man. In his letter to the duke of Ferrara he spoke strongly of prison as
a fit punishment. His role as protector of the Lateran Canons, however, offered him a convenient means of avoiding imposition of such
a penalty.

At issue in Gonzaga's letter to his cousin were the religious position of Renée of France and the relationship between the ruling fami-

109. Pagano, 269, n. 49.

110. Pagano, *Secondo Costituto di Endimio Calandra,* March 27, 1568, 254. BAV,
Barb. Lat., codex 5793, ff. 48v–49v, Ercole Gonzaga to Ercole d'Este, November 26,
1545.

111. On Renée see Emmanuel Rodocanachi, *Une protectrice de la Réforme en Italie
et en France. Renée de France, duchesse de Ferrare* (1896; reprint, Geneva: Slatkine Reprints, 1970). For further bibliography see Charmarie Jenkins Blaisdell, "Politics and
Heresy in Ferrara, 1534–1559," *Sixteenth Century Journal* 6 (1975): 67–93.

112. BAV, Barb. Lat., codex 5793, ff. 48v–49v, Ercole Gonzaga to Ercole d'Este,
November 26, 1545. "Non molto dotto, ma tanto posto in queste nuove dottrine." f.
48v.

113. Ibid., ff. 48v–49r. Ercole Gonzaga to Ercole D'Este, November 26, 1545.
"Alcune cose che non bene haveva dette et ancho per honore della sua religione, certo
l'haverei fatto impregionar, pure me ne ritenni per li sopradetti rispetti."

lies of Mantua and Ferrara. The duchess was a Calvinist who resisted her husband's attempts to have her return to Catholicism. After his death she returned to France and practiced her faith more freely. It is not surprising that Gonzaga would not want Don Costantino preaching to her. He may have been unwilling to arrest the man, but the religious and political stakes in Ferrara seemed high enough to advise against Costantino's presence there. Of the duchess's religious views Gonzaga wrote that "she assents willingly to one who speaks of these new doctrines perhaps with good zeal but not with much prudence, things being what they are."[114] Gonzaga saw the need for caution particularly on account of the social position of Renée. She was his cousin's wife, a member of "a very Catholic house." He would not act without Ercole d'Este's consent and would follow his cousin's lead.[115] He first suggested that if the duke did not consider it appropriate for this man to preach to the duchess, Gonzaga would respond to her by saying that he had already removed the man's license to preach on account of his "impurity of doctrine," and would therefore not tolerate that he ever preach in her presence. But if the duke consented to the man's coming to Ferrara, Gonzaga would be willing to allow it. He would do this, however, on the condition that if Costantino said anything that was "not Catholic," the duke of Ferrara would put him in prison and punish him as he deserved.[116]

The content of Don Costantino's preaching must have been clearly heretical. Gonzaga had already taken action by removing his license to preach, not an insignificant act of discipline. But for one who has been characterized as ruling his diocese with a rod of iron, the punishment was rather light. In order to preserve the honor of the Lateran Canons Gonzaga did not confine the man in prison. Nor did Gon-

114. Ibid., ff. 48v–49v. Ercole Gonzaga to Ercole d'Este, November 26, 1545. "Assentire volentieri a cui parla d'esse nuove dottrine forse con buon zelo, ma non già con molta prudentia correndo i tempi che corrono." f. 49r.

115. Ibid., ff. 48v–49v, Ercole Gonzaga to Ercole d'Este, November 26, 1545. "Essendo moglie di chi elle è et di quella casa tanto catholica, non me ne son voluto risolvere se prima non ne intendo l'openione di vostra eccellenza." f. 49r.

116. Ibid., codex 5789, f. 49r, Ercole Gonzaga to Ercole d'Este, November 26, 1545.

zaga's challenge eliminate the possibility that Don Costantino might continue his career under the right circumstances. If someone else would take responsibility for the man's conduct, Gonzaga was quite willing to let him again ascend the pulpit. Certainly he was concerned about the import of sending a Protestant preacher to the Este court. But even when characterizing the theological views of the duchess he seemed more concerned about a lack of prudence than with the actual content of the sermons. How strenuously he pursued the heresy of Don Costantino depended largely on the political situation.

Gonzaga's hesitancy to pursue those accused of heresy is further illustrated by his relationship to the Augustinian Frate Stefano da Mantova. Gonzaga apparently intended to hire the man for "certain pious works." In August of 1545 the inquisitor in Mantua wrote to Gonzaga of his concerns about Frate Stefano, saying that he had been tried for heresy in Ferrara and that he had not been acquitted. The inquisitor did not say that he was a heretic, but that he was suspect and indicted as a heretic and that his religious order had paid a bond of one hundred scudi and promised to present him to the inquisitors.[117] He added that Frate Stefano continued to preach Lutheran doctrine privately. The inquisitor requested that Ercole banish the man on account of his failings. Nearly six months later Gonzaga sought the opinion of Cardinal Salviati, the archbishop of Ferrara, who declared that the case never came to trial. He further stated that the things Frate Stefano had preached were not Lutheran, nor even scandalous.[118] Two years later Frate Stefano's orthodoxy was still in question. Gonzaga's brother Ferrante had written that the Augustinian had preached "Lutheran" doctrine in the Mantuan town of Bozzolo. Ferrante had also suggested that the man had associated himself with Cardinal Gonzaga in the course of his preaching to make it appear that Gonzaga held the same views. Cardinal Gonzaga vouched for Frate Stefano's orthodoxy on

117. Frate Ambrosio to Ercole Gonzaga, August 3, 1545, in Bertazzi Nizzola, 7 (1957), 223.

118. ASM, AG, b. 1915, ff. Giovanni Salviati to Ercole Gonzaga, February 3, 1546, in Bertazzi Nizzola, 7 (1957), 223.

the basis of personal knowledge: "He is my friend and learned and he went to Bozzolo with my permission." Gonzaga admitted that what Frate Stefano said may have been scandalous, but it could not have been heretical. More likely, he suggested, other friars had purposely spoken ill of Stefano to Ferrante. Therefore, he asked Ferrante not to bother the man.[119] These letters illustrate that Gonzaga did not assiduously pursue accusations of heresy. Further, he clearly made a distinction between heresy and scandal. Again, one hears the echo of the emphasis laid on careful preaching of scripture as outlined by Contarini. Giving scandal to the people would be unproductive even if it were theologically accurate.

This relationship between religious and political commitments influenced Gonzaga's involvement with the Benedictine monks Luciano Degli Ottoni and Benedetto Fontanini. Both monks belonged to the Cassinese Congregation of Benedictines who had a noted monastery in Mantuan territory, San Benedetto in Polirone,[120] and both were Mantuans who made significant contributions to the religious thought of their day. Fontanini wrote the original draft of the *Beneficio di Cristo*. Degli Ottoni edited a commentary of John Chrysostom on Paul's epistle to the Romans that was placed on the Index of Prohibited Books of 1559, and he produced a Latin translation of the heretic Giorgio Siculo's *Trattato de iustificatione*.[121] While at San Bene-

---

119. Ibid., b. 1917, unnumbered fascicle labeled "Minute di lettere a diversi, copie di lettere di varie provenienze e lettere decifrate," Ercole Gonzaga to Ferrante Gonzaga, April 30, 1548. "Di quel Frate Stefano da Mantova che ha predicato a Bozzolo lutheranamente miscolando il nome mio con la dottrina sua et per dire il vero a vostra eccellenza io non ne credo niente per che il Frate è amico mio et dotto et è andato a predicare in Bozzolo di mia licenza et avertito a dire cosa che fusse non che heretica ma scandalosa."

120. On this congregation see Barry Collett, *Italian Benedictine Scholars and the Reformation: The Congregation of Santa Giustina of Padua* (Oxford: Oxford University Press, 1985).

121. On the edition of Chrysostom see CT, 1: 206, n. 8. On the translation of Siculo see Luciano Degli Ottoni to Ercole Gonzaga, December 6, 1550, in Carlo Ginzburg and Adriano Prosperi, "Le due redazioni del 'Beneficio di Cristo,'" in *Eresia e riforma nell'Italia del Cinquecento* (Florence: Sansoni, and Chicago: The Newberry Library, 1974), 202–3.

detto in Polirone, Degli Ottoni assisted Gonzaga in his attempts to maintain a resident philosopher.[122] He also attended the first sessions of the Council of Trent in 1545 and 1546 where he came under suspicion of heresy for his thoughts on justification, expressing the view that if one had faith one would not sin. The idea was rejected by the council and he retracted the thesis the next day.[123]

In April of 1549 the monks of the monastery of San Benedetto in Polirone met in chapter to elect a new abbot. Gonzaga wrote to Cardinal Pole, the protector of the Cassinese congregation, appealing for the election of a Mantuan whom he could trust and naming two monks as acceptable candidates. Unfortunately we no longer possess that letter. Pole's response was positive but did not entirely guarantee that Gonzaga's preferences would be selected.[124] Gonzaga then sent an emissary to the monastery to urge his case directly. In response, seven monks wrote to Gonzaga assuring him that they would assist him as they could. As a result of this lobbying, the monks elected Luciano Degli Ottoni as abbot. It seems that he was one of Gonzaga's candidates since the cardinal later referred to him as "that abbot that they conceded to me."[125]

The most revealing moments in this relationship surfaced approximately a year after the election of Degli Ottoni, when the monks of the monastery deposed him. They accused him of permitting the circulation of suspect books and of permitting disorders such as eating meat without permission. Gonzaga reacted negatively to this action: public accusations of unorthodoxy disturbed him, but the deposition was also an affront to his dignity as ducal regent. The monks had treated him as if he were a "plebeian,"[126] because Degli Ottoni was

122. ASM, AG, b. 1919, ff. 63r–63v, Luciano Degli Ottoni to Ercole Gonzaga, September 30, 1549.

123. CT 5: 473–76, 659–60.

124. Mayer, *The Correspondence,* 2: 23. Reginald Pole to Ercole Gonzaga, April 26, 1549.

125. ASM, AG, b. 1945, ff. 16r–17v, Ercole Gonzaga to Galeazzo Florimonte, June 29, 1550. "Quell'abbate che m'havevano concesso." See also Ginzburg and Prosperi, 200.

126. Ibid.

Gonzaga's man at San Benedetto in Polirone. Further, despite the advice of some of the monks there, Gonzaga did not maintain his distance from Degli Ottoni. Gigliola Fragnito has suggested that he may have negotiated with the Benedictines to provide the deposed abbot with a new post.[127]

The problems of Degli Ottoni worsened when his fellow Benedictine Giorgio Siculo testified against him and Benedetto Fontanini during his own heresy trial in September of 1550. Both Degli Ottoni and Fontanini were then arrested. Degli Ottoni interpreted this action as an attempt by the monks to justify themselves for overthrowing his leadership.[128] He wrote to Gonzaga twice in December of 1550 to plead that he and Pole hear the case, rather than his fellow monks, whose privilege it ordinarily was to try their own. At this point Gonzaga's actions begin to reveal his way of operating when dealing with questions of heresy. Gonzaga responded to Degli Ottoni with a rather harsh rejection of the suggestion that Gonzaga judge the case. In the matter of Siculo's accusations he had already asked the inquisitor in Ferrara to come to Mantua to explain the details of the case. The inquisitor had sent a subordinate in his place. During that meeting Ercole and his own suffragan and inquisitor in Mantua had the opportunity to examine the documents of Siculo's case that pertained to Degli Ottoni and Fontanini. Having seen the documents, Gonzaga told Degli Ottoni that he considered the charges reasonable and that he should be punished according to the law.[129] He refused to take part in the trial and encouraged the Benedictine officials to proceed. But he promised Degli Ottoni that he would encourage the judges to act with "equity, justice and charity" or he would have recourse to the pope.[130] Despite his refusal to intervene, Gonzaga nevertheless assisted

127. Gigliola Fragnito, "Ercole Gonzaga, Reginald Pole e il Monastero di San Benedetto Polirone. Nuovi documenti su Luciano Degli Ottoni e Benedetto Fontanini. (1549–1551)," *Benedictina* 34 (1987): 257.

128. Luciano Degli Ottoni to Ercole Gonzaga, December 6, 1550, in Ginzburg and Prosperi, 202–3.

129. Ercole Gonzaga to Luciano Degli Ottoni, January 3, 1551, in Fragnito, "Ercole Gonzaga," 269.

130. Ibid., 269.

Degli Ottoni and Fontanini in a significant way. In keeping with the norms of inquisitorial procedure, Gonzaga supplied the accused with the depositions taken against them, saying that he would always offer them if they are able to justify themselves.[131] Thus, the accused had an advantage as they prepared to defend themselves. In the end, the two monks received relatively light sentences when compared to their principal accuser, Siculo, who died by hanging in Ferrara in February of 1551. Degli Ottoni lost his offices but died in a monastery of natural causes. Fontanini was eventually freed from prison.[132]

Gonzaga took with one hand and gave with the other. In this way he held himself above the fray and avoided any public forum in which his own actions and words could be scrutinized. He had already acted on behalf of Degli Ottoni when accusations of irregularities were as yet intramural. A second public defense might bring difficulties and dishonor upon his family and duchy. Yet when he backed Degli Ottoni as a candidate to be abbot of San Benedetto in Polirone, Gonzaga must have been aware of the accusations made against him at Trent. Gigliola Fragnito has suggested that Gonzaga may have shared in the heretical views of Siculo, Degli Ottoni, and Fontanini, and that such a shared theological outlook would explain Gonzaga's support of Degli Ottoni as abbot.[133] If one considers only this episode, such a conclusion might seem tenable. Although some doubted Gonzaga's orthodoxy, the best contemporary evidence we have attests to it. There is no direct evidence that he shared in heretical views, while there are specific indications to the contrary. If he had held any heretical views, it seems unlikely that he could have been chosen as papal legate to the Council of Trent in 1561, no matter how repentant he might have been by that time. Gonzaga was, however, unintimidated by reasoned discussions of questionable orthodoxy when they were carried on in

131. Ibid., 270.
132. Ibid., 263.
133. Ibid., 265. If Gonzaga did share Siculo's views he manifested a particularly cold-blooded attitude toward his plight when he urged Ercole d'Este to cooperate more fully with the inquisitors in Siculo's prosecution. See ibid., 262, and Blaisdell, "Politics and Heresy," 81.

a suitably elite forum. Participation in such discussion must not have eliminated the speaker from his good graces. Gonzaga was also powerful enough politically to give shelter. Mantuans such as Degli Ottoni and Fontanini most likely perceived that and sought his aid.

Given all of this ambiguous activity, it is not surprising that Reginaldo Nerli wondered about the orthodoxy of his Mantuan patron. Gonzaga himself had no doubts about it. Yet his protest that membership in the "Company of Christ" should be sufficient indication of orthodoxy also has an Erasmian tone, with its lack of emphasis on external norms. Admission that he had someone in his household to teach him what he should say and think as a Catholic reveals Gonzaga as both not utterly certain of what the details of that allegiance might entail and committed to understanding it as fully as possible. Nevertheless, if some had doubts about Gonzaga, he was not without defenders among even the most conservative elements in the Church. In 1554, Girolamo Muzzarelli, O.P. (d. 1561), master of the Sacred Palace, attested to his orthodoxy.[134] Muzzarelli wrote to Marcello Cervini: "In Mantua I have seen the Catholic zeal of the cardinal. . . . I think that his reverend lordship has no need of the spur."[135]

Gonzaga presents difficulties for the historian precisely because he held to generally conservative theological views while at the same time offering shelter and support not only to figures such as Contarini and Pole, whose adherence to the papacy and the Church was without question, but also to an array of individuals who either left the Church or continued to profess heretical doctrines well into the 1550s. The fact that Gonzaga, a man whose orthodoxy was far enough above suspicion as to be selected papal legate to the Council of Trent in 1561, moved with regularity and apparent ease in the company of these individuals, reveals a religious world in which many personalities escape

---

134. See Jacobus Quetif and Jacobus Echard, *Scriptores ordinis praedicatorum recensiti, notisque, historicis et criticis illustrati*, 2 vols. (1719–23; reprint, New York: Burt Franklin, 1959–61), 2/1: 179.

135. Girolamo Muzzarelli to Marcello Cervini, 13 February 1554, in Buschbell, 321. "In Mantova ho conosciuto il zelo catholico del cardinale . . . ho giudicato Sua Signoria Reverendissima non haver bisogno de sproni."

easy categorization. The key to understanding this conundrum lies in two important facts of Gonzaga's life: his role as a great lord of northern Italy and his education. As the regent for his nephews, Gonzaga's political role was, quite literally, conservative. His responsibilities entailed preserving intact the principality that his brother Federico had left behind. Cardinal Gonzaga strenuously opposed any activity that threatened that inheritance. Preaching that by the standards of Catholic orthodoxy might be seen as scandalous or imprudent could present such a threat to the civil and religious stability of Mantua. Mantuan society and his role as ruler of it served as the ground for Gonzaga's understanding of reform because awareness of the role of his family in the affairs of Italy and Europe was the foundation of his outlook on life.

Limiting analysis of Gonzaga's activities in relation to heresy to the sphere of politics, however, leaves a great deal out of consideration. If politics and political stability were his only concerns, then he could easily have taken far more severe measures than he actually did against heresy in his diocese. Gonzaga's restraint when confronting those who lacked orthodoxy gives evidence of one who, well into the 1550s, maintained a broad-mindedness in matters of religion. This openness resulted in part from early training received from Pomponazzi. The philosophical skepticism that Pomponazzi exhibited on the question of the immortality of the soul may have taken root in Gonzaga. According to Endimio Calandra, Gonzaga expressed a willingness to pay five hundred scudi to know the fate of the souls of a group of executed heretics.[136] This is a remarkably skeptical admission by a high-ranking churchman about the souls of heretics. It is the expression, perhaps, of one in whom philosophical skepticism had spread beyond matters of natural philosophy and into the realm of theology. It is consistent with his interpretation of Paul's letter to the Romans and the inscrutability of God's designs. Gonzaga's observations, if we can take Calandra's testimony as accurate, indicate that he either could not know for certain that those convicted heretics were in error,

---

136. Pagano, *Nona Costituto di Endimio Calandra,* May 3, 1568, 350.

or, if he were certain of their error, what effect it would have on their salvation, however comfortable he might feel in his own conservative beliefs.[137] The humanistic and philosophical foundation that he laid at Bologna in the 1520s continued to influence Gonzaga's ongoing theological studies and enabled him to engage in dialogue with many religious figures whom he met in his lifetime. Close contact with Contarini, Pole, Morone, Ochino, Vergerio, and others introduced Gonzaga to individuals whose lives and thought raised significant questions about the religious standards with which he had been raised. Gonzaga personally rejected the doctrines of Protestant theologians and willingly took action when those teachings threatened the social order for which he was responsible. But when those matters of faith were discussed in a circumspect manner by members of an intellectual or social elite, Gonzaga stayed his hand. Gonzaga's conservatism was that of a Renaissance lord and lacked the dogmatism of an inquisitor. His relationships with religious dissenters throw into relief the various influences of Italian humanism, Catholic reform, international politics, and dynastic responsibility in the career of an aristocratic cardinal of the late Renaissance.

137. It is worth noting the account of Pomponazzi's death in the context of Gonzaga's questions about the fate of the heretics. In his last illness an associate asked Pomponazzi where he was going. The philosopher responded enigmatically, "Where all mortals go." When pressed as to where that was he added, "Where I am going and all others have gone." See Pine, 51.

CHAPTER 5

THE REGENCY IN MANTUA

Ercole Gonzaga played a role as bishop of Mantua that was normative for younger sons of the Gonzaga family. For generations a member of the Gonzaga family had acted as the ecclesiastical ruler of the diocese. Gonzaga's responsibilities toward his family were not limited to his administration of the local church, however. He also acted as tutor and regent for his nephews during their minorities. This in itself was not unusual either. It was the length and influence of Gonzaga's regency, which extended almost without a break from 1540 through 1556, that made Gonzaga's career unique in the history of his family. For those seventeen years Ercole Gonzaga ruled Mantua both temporally and spiritually. It is in this area of his career that his role as the preeminent member of his family led Cardinal Gonzaga to engage in politics on a broader geopolitical level. Here he dealt not simply with recalcitrant cathedral canons but with the nettlesome and indeed dangerous issues of maintaining Gonzaga power in the midst of the Habsburg-Valois wars.[1] The longstanding Gonzaga tradition of avoiding firm commitments to greater powers and the willingness to shift allegiances allowed them to maintain the independence of their small principality for more than two hundred years. Their entry into the imperial camp in the 1520s complicated but did not extinguish this tradition, which Ercole Gonzaga maintained during his regency of Mantua.

1. On these political conditions see Mazzoldi, *Mantova: La Storia,* and Cesare Mozzarelli, *Mantova e i Gonzaga dal 1382 al 1707* (Turin: UTET Libreria, 1987) (hereafter cited as Mozzarelli).

Federico Gonzaga, Duke of Mantua

Ercole's older brother, Federico, had been groomed for the role of Mantuan ruler from infancy. His preparation included not a little drama. Although he received literary training from a local humanist in Mantua in his youth, the experience he gained as a courtier was more significant for his career. When Marquis Francesco II Gonzaga was captured in battle by the Venetians in 1510 he gained his freedom only by offering his son Federico as a hostage to be held by the pope in the Vatican. Federico then spent several years in the Rome of Julius II and Leo X. He later went to the French royal court as a hostage of King Francis I from 1515 to 1517, where his presence was intended to ensure Gonzaga cooperation with Francis I after French victories in Italy. In the spring of 1517 when Federico's time as a hostage ended, he took up a place as a courtier in the royal court and then stayed on to congratulate the French king on the birth of a son.[2] He was not permitted to return to Mantua until he had agreed to marriage with Maria Paleologa, the daughter of the French ally the Marquis of Monferrato. Thus he received an education that was courtly rather than humanistic and initially displayed a noteworthy closeness to the king of France. Federico's reputation as a courtier and prince found expression in the words of Baldassare Castiglione, who described him in *The Book of the Courtier:*

In addition to the fine manners and discretion he shows at so tender an age, those who have charge of him tell wonderful things about his talent, his thirst for honour, his magnanimity, courtesy, generosity and love of justice.[3]

Federico succeeded his father, Francesco, in 1519 at the age of nineteen. Charles V and Francis I had reached a temporary truce at Noy-

2. On Federico's time in France see Raffaele Tamalio, *Federico Gonzaga alla corte di Francesco I di Francia: nel carteggio privato con Mantova (1515–1517)* (Paris: Champion, 1994), and Anthony B. Cashman III, "Performance Anxiety: Federico Gonzaga at the Court of Francis I and the Uncertainty of Ritual Action," *Sixteenth Century Journal* 33, no. 2 (2002): 333–52.

3. Baldessare Castiglione, *The Book of the Courtier,* trans. George Bull (New York: Viking Penguin, 1967), 36.

ons in 1516, which restored a semblance of tranquility to the Italian peninsula after more than twenty years of almost continuous warfare and made the early years of Federico's reign relatively peaceful. He continued the Gonzaga practice of acting as a mercenary captain in a way that, at least initially, was compatible with French interests. He entered into a contract with Pope Leo X, then an ally of Francis I, who made Federico the captain general of the papal armies. Leo sweetened the offer by giving Ercole Gonzaga control of the diocese of Mantua and offering the promise to make him a cardinal at some point in the future. Further, in a secret clause of the agreement, Leo insisted that in the event of a conflict between the pope and the emperor, Federico should fight for the papacy. In return, Federico was to receive possession of Parma and Piacenza. His position was to become increasingly difficult for one whose feudal lord and legitimate sovereign was Charles V.[4] The contents of that secret chapter had not come to light during the lifetime of Leo X, who died in December of 1521, and the Gonzaga took pains to acquire the document containing the arrangement. Isabella d'Este destroyed it with her own hands.[5]

Federico continued to serve as captain general of the Church during the reign of Leo's successor, Adrian VI, Charles V's old tutor. To this command he added that of Florence. Thus as the French once again invaded Italy in 1523, Federico Gonzaga was one of the most significant commanders in the peninsula. The events of the 1520s were to bring an end to Federico's association with the French. Florence had already entered into the League of Venice to prevent the French from seizing Milan. Federico could not have been enthusiastic about confronting the French and his response to the crisis was something less than energetic. He spent much of his time during this stage of the Italian Wars claiming to be unable to act on account of illness.[6]

---

4. On the diplomatic arrangements for Ercole Gonzaga's promotion see Mazzoldi, *Mantova: La Storia,* 2: 271.

5. Ibid., 280.

6. M. J. Rodríguez-Salgado, "Terracotta and Iron," in *La Corte di Mantova nell'età di Andrea Mantegna: 1450–1550/The Court of the Gonzaga in the Age of Mantegna: 1450–1550,* Atti del convegno (Londra, 6–8 marzo 1992/Mantova, 28 marzo 1992),

After the death of Adrian VI, the new pontiff, Clement VII, renewed Federico's contract as captain general of the Church, which
made him commander once again for a pope who resisted rather than
supported the policies of Charles V. The position did not, however,
prevent him from maintaining the old Gonzaga tradition of avoiding binding commitments when necessary. Charles's victory over the
French at Pavia in 1525, for example, would seem to have demanded
action on Federico's part to defend the interest of his employer, the
pope. Nevertheless, in the tradition of earlier Gonzaga lords he acted
only when it was convenient. Federico sought to maintain a degree of
freedom in the political struggles between the emperor and the pope
by insisting that the pope agree to a secret clause in his contract that
freed Federico from the necessity of fighting his sovereign, Charles V.
In fact, Federico did little to impede the advance of imperial troops as
they descended upon Rome in the spring of 1527.

The course of the Habsburg-Valois wars in Italy in the 1520s largely determined Gonzaga policy for the remainder of the century. The
new conditions allowed much less space for the cagy neutrality that
they traditionally displayed. Or perhaps the neutrality they had earlier
shown was less necessary to Federico after 1527, since Charles's power
in Italy had increased dramatically. In either case, in the aftermath of
the imperial victories in Italy, Federico drew closer to the Habsburgs.
He rejected the planned marriage to Maria Paleologa, which had been
arranged as part of an earlier French policy, in order to marry a cousin
of Charles V. The emperor himself, however, seemed to recognize that
his overwhelming power in Italy made it necessary to assuage the fears
of Italians that he might swallow all of the northern Italian states. As
a part of this program, he elevated Federico to the dignity of duke in
1530 and did not oppose Federico's renewal of a marriage alliance with
Maria Paleologa, or when she died, with her sister Margherita.

These developments brought Cardinal Gonzaga to a political turning point. In the early years of his career he moved within French

ed. Cesare Mozzarelli, Robert Oresko, and Leandro Ventura (Rome: Bulzoni, 1997),
37 (hereafter cited as *La Corte di Mantova*).

circles at the papal court. The Spanish cardinal of Osma, García de Loaisa, observed that he was "more French than the French ambassador."[7] For a time, the political climate allowed him to maintain such attachments and they were not inconsistent with the tendency of the Gonzaga to leave all their options open in the midst of the Italian Wars. The victories of Charles V and Federico's desire to possess the marquisate of Monferrato made a closer alliance with the emperor politically expedient. Hence, Cardinal Gonzaga was present in Bologna for the imperial coronation of Charles in 1530 and then accompanied him to Mantua for his brother's investiture as duke.[8] In return for continued loyalty, Federico eventually received the title of Marquis of Monferrato in 1536. This new political situation required Ercole Gonzaga to distance himself from the French. As a condition for acquisition of Monferrato, Federico was bound to provide Charles V with all of the support of his duchy and family. An independent foreign policy by Ercole was no longer possible. In these years the entire Gonzaga family began to serve imperial interests. Ferrante Gonzaga had already embarked upon a career of military service to Charles V and Cardinal Ercole Gonzaga permanently joined the imperial faction in the college of cardinals.

The court of Mantua under Federico attained an unprecedented splendor as increasing sums poured into the maintenance of an enormous household for such a small principality. It is estimated that at Federico's death the ducal household numbered as many as eight hundred members. He employed as his official architect Giulio Romano, whose work at the Palazzo del Te in particular distinguished the Gonzaga capital. This display of pomp was part of a calculation to present an image of princely splendor and thereby secure his fortune. A remarkable example of this image was the celebration Federico orchestrated on the occasion of the visit of Charles V to Mantua in

7. García de Loaisa, *Documentos ineditos para la historia de España,* vol. 14, *Correspondencia del Cardenal de Osma con Carlos V y con su secretario Don Francisco de los Cobos, Comendador Mayor de Leon,* ed. Miguel Salvá and Pedro Sainz de Baranda (Madrid: Imprenta de la viuda de Calero, 1849), 21.

8. Mozzarelli, 52.

1530. Upon his entry to the city, Charles was met by crowds of nobles among whom were more than one hundred Gonzaga relatives of Federico. Knowing the emperor's tastes, Federico also arranged for packs of hunting dogs, falcons, and horses to be at the ready. Triumphal arches and statues celebrating the emperor and the Gonzaga decorated the city. The results were what Federico had wanted. Charles stated that there was no city in Italy that pleased him as much as Mantua.[9] The success of the visit, especially the hunting parties, was such that Charles returned in 1532 for similar festivities. The detachment that the Gonzaga had traditionally shown toward greater powers was, for a time at least, set aside and Federico established a firm commitment to the Habsburgs.

The Regency

In 1540 Duke Federico died, leaving his seven-year-old son, Francesco, as heir. The regency was conferred upon Ercole, Ferrante, and the Duchess Margherita Paleologa. In keeping with their princely status, the cardinal and the duchess presided at audiences in the ducal palace each week during which any of their subjects might approach them and ask for favors or report malfeasance by ducal administrators.[10] In practical terms, however, on account of Ferrante's absence in Sicily and Margherita's in-law status, as well as general distrust of women in the Renaissance, the governance of the duchy of Mantua remained largely the responsibility of Cardinal Gonzaga,[11] who held the posts of regent and official tutor of his nephews until 1557. During this period he wielded supreme authority in the duchy of Mantua in both the temporal and the spiritual spheres. These years witnessed his maintenance of the Gonzaga family's interests in Lombardy and their

9. Ibid., 42–44.

10. ASM, AG, b. 2038–2039, f. 15r, August 7, 1540. On Margherita Paleologa see Louisa Parker Mattozzi, "The Feminine Art of Politics and Diplomacy: Duchesses in Early Modern Italy" (Ph.D. diss., University of Virginia, 2003).

11. Castellani, *Vita*, 15. "Fù necessario al cardinale Ercole di pigliar sopra sè la maggior parte del carico, che seco tal tutela portava, e tanto governo."

commitment to imperial interests in Italy. This additional responsibility confirmed his role as a patrician reformer. His work in the Church was as much a matter of dynastic duty as it was one of ecclesial concern.

The prospect of governing Mantua was not an altogether pleasant one for Cardinal Gonzaga. He wrote to Cardinal Contarini just two days after the death of Federico to inform his friend of this development and to seek his assistance. He expressed his concern that this new duty was "truly a weight as burdensome on my back as it is different and contrary from the quiet life that I have led up until now."[12] Contarini responded with encouragement for Gonzaga as he took up those responsibilities:

God has given Your Lordship many talents, perhaps more than to anyone of your house for many years he has given you the greatest way of expending them in his honor, for the benefit of your *patria,* of which you now hold the spiritual and temporal government. It is time to expend them, to give them *ad usura,* so that they multiply for the patron by the fruit and profit that they will provide for so many of your family, and these gifts will increase for Your Lordship by spending them. "To those who have it is given."[13]

These sentiments were echoed by those of Gregorio Cortese, who expressed his approval of what Gonzaga had already begun in terms of religious reform and stated his hopes for what could happen when Gonzaga was also the regent. He expressed confidence in Gonzaga's "effective example to all the other princes."[14] Here an important con-

12. Ercole Gonzaga to Gasparo Contarini, June 30, 1540, Friedensburg, 52. "Peso veramente più grave alle spalle mie quanto è più diverso et contrario alla quieta vita che ho fatto fin qui."

13. Gasparo Contarini to Ercole Gonzaga, July 13, 1540, Friedensburg, 53–54. "Dio ha dato a V.S. molti talenti, et forsi più che ad alcuno di casa sua già molti anni li ha dato grandissimo modo di spenderli in honore suo, in beneficio della patria sua, della quale hora ha il governo spirituale et temporale. tempo è da spenderli, di darli ad usura, ad ciò multiplicino al patrone per il fructo et guadagno che faranno tanti et tanti della sua familgia [*sic*], et a V.S. acresceranno spendendoli. habenti dabitur."

14. "Efficace esempio a tutti li altri Principi." Cited in Gigliola Fragnito, *Il Cardinale Gregorio Cortese (1483?–1548) nella crisi religiosa del cinquecento* (Rome: Abbazia di S. Paolo, 1983), 74.

temporary saw Gonzaga's work of ecclesiastical reform within a broader context of reform of and by the princes. Whatever his initial doubts,
Cardinal Gonzaga did carry out his duties with great care.

As regent, Ercole took up a complicated set of rights and policies
that the Gonzaga had established over the course of the fourteenth
and fifteenth centuries. In essence Mantua and its surrounding territory functioned as a bastion from which the Gonzaga could operate as
condottieri for a variety of Italian states. Earlier Gonzaga rulers such as
Ludovico and Francesco I had served Milan, Venice, and the papacy
while technically being vassals of the emperor. In many respects this
regency reflected both the present needs of the young dukes and the
traditional policies of the Gonzaga. One matter had become increasingly clear by 1540—the need to effect administrative and fiscal reform in Mantua. Essentially this need led Ercole Gonzaga to pursue a
conservative policy of preserving the Mantuan state and avoiding any
dramatic foreign adventures. All the while, he and Pope Paul III complicated each other's efforts by their long-standing feud.

A valuable source on the state of affairs in Mantua at the time Cardinal Gonzaga assumed the regency in 1540 is the diplomatic correspondence of Bernardo Navagero, Venetian envoy to Mantua at the
time of Federico's death. Navagero included a careful description of
the duchy and the cardinal regent in his letters to the Senate. The ambassador described him in uniformly positive terms, a man gifted in
mind and body. He characterized Ercole's administration by two principal features. First, he put Mantuan public finances in order. The Venetian described Cardinal Gonzaga as one who today might be called
a fiscal conservative, who lowered taxes and eliminated monopolies in
order to solve the financial problems of the ducal government.[15] Second, he ensured that in the conflicted atmosphere of sixteenth-century Italy Mantua did not become entangled in wars or crises elsewhere
in the peninsula. This detachment required a diplomatic position

15. Albèri, *Relazioni*, 16–17. "Vuole che la mercanzia sia libera." Navagero himself later became a cardinal and succeeded Gonzaga as legate to the Council of Trent
in 1563.

verging on neutrality on the part of Mantua for the duration of the regency, notwithstanding Gonzaga commitments to Charles V. In short, during the regency Gonzaga policy was characterized by cautious negotiation between rival powers that had been the heart of their diplomacy before 1530. It should be noted that Cardinal Gonzaga brought to Mantuan government during the regency a preparation far different from that of his brother or his father. He was not trained as a soldier and had a much more extensive academic background. The years spent in Rome had introduced him to the workings of a highly organized bureaucracy. This training and his role as a cardinal equipped him with skills that his brother Federico had lacked and allowed him to avoid some of the greater costs of the life of a Renaissance warrior. Consequently the regency not only maintained Gonzaga status but also achieved a significant reform of ducal government.

Domestic Administration

For all of the difficulties bequeathed by Federico, ducal revenue was not a complete disaster. Navagero estimated the annual revenue of the duchy at ninety thousand to one hundred thousand scudi. The single largest source was the tax on salt, which alone provided upward of thirty thousand scudi. Expenses during the life of Federico, however, had been quite onerous. Navagero explained to the Venetian government that they were very high because Federico spent much on horses, buildings, and maintaining a large court. In addition to the cost of raising his heir, Francesco, Federico had also left two younger legitimate sons, Guglielmo and Ludovico, each of whom was entitled to eight thousand ducats per annum, and a daughter, Isabella, whom Federico had provided with a dowry of twenty-five thousand ducats. Further, at Federico's death, the Duchess Margherita was pregnant and that child would have to be cared for in a manner similar to that of the older siblings. These expenses for the immediate family were accompanied by legacies that Federico had provided for servants and his natural son, Alessandro. The result was a seriously unbalanced budget. Given all of this, the cardinal explained to Navagero, it was necessary for him to be very economical if he hoped to leave anything for his nephew Francesco.[16]

Cardinal Gonzaga wasted no time in addressing the fiscal problems of the duchy. When Navagero arrived in Mantua to offer his condolences on the passing of Federico and to assess the economic and political condition of the Mantuan state, Cardinal Gonzaga had already reduced the size of the ducal court from about eight hundred to about three hundred fifty people. This reduction constituted what Navagero called the removal of "superfluous provisions to men of little usefulness." Among these, the regents ousted the treasurer Carlo Bologna and the *sindaco* Antonio Delfino, both of whom were found guilty of extortion and other crimes. Navagero characterized this fiscal conservatism as providing only for governmental officers such as judges, government ministers, and other necessary officials. Navagero estimated the cost of this reduced staff at between thirty thousand and thirty-five thousand ducats per annum. These economies would have, therefore, provided for an annual surplus of between fifty-five thousand and seventy thousand scudi per annum.[17] Navagero had discussed these measures with Gonzaga himself. The cardinal regent explained that they were necessary given the debts that his brother had left behind, all of which had to be paid. In a decree of 1543 the regents reiterated their commitment to balancing the books and indicated that in order to do so they would need to limit expenses further by reducing provisions to courtiers and "doing away with superfluous officials, gentlemen, and other salaried officials."[18]

Cardinal Gonzaga not only addressed problems of the duchy through a reduction in expenditures but also undertook a significant reform of the ducal administration that rationalized and professionalized the government. The basic apparatus of Mantuan government in the mid-sixteenth century was largely unchanged from the time

16. Ibid., 11–12.
17. Ibid. On the actions against Bologna and Delfino see ibid., 17.
18. ASM, AG, b. 2047, September 2, 1543, cited in Marzio A. Romani, "Finanze, Istituzioni, Corte. I Gonzaga da Padroni a Principi (XIV–XVII sec.)," in *La Corte di Mantova*, 101–2.

of Francesco IV Gonzaga, *Capitano del Popolo* (1383–1407), who re-formed the communal statutes to reflect the presence of the Gonzaga rulers. Even then, much of the communal governmental machinery remained intact, although it became much more the tool of the Gon-zaga princes.[19] Cardinal Gonzaga initiated reforms that rendered the Mantuan government more efficient and increased professional dis-tinctions among civil servants. The ducal chancellery was reorganized by establishing four secretaries whose prominence was enhanced by the subsequent choice of the regents to leave the old post of *capo della segreteria* vacant and allowing the secretaries to speak for themselves in government councils. Qualifications for office were also raised. Fed-erico had begun the practice of selling offices, a common one among early modern states. Ercole stopped this practice and placed officers of proven ability, even if they were not Mantuans, in positions of re-sponsibility. Term limits were set at two years for offices in the duchy and they were to go to nobles who were in need. In 1546 the regen-cy government issued new norms for those who would work as du-cal notaries. Among qualifications demanded by the regents was that a candidate be *"litteris latinis convenienter instructus"* as well as at least twenty years of age and have at least two years of prior experience.[20] These changes suggest an increased emphasis on professionalization in Mantuan temporal government that is analogous to the higher de-mands that Cardinal Gonzaga simultaneously placed on his clergy. In addition to these lesser officers, Cardinal Gonzaga saw to an innova-tion at the highest levels of the government. The 1540s saw the growth of a new council of government, the *Consiglio segreto*. This council be-came the primary instrument of ordinary government, over which the regents themselves presided. The older *Consilium domini* now came to focus entirely on judicial matters.[21]

This care for fiscal and administrative prudence extended to deci-

19. Mozzarelli, 3–21. See also Mario Vaini, "Gli statuti di Francesco Gonzaga IV Capitano. Prime ricerche," *Atti e memorie dell'Accademia Virgiliana di Mantova*, n.s., 56 (1988): 187–214.

20. ASM, AG, b. 3581, "Ordines admittendi notarios in collegio."

21. Mozzarelli, 62–63.

sions about Mantuan diplomatic representation abroad. In a letter to Cardinal Gonzaga, Ferrante summed up regency practice by judging three ambassadors to be sufficient. One was to be present at the court of Francis I of France and would be sent in the name of Margherita as the Marquise of Monferrato and with the agreement of Charles V. This solution apparently satisfied Ferrante, who had initially opposed the sending of any ambassador to the French court since it might send the wrong signal to the imperial court. A second ambassador was to be at the court of Charles V at the expense of the duke himself, but in the name of Ercole, who was the *governatore* of Mantua. This diplomat was to show that the young duke's "soul would be firm and sure in the service of His Majesty and that he had no desire to depend on others than him, by which he would be able to bring himself honor and service."[22] A third ambassador was to be sent to Venice. Diplomatic representation in Rome was to be handled by Ercole's own agent there at the time, Nino Sernini.

Often in the past scholars have credited Cardinal Gonzaga's fiscal-mindedness to a form of Counter-Reformation rigor. He has been referred to as a stern "Counter-Reformation cardinal." Thus his economies have been attributed to his religious views rather than to political or economic necessity.[23] Given the realities of Italian politics in the mid-sixteenth century, however, it is more reasonable to view his reforms in a secular light. Gonzaga never expressed any religious concern in his reforms of the Mantuan chancery. These were practical measures and they were effective. Indeed, if the tale of Gonzaga rulers was one largely of leaving behind the modest status of *Capitano del*

22. Instruction of Ferrante Gonzaga to Federico Cavriani, July 28, 1540, ASM, AG, b. 910. Cited in Mazzoldi, *Mantova: La Storia,* 2: 311–12 "Che l'animo suo fosse fermo et stabilito sul servicio de Sua Maestà et di non voler dependere da altri che da lei, la qual cosa potria sperare che in breve li recasse honore et utile." Ferrante seems to have been concerned about unspecified bad habits that the seven-year-old duke had already cultivated. He believed it necessary "per ritirarlo da quella mal creanza che si vede havere presa fin al presente, et riducerlo su la buona via, perchè seria pur troppo errore a lascialo precipitare in quei pessimi costumi et farsi un bufalo come si va facendo."

23. See Frederick Hartt, *Giulio Romano* (New York: Hacher Art Books, 1981), 234.

Popolo in order to establish themselves as sovereign princes, then the period of Cardinal Gonzaga's regency can be viewed as a significant chapter in that history.

Cardinal Gonzaga's Foreign Policy

Mantuan foreign policy under Cardinal Gonzaga was simple in purpose and complex in execution. His intention was to conserve and strengthen his nephew Francesco's inheritance until the boy attained his majority. Achieving that goal was made difficult by the realities of the Habsburg-Valois wars in Italy during the regency and the tensions between Charles V and Pope Paul III over reform of the Church. Ercole Gonzaga never placed the fundamental loyalty of his family to the Habsburgs in jeopardy. However, his avoidance of dangerous conflicts did lead others to wonder if he might be more independent than he was in fact. The Gonzaga owed previous titles to earlier emperors and their ducal title to Charles V himself. Habsburg forces occupied neighboring Milan. Ferrante's close personal relations with the emperor sustained these political ties, and Cardinal Gonzaga's own distaste for the politics of Paul III also reinforced the Gonzaga adherence to imperial interests. Nevertheless, the presence of French troops in Italy and the possibility that they might defeat the Habsburgs meant that simultaneously Cardinal Gonzaga had to avoid offending Francis I. Apart from a perennial hesitancy to engage in war in defense of Habsburg interests, the most obvious gesture to France during the regency was the decision by Cardinal Gonzaga and Margherita Paleologa to permit Francesco's younger brother Ludovico to go to France in 1549 to claim an inheritance from his French grandmother and eventually to marry the heiress to the French duchy of Nevers.[24] These actions rekindled suspicions among the Habsburgs that Cardinal Gonzaga was a francophile. In general, therefore, Gonzaga pursued a policy that verged on neutrality. He dared not take any action that

24. On Ludovico Gonzaga and the political significance of his marriage see Mozzarelli, 114–17.

would imperil his nephew's inheritance. Yet he could not avoid showing some signs of support for the imperial camp. This need to maintain a delicate diplomatic balancing act largely explains the actions of
Cardinal Gonzaga in foreign policy.

The defense of Mantua was a complicated problem given the city's
location in the middle of northern Italy. When Navagero assessed the
Mantuan state for the Venetian government he pointed out that the
Gonzaga commanded a significant military force of their own. In 1540
this force included three hundred *"uomini d'armi"* whom Navagero
described as *"gentilhuomini o buoni cittadini,"* five hundred light caval-
ry, and about seven hundred infantry. These forces also enjoyed the use
of one hundred eighteen pieces of *"munizione,"* both large and small.
Perhaps the greatest military advantage of Mantua was that provided
by nature. The city itself occupied what, for all intents and purposes,
was an island in the Mincio River. Not surprisingly, the Venetian ambassador duly noted these walls of water. In addition to the river, the
Gonzaga had established significant man-made bastions. Navagero's
observations on the military significance of Mantua also highlight its
political relevance to other northern Italian powers. As a friend, Navagero wrote, Mantua could be of assistance to all of Lombardy and
the Venetian mainland as well. As an enemy it was close enough to
threaten Venetian cities such as Verona, Brescia, and Padua, as well as
other Italian cities such as Milan, Parma, Reggio Emilia, and Ferrara.
It was for this reason, Navagero argued, that the imperial general Prospero Colonna had urged Pope Leo X to make Federico captain general
of the Church in 1520. Mantua may have been a small state in comparison to Milan, Venice, or the Papal States, but its relative wealth
and its location made the duke an attractive ally in the Italian Wars
of the sixteenth century. These circumstances required great attentiveness on the part of Cardinal Gonzaga as he attempted to simultaneously maintain Gonzaga power and avoid military and diplomatic en-
tanglements in the region.[25]

The impressive display of military might that Navagero saw at the

25. Albèri, *Relazioni,* 12–13.

time of Federico's funeral in 1540 was maintained only long enough to impress those who came for the event. It becomes clear from the correspondence of the ducal chancery in the following years that the regents drastically reduced military expenditures. By late summer of 1541 the actual defenses of Mantua itself were so weakened that the duchy could not afford to offer assistance to the emperor for his war in Hungary. The Habsburgs had sent a request to their allies asking for both financial and military help. This included an appeal for twenty thousand scudi in silver, gunpowder, and *bombardieri,* or artillery personnel. Perhaps not wanting to be the bearer of bad news, Ercole left it to the Duchess Margherita to respond. In her letter to the imperial court she expressed surprise that the difficulties of Mantua were not already known there. She added the excuse that she and Ercole were not "absolute patrons, but only tutors" and her children were quite small. Moreover, the young duke was responsible for the debts of his father, so that even if he were a grown man she did not know how he would be able to afford to send those funds. She added that they had little gunpowder and that since Federico's death the court had been so reduced that she could only remember having two *bombardieri* in the household at that time.[26] These protests to the imperial court were more than a careful and disingenuous means of avoiding the supply of men and money to the emperor. The same week that Margherita wrote of the financial and military constraints of the duchy the regents received news of a mutiny of soldiers in the duchy because they had not received their pay. The matter was settled only when Cardinal Gonzaga released the funds to mollify the troops.[27]

It seems that rumors of those military weaknesses had begun to circulate as early as the spring of 1541. In a dispatch from Benedetto Agnello, Mantuan ambassador at Venice, Cardinal Gonzaga learned of the Venetian Senate's interest in these matters. Agnello communicated the great distrust the Venetians had for Charles V. Moreover, he

26. ASM, AG, b. 2194, ff. 1013–1016, fascicle labeled "Minute della Cancelleria," September 10, 1541, from Margherita Paleologa without salutation.

27. Ibid., f. 1018r, fascicle labeled "Minute della Cancelleria," anonymous enclosure with a letter from Margherita to her mother, September 6, 1541.

added, they were concerned with Mantua's defenses. In a private conversation with Francesco de Priuli, procurator of San Marco, the Venetian began to question Agnello in an unusual manner on these military issues. He inquired about the strength of Mantua's defenses and how many troops the duchy could field. Agnello responded to Priuli by making the Mantuan defenses sound especially strong, thus exemplifying the description of an ambassador as a man who lies abroad for his country.[28]

The defense of Mantua required careful attention also to visits there by foreign powers and the nearly constant presence of the regents. Cardinal Gonzaga quickly put an end to discussions in 1542 about Mantua as a possible site for the proposed reform council. His first excuse for this was that he would not go against the explicit wishes of his deceased brother Federico, who opposed a council in Mantua in 1537. Moreover, the thought of Mantua being filled with a large number of armed men under obedience to foreign princes at a time when Mantua's military forces were significantly weakened did not seem conducive to Mantuan security.[29] Indeed, Cardinal Gonzaga's concern for the security of the city was so great that he believed it required denying the emperor entrance in 1541, a position that Ferrante insisted was not necessary or feasible given the Gonzaga family's debt to Charles V.[30]

Cardinal Gonzaga not only desired to avoid any difficult visits from foreign dignitaries but also avoided leaving Mantua, especially after the reopening of hostilities between Charles V and Francis I in July of 1542. During this period Cardinal Gonzaga displayed great anxiety about his nephew's inheritance, even after he had been assured by Alfonso d'Avalos, the Marquis del Vasto and Pescara and Charles V's governor in Milan, that it was not likely that much fight-

28. ASM, AG, b. 2195, ff. 984r–985r, March 12, 1541, Benedetto Agnello to Ercole Gonzaga and Margherita Paleologa.

29. BAV, Bar. Lat., codex 5790, ff. 112v–113v, Ercole Gonzaga to Gasparo Contarini, January 18, 1542. On the implications of this for the council see Chapter 6.

30. ASM, AG, b. 1911, Ferrante Gonzaga to Ercole Gonzaga, March 8, 1541, cited in Mazzoldi, *Mantova: La Storia*, 2: 313.

ing would go on in Italy itself. In November of 1542 Paul III asked Cardinal Gonzaga to come to Rome for consultations, but Nino Sernini, his agent in Rome, secured permission from the pope for him not make that journey.[31] Only on rare occasions, such as the meeting of Paul III and Charles V at Busseto in June of 1543, did he overcome his hesitancy to leave the duchy. Gonzaga watched with interest to see how they would direct imperial and papal policy in Italy. On June 16 he had gone as far as Parma, where the pope awaited the arrival of the emperor. There Gonzaga made an act of loyalty to the pope, perhaps in response to concerns about him at the time of the flight of Bernardino Ochino.

Efforts to establish a nearly neutral policy did not preclude solidification of Gonzaga-Habsburg ties. That same summer of 1543 the emperor announced plans for the marriage of his niece Catherine of Austria, the daughter of Ferdinand I, to the young Duke Francesco Gonzaga. Betrothal of these ten-year-olds further cemented the alliance between the Habsburgs and the Gonzaga. The acrimonious relationship between Cardinal Gonzaga and the pope made this alliance even more welcome. Thus it is no surprise that the Mantuan cardinal willingly paid agents to gather information on the relationship between Paul III and Francis I. He wrote to his brother Ferrante in January of 1544 that he paid these spies "at my own expense and [with] the great trouble and danger of the one who gathered it."[32] But Cardinal Gonzaga believed that his information was not being taken seriously enough at the imperial court. This belief enhanced the cardinal's fears about the security of Francesco's inheritance even as he solidified the Habsburg alliance.

These fears were not diminished when, contrary to the prediction of the Marquis del Vasto, the French did wage war in Italy. Specifically, they defeated the Marquis del Vasto himself in April of 1544, leaving Monferrato dangerously exposed to French troops. The principal fortress defending the region was Casale. In order to secure it,

31. Ibid., 313–14.

32. ASM, AG, b. 1914, Ecole Gonzaga to Ferrante Gonzaga, January 9, 1544, cited in Mazzoldi, *Mantova: La Storia,* 2: 314.

Cardinal Gonzaga agreed with the Marquise Anna Paleologo of Monferrato, Federico's mother-in-law, that it should be considered neutral and that imperial troops should not occupy it. This agreement might have had the effect of removing a French rationale for attacking it in the first place. It was also a rationalization for Cardinal Gonzaga's not being more vigorous in his defense of Habsburg interests. As he expressed it in a letter to Ferrante of April 30, 1544, "when things are in our own hands we will not give any material for either party to be disappointed in us."[33]

As French troops drew closer to Mantua itself, Cardinal Gonzaga found himself in the awkward position of trying to maintain this nearly neutral policy without raising the suspicions of the emperor. In May of 1544, when French troops crossed the Po and came within a three-hour march of Mantua, the Marquis del Vasto requested troops from the cardinal. Gonzaga found this request rather difficult to fulfill. He wrote to Ferrante that on the one hand he did not want to bring about the ruin of the whole Mantuan state by inviting French reprisals. The French were so close that if they initiated war the Gonzaga would be forced to battle the French in their own territory, something that would surely threaten his nephew's inheritance. On the other hand he recognized that imperial forces had to make some sort of response. He made the modest proposal of sending reinforcements to the imperial-held city of Cremona, outside of Mantuan territory. He explained himself to his brother Ferrante, perhaps with an eye to criticism of his actions by some at the imperial court, by insisting that he still remained loyal to the emperor and would carry out all that he could do well and justly without risking more than he had received from the emperor. In short, regardless of the benefits that Charles V had bestowed upon them over the previous generation, they did not justify, in the mind of Cardinal Gonzaga, imperiling the security of the Gonzaga themselves.[34] Gonzaga did not have to endure this uncomfortable fence-sitting for long. War did not spread to the duchy

33. Ibid., 316.

34. ASM, AG, b. 1914, Ercole Gonzaga to Ferrante Gonzaga, May 5, 1544, cited in Mazzoldi, *Mantova: La Storia,* 2: 316–17.

of Mantua and by August of 1544 Charles V and Francis I had, at least temporarily, ended the conflict. The Gonzaga alliance with the Habsburgs was not definitively put to the test. In fact, it was further enhanced in 1546 when Charles V chose Ferrante to serve as his governor in Milan.

Gonzaga and the Farnese

In August of 1545, while reflecting on his relationship with Pope Paul III, Ercole Gonzaga went so far as to claim: "We have not had one happy moment in the eleven years of this papacy."[35] To a considerable extent Gonzaga's unhappy relationship with Paul III influenced his views on the reform of the Church and his efforts as regent of Mantua. It contributed to his return to Mantua in 1537 and greatly influenced his association with individuals such as Pier Paolo Vergerio and Bernardino Ochino. From the election of the Farnese pope in 1534 until his death in 1549 it is difficult to isolate Gonzaga's opinions on reform or much of his work as regent of Mantua from his many uncomfortable moments with the Farnese family.

Cardinal Gonzaga's relationship with Paul III became strained for two reasons in particular: Gonzaga's fidelity to imperial interests in Italy and his discomfort, like that of many others, at Paul III's largess toward his own family. That strain is typified by a struggle between the Farnese and the Gonzaga over a benefice in Duke Federico's marquisate of Monferrato. The Cistercian abbey of Santa Maria di Lucedio in Casale, most often referred to in Gonzaga's correspondence simply as Lucedio, had been in the hands of Cardinal Agostino Trivulzio but was, strictly speaking, in the gift of the Emperor Charles V.[36] As early as 1533, transfer of the monastery came into dispute, at first

35. BAV, Barb. Lat., codex 5793, ff. 11r–13r, Ercole Gonzaga to Ippolito Capilupi, August 31, 1545. "Non havendo noi goduto delle felicità d'undici anni del Papato, ma piutosto ricevuti scorni e affronti insieme con molti danni." f. 12v.

36. ASM, AG, b. 1907, Bernardino de Plotis to Ercole Gonzaga, April 10, April 22, May 12, August 20, August 26, September 25, October 12, 1538. These letters discuss, among other things, the monastery of Lucedio that Gonzaga was still trying to secure.

between Cardinal Ippolito de' Medici and Cardinal Gonzaga.[37] It was this dispute that gave Paul III a rationale for attempting to acquire it for his own family.

In February of 1535 Gonzaga wrote to Francesco II Sforza, Duke of Milan, to explain how this dispute came about. He informed the duke that Paul III had instructed his ambassador at the imperial court to influence the conferral of the monastery. The pope had argued that since both Gonzaga and Medici were "of great significance and great lords," the emperor could not give the monastery to one without offending the other. The better solution, the pope submitted, was to confer the monastery on his own grandson, Alessandro Farnese. In that way Charles could keep all parties in peace.[38] The conflict was somewhat simplified by the death of Cardinal de' Medici in 1535, so Gonzaga and Alessandro Farnese were left as the principal claimants to the monastery. Much to Cardinal Gonzaga's chagrin, his brother Federico, as the Marquis of Monferrato, also sought the revenues of the monastery.[39] This struggle continued with all parties seeking diplomatic advantage. Gonzaga noted in a letter of January 1537 that the Marquis del Vasto was assisting Cardinal Farnese in attaining Lucedio.[40] In order to counter this Farnese effort, Gonzaga appealed to Francisco de los Cobos, Charles V's secretary for Italian affairs. He asked the Spanish official to look after his interests in the abbey and expressed hope that the

37. Ibid., b. 1155, unnumbered fascicle, Ercole Gonzaga to Giovanni Jacomo Calandra, February 11, 1533.

38. BAV, Barb. Lat., codex 5788, ff. 96v–97v, Ercole Gonzaga to the Duke of Milan, February 6, 1535. "Ho inteso ch'l Papa tra l'altre sue commissioni date al Nuntio che manda all'Imperatore una delle principali è questa di chiedere in gratia a Sua Maestà la Badia di Lucedio per un suo nipote allegando che per essere in lite tra Medici et me che ambi duo siamo di molto momento et gran signori over usare le proprie sue parole, non potra fare che dandola ad uno, non offenda gravemente all'altro et gratificandone l'uno di noi verrà a perdersi l'altro. Ma che se a Sua Santità la concede per uno Cardinale suo nipote ogniuno piu facilmente s'acquietarà et tanto più ch'lla troverà molto farli stare tutti contenti."

39. ASM, AG, b. 887, ff. 150r–150v, Ercole Gonzaga to Isabella d'Este, January 5, 1537.

40. BAV, Barb. Lat., codex 5789, ff. 8r–11v, Ercole Gonzaga to Sagunta, January 16, 1537. Cardinal Farnese had sought the possession of the abbey of Lucedio "col favore del Signore Marchese de Vasto," f. 8r.

emperor and his servants would prevent the pope from carrying out his "fantasia."[41] The struggle over Lucedio is a part of the larger history of interdependence between secular and religious institutions and the grant of the right of *juspatronato* was closely connected to the issue of Gonzaga status. Gonzaga security in Monferrato was at the core of the dispute and to deny a "great lord" such a privilege would be an affront to Gonzaga dignity. Thus one reason for the length and bitterness of the episode lies in the struggle of the Gonzaga to attain or maintain their status as great lords.[42]

Gonzaga's concern over the pope's activities extended to the difficulties that some of his colleagues were experiencing under Paul III. One of Gonzaga's closest associates in the early part of his career was Benedetto Accolti, cardinal of Ravenna and the papal legate to the Marche of Ancona. Soon after his election, Paul III began to investigate Accolti's fiscal administration of Ancona. At the same time that Gonzaga was carrying on correspondence about the abbey of Lucedio he wrote to Accolti about that cardinal's conflict with the Farnese. Accolti had sought a pension from the cathedral of Monreale in Sicily for a friend and Gonzaga had intervened with the pope on his behalf. Gonzaga refers to the "crime" that Paul III committed every time that he overlooked the opportunity to assist Accolti. In a letter to his brother Federico from Rome, Cardinal Gonzaga expressed his disgust that "in this court a way is found every day to do evil and to bury the truth."[43] Gonzaga's problems over Lucedio, therefore, fit into a broader experience of those who saw the Farnese as taking care of their own while at the same time ignoring the needs of the cardinals appointed by Clement VII.[44]

41. Ibid., ff. 13r–14v, Ercole Gonzaga to Francisco de los Cobos, the Commendador Mayor de Leon, January 22, 1537.

42. On this relationship between political status and benefices see Flavio Rurale, "Chiesa e Corte," in *La Corte di Mantova*, 105–24.

43. ASM, AG, b. 887, ff. 139r–142v, Ercole Gonzaga to Federico Gonzaga, January 3, 1537. "Et in questa corte trovassi ogni di più la via di fare male et di tenere sepulta la verità." ff. 142r–142v.

44. BAV, Barb. Lat., codex 5789, ff. 15v–16v, Ercole Gonzaga to Benedetto Accolti, January 27, 1537.

By February of 1537 the Gonzaga family had nearly despaired of obtaining the monastery for Ercole. In that month they began to change their tactics in order to ensure, at the very least, that the monastery would not fall into the hands of the Farnese. The method was to present Ercole not as one who was defending his own interest but as one who intended to cede the monastery to a deserving cleric. As Cardinal Gonzaga himself stated, "If they [the Farnese] want to litigate this matter, they will obtain less when opposing another than they would against me."[45] Even this concession did not relieve the Gonzaga of their difficulties. After this change in strategy the Farnese tried to secure for themselves at least the castles that pertained to the abbey, an arrangement that Federico, as Marquis of Monferrato would not permit. Nor, it seemed, would the emperor who was concerned about the Italian policy of the Farnese.[46] By the end of 1539 negotiations had reached the point where the Farnese seemed willing to forgo their claim on the abbey, but only with the guarantee of a four thousand *scudi* pension for Cardinal Farnese in order to satisfy their "black honor," as Cardinal Gonzaga put it.[47]

Not until after the death of Federico Gonzaga in 1540 did much progress take place on the matter of Lucedio. In August of that year Cardinal Gonzaga made an offer that was an attempt to please both the Farnese and the Gonzaga. According to the proposal, Cardinals Gonzaga and Farnese were to divide equally the income of the monastery. Gonzaga was to retain the title of the monastery and the right to cede it to another. According to Ludovico Strozza, Gonzaga's representative in Rome, even Pier Luigi Farnese, father of Cardinal Farnese, agreed that Cardinal Gonzaga had good reason to maintain posses-

---

45. ASM, AG, b. 887, f. 208r, Ercole Gonzaga to Federico Gonzaga, February 26, 1537. "Perche se costoro voranno litigare, men frutto faranno sempre contra un altro che non fariano contra di me."

46. BAV, Barb. Lat., codex 5789, ff. 79r–81r, Ercole Gonzaga to Nino Sernini, November 16, 1537.

47. ASM, AG, Carteggio di Ercole Gonzaga, b. 1908, unnumbered fascicle, copy of a letter from Ercole Gonzaga without indication of the addressee, December 1, 1539. "Si vede chiaramente che Farnese disse che ne pigliarebbe di pensioni 4 mille scudi con li quali il loro negro honor si vederebbe."

sion of the abbey.[48] This arrangement was accepted and by February of 1541, Bernardino de Plotis, one of Gonzaga's agents in Rome, wrote to him on the matter of reforming the monastery.[49]

Cardinal Gonzaga's difficulties over the abbey of Lucedio did not end there, however. While a general settlement had been reached, the agents of Cardinal Farnese continued to seek advantage. They refused to pay his share of a previously established pension for Cardinal Trivulzio.[50] Furthermore, in early 1544, Gonzaga learned with displeasure that Paul III had arranged that Cardinal Farnese would secretly maintain for himself the right to the regress of the monastery in contravention of the official agreement with Gonzaga, that is, if Gonzaga were to cede the title to the monastery, it would of necessity go to Cardinal Farnese. Gonzaga credited the pope's actions to his *"malignità."*[51] In May of that year Gonzaga wrote to Ippolito Capilupi to outline his future strategy, including a willingness to renounce his titles to the abbeys of San Tommaso in Acquanegra and Felonica if the pope would give way on Lucedio. He told Capilupi to delay on the first two until Gonzaga had received assurances from the pope on the third. It was his intention to provide his nephew, the future Cardinal Francesco Gonzaga, the son of Ferrante, with that benefice.[52]

Some progress in the discussions took place the following spring. Gonzaga and Farnese had the opportunity to negotiate in person when Farnese stopped in Mantua on his way to Germany. Gonzaga described Farnese as having performed a miracle, because before he left Rome he sealed the cession of the regress of Lucedio. In Mantua

48. Ibid., b. 888, ff. 50r–53v, Ludovico Strozza to Ercole Gonzaga, August 7, 1540.

49. Ibid., b. 1911, ff. 11r–11v, Bernardino de Plotis to Ercole Gonzaga, February 25, 1541.

50. BAV, Barb. Lat., codex 5790, ff. 45r–47v, Ercole Gonzaga to Agostino Trivulzio, March 7, 1541.

51. Ibid., codex 5792, ff. 11v–12r, Ercole Gonzaga to Ippolito Capilupi, February 2, 1544.

52. Ibid., ff. 54v–55v, Ercole Gonzaga to Ippolito Capilupi, May 7, 1544. In 1552 the abbey went to another relative, Cardinal Federico Gonzaga. For the bull of collation see ASM, AG, b. 3345, part XVIII, "Abazzia di Santa Maria di Lucedio 1552," January 29, 1552.

Farnese offered to do as Gonzaga wished about his share of the income
of the monastery. Nevertheless, Gonzaga was hesitant to agree completely, since he did not yet have complete information on the income
of the monastery.[53] An assessment of its wealth, prepared for Gonzaga
in 1545, showed the total income of Lucedio was 4,730½ scudi per annum. Expenditures for the previous year had amounted to 3,047 scudi, leaving a total of 1,683½ scudi to be shared between the two cardinals.[54] They finally settled on this income-sharing arrangement, and
Alessandro Farnese continued to enjoy the fruits of the monastery of
Lucedio into the 1570s.[55] The ten-year struggle over Lucedio serves to
illustrate the obstacles to reform in the years immediately before the
opening of the Council of Trent and how those obstacles intersect-
ed with the political aspirations of the Farnese, the Gonzaga, and the
Habsburgs.

The conflict between the Gonzaga and the Farnese was bitter
enough because of financial competition, but it worsened as a result
of Gonzaga involvement in the murder of Pope Paul III's son, Pier Luigi Farnese, and later in the War of Parma. Ferrante Gonzaga played
a central role in both events, which resulted in even greater enmity
between the rival families. By the 1540s Ferrante had already spent a
large part of his career in service to the Emperor Charles V. For many
years he had held the post of viceroy of Sicily. Upon Charles V's appointment of him as governor in Milan and captain general of imperial forces in Italy, Ferrante involved himself more deeply in the conflict between the houses of Habsburg and Valois. During these years

53. BAV, Barb. Lat., codex 5792, ff. 165r–168r, Ercole Gonzaga to Ercole d'Este,
April 26, 1545. "Nei nostri poi parmi ch'egli habbia fatto miracoli perche prima che
sia partito di Roma, ha segnata le ceduta della cessione del regresso di Lucedio et qui
s'è offerto di fare tutto quel ch'io voro de suoi mezzi frutti sopra quella Badia." Upon
his return from Germany in June, Cardinal Farnese repeated his assurance to Gonzaga.
See ibid., ff. 170v–171r, Ercole Gonzaga to Ercole d'Este, June 4, 1545.

54. ASM, AG, b. 1915, ff. 180r–181v, expenses and income of the abbey of Lucedio for 1545.

55. A. Edith Hewett, ed., "An Assessment of Italian Benefices Held by the Cardinals for the Turkish War of 1571," *English Historical Review* 30 (1915): 488–501. For
Lucedio see 489; Hallman, 39; see also A. V. Antonovics, "Counter-Reformation Cardinals: 1534–1590," *European Studies Review* 2 (1972): 319–22.

of service to the Habsburgs, Ferrante encountered Pier Luigi Farnese and formed a visceral dislike for the man.

Pier Luigi Farnese owed his rise in the world to the elevation of his father, Alessandro Farnese, to the pontificate in 1534. The pope then lavished the material wealth at his disposal on this unpleasant individual. For many years Pier Luigi had acted as a diplomatic representative of the pope. In 1545, Paul III obtained a cherished objective for Pier Luigi by alienating the duchy of Parma and Piacenza from the states of the Church and bestowing it on his son. Many members of the college of cardinals opposed this act of nepotism. It was widely doubted that the pope, as trustee of the papal states, had the right to alienate any of its territory. Cardinal Gonzaga also expressed dismay at the investiture of a duchy so close to the borders of Mantua upon a member of a rival house. He wrote of the pope and his son to his cousin the Duke of Ferrara:

That old man intends to make . . . the future Duke of Parma the King of Spain, of France, and of the whole world, since everything turns out well for him. To us who do not have such luck and hold our states by ancient right and much labor and effort, and with so many other worries, it seems strange to see a duke of two such cities sprout up in one night like a mushroom.[56]

Since Charles V never assented to this transfer of jurisdiction, Pier Luigi soon associated himself with France. Incidents followed in which Farnese harried the borders of the duchy of Milan, which was by then a Habsburg possession. Ferrante Gonzaga urged the emperor to expel Pier Luigi from the duchy. The emperor at first indicated that he preferred to wait until after the death of the pope. By spring of 1547, however, Charles was ready to approve a plan by Ferrante to drive the Farnese out of Parma and Piacenza by means of a local re-

56. BAV, Barb. Lat., codex 5793, ff. 6v–7r, Ercole Gonzaga to Ercole D'Este, August 23, 1545. "Certo ch'l vecchiarello ha molto ragione di far il futuro duca di Piacenza re di Spagna, di Francia et di tutto, poi ch'ogni cosa gli riesce così bene. A noi altri, che senza tanta buona sorte habbiamo i stati per li nostri antichi con tante fatiche e stenti guadagnati et che con altre tante angoscie si conservano, pare strano cosa vedere far un duca di due simili città in una notte come nasce un fungo." Also in Pastor, 12, appendix #29, 675–76.

volt of disgruntled nobles. Charles insisted, however, that the revolt
not result in the execution of Pier Luigi. Ferrante, for his part, was unable to extract such a promise from the conspirators in Parma and did
not insist upon a guarantee of safety for Farnese.[57] Perhaps the guarantee was not that important to him. He did promise immunity from
prosecution for all those who participated in the coup d'etat, however. On September 10, 1547, the conspirators entered the citadel at
Piacenza where Pier Luigi was then staying, murdered Farnese in his
bedroom, and then threw his bloody corpse from a window of the fortress. Word of the revolt reached Milan the same day and Ferrante intervened to secure imperial interests. He immediately informed Ercole
of the death of Pier Luigi and told his brother that he intended to go
to Lodi to ensure that only imperial allies took control of Piacenza.[58]
By September 12 Ferrante had occupied Piacenza in the name of the
emperor. Parma, meanwhile, resisted an imperial occupation and Pier
Luigi's son Ottavio arrived in the city on September 16.

Cardinal Gonzaga responded with advice for his brother to be-
ware of the Farnese, whom he felt sure would blame Ferrante for the
assassination, a prediction that proved correct. Upon receiving news
of Pier Luigi's death, Paul III declared that he had no greater enemies
in the world than Ferrante and Ercole Gonzaga.[59] Gonzaga agents in
Rome informed the cardinal of discussions in the curia about excom-
munication of the conspirators and the desire of Paul III to place Ferrante's name at the head of the list. Indeed, some of the Farnese had
said that if the emperor died before Paul III, the pope would destroy
the house of Gonzaga.[60] This event brought Cardinal Gonzaga's relationship with the pope to its lowest ebb and at the same time gave de-
monstrable, if distasteful, proof of Gonzaga fidelity to Charles V's in-

57. Tamalio, *Federico Gonzaga*, 28.

58. ASM, AG, b. 1916, unnumbered fascicle, Ferrante Gonzaga to Ercole Gonzaga, September 10, 1547.

59. Angelo Cocconcelli, *Le Rivaltà dei Gonzaga coi Farnese e la riconciliazione voluta da Pio IV a mezzo di San Carlo Borromeo e del Cardinale di Mantova* (Reggio Emilia:
Tipografia Mario Corsi, 1937), 4–5.

60. ASM, AG, b. 1916, unnumbered fascicle of drafts of letters and minutes of
letters from Rome, letter without name of author or addressee, October 14, 1547.

terests in Italy as well as his family's sense of *realpolitik*. As bitter as the enmity between the two families was, a continued and open breach between the pope and such an influential family as the Gonzaga was inadvisable. Cardinal Gonzaga started to make efforts to reconcile as early as 1548. Nevertheless the conflict between the houses of Farnese and Gonzaga did not completely end until the pontificate of Pius IV in the 1560s.[61]

Apart from this bitter rivalry with the Farnese, however, Cardinal Gonzaga managed to avoid any serious conflicts with the major powers of Europe or with Mantua's smaller neighboring states. The remainder of Duke Francesco's minority was, therefore, peaceful and optimistic. The year 1549 should have been a signal one for the young duke and the cardinal regent. In January they hosted Charles V's heir, Philip II, for three days in Mantua. Lavish displays of pomp and ceremony ritualized the now solid connection between the two families. Later that year Francesco welcomed to Mantua his Habsburg bride, Catherine of Austria. Celebrations surrounding the marriage continued for a week's time. Not surprisingly, those present at the wedding feast were not inclined to set aside the celebrations when news reached them that Pope Paul III had died on November 10. They only reluctantly ceased their revels as they took up the duty of mourning over the death of a pope who was no friend to the Gonzaga.

Toward the end of 1549, therefore, Cardinal Gonzaga must have seen himself as reaching a turning point in his life. His nephew Francesco was entering into his majority and the responsibilities of the regency would soon be a thing of the past. The death of Paul III freed Gonzaga of his greatest nemesis. As he set out for the conclave that was to select Paul's successor, he could take satisfaction in knowing that he was himself an influential figure in the upcoming election. Even his preferences in the election demonstrate a certain political

61. Ibid., b. 1917, unnumbered fascicle of minutes and drafts of letters, Ercole Gonzaga to "Capilupi," November 26, 1548. "Ho visto quello che m'havette scritto essere passato fra noi et Montesa intorno alla reconciliatione di cotesti signori Farnese con il Signore mio Fratello et certo ho preso piacere grande." Fernando Montesa was the secretary of Cardinal Francisco de Mendoza.

neutrality within a largely imperial commitment that was consistent with his work in Mantua. At the outset he, along with the other imperial cardinals, supported the unsuccessful candidacy of his old friend Reginald Pole. Later in the conclave he supported another old friend, Cardinal Giovanni Salviati, despite Charles V's explicit exclusion of the man. As the long conclave drew to a close Gonzaga was one of a handful of cardinals who stood resistant to the acclamation of Cardinal Giovanni Maria Del Monte as Julius III (1550–55), one whom Charles V also opposed. Even this opposition to Del Monte did not cost Gonzaga the friendship of the new pope, who presented him with an ancient Roman emerald valued at three thousand scudi.[62]

Reports from Rome indicated that Gonzaga was in a jocular mood. The diarist Angelo Massarelli described an instance during the conclave when Cardinal Niccolò Gaddi disturbed the solemnity of the papal election by clumsily knocking over his writing table and spilling all of his writing materials on the floor as he rose to deposit his ballot during one of the scrutinies. "His inept picking up of them moved their Reverend Lordships to laughter more than the fall of the table, especially the Cardinal of Mantua, both because he was nearby and because he is by nature rather prone to laughter."[63] Gonzaga's willingness to find humor at the expense of others manifested itself again upon the arrival of the cardinal of Rouen, in Latin the cardinal *"Rothomagensis."* Another observer reported: "Great laughter was provoked among the cardinals on account of Mantua, who said that the see of the Cardinal *'Rhothomagensem'* was as ridiculous as his face."[64] But Cardinal Gonzaga suddenly saw his reasons for optimism and good humor evaporate. On

62. On the conclave see Massarelli, CT 2: 3–145; Pastor, vol. 13, 1–44. On the gift of the emerald see ibid., 52, #3. See also Thomas F. Mayer and Peter E. Starenko, "An Unknown Diary of Julius III's Conclave by Bartolomeo Stella, a Servant of Cardinal Pole," *Annuarium Historiae Conciliorum* 24, no. 2 (1992): 345–75.

63. Massarelli, CT 2: 73, December 24, 1549. "Quae dum ineptus colligit, non magis quam ex casu scanni risum movit R.mis. Dominis, Manutano praesertim, et ut vicino, et ad risum proniori natura ipsa."

64. Massarelli, CT 2: 76, n. 6. Petrus Paulus Gualterius reported "magnus risus excitatus est inter cardinales Mantuano auctore, qui dixit cardinalem Rothomagensem cuidam suo villico similem esse ob faciem ridiculam."

December 9, 1549, Duke Francesco fell into the chilly waters of the Mincio while hunting and came down with a severe fever. After lingering on his sickbed for more than two months, he died on February 21, 1550, while Cardinal Gonzaga was still in Rome. Francesco's untimely death held Cardinal Gonzaga in Mantua once more, this time as the regent for his younger nephew Guglielmo.

The Regency of Guglielmo

At the time of his older brother's death, Guglielmo Gonzaga did not appear very impressive. The twelve-year-old was hunchbacked, as were several of his ancestors, and therefore unable to bear arms. Fearing that he would be unable to rule effectively, Cardinal Gonzaga and Duchess Margherita tried unsuccessfully to convince the boy to abdicate in favor of Federico's third son, Ludovico. Guglielmo, however, firmly refused to take their advice. Thus began the second stage of Ercole Gonzaga's work as regent of Mantua. Guglielmo's regency was characterized by much the same foreign and domestic policy as Francesco's had been. Cardinal Gonzaga affirmed the family's alliance with the Habsburgs while at the same time retaining as great a degree as possible of practical neutrality in the Habsburg-Valois conflict.

The most immediate example of this foreign policy during the regency of Guglielmo involved tensions with the Farnese and the complexity of maintaining the Habsburg alliance in the midst of the Italian Wars, in particular the struggle over the duchy of Parma and Piacenza. In the aftermath of Pier Luigi Farnese's death in 1547 the competition for Parma and Piacenza intensified. King Henry II of France demanded that both Parma and Piacenza be given to the French king's new son-in-law, Orazio Farnese. Paul III, meanwhile, who had initially agreed to accept a partition of Piacenza from Parma on the suggestion of Charles V, reversed himself before he died in 1549 and declared Ottavio Farnese the heir to the entire duchy. Upon his election as pope in 1550 Julius III confirmed Ottavio Farnese in possession of the duchy and made him captain general of the Church. Charles V, for his part, remained determined to acquire both Parma and Piacenza. When he made them a condition of his agreement to the reopening of the Council of Trent, Julius III reversed his initial commitment to Ottavio Farnese and backed the emperor's claims to the whole duchy. In these circumstances Ottavio Farnese sought the assistance of Henry II. The pope, who now supported imperial policies, recalled Ottavio to Rome. When he refused to present himself, Julius declared Farnese a rebel and revoked his right to hold Parma as a fief of the papal state. The pope then sought the military assistance of Charles and his governor in Milan, Ferrante Gonzaga. Hostilities broke out on June 12, 1552, when Farnese moved his troops into the papal state itself and carried out raids near Bologna. Ferrante Gonzaga sent troops to join the papal forces and challenge Farnese.[65]

Once again, in the midst of war, imperial interests required Gonzaga support. Again Cardinal Gonzaga faced decisions affecting the inheritance of his nephew. In this case he not only elected not to intervene in the conflict, but also ordered the destruction of the Gonzaga's own castle at Sermide in order to remove it as an attractive stronghold for either side.[66] Gonzaga's continued avoidance of conflict became even more difficult when the French invaded Monferrato to assert themselves in northern Italy and support Orazio Farnese's claims. Although Cardinal Gonzaga at first hoped that imperial troops from Milan under the command of Ferrante would successfully counter the French, he nevertheless found himself in the position of having to offer direct military assistance to the imperial forces. He was only spared further involvement in this military crisis as external factors brought it to a close: opposition to the war had grown in the Roman curia on account of its cost to the papacy, rebellion in Germany distracted Charles from Italian affairs, and Ferrante Gonzaga sought a truce when his forces experienced reverses at the hands of the French in Piedmont.

These challenges did not directly touch Guglielmo Gonzaga's inheritance but they exposed a weakness in Cardinal Gonzaga's diplo-

---

65. On this conflict see Mazzoldi, *Mantova: La Storia,* 2: 4–6; Pastor, 13: 129–57.
66. ASM, AG, b. 2549, Antonio Pavese to Ercole Gonzaga, cited in Mazzoldi, *Mantova: La Storia,* 2: 5.

macy. The Habsburg alliance had been fundamental to Gonzaga polit- ical activity since at least the 1520s. Nevertheless, Cardinal Gonzaga's need to maintain some distance from conflicts that would threaten his nephew's inheritance and his willingness in 1549 to permit the mar- riage of his nephew Ludovico Gonzaga to a French princess had be- gun to raise questions about his loyalty in the minds of Charles V and Philip II. By the 1550s this relationship was complicated by a weak- ening of the political connections that bound the two families, the friendship and confidence that Ferrante enjoyed with Charles V in particular. Ferrante's relationship to Philip II had never been partic- ularly intimate. As Philip emerged as a ruler in his own right during the 1550s, Ferrante, and the Gonzaga as a whole, experienced a corre- sponding diminution in influence among the Habsburgs.[67]

A crisis in the relationship between the Gonzaga and the Habsburgs occurred toward the close of the War of Parma in 1553. Philip II held Ferrante Gonzaga personally responsible for Habsburg defeats in Pied- mont. At the same time Philip had been urging his father, Charles, to reform administration of the Italian Habsburg territories by removing Ferrante Gonzaga from office in Milan and replacing him with one of Philip's own servants. An important advisor to Philip in this mat- ter was the Duke of Alba, who had become a rival of Ferrante at the imperial court. By late 1553 a charge of corruption in office had been made against Ferrante. This charge gave Philip the opportunity to ini- tiate his proposed reforms. In January of 1554 Charles summoned Fer- rante to the imperial court, ostensibly to seek his advice in planning Charles's next northern military campaign. When he arrived Ferrante asserted his innocence of the charges against him and demanded res- toration to office. These arguments persuaded Charles of the inno- cence of his old comrade and he ordered Philip to reinstate Ferrante in Milan. By that time, however, Philip had removed him from of- fice, rejected his father's request, and effectively signaled Ferrante's fall from power. In 1554 Ferrante withdrew from active imperial service for the first time in decades and returned to his own lands.[68]

Cardinal Gonzaga saw the challenge that these changes in imperial administration might bring to the Gonzaga themselves. As early as 1551, it seems, opposition to Ferrante had already surfaced in the circle around Phillip and led Ferrante to consider retiring. In a letter of November 20, 1551, Ercole encouraged his brother and stated that under no circumstances should he leave imperial service. He reiterated these thoughts in a letter written in his own hand a few weeks later, stating not only that Ferrante should not retire but also that he should show greater diligence than ever.[69] As Ferrante's position continued to deteriorate, Ercole addressed Charles V directly. In July of 1554 he wrote to the emperor and defended Ferrante against the accusation that he would have betrayed the Habsburgs and sought the duchy of Milan for himself. Ercole argued against the probability of that by reference to Ferrante's actions during the revolt against Pier Luigi Farnese in 1547:

If my brother had had a different attitude than he did toward the service of Your Majesty it would not have been difficult to inform Pope Paul and Pier Luigi secretly of the attempts that the plotters had to give Piacenza to Your Majesty in order to oblige the pope and his son to help him be made Duke of Milan with the importance of that city that is in the heart of that state. But not only did he not do this, rather he adroitly and prudently brought that plan to a conclusion that was in service to Your Majesty and the preservation of the state of Milan. By this he earned the enmity of the pope and his house which endures still now.[70]

68. Rodríguez-Salgado, "Terracotta and Iron," 53.

69. ASM, AG, b. 1921, ff. 551–555r, Ercole Gonzaga to Ferrante Gonzaga, November 20, 1551; ibid., ff. 571r–581v, Ercole Gonzaga to Ferrante Gonzaga, December 11, 1551.

70. ASM, AG, b. 1926, ff. 445r–448v, Ercole Gonzaga to Charles V, July 8, 1554. "Dico che quando il Signore mio fratello havesse havuto altro animo che quello che ha et hebbe sempre verso il servigio di Vostra Maestà non gli sarebbe stato dificile il far secretamente intendere a Papa Paulo et a Pier Luigi el trattato che menavano li coniurati di dar Piasenza a Vostra Maestà per obbligarsi el Papa et el figliuolo ad aiutarlo

As improbable as Gonzaga's assertion that the Farnese might under any circumstances assist Ferrante in becoming Duke of Milan, this statement does highlight how he found merit in Ferrante's involvement in the death of Pier Luigi Farnese. Cardinal Gonzaga pointed out to the emperor that if Ferrante had not been so loyal to the Habsburgs he could have easily betrayed the conspiracy to Paul III and to Pier Luigi. Rather than that, Ferrante had acted to secure imperial interests in Milan. Indeed, by seeing his brother's actions as a sign of fidelity to the imperial family, he virtually approved the assassination of Pier Luigi.

Ferrante's retirement until his return to military service in the Netherlands in 1557 signaled a decline in trust between the Gonzaga and the Habsburgs. With Ferrante's death that same year there was an unaccustomed lack of Gonzaga presence among the military leaders of Habsburg Italy. The French invasion of Monferrato in 1557 highlighted the lack. Monferrato was lost to the Gonzaga until the Peace of Cateau-Cambresis in 1559. This lack of Gonzaga influence at the Habsburg court may also have reduced their significance as allies in the mind of Philip II and others. The Venetian ambassador to Mantua in 1557 wrote to the Venetian Senate that it was unclear to him whether the Gonzaga stood with the French or the Habsburgs.[71] Thus Ercole Gonzaga's policy of near neutrality during the regency of Mantua undermined his credibility as a Habsburg ally, although he never entertained the possibility of an alliance with the French and worked to maintain his brother Ferrante's role in imperial politics. By the mid-1550s it was becoming apparent that the Gonzaga would need to be doubly careful to ensure that their relationship to the Habsburgs not be misunderstood. Ercole Gonzaga increased his efforts to ensure it. The fall of Ferrante from power highlights not only the waning of

con l'occasione a farsi Duca di Milano colla importanza di quella città ch'è nel cuore di quel stato. Ma non solo non fece questo, anzi destramente et prudentemente condusse quella pratica al fine che ne seguì in servigio di Vostra Maestà et conservatione dello stato di Milano: per qual impresa s'acquistò la inimicitia del Papa et di casa sua, che anchora dura." ff. 445v–446r.

71. Rodrìguez-Salgado, "Terracotta and Iron," 53.

Charles V's real power but reveals changes in the political context in which Ercole Gonzaga concluded his regency for Guglielmo. With the passing of Ferrante in 1557, the friendship between Ferrante and Charles, which had provided a firm link with the Habsburgs and overcome many suspicions of Gonzaga loyalty, was now in the past. It must have come as a great relief later that year, when Ercole Gonzaga witnessed Duke Guglielmo Gonzaga attain his majority and begin to rule in his own right.

Complexities of these political relationships played themselves out in the papal conclave that followed the death of Pope Paul IV.[72] This conclave convened on September 5, 1559, and lasted for nearly four months. The Venetian ambassador, Alvise Mocenigo, characterized it as "the most open and licentious that there ever was either in memory or writing."[73] The cardinals were divided into three principal factions: the Spanish or imperial faction led by Cardinal Guido Ascanio Sforza; the French led by Cardinal Ippolito d'Este; and that of the Carafa led by Paul IV's nephew Cardinal Carlo Carafa. This division prevented any one candidate from attaining the necessary two-thirds majority for a long time. It appeared for a while, however, that Isabella d'Este's hopes for her son's elevation to the pontificate were not greatly misplaced. His standing in the college of cardinals as early as 1549 had been sufficient to elicit a response from Pasquino, the ancient Roman statue that served as the mouthpiece for innumerable anonymous political barbs: "He became a great tyrant at the expense of his nephew in less than a year. Don't make him pope!"[74] Others hoped for his election. Cardinal Cristoforo Madruzzo of Trent shared with one of Gonzaga's servants in Germany his expectation that "when our diligence is governed by the wisdom of the Cardinal of Mantua we will turn things around nicely."[75]

---

72. On this conclave see Pastor, 15: 1–65, and Roberto Rezzaghi, "Cronaca di un conclave: l'elezione di Pio IV (1559)," *Salesianum* 48 (1986): 539–81.

73. Albèri, *Relazioni,* 43.

74. Jedin, "Il Figlio," 506.

75. ASM, AG, b. 1915, f. 323v, Camillo Capilupi to Ercole Gonzaga, April 11, 1546.

The near neutrality of Cardinal Gonzaga's political activity as regent may have eliminated the sort of opposition that would have arisen had he been more clearly partisan in his activities between 1540 and 1557. Only the Farnese showed implacable hostility to Gonzaga. Thus, the near neutrality made his candidacy more acceptable to a majority. However, it appears simultaneously to have lessened the enthusiasm for a Gonzaga pope among the various factions of the conclave, thus rendering Gonzaga's candidacy too weak to attain victory. The French viewed Gonzaga as acceptable but as their third candidate after Cardinal Ippolito d'Este and Cardinal François de Tournon. He was also acceptable to the cardinals who formed the Spanish faction, but not, as the conclave proceeded, to the Spanish ambassador. When scrutinies of the first three weeks proved unsuccessful, leaders of the French and the Spanish parties agreed to Gonzaga as an acceptable alternative.[76] Since Gonzaga's name had surfaced rapidly, the faction leaders sought to arrange his election at night by means of adoration in the Pauline Chapel of the Vatican to allow them to avoid the necessity of a ballot and to evade the opposition of Cardinal Alessandro Farnese, who generally worked in association with Carafa. Late on the night of September 25 Gonzaga was led into the chapel and cardinals assembled to proclaim him pope. Not all of the Spanish faction came into the chapel, however. Only twenty-three cardinals were present to acclaim Gonzaga pope, an insufficient number.[77] Supporters of Gonzaga such as Cardinals Sforza and Sermoneta went out of the chapel to find more votes. Cardinal Madruzzo sought to ram the election through by crying out that Gonzaga was already elected. When Farnese learned of these efforts he "jumped out of his bed in fright" and began to assem-

---

76. Pietro Carnesecchi acknowledged in his testimony at his heresy trial in 1566 that Morone and Gonzaga were his favored candidates. He favored Gonzaga because "dovesse essere un buon papa et perché mi promettevo di lui ogni gratia et favore." LXVIII Costituto di Pietro Carnesecchi, December 18, 1566, Massimo Firpo and Dario Marcatto, *I Processi inquisitoriali di Pietro Carnesecchi,* 3 vols. (Vatican City: Archivio Segreto Vaticano, 1998–2000), vol. II/2, 701 (hereafter Firpo and Marcatto, *Carnesecchi*).

77. On the vote total see Pastor, 15: 22.

ble his supporters in the Sistine Chapel.[78] Alessandro Farnese's brother, Cardinal Ranuccio Farnese, who was then ill, raised himself from
his sickbed and took up a position in the door of the Pauline Chapel
in order to block the entrance of any further supporters of Gonzaga
for the attempted acclamation. Alessandro Farnese successfully separated the Spanish cardinals Pacheco and Cuevas from Gonzaga. One
witness to these events wrote that Gonzaga had come so close that if
Pacheco and Cuevas had supported Gonzaga "the unfortunate Farnese
would have had to say good night."[79] Thus, by a narrow margin the
candidacy of Gonzaga fell short.

Gonzaga's hopes for the papacy did not collapse altogether as a result of his failed adoration, however. Many still supported him, but
in the days after September 25 his election encountered more serious
obstacles. The Farnese and the Carafa remained opposed to him. On
September 25 itself the new Spanish ambassador, Francisco de Vargas,
arrived in Rome and began heavy-handed lobbying for a loyal Spanish candidate. Vargas made a habit of entering the conclave by night
in order to argue his case directly to the cardinals. Compromise with
the French cardinals was not necessary in his mind. As for the candidacy of Gonzaga, the Spanish ambassador made it clear that the Mantuan was unacceptable to him. The lack of clear instruction from Philip II to Vargas as to the king's opinion of Gonzaga, however, assisted
in prolonging Gonzaga's candidacy.[80] Meanwhile, supporters of Gonzaga sent letters to the king. Cardinal Sforza, the leader of the Spanish
party in the conclave, wrote to Philip with complaints about Cardinal
Farnese, whose opposition to Gonzaga was personal, and of Gonzaga's proven loyalty to the Habsburgs. The emperor Ferdinand wrote
to several imperial cardinals urging them to vote for Gonzaga. Thus
the conclave was in suspension until Philip's couriers arrived, and they
were not expected until the middle of October. All in the conclave
hoped that news would clarify the situation. The more time passed,

78. See letter of Thomaso Vertua in Rezzaghi, "Cronaca," 560. "Farnese no solo
svegliato ma spaventato subito saltò di letto."
79. Ibid., 562. "Il sfortunato Farnese poteva dire buona notte."
80. On Vargas's arrival at and activities in the conclave see Pastor, 15: 25–26.

however, the more opportunity there was for alternative alliances to form. Cardinal Carafa began to work for an alliance with the French and draw them away from Gonzaga.[81]

When the couriers finally arrived on October 27 Philip's letters, dated October 8 and 9, contained no comment on Gonzaga's candidacy. It may be that Philip, who opposed Gonzaga, hoped that the cardinals would exclude him without the Spanish king's having to explicitly indicate his own opposition. The cardinals remained deadlocked. Only on October 20 did Philip explicitly oppose Gonzaga in a letter to Vargas. The ambassador did not, however, make this opposition known and made it otherwise appear that Philip was favorable to Gonzaga. This double game did not last long. On October 27 Philip wrote to Vargas and again expressed his opposition to Gonzaga. This time, however, he did not repeat the instruction that Vargas was to keep the secret. As it turned out, the second of these letters was the first to arrive, on November 11, and Vargas used it as a means to explicitly exclude Gonzaga, who had already chosen to remove himself from formal candidacy on November 8, possibly in recognition of the futility of his candidacy but more likely as a means of gaining favor through a show of humility.[82] The ongoing negotiations among the French, Carafa, and Sforza prolonged Gonzaga's candidacy, and in mid-December it appeared to many that he would be elected. Only when Cardinal Carlo Carafa successfully drew Sforza and the Spanish faction away from Gonzaga with a promise not to support any candidate opposed by Philip did the election definitely slip away from Gonzaga.[83]

The failure of his candidacy illustrates both the strengths and the weaknesses of Ercole Gonzaga's role in the Church and in the global politics of his day. His place at the head of a great family of Italy had

---

81. Ibid., 29–30.

82. Pietro Carnesecchi interpreted this withdrawal from candidacy as a strategy to gain support by a show of humility in a letter to Giulia Gonzaga: "Molti suspicano che habbia ciò fatto per una modestia più presto simulata che vera, pur apresso l'universale ne ha acquistato laude." Firpo and Marcatto, *Carnesecchi,* II/2: 741.

83. Pastor, 15: 47.

assured him of considerable support. The fact that he had spent many years carefully avoiding direct conflict with the French while at the same time maintaining an alliance with the Habsburgs during the regency allowed him to be placed on the lists of acceptable candidates of both camps. Nevertheless, these same aspects of Gonzaga's career also undermined his candidacy. In the conclave Gonzaga faced the implacable opposition of the Farnese as a result of many years of mutual hostility. As a member of a ruling family in Italy, moreover, his election could be seen as a threat to Spanish power there. The doubts that Philip II and the Duke of Alba had harbored about the loyalty of Ferrante Gonzaga and, by extension, the loyalty of Ercole, meant that he was not perceived as totally acceptable from the perspective of the Spanish court. Philip II's own hesitation to exclude Gonzaga publicly suggests that his candidacy was a serious one, however. In a set of diplomatic instructions about the future course of the conclave that were not sent once the king learned the result of the election of Pius IV, Philip allowed that he would not prefer Gonzaga but could live with his election.[84] This concession came too late for Gonzaga but is exemplary of his position in both European and ecclesiastical politics.

84. Ibid., 64.

CHAPTER 6

GONZAGA AND THE COUNCIL
OF TRENT

In many respects Ercole Gonzaga reached the zenith of his career as papal legate at the Council of Trent from December 1561 until his death in March 1563, but his involvement in conciliar issues began long before the opening of the council itself. Gonzaga's views on the council, both while he was still resident in Mantua and after he went to Trent, were shaped by his upbringing in a princely family, his philosophical and humanistic training, and his own experience as a resident bishop, forces that had shaped other areas of his life and work. The Gonzaga policy of carving out for themselves a secure place in the midst of the Italian Wars also influenced his attitude toward the Council of Trent. As an imperial cardinal, Gonzaga faced the challenge of negotiating between the often conflicting interests of emperor and pope. Thus his views on the council were based not only on what was theologically consistent or acceptable but also on what would be practical.

Gonzaga and the Proposed Council of Mantua

The Church's efforts to assemble and hold a council were a part of Gonzaga's career long before his time as papal legate. As early as 1530 Mantua had been under consideration as a site for the assembly. On June 2, 1536, Pope Paul III issued the bull *Ad dominici gregis curam* formally convoking a reform council and calling for it to meet in Man-

tua the following year. From early in his career, therefore, Gonzaga involved himself in negotiations over the location and the timing of the
council. His earliest known thoughts on the subject come from a letter of 1536 to Cardinal Girolamo Aleandro in which he responded to
the draft of the original bull of convocation. He expressed adherence
to Catholic theology, showed his displeasure with the Farnese papacy,
and made two suggestions for changes in the wording of the bull. The
first demonstrates his conservatism and opposition to Protestants on
principle. Gonzaga objected to the term "schismatics," as used in the
bull, for Protestants. He argued that the term was open to the relatively mild interpretation that Protestants were merely separated from
obedience to the See of Rome but were still *"inter capita ecclesia"* and
not heretics in a doctrinal sense. This statement indicates a distinct-
ly critical attitude toward Protestants on a doctrinal level well before
the events of the 1540s. Gonzaga's other suggested change of wording
sought to recall the memory of Pope Clement VII, his own benefac-
tor, and that pontiff's desire for a council.[1] Gonzaga found it distasteful that all the credit for this council go to Paul III.

The duchy of Mantua's location initially made it a suitable compromise site for both the papal curia and the interests of the emperor
and other Germans: Mantua was nominally within the borders of the
Holy Roman Empire, ducal status for the state had recently been conferred by the emperor, and the city lay within Italy. That council never took place, however, in large part because negotiations between the
pope and the emperor failed and the French king, Francis I, opposed
it. But difficulties arising from Duke Federico Gonzaga's demands also
obstructed the opening of the council. Cardinal Gonzaga's role in this
episode was one of negotiating between a pope whom he detested and
his brother, the ruler of Mantua.

From the beginning of discussions about Mantua, Federico had re-

---

1. BAV, Barb. Lat., codex 5789, ff. 178r–178v, Ercole Gonzaga to Girolamo Aleandro. The date is unclear. It must have been written between April 1536, when Aleandro wrote a draft bull, and June 2, 1536, when the bull *Ad dominici gregis curam* was
promulgated. "Quia hoc verbum frequentius usurpatur in illa divisione qua est inter
capita Ecclesia." f. 178r.

peatedly demanded that he command a large body of papally financed troops that would guard the council. The pope wanted Federico to provide security but did not consider a large body of troops either necessary or desirable.[2] Throughout January and February of 1537 Cardinal Gonzaga kept his brother informed of papal plans for the council. He also requested that Federico moderate his request for troops so that Paul III would have no reason to attack him for obstructing the council. Federico's demands could give the pope an excuse to cancel his journey to Mantua and to delay the council again. He told Federico that more modest defense proposals would place responsibility for the council in the pope's hands. If Paul III did not come, then the fault would lie with Rome. Further, Federico must remember his priorities: "Be assured that this is your responsibility, both to be of service to the emperor and be resolved to do what appears best." He urged Federico to send another envoy to represent his position to the pope, claiming that an agent other than Cardinal Gonzaga could handle the situation more effectively. The cardinal also suggested that Federico investigate how preparations were made in other cities in Italy for councils such as this.[3] It was in response to this last suggestion that Federico repeated his request that the papacy provide funding for troops for the duration of the council and it was on this request that negotiations for the proposed Council of Mantua foundered. Ercole's advice was intend-

2. For a general assessment of the negotiations over Mantua as the venue for the council see Jedin, *History,* 1: 324–28.

3. BAV, Barb. Lat., codex 5789, ff. 22v–23r, Ercole Gonzaga to Federico Gonzaga, February 16, 1537. "Non è senon bene a mio giudicio che vostra eccellenza si moderi talmente nelle conditioni d'accomodare di Mantova al Papa per lo concilio ch'egli non habbia ragione d'attaccarvisi sopra senon viene a cominciarlo, et rivoltarne la colpa sopra di lei, che altramente poro servigio si verrebbe a fare all'Imperatore et assi a costoro quali non cercan'altro che un simile attaco per fuggire la scola et che non para che dalloro manchi: vostra eccellenza donque ha d'assicurarsi, che questo è il dovere, et poi pensare al servigio di Sua Maestà et risolversi in quello que le parerà migliore, rispondendo quanto piu tosto le sarà possibile a Sua Santità con le quale mi piaciarebbe per l'importanza del negotio et per la brevita del tempo che vostra eccellenza mandasse qua un suo trattarlo perche a me non così è conveniente come sarebbe ad un'altro che fosse qua mandato dal Lei a questo effetto per dire che replicare quanto fosse necessario che si dicesse et replicasse al Papa in nome di lei." ff. 22v–23r. This letter also appears in CT, 4: cxxxiii.

ed to encourage his brother to refrain from anything that would turn others away, something that Federico did anyway. The pope continued to reject the notion of an "armed council." When it became clear that Federico did not intend to change his mind the pope prorogued the council.[4] Thus Cardinal Gonzaga himself inadvertently elicited his brother's demands on the security of the council.

This breakdown in negotiations over the proposed Council of Mantua contributed to Cardinal Gonzaga's decision to leave Rome, since the failed negotiations between his brother Federico and Paul III contributed to the enmity between the Gonzaga cardinal and the Farnese pope. On March 30 he had informed his mother of his decision to return to Mantua.[5] While discussions over opening the council at Mantua proceeded, the Gonzaga were also struggling with the Farnese over control of the abbey of Lucedio, further complicating the negotiations. Cardinal Gonzaga's views on Mantua as the site of a general council of the Church developed in response to the needs of the Gonzaga family and the interests of the emperor. He knew where his family's political interests lay and he knew that Federico's demands did not further those interests. Conciliar politics on the one hand and rivalry between the Farnese and the Gonzaga on the other contributed to the breakdown in negotiations over a Mantuan council.

These issues arose one last time in 1542 when the pope again addressed the possibility of opening a council at Mantua. Gasparo Contarini wrote to Cardinal Gonzaga about discussions at the papal court over when and where to open the long-delayed council and that Mantua was one of the locations under consideration.[6] By that time Gonzaga was himself the ducal regent and would have had authority to permit the convocation there, but he refused to do so. In response to Contarini he argued against Mantua as the site of the council for several reasons. First, Mantua could not physically accommodate the council. Second, he had the example of his late brother Federico, who

4. See Pastor, 11: 97–100.

5. ASM, AG, b. 887, f. 252r, Ercole Gonzaga to Isabella d'Este, March 30, 1537.

6. Gasparo Contarini to Ercole Gonzaga, January 7, 1542, Friedensburg, 217–18.

in the end refused to host the council and could not resolve it otherwise. Third, the best argument for having the council in Mantua had been that it was technically in imperial territory and the German Protestants could not reasonably refuse to come. But since he, the regent, was a cardinal, Protestants might see that fact as an excuse to refuse to come. Finally, he argued that the king of France wished to attend the council and Gonzaga did not believe that the honor of the king could be maintained if he were required to bring an armed escort smaller than that maintained by Gonzaga himself. For his part Cardinal Gonzaga could not allow the city to be effectively in the power of the king of France.[7] Dynastic considerations, respect for his late brother's wishes, and a cautious foreign policy limited Cardinal Gonzaga's freedom to affirm plans for a council in Mantua. In addition, Cardinal Gonzaga was working to secure his nephew's inheritance and restore the finances of the duchy after the death of his brother Federico. A council in Mantua could have presented obstacles to achieving these two ends, given its cost and the presence of foreign princes and their representatives.

Paul III did not publish a formal bull of convocation for a council in the city of Trent until June 29, 1542. Even with an agreement over location, international events delayed the council's opening sessions. Only after peace had been established between Francis I and Charles V in September of 1544 did the likelihood that the council would meet increase. The pope published another bull of convocation, *Laetare Jerusalem,* in November of 1544 but significant activity at Trent did not begin until December of 1545, when the council assembled. Among the issues under discussion during the months before the opening of the council were the role of the pope and the participation of the Protestants. In addition, at the Diet of Speyer in 1544 Charles V had promised the Protestants in Germany that religious questions would be dealt with in a future diet that was to take place at Worms in 1545. Paul III opposed any religious discussions at the diet as derogating from his authority and that of the council.

7. BAV, Barb. Lat., codex 5790, ff. 112v–113v, Ercole Gonzaga to Gasparo Contarini, January 18, 1542.

Cardinal Gonzaga did not go to Trent at its opening in 1545 because of responsibilities as regent in Mantua.[8] He limited his participation in council matters prior to its third period of activity to seeking information from others or giving them advice.[9] Just as the Gonzaga family had navigated the waters of temporal politics in order to avoid being swamped by larger competing powers, so Ercole Gonzaga sought to navigate between imperial and papal policies toward the council and still protect Gonzaga interests. He held to a moderate papalist position that nevertheless contained significant criticism of the specifics of Paul III's conciliar policy and his exercise of papal authority. Gonzaga committed himself to reform by means of a council but viewed the issues surrounding its convocation in the light of his experience as a servant of Charles V. On October 14, 1544, Gonzaga wrote to his cousin the Duke of Ferrara on the impending council and on the imperial diet to be held at Worms in January of 1545. This letter was written a month before publication of the bull *Laetare Jerusalem* and reflects uncertainty over the future path of reform. Cardinal Gonzaga informed his cousin that since the pope had arranged for the council in Trent and Trent had been accepted by Charles V, the emperor's brother Ferdinand, and the Catholic princes of Germany, it did not seem likely that Paul III would be able to transfer the council to another city without the consent of those princes. The current peace between the Habsburgs and the Valois also removed the fear that the French would threaten the council as a rationale for moving it.[10]

Gonzaga also took note of the ecclesiological issues at stake. The experience of conciliarism during the fifteenth century had made

---

8. Ibid., codex 5792, ff. 135r–135v, Ercole Gonzaga to Paul III, January 17, 1545. Gonzaga explained that he could not attend the council because of his obligations as regent, but promised all the support he could as "uno devotissimo cardinale et da un Gentilhuomo nato da sangue ch'a servito alli predecessori di Vostra Santità molte volte con lo stato et con la vita propria." f. 135v.

9. Although Gonzaga communicated extensively with others about matters during the first period of the council, there is almost no record of his thoughts about issues raised during the second period. The one exception to this is a letter of Gonzaga concerning a benefice in Monferrato. ASM, AG, b. 1945, ff. 119r–119v, Ercole Gonzaga to Ippolito Capilupi, March 17, 1552.

10. Ibid., f. 112v, Ercole Gonzaga to Ercole d'Este, October 14, 1544.

popes extremely sensitive to questions of their own authority. One reason why the council did not open until 1545 was papal concern about how a council might challenge papal authority. Protestant critiques of the papacy had added to this concern. When Gasparo Contarini went to Regensburg to negotiate with the Protestants in 1541, he received instructions on this very issue from Cardinal Marcello Cervini, who insisted that Protestants must uphold papal authority. Cervini served as legate to the council in its first sessions and reiterated these views soon after Paul III convened the council: "It is time with all diligence to hold this body united and obedient to the pope." This issue of papal authority was the single most important point of division between the imperial party and the papal, or curial, party.[11]

Gonzaga was also aware of these issues but viewed papal authority itself as a potential obstacle to the successful outcome of the council. The pope had many enemies, he argued, because the papacy enjoyed such absolute power that many times that power was used "for destruction and not edification, as St. Paul would say."[12] Among these enemies Gonzaga numbered Catholics who, he insisted, were more opposed to the power of the pope than the Lutherans were. Presumably he meant German and Italian Catholics, since he excluded from this group the French and the Spanish, who had already effectively separated themselves from much of the pope's authority by means of concordats and royal pragmatics. This was a concern of Gonzaga as he looked forward to the council:

Therefore, it seems to me that in Trent we will do very badly and perhaps only a little better in any other place because our conduct, both in temporal government as vassals and in the spiritual government of all of Christianity, [is] as contrary to the dispositions of canons made by our ancestors and of those good and holy councils as the good [is] contrary to the bad. From now on it is necessary that there be born a reform of our abuses that will cut the claws more perfectly. And if the pope were what he ought to have been, at

11. On the issue of papal authority and control over the council, as well as Cervini's role there see Hudon, *Marcello Cervini*, 46–70, 72–81.

12. BAV, Barb. Lat., codex 5792, f. 112v, Ercole Gonzaga to Ercole d'Este, October 14, 1544.

least after having enriched his own, he would have carried out that reform of our abuses that now he speaks of doing, despite his corruption, and it would have appeared then to have been voluntary what now is judged to be by necessity.[13]

Gonzaga thus viewed the position of the papacy by 1544 as relatively perilous. He did not hesitate to criticize his Farnese opponent for delay in summoning the council and for his continued nepotism, but he presented himself as a papalist concerned about the potential loss of legitimate power by the papacy. He believed that the pope might try to transfer the council to another Italian city and thereby obtain a better outcome from a papal perspective. For his part, Gonzaga foresaw some curtailment of papal power as a necessary means to avoid the loss of all of it.[14] He also suggested that when the council convened in Trent it would be better for the pope to remain in Rome and at the same time avoid becoming the object of a summons by the council, the refusal of which would make him appear contumacious. Gonzaga concluded his letter with two pieces of advice for his cousin, the Duke of Ferrera. First, he suggested that the duke have someone read to him from the acts of the Councils of Constance and Basel. Second, if the duke wished to know more about these conciliar matters, both in what favored the pope and what worked against him, Gonzaga would be happy to send a theologian to explain them more fully.[15] Reading and discussion over the previous years had made Gon-

13. Ibid., ff. 112r–114r, Ercole Gonzaga to Ercole d'Este, October 14, 1544. "La onde mi pare di potere concludere che in Trento il faremo assai male et forse poco meglio in qual'si voglia altro luogho che sia per essere in fatti lo procedere nostro et nel governo temporale de vasalli et nello spirituale di tutta la christianita così contrario alla dispositione de canoni fatti da nostri maggiori et delli concilii buoni et santi, com'è il bene contrario al male: Di qui bisogna necessariamente che nasca una reforma la quale mozzi l'ungie a più di sette. Et s'el Papa fosse stato quel che doveva essere, almeno dopo l'havere arricchiti i suoi, egli haverebbe fatta quella reforma degli nostri abusi che mo converra fare al suo marzo dispetto et sarebbe paruta all'hora voluntaria che adesso sarà reputata fatta per necessità." f. 113r.

14. Ibid., Ercole Gonzaga to Ercole d'Este, October 14, 1544. "Ma con tutto non veggo sia per fare altramente che di quel che si dice del castoro, cioe che non si taglie una a gran parte d'essa sua assoluta potestà per non essere poi toccato nel resto." f. 113v.

15. Ibid., ff. 112r–114r, Ercole Gonzaga to Ercole d'Este, October 14, 1544.

zaga familiar with the conciliar issues that the Church faced as it went
to Trent. This is an early example of Gonzaga's enduring commitment
to Trent as the location for the council as well as his willingness to distance himself from papal policy.

Nearly two weeks later Gonzaga again expressed his views to his
cousin in Ferrara, particularly about the upcoming Diet of Worms.
Charles V still intended that religious questions be addressed at the
diet. At the preceding Diet of Speyer of 1544, he had promised the
Protestants at least an interim reform. Paul III initially opposed discussion of religious issues because he held that an imperial diet was
not the appropriate forum for it, and for a time refused to send a legate to Worms.[16] In his second letter on the topic to the Duke of Ferrara, Cardinal Gonzaga argued several points on which he agreed with
imperial interests. First, he stated that it would be wise for papal legates to attend the imperial diet to discuss matters because there was
no alternative. Second, those permitted to speak in a council were also
a matter of dispute and the question of their status would have to be
raised at Worms. Gonzaga was not concerned about such matters being taken up at the diet since they would all have to be revisited later
at the council itself. Further, he believed that the council should open
within three months and that the pope should hold firmly to Trent
as the location. Then in summing up his position, Gonzaga offered a
prediction of what would follow:

I am of the opinion that they ought to discuss as soon as possible both of the
two questions in dispute because as far as the material to be treated, ours [our
coreligionists] will say that there is no need that the council discuss matters
covered and determined at other times in past councils, the majority of which
are the issues that the Lutherans have raised. But it seems to me a good idea
to hear, nevertheless, many disputes and words because we want every person of ecclesiastical rank to have a voice in the council. And the Lutherans
say that it is not right that we are both judges and parties to the controversy,
and that any person that knows how to speak of the things of faith ought to
speak in the council. And it appears to me to see that they [the Lutherans]

16. On the relationship of the Diet of Worms of 1545 to the Council of Trent see
Jedin, *History,* 1: 506–7.

will withdraw and that the council will take place without them with the design then that when the Lutherans refuse to accept what has been determined there, they will have to be made to accept it by other means than words.[17]

Gonzaga's views supported those of the imperial diplomats who sought papal representation at the diet as a part of a policy of keeping the Protestants at ease until the emperor could deal with them by force. Gonzaga was quite willing, as a procedural matter, to give a hearing to the Protestants before and during a council. His statement that the Protestants will have to accept what is determined at the council by other means than words suggests, however, that he was aware of imperial intentions to use force when expedient to return the Protestants to unity with the Church.

Gonzaga may have supported some diminution of papal power and differed with Paul III on certain specifics concerning the convocation of the council and preliminary discussions with the Protestants, but he remained committed to papal leadership in the council itself. Gonzaga took note of the mission in 1544 of Juan de Vega, the imperial ambassador to Rome, and Archbishop Georges d'Armagnac, French ambassador to Rome, to convince the pope to convene the council within three months. Gonzaga considered this good news for those like himself who looked to the pope for leadership. As much as Gonzaga may have supported the political interests of the emperor, he nevertheless sought a council over which the pope or his representatives would preside. The pace of negotiations over the council and the peace that then held between the Habsburgs and the Valois seem to have

17. BAV, Barb. Lat., codex 5792, ff. 116v–117v, Ercole Gonzaga to Ercole d'Este, October 27, 1544. "Io mo son d'openione che di bello primo tratto saranno in l'una et l'altra di queste due cose discordi et n'ho le ragione prontissime perche quanto alle materie da trattarsi i nostri diranno che non è di bisogno che siano le medesime de quali altri volte s'è parlato nei concili passati et fattene terminationi et la maggior parte d'esse sono quelle che Lutherani hanno suscitate, perho mi par d'udire tuttavia dispute et parole assai, perchè noi vogliamo ch'ogni persona di grado ecclesiastico habbia voce in concilio. Et Lutherani dicono che non è honesto che siamo giudici et parte et che nel concilio deve intravenire ogni persona che sappia parlare delle cose della fede et parmi veder ch'essi si ritiranno da parte et che converra ch'l concilio si faccia senza loro con disegno poi che quando Lutherani non volessino accettare quel che in esso sarà terminato glielo havessino da fare accettare con altro che con parole." f. 117r.

given him a good deal of hope that real reform would take root in the Church and in the curia. He stated to Ippolito Capilupi, with what appears to have been genuine optimism, that the pope can now "without prejudice to the Contarini wing, cast down that office of wickedness called the Penitentiary and take away much of the bad name that we have before all the world."[18] Gonzaga shared with many others a desire to see a reform of the practices of the Papal Penitentiary, the office that granted dispensations from obligations under canon law, such as vows of religion or marriage, and provided for much revenue in the curia. Four years earlier he had discussed with Cardinal Contarini the reform of that institution.[19] Reference to Contarini in the context of the reform of the Penitentiary points to Gonzaga's ongoing reliance on the thought of the Venetian cardinal. In December of 1544 he wrote again to the Duke of Ferrara about the procedures of the council. He suggested that the duke study what Contarini had written in a summary of the councils that the late cardinal had compiled for the pope. Gonzaga had received a copy of this summary from Contarini himself for his personal library and had already arranged for a transcript of it to be made available to the duke. More than two years after his death, Contarini's ideas on the work of the council were still current enough for Gonzaga to use them in advising his cousin in Ferrara.[20]

After the council opened in December of 1545, Cardinal Gonzaga shifted his attention from issues surrounding its convocation, who might participate, and who would lead it, to the theological issues that were to come under discussion. These included both disciplinary and

18. Ibid., ff. 116r–116v, Ercole Gonzaga to Ippolito Capilupi, October 25, 1544. "Assai buon segno mi pare per noi altri che si faccia capo a Sua Santità la quale se fara quel che deve, massimamente hora che puo senza pregiudicio della gamba contarina butterà a Terra quella officina di sceleragini detta penitentieria so certo che leverà assai del mal nome ch'abbiamo appress' a tutt'il mondo." f. 116r.

19. See Ercole Gonzaga to Gasparo Contarini, April 18, 1540, Friedensburg, 203–6.

20. BAV, Barb. Lat., codex 5792, ff. 120v–121v, Ercole Gonzaga to Ercole d'Este, December 4, 1544. "Ho trovato ne' miei libri un sommario de concilii che fece il Cardinale Contarino al papa molto brieve et bello che da luce di pure assai belle cose, et ho posto ordine che sia transcritto per mandarlo a vostra eccellenza perchè so certo che molto le piacerà." f. 121v.

dogmatic matters. As early as January 21, 1546, Gonzaga wrote about them to Cardinal Pole, one of the papal legates at Trent. Pole had just given an opening exhortation to the council on behalf of all of the legates. Gonzaga remarked upon Pole's "singular prudence and piety," for which he thanked God. He stated that the need of their day was not only to have someone who knew what to say but one who freely wished to uncover the plagues that threatened the Church. Pole fitted this description in Gonzaga's estimation. Gonzaga further admitted that he had had a part in the problems in which the Church found itself and pledged to work to remedy them, knowing that, if he did not, not only would he be at fault himself but these evils would worsen.[21] Gonzaga concluded his letter by indicating that by means of Bishop Pietro Bertano he would maintain contact with Pole and the council and make specific observations on what the council should do.[22] Gonzaga considered Bertano to be his agent at the council and trusted him to convey his own views on the reform of both discipline and doctrine during its early sessions.[23]

He first communicated with Bertano at Trent on January 26, 1546, a moment when it was still unclear whether the council would discuss doctrine or disciplinary reforms first. The pope and the emperor were divided on this question. Charles V wanted the council to discuss disciplinary questions first as a way of appealing to the Protestants. This discussion would postpone dogmatic matters that clearly divided the Protestants from the Catholics while accomplishing the emperor's purpose of finding some common ground where the divided religious parties could agree on practical matters before proceeding to thornier dogmatic questions. Paul III, on the contrary, wanted the council to begin by addressing dogmatic issues, especially doctrinal challenges to Catholicism. The pope's policy sought priority for ques-

21. Ibid., codex 5793, ff. 81r–81v, Ercole Gonzaga to Reginald Pole, January 21, 1546. Pole delivered his exhortation on January 7, 1546, during the second session of the council. See Pastor, 12: 248.

22. BAV, Barb. Lat., codex 5793, f. 81r, Ercole Gonzaga to Reginald Pole, January 21, 1546.

23. Ibid., f. 157v, Ercole Gonzaga to Camillo Capilupi, August 13, 1546.

tions on justification and the sacraments as central to the tradition of the Church. By February of 1546 a compromise had been reached whereby the council would address dogmatic and disciplinary matters simultaneously, but on the pope's insistence, dogmatic matters would be considered more important.[24]

Gonzaga did not explicitly address the issue of negotiations between pope and emperor over the agenda in his letter to Bertano. The order in which he outlined his own opinions, however, may be taken as an indication of a preference for the imperial policy. The first items that he mentioned to Bertano were disciplinary, in particular the life of the clergy. Gonzaga, like many others of his day, proposed a conservative policy that did not require much in the way of new laws in order to reform the clergy. He advised Bertano that the prelates at Trent should follow instructions laid down in earlier councils and synods, with the addition or subtraction of certain things to ensure that the Church address current problems. If, however, the council should choose to set aside the regulations of the past, then it would be necessary to consider what should remain in place and what should change, a time-consuming exercise in Gonzaga's estimation. Further, there was the possibility of confusion in such debate, given that all of the things needing reform would have to be discussed precisely by those who were in need of reform themselves. Each one, he suggested, would debate in his own way "without that charity that edifies but with that knowledge that is given to pride." If that happened, Gonzaga argued, much time would be spent without accomplishing very much.[25] Gon-

24. On the question of the agenda at the Council of Trent see Jedin, *History,* 2: 29–35.

25. BAV, Barb. Lat., codex 5793, ff. 81v–83v, Ercole Gonzaga to Pietro Bertano, January 26, 1546. "Se ancho concludesse che non si havesse a stare alli concili et canoni passati in ogni cosa ma solamente in alcune cose, saria bene ordinare che ogniuno pensasse quali sono quelle che si vogliono lasciare ferme et quali quelle che si vogliono mutare, et a questo modo s'avanzarebbe un gran tempo e schifarebbe una gran contentione et forse confusione, dubitandomi io che come si viene a questo chaos di fare deliberatione di tante cose che si debbano reformare quante sono quelle che ne hanno dibisogno. Ogniuno non voglia dire a suo modo senza quella carità che edifica ma con quella scientia che gonfia et così con fare poco frutto si perde infinito tempo." ff. 81v–82r.

zaga's views on previously established decrees of the councils and synods place in perspective his more conservative approach to reform of
the clergy. The old canons and laws on clerical discipline do not seem
to have been of significant value to him simply because they represented ancient traditions. Changes were necessary in order to meet the
needs of the Church of his own day. The difficulty was in determining
which changes were to be made. He recognized the value of the older
canons but, above all, he presumed that a Church whose very leadership was enmeshed in the abuses that were to be eradicated might be
incapable of establishing appropriate new regulations.[26]

Following this advice on the disciplinary reform of the clergy, Gonzaga proposed an agenda for treating dogmatic issues. First, he wanted
the council to address the issue of justification. He recognized the Lutheran teaching on justification as the foundation of Protestant theology and saw that it was upon that issue that the Lutherans rejected the other doctrines of the Church.[27] He also linked theologically
the discussion of justification with consideration of the sacraments. In
consequence, once the council had addressed the issue of justification,
Gonzaga wanted it to address the sacraments, both their number and
their place in the Church. As an authority for this procedure he proposed the decrees of the Council of Florence, which had provided a
model of union between the Church of Rome and a variety of Orthodox Churches. In its decree on union with the Armenians in 1439, the
Council of Florence included a brief statement of sacramental theology based upon a Thomistic model that included their number and
role in the life of the Church.[28] After determining the issue of the sac-

26. Gonzaga was no doubt aware of the thought of Egidio da Viterbo who, in his
opening address to Lateran Council V, urged reform based upon traditional models.
Viterbo had stated on that occasion: "Men must be changed by religion, not religion
by men." Egidio da Viterbo, "Address to the Fifth Lateran Council," in Olin, 45.

27. BAV, Barb. Lat., codex 5793, f. 82r, Ercole Gonzaga to Pietro Bertano, January 26, 1546.

28. On the decrees of the Council of Florence on the sacraments see J. Neuner,
S.J., and J. Depuis, S.J., *The Christian Faith in the Doctrinal Documents of the Catholic
Church* (Bangalore: Theological Publications in India, 1973), 348–50, 370–72, 388–
90, 430, 465–66, 492–93.

raments, Gonzaga wanted the fathers of the council to make a declaration on the doctrine of purgatory and prayers for the dead.[29] Gonzaga considered all of these to be threatened by the doctrine of justification by faith alone. Surprisingly, given his interest in scripture studies, Gonzaga did not make any reference at that time to the discussions over the canon of scripture, which turned out to be the first controversial issue taken up by the council.

Gonzaga also made suggestions to Bertano on the question of the authority of the pope in relation to the council. More than a year earlier he had suggested to the Duke of Ferrara that some reduction in papal authority might be necessary in order to safeguard most of it. Gonzaga had also written to Bertano in August of 1545 on the status of papal authority. He mentioned that he had heard a rumor from Rome of a statement by French theologians on papal authority that did not please the pope, namely that "the pope is the Vicar of Christ with the ministry only of the other bishops, the power of this one being for edification and not destruction." He then asked Bertano to familiarize himself with this thesis in order to speak to Gonzaga thoroughly on it.[30] In a letter of January 26, 1546, Gonzaga suggested that the prelates at Trent debate whether the council and the pope are capable or not of obligating a Christian in matters that are indifferent as far as the Gospel was concerned. As examples he suggested regulations concerning whom one might marry or abstinence from meat on Fridays and during Lent. This focus on disciplinary matters, rather than doctrine, may have come from his support of imperial interests. He then suggested that the council should avoid the question of whether the pope is above the council or not, except indirectly. He doubted that directly addressing this topic would do much good since it had not at the Council of Basel, where it led to dissolution of the council and

29. Three years earlier Gonzaga had insisted that Frate Andrea Ghetti da Volterra preach on this doctrine during Lent. Gonzaga's secretary Calandra quoted the cardinal as saying "vi era il purgatorio et guai a noi se non vi fusse stato purgatorio." Pagano, *Secondo Costituto di Endimio Calandra,* March 27, 1568, 253.

30. BAV, Barb. Lat., codex 5793, ff. 8v–9v, Ercole Gonzaga to Pietro Bertano, August 30, 1545. "Papa est vicarius Christi cum ministerio tantum ceterorum Episcoporum huius potestate in aedificationem et non in destructione." f. 9r.

impeded other valuable work. Gonzaga preferred that, after the council formulated its decrees on abuses in the Church and dogmatic matters, it discuss whether the pope has the power to revoke anything that the council has declared.[31]

Gonzaga's own views on the pope's role in the council appear ambivalent. He argued that in the past when it was decided that the pope could not revoke conciliar decrees, he was seen as under the authority of the Church as a whole. This decision resulted in a decline in his legitimate authority to build up the Church. If, however, it were determined that the pope did have the power to revoke conciliar decisions, not when he wanted to for his own personal reasons but rather for the good of the Church, then the council should determine the situations in which the pope can depart from the decisions of the council and those in which he cannot. Gonzaga added that the council can:

bind his [the pope's] hands in such manner that he would not be able to ruin once again what has been determined in holiness and reduce or lower the Church again to those evil conditions in which she now finds herself, for the elimination of which the council was convoked.[32]

Gonzaga saw that blanket denials of the pope's authority to limit the decrees of the councils could also reduce those powers that he held to be divinely instituted. Nevertheless, he favored a limitation on the authority of the pope over the council as long as the areas of authority were made specific.

As a political matter, however, Gonzaga was keenly aware that his suggestions could be taken as a challenge to papal authority in general. Therefore he encouraged Bertano to write to the pope and the college of cardinals to assure them that the Mantuan cardinal did not rea-

31. Ibid., ff. 81v–83v, Ercole Gonzaga to Pietro Bertano, January 26, 1546.
32. Ibid., f. 82v, Ercole Gonzaga to Pietro Bertano, January 26, 1546. "Si potrebbe all hora determinare ancho quali sieno quei casi in che il papa puo et deve derogare alli concilii et quali no. Nel resto pensare tutti i modi possibili per li quali gli si legassero le mani talmente che se bene volesse non potesse rovinare un'altra volta quel che fosse stato santamente determinato, et riducere la chiesa di nuovo a quei mali termini dove hora si truova per l'estirpatione de quali fosse stato necessario convocare il concilio."

son in this way for a "bad end," but only for the service of God. He felt sure that the pope would take this disclaimer in the proper spirit and not be displeased by such a tempering of papal authority, but rather would rejoice that such an occasion for disservice to God and scandal to the Church had been taken away.[33] It is not difficult to read this last thought as an ironic criticism of Paul III. Gonzaga's further statement seems to confirm that it was: "If, however, the pope wants a council in word but not in effect, a thing that I am sure he does not want, to what purpose would it be done but that His Holiness and the popes that succeed him can depart from the council at their pleasure?"[34] In the midst of his conflicts with the pope over the monastery of Lucedio and the duchy of Parma and Piacenza, Gonzaga's criticisms of papal prerogatives expressed the bitterness of one who had already confronted the reality of papal privilege. Nevertheless, he did support papal authority in principle for the greater good of the Church.

For all of his support of the emperor's policies on the council, Gonzaga could also manifest a degree of independence from Habsburg interests. In 1545 and 1546 Charles's attitude toward the council was largely determined by his desire to solve the religious question in Germany by force of arms. While the council was in session he still offered the Protestants the opportunity of a hearing in Germany. His opposition to having the council address dogma stemmed from his desire to delay as long as possible the Protestant rejection of Catholic conciliar policy and theology. He blocked the participation of German bishops at Trent until it suited the emperor's purposes. As much as Gonzaga might have seen the council at least in part as an opportunity to mod-

---

33. Ibid., ff. 82v–83r, Ercole Gonzaga to Pietro Bertano, January 26, 1546. In a letter to the Duke of Ferrara the previous spring Gonzaga had been less charitable toward Paul III. He then wrote that he understood that the pope wanted to have the council declare that the pope was superior to it and that those theologians who agreed would be rewarded with red hats. "Beati quei frati et dottori che diranno con loro perchè tutti saranno incapellati." Ibid., codex 5792, ff. 165r–168r. Citation on f. 166v.

34. Ibid., codex 5793, f. 83r, Ercole Gonzaga to Pietro Bertano, January 26, 1546. "Se ancho desidera il concilio in parole et non in effetto cosa che non credo, a che proposito farlo perchè fatto che sia et Sua Beatudine et i Papi che saranno dopo lei vi possano derogare a piacere loro."

erate papal prerogatives, he did not want it to fail in reforming the Church and addressing the challenge of the Protestants. On a theological level his views on justification and the sacraments illustrated this wish. Further, in February of 1546 he wrote to Giovanni Girolamo de' Rossi, bishop of Pavia and another prelate who had fallen afoul of Paul III, warning that unless the emperor adjusted his conciliar policy, the Council of Trent would be a greater failure than the Fifth Lateran Council (1512–17), which the popes left "with an infinite number of good ideas in order to call down the Holy Spirit with a large number of angels. But nothing was done in the council, not even a way of doing something."[35] Gonzaga's attitude toward the council, like many other parts of his life, manifested a divided concern for both the interests of the imperial party in Italy and the need for reform in the Church. His actions and thought were not alien to the spirit of generations of Gonzaga diplomacy in northern Italy.

Once the Council of Trent opened, Gonzaga's opinions were increasingly responses to what was actually taking place there. Early in its deliberations, the council addressed the related issues of scripture and tradition.[36] The emphasis that Protestants had laid upon the sufficiency of scripture alone as an authority in matters of faith made some response by the Catholic Church necessary. The council chose to reaffirm the Latin Vulgate text of the Bible that had been in use throughout the Middle Ages. It continued to accept those books of the Bible that Protestants rejected as apocryphal. In addition the council established a decree on the authority of unwritten traditions that the Church held to have come from the apostles. The fathers of the council intended to defend the nonscriptural traditions of the Church against Protestant assertions that they were merely human inven-

35. Ibid., ff. 101v–103v, Ercole Gonzaga to Monsignore de Rossi, February 25, 1546. "Vi posso affermare di certo ch'l concilio tridentino sarà maggiore barro che non fu quell'ultimo lateranense ove i Papi andavano con una infinita moltitudine di buone robbe avanti per provocare tanto meglio lo spirito santo con sì bel numero d'angeli, onde non si facendo in concilio cosa alcuna neancho essendovi maniera di farla." f. 102r.

36. Tanner, 2: 663–65. On discussion of traditions at Trent see Jedin, *History,* 2: 52–98.

tions. On the latter of these two issues there was significant discussion among the prelates and theologians in Trent. It was not precisely clear what the term *tradition* meant or which teachings and practices should be accepted as of apostolic origin. Ultimately the council defended the place of tradition in principle without giving any specific examples.

Gonzaga corresponded with Pietro Bertano on the question of tradition during the weeks when it was debated at Trent. Bertano had written to Gonzaga on February 26, 1546, on the debates over the relationship of scripture and tradition. He disagreed with the proposed decree that seemed to equate the value of the two and pointed out that certain apostolic traditions had fallen into disuse, such as communion under both species and married clergy. Bertano wondered how the Church was to explain and permit those lapses in keeping tradition if it also claimed equal authority for both scripture and tradition. If the bishops of the council were to approve as exceptions only those changes that had already taken effect, he argued, they would simply be formulating conciliar decrees based on their own arbitrary choices. Bertano further warned that this inconsistency might also provide the Germans with a justification for offering communion under both species and allowing the marriage of priests.[37]

Gonzaga's response to Bertano included an admission that he did not understand the question very well. Nevertheless, he offered his own opinion on the value of the nonscriptural traditions in the Church. Gonzaga agreed with Bertano's opposition to the preliminary decree, since the Church had never been in total agreement on the issues of communion under both species, the marriage of clergy, and other issues. The use of the term "Church" in those discussions would produce dissension in the council, in his view. It would allow some to criticize the Eastern Church, which maintained those traditions, while others might criticize the Latin Church for having abandoned them.[38] Gonzaga preferred that the fathers of the council remain completely

37. See Jedin, *History,* 2: 83–87.
38. BAV, Barb. Lat., codex 5793, ff. 103v–106r, Ercole Gonzaga to Pietro Bertano, February 28, 1546.

silent on the traditions of the Church. If they had to address the issue, however, he suggested that they speak not in general terms but very specifically. He believed that the council had two options. Either it would impose its own judgment on the traditions in place of the various opinions in the Church, or suspend judgment and wait for a more opportune time. If the council wanted to proceed with defending the authority of the apostolic traditions at that moment, Gonzaga argued, it would not be enough to determine that there are such traditions and that they should be shown the same reverence as scripture. In addition, he insisted, the council should specify what those traditions were. As an example Gonzaga turned to the question of the sacrificial nature of the Eucharist. He suggested that it would not be enough to say that Christianity has a sacrifice as the Hebrews did. It would also be necessary to say that the Christian sacrifice is the sacrifice of the altar, the grace of which, according to apostolic tradition, is efficacious for both the living and the dead. This statement would permit the Church to value the sacrifice of the altar as if it were confirmed "by the word," that is, scripture, given that the Church, Gonzaga argued, knows it has learned of it from the "living word" and not from the scriptures. At least, Gonzaga added, this would remove the argument of the Lutherans that in Christianity there is no other sacrifice than that which Christ offered on the cross and that Catholics were claiming multiple sacrifices of Christ each time they said mass.[39] In any event, the council did not choose to follow the advice of Gonzaga and Bertano: it simply asserted the authority of ancient traditions without offering any specific examples.

Gonzaga also commented upon deliberations over the decree on sacred scripture. He would have preferred that the council address that issue before dealing with traditions. Then it could have gone on to the apocryphal scriptures. He advised that the council determine which were apocryphal and remove them immediately and without delay from the Church's official text of scripture. That, he added somewhat caustically, would offer the advantage of allowing the council to have

39. Ibid.

actually accomplished something.[40] In this advice Gonzaga differed from the ultimate decision of the council to retain all of the books contained in the Vulgate, and he was not alone. Bertano had shared his views along with several other members of the council including Reginald Pole and Girolamo Seripando. Seripando had sought at least that the council recognize that the apocrypha carried less authority than the rest of the canonical texts. This qualification was important not only for specifying the canonical books for the sake of countering the Protestants, but also as a priority among Catholic scholars who were influenced by humanist biblical scholarship, such as the work of Erasmus. That Gonzaga would hold this opinion on the scriptures is not surprising. The combination of humanistic study in his youth and scripture study in Mantua made him receptive to humanist and evangelical critiques of the biblical canon.[41] His attitude toward the Bible was as open to revision of the apocrypha as that of any prelate at Trent. He sought a greatly modified Vulgate and preferred silence by the council on the matter of tradition. In the end the Council of Trent did not accept the advice of Gonzaga and others. It reaffirmed the authority of the Vulgate and established the principle of nonscriptural traditions in general.

As the prelates and theologians at Trent continued their work they eventually approached the dogmatic questions that most divided Christendom. Among these was the definition of original sin. This dogma was central to both Catholic and Protestant views of justification, though the two sides differed over the severity of its effects. The Lutheran position was that human beings were so affected by original sin that they could not avoid sinning. In this view, concupiscence, the human inclination toward sin and one of the effects of original sin, was itself sin. It was the presence of concupiscence that rendered the

40. Ibid., ff. 105–106, Ercole Gonzaga to Pietro Bertano, February 28, 1546. "Haverei voluto che si fosse diferito il parlare delle traditioni in generale et per hora, poi che il concilio haveva determinato quel che si deve tenere per scrittura canonica, poteva seguira a determinare quali erano le scritture apocrife et false et in questo fare uno decreto col quale tutte si fossero remosse dalla chiesa senza dilatione di tempo." ff. 105r–105v.

41. On Seripando's attitudes toward the biblical canon see Jedin, *History,* 2: 57.

human essentially sinful. The individual saved by faith remained *simul justus et peccator,* in Luther's words. On the whole, Roman Catholic theology held a less negative view. The Council of Trent did not consider concupiscence to be sin, properly speaking. Rather, the council held, concupiscence was the effect that acted as *fomes peccati,* or "tinder" for the fires of sinful desires. The human capacity to avoid sin was still intact, even if the will to do so was weakened.

The council discussed this issue between May 28 and June 16, 1546. The papal legates at Trent ordered a draft decree prepared on the issue. On June 6, this draft was shown to Pietro Bertano, who forwarded a copy to Gonzaga.[42] That decree argued that baptism removed original sin so completely that there was nothing left in the individual that was detestable to God. The decree also referred to the residue of original sin. The seeming contradiction between these two theses was the source of dispute at the council during the ensuing debate on June 14. Many theologians at Trent held an Augustinian position, among them Girolamo Seripando, who wished to eliminate the contradiction in the proposed decree by removing the phrase that described baptism as taking away original sin completely. Others, Bertano included, rejected the Augustinian notion of concupiscence.

On June 11, Gonzaga wrote again to Bertano, after having reviewed the preliminary draft of the decree. Like Bertano, he opted to oppose an Augustinian definition of original sin. He informed his Dominican colleague that he was generally pleased with the decree, but wished to add a few words to it in order to correct those who were persuaded by the "new German doctrine" that *fomes peccati,* or concupiscence, is itself sin, that it is not simply the effect of the sin of Adam and is therefore the reason for all of the present sins that human beings commit. Gonzaga sought a clear condemnation on this point. His suggested addition read: "And this holy synod rejects the opinion of those who affirm that *fomes* is truly sin and worthy of the hatred of God, lest in perpetuity it [the Protestant opinion] be condoned."[43] Gonzaga cit-

42. Jedin, *History,* 2: 125–65.
43. BAV, Barb. Lat., codex 5793, f. 142v, Ercole Gonzaga to Pietro Bertano, June 11, 1546. "Vorrei aggiungervi alcune parole per sanare molti ingegni quali per-

ed the African councils at the time of the Pelagian controversy as an example of how the Church should proceed against the Protestants by condemnations of specific theses.[44] The Mantuan cardinal was not alone in this concern. During the debate of June 14, a canon was added to the decree on precisely that point. It anathematized those who held that there was anything reprehensible in those who had been baptized. This canon included the statement: "This concupiscence, which the Apostle sometimes calls sin, the holy council declares the Catholic Church has never understood to be called sin in the sense that it is truly and properly sin in those born again, but in the sense that it is of sin and inclines to sin."[45] Gonzaga's advice to Bertano on June 11 may have reached Trent in time to have some effect on the reformulation of the decree. At the least, Gonzaga's communication with Bertano demonstrates his rejection of an Augustinian teaching on original sin and his agreement with the majority of the prelates and theologians at the Council of Trent on this matter.

Along with dogmatic issues, the Council of Trent in its earliest sessions also addressed questions of practical reform. While members of the council were discussing scripture, tradition, original sin, and justification, they also tried to confront earthier matters of ecclesiastical finance and discipline. In particular, the Spanish bishops sought to discuss the residence of bishops while the Roman curia studiously avoided confronting that issue. An indirect way of approaching the problem was to eliminate the excuses used by bishops for not being present in their dioceses. Among these was the claim that the Roman curia and the popes had removed local episcopal control over the cler-

---

suasi dalla Dottrina nuova di Germani pensano certo ch'l fomite sia veramente peccato et non effeto del peccato del primo nostro padre et ragione poi di tutto gli attuali che noi adulti commettiamo: le parole sono queste, Et haec sancta sinodus reprobat opinione illorum qui affirmant fomitatem esse vere peccatum et dignum odio Dei nisi perpetuo condonet."

44. In 416 local councils took place at Carthage and Milevis in North Africa. Those councils condemned specific theses of the Pelagians concerning free will, infant baptism, and the power of prayer. These condemnations were subsequently approved by Pope Innocent I in 417.

45. Tanner, 2: 667.

gy by reinforcing the independence of the exempt religious orders and by granting benefices to individuals who had no intention of residing and carrying out the *cura animarum* for which the benefices existed—thereby leaving little reason for a bishop to reside in his diocese. If those practices of the pope and the curia could be eliminated, many argued, it might be easier to encourage bishops to take up residence.

In his letter of February 28, 1546, Gonzaga informed Bertano of his disappointment over a decision by the cardinals in Rome and by Pope Paul III not to eliminate the abuse of granting "expectative graces." The traffic in expectative graces was essentially the practice of maintaining a futures market on lesser ecclesiastical offices. In essence, the pope would promise to grant an ecclesiastical post when it became vacant by the death of its present holder in return for a fee from the individual seeking the benefice.[46] Gonzaga informed Bertano that the decision had been made in order to maintain the authority of the Apostolic See and out of concern that, now that the Council of Trent was in session, a papal decision to renounce the practice of expectatives would give the impression that the pope was admitting himself to be under the authority of the council.[47] Gonzaga claimed to be greatly saddened by this decision since at the council they identified "the authority of the pope with the abuse of his authority because in many respects the abuse is so great."[48] Gonzaga went on to say that papal abuses could not be greater, more scandalous, or more contrary to the doctrine of Christ and of the apostles who "cry out with one voice 'feed those who are your flock.'"[49] But the pope, he complained, gave the expectatives to those who fed themselves, bestowing them

46. On expectative graces and other sources of ecclesiastical wealth see Hallman, 43–46.

47. BAV, Barb. Lat., codex 5793, ff. 103v–106r, Ercole Gonzaga to Pietro Bertano, February 28, 1546.

48. Ibid., Ercole Gonzaga to Pietro Bertano, February 28, 1546. "Si conosce che di la pongono l'autorità del Papa nell'abuso dell'autorità sua per essere in molte cose grandissimo." f. 106r.

49. Ibid., Ercole Gonzaga to Pietro Bertano, February 28, 1546. "Ne più contrario alla Dottrina di Christo e degli apostoli i quali tutti ad una voce gridano pascite qui in vobis est gregem." f. 106r.

"for money to merchants who buy them and to those who are unknown."[50] Given Gonzaga's own involvement in the traffic in benefices, it is not difficult to see that this complaint arose not solely from a genuine concern to eliminate this abuse, but also from the experience of Paul III's involvement in the affairs of the abbey of Lucedio.

After the council formulated its views on the nature of original sin, it proceeded to what had been the central theological challenge of the Protestants, justification. Gonzaga's comments on that doctrine are brief but reveal him to be soundly opposed to compromise with the Protestants. In his letter to Bertano on the agenda of the council he wanted justification to be treated first among the dogmatic issues since it was of fundamental importance. He added that it was on this ground that the Lutherans wanted to cast down anything else that might have been agreed upon.[51] Gonzaga did not elaborate further on his understanding of justification, but these statements confirm that he did not hold the fundamental views of the Protestant Reformers, notwithstanding his association with a number of Italian Protestants. In late 1546 and early 1547 the more important issue, however, was when the council would address justification. The emperor continued to oppose an early treatment of the topic in order to avoid alienating the Protestants, while the pope wanted the prelates at Trent to deal with the question without delay. Gonzaga's interest in addressing justification again highlights his willingness to differ with imperial policy when necessary.

In the midst of that difference of opinion, the further matter of suspending or transferring the council arose. The pope showed interest in this move in order to maintain papal control over the assembly. The emperor wanted the council to remain in Trent so that it would continue to meet in imperial territory. Gonzaga preferred a solution that would mediate between the interests of the emperor and the pope. In July of 1546 he wrote to Camillo Capilupi on the status

---

50. Ibid., Ercole Gonzaga to Pietro Bertano, February 28, 1546. "Sono date solamente per denari a mercantanti che le comprano et a quelli che non sono conosciuti." f. 106r.

51. Ibid., f. 82, Ercole Gonzaga to Pietro Bertano, January 26, 1546.

of negotiations. He expressed his appreciation for the emperor's preference for not dealing too hastily with justification. He understood the value of not acting, because it avoided giving the Protestants an opportunity to claim that a decision was made without their opinions having been heard. Gonzaga also saw, however, that each time the emperor successfully delayed debate on justification he gave the king of France the opportunity to withdraw his bishops on the grounds that nothing was happening at the council. This situation, he argued, could lead to two problems. First, since the pope was already inclined to transfer the council from Trent, departure of the French would give him the opportunity to leave on the grounds that the council was no longer universal, an event that Charles hoped to avoid. Second, if the emperor's desire was to force the Protestants to participate in a universal council, departure of the French would deprive the council of precisely that universal character. Therefore, Gonzaga argued, it would be better for the emperor to allow the council to do something on justification. If he wanted to bring the Protestants to Trent later, they could come and dispute the same things that had already been determined by the council and put forward new arguments that might not have been understood before. Then the council could again deliberate and Protestants could not claim that their views went unheard. That accomplished, Gonzaga stated bluntly, the emperor could force them to do as he wished.[52] This plan would gain the pope a decree on justification and guarantee the emperor that the council would remain in Trent. Gonzaga balanced the needs of the papacy with those of the emperor and skillfully avoided alienating either party.

In 1546 and 1547 political realities in Germany and Italy led to the transfer of the council from Trent. The War of the Schmalkaldic League presented a threat to the safety and progress of the council. Disease also threatened those in Trent. For these reasons the legates and the assembled prelates voted on March 11, 1547, to move to Bologna. This decision was fraught with diplomatic difficulties. The emperor refused to recognize the legality of the transfer. He had prom-

---

52. Ibid., ff. 153v–154v, Ercole Gonzaga to Camillo Capilupi, July 23, 1546.

ised the Protestants a council in the empire, and Trent fulfilled that promise. The pope had feared imperial dominance of the council and the possibility that too many concessions might be made to the Protestants under an imperially controlled council. Hence Paul III viewed Bologna, a city within the papal state, as more amenable to papal ends. The victory of Charles V over the Schmalkaldic League at Mühlburg in April of 1547, however, and the subsequent surrender of the Protestant princes in May and June changed the climate at the council. The pope now feared the overwhelming influence of the emperor in the affairs of the council more than military threats from the Protestants. Not until 1548, after a significant period in Bologna, did the council return to Trent.

Cardinal Gonzaga found himself in the somewhat uncomfortable position of having to defend the council's liberty from the emperor while simultaneously defending the emperor's interests. As early as 1544 he had advised the Duke of Ferrara on the possibility of the council's being held in that city, but denied that Ferrara would be possible because of the demands of the Lutherans.[53] Two years later, when a transfer of the council was under discussion and some mentioned Ferrara again as a possible venue, Cardinal Gonzaga gave reasons both for and against such a move, but his arguments against it predominated. He expressed his belief that the council could not be held there, given the demands of the Lutherans for a council in Germany. His argument is consistent with the imperial position on having the council within the empire.[54] His thoughts on the council's meeting at Bologna were quite bitter indeed. In a letter of July 17, 1547, to the Duke of Ferrara, Gonzaga characterized it as "that little council in Bologna and almost entirely of Italian bishops, and there is no doubt at all that it will be carried out in our fashion and will therefore be no hindrance at all."[55]

53. Ibid., codex 5792, ff. 118r–118v, Ercole Gonzaga to the Duke of Ferrara, November 9, 1544.

54. Ibid., codex 5793, ff. 161r–162r, Ercole Gonzaga to Ercole d'Este, August 17, 1546. As late as the summer of 1547 Ferrara came under consideration as a possible compromise between Paul III and Charles V, the former having defended the location of Bologna and the latter insisting on a return to Trent. See Jedin, *Storia*, 3: 129.

55. ASM, AG, b. 1916, unnumbered fascicle of letters of Ercole Gonzaga, Ercole Gonzaga to Ercole D'Este, July 17, 1547.

When the War of the Schmalkaldic League broke out, Gonzaga firmly supported Charles V's undertaking. In a letter to Ippolito Capilupi he expressed his amazement that members of the Council of Trent were so hesitant to offer the Church's financial support for the war effort. He argued that the current situation was very clear and that the Protestants were enemies of the Church.[56] Further, even after the transfer of the council to Bologna, Cardinal Gonzaga held to the imperial position that it should continue in Trent. Between March of 1547, when the translation of the council took place, and early 1548, the pope and the emperor resisted each other's demands on the location of the council.

In November of 1547 the emperor sent Cardinal Cristoforo Madruzzo of Trent to Rome to offer a proposal for returning the council to Trent. At the same time Gonzaga intervened to help negotiate a way around the impasse. In a letter to the imperial ambassador to Rome, Don Diego Hurtado de Mendoza, Gonzaga informed the emperor of papal policy on Bologna. The pope was still trying to gain imperial recognition of the transfer of the council to Bologna. To that end, Gonzaga informed the ambassador, Pope Paul III was attempting to bring the deliberations at Bologna to a close in order to present Charles V with a *fait accompli*. Charles had continued to obstruct participation of German bishops at Trent until after he had come to an understanding in Germany on Protestant participation. Paul III had pointed to this lack of German participation by either Catholic bishops or Lutheran representatives as a rationale for moving the council. Gonzaga's advice to Mendoza was to have the emperor order at least some Germans, Protestants included, to Trent as soon as possible in order to strengthen the argument for continuing the council there. If the emperor did so, the pope's arguments for transferring the council would be significantly weakened.[57] This advice highlights the delicate position in which Gonzaga found himself as a cardinal in the imperial camp. The letter to Mendoza ostensibly supported the emperor and

56. BAV, Barb. Lat., codex 5793, ff. 151r–152r, Ercole Gonzaga to Ippolito Capilupi, June 28, 1546.

57. ASM, AG, b. 1916, unnumbered fascicle of letters of Ercole Gonzaga, Ercole Gonzaga to Don Diego Hurtado de Mendoza, November 2, 1547.

suggested a means of returning the council to Trent. In urging the emperor to provide for a German presence at Trent, however, he was also implicitly affirming one of Paul III's principal criticisms of the proceedings at Trent and the emperor's involvement. As an imperialist he sought to maintain the position of the emperor, but as he made clear in his suggestions to Pietro Bertano, Gonzaga also favored a council led by the pope that could effectively deal with the doctrinal issues of the day. Just as Gonzaga's commitment to reform within the diocese of Mantua and in matters relating to his own benefices involved a balance between the social and political needs of his family and the requirements of reform, so too is this mixture of interests evident in his views on the Council of Trent.

Gonzaga at Trent

Gonzaga's most significant involvement in the council came during its third period. It was then that Gonzaga the papal legate came most fully to the center of European and ecclesiastical politics. It is this period of his career for which Gonzaga is best known and most strongly criticized. Under his leadership the council entered into conflicts over reform that nearly destroyed it. The almost irreconcilable differences among many of the prelates were too great to bridge, even for one as skilled at compromise as Ercole Gonzaga.

Gonzaga's experience in conciliar matters before he arrived at Trent was surely not as extensive as that of many other prelates. Nevertheless, he was not without valuable experience and knowledge. He had kept himself closely informed of events at the council. His friends there, including Pietro Bertano and Cardinal Cristoforo Madruzzo, wrote to him frequently on matters under discussion. His earlier studies and his personal library demonstrate a long-term interest in conciliar theology. Beyond these strictly professional reasons for Pius IV's selection of Gonzaga as legate stood economic and social ones. During the previous years Gonzaga had offered significant financial support for the council. He had made grain from Mantua readily available to those gathered in Trent. Further, his wealth also assured the pope that the

Mantuan cardinal would be able to pay for his own expenses while in Trent and not have to rely upon the Roman curia. In fact, Gonzaga's retinue of one hundred sixty men and twenty horses was the largest of any prelate at the council.[58] Family connections also offered a basis for trust between the pope and the cardinal. The marriages of Cardinal Gonzaga's niece Virginia della Rovere to the pope's nephew Federico Borromeo, and of Federico's sister Camilla to Ercole's nephew Cesare Gonzaga, sealed the accord between the two families. In February of 1561 Pius IV elevated Ercole's nephew Francesco Gonzaga, son of Ferrante, to the cardinalate. He subsequently took up residence in Rome and played an important role in communications among the legates in Trent, the pope, and the pope's nephew Carlo Borromeo. At first Gonzaga tried to resist the papal mandate. He assented only after the pope called him to Rome to explain his hesitancy. Gonzaga later said that he gave in before traveling there because he did not want it to seem that he was being summoned to Rome for disobedience.[59] Selection of Gonzaga did not go unopposed. Philip II, who had effectively blocked Gonzaga's candidacy for the papacy in the previous conclave, also opposed his appointment as legate because of the Spanish king's distrust for Pius IV and because it could renew Gonzaga's hopes for the papal tiara. Gonzaga's association with the *spirituali* and his support of Morone had also, among some, brought suspicion of heresy upon him. The Farnese tried to block the selection of Gonzaga ostensibly for the same reasons, and also because of their old vendetta with him.[60] Pius IV's support overcame this opposition, and Gonzaga made his solemn entrance into the city of Trent on April 16, 1561, when he joined his fellow legates Cardinals Ludovico Simonetta, Stanislaus Hosius, and Girolamo Seripando.

Gonzaga's work at Trent continued his policy of seeking a reform that balanced imperial and papal interests. The Europe of the 1560s

58. On Gonzaga's supplying the council see Reginald Pole to Paul III, May 11, 1545, CT 4: 419.

59. On Gonzaga's selection as legate and arrival there see Jedin, *Storia,* 4/1: 132–36; Scaduto, 4: 62.

60. Scaduto, 4: 62–63.

was a different place from that of the 1540s and 1550s, however. The Gonzaga family that had solidified its alliance with Charles V in the 1530s now found itself relating to a more remote and less familiar Philip II. The friendship between Charles V and Ercole's brother Ferrante was now of no account since both men had died. The old suspicions on the part of the Habsburgs that the Gonzaga, and Cardinal Gonzaga in particular, were crypto-francophiles once more complicated Gonzaga diplomacy. Nevertheless, the old Gonzaga tradition of walking a tightrope between competing interests still seems to have strongly influenced Cardinal Gonzaga's work at Trent. His involvement in matters discussed at the council, therefore, may be more fully understood when viewed in the light of his earlier career. He proceeded with a pragmatic attitude that sought compromises that were as much diplomatic as theological. This pragmatism included a flexibility that at times engendered suspicions in Rome concerning his loyalty to the pope. The best examples of his pragmatism may be seen in Gonzaga's support for attempts to use the council's work on the revision of the Index of Prohibited Books as a way to reconcile Protestants to the Church, and in his conduct during deliberations over the obligation of residence for bishops. The latter gave rise to his greatest difficulties, but in both instances Gonzaga's actions followed patterns of behavior and thought that had long held a place in his life.

As the council opened, the legates received orders from the pope to begin "the treatment of the dogmas and of the reforms that were left unfinished by the Council of Trent."[61] This vague formulation was meant to avoid conflict between the Spanish, who sought a clear statement that the new sessions of the council were a continuation of the previous council, and the French and imperial factions, which sought a new council altogether and the liberty to address issues that had been decided at earlier sessions. Gonzaga had referred to this issue implicitly in a letter to Cardinal Francesco Gonzaga of February 11, 1562, when, in keeping with his diplomatic practice of compromise, he suggested that the pope confirm all of the decrees of the earlier sessions

61. Ibid.

to satisfy the Spanish bishops while at the same time showing that the pope "wants to do what his predecessors did not do."[62] He also emphasized that this confirmation should be done in such a way that it would give neither the French nor the Protestants an excuse for not coming to the council. The decision to address issues still unresolved in 1552, however, left a door open to supporters of what became the most explosive issue before the council: debate over episcopal residence and whether it is an obligation *jure divino.*

To avoid direct confrontation at the beginning on these two views on the continuation of the council, the legates chose to address an apparently more innocuous issue, revision of the Index of Prohibited Books established by Paul IV in 1559, and then withdrawn upon his death that same year.[63] To some this issue seemed less controversial than confronting the political forces of Europe. Nevertheless, the proposed revision stirred up strong feelings. Some argued that the council was not an appropriate place to carry out such work because many books listed on the Index could not be found at Trent. Others believed that the universities should do the revision.[64] Moreover, such a revision at the council seemed to require the presence of authors whose works were under suspicion as well as those whose books had already been condemned. Thus the issue of offering a safe conduct to Protestants to come to the council to defend themselves, as well as the authority of the council to reconcile any individuals separated from the Church who came to Trent with that intention, was placed in discussion. These were originally clauses in the proposed decree on the Index. The Holy See had already granted the legates authority to reconcile those from Germany, Poland, and elsewhere in northern Europe, even if they had already been convicted by the Roman Inquisition. Rome excluded from this invitation for reconciliation those who

62. Giovanni Drei, "La corrispondenza del cardinale Ercole Gonzaga, presidente del Concilio di Trento," part 1, *Archivio per le Provincie Parmensi* 17 (1917): 198–99.

63. See Jedin, *Storia,* 4/1: 153–62. On the Index of 1559 see Paul F. Grendler, *The Roman Inquisition,* 115–27.

64. See De Bujanda, *Index des livres interdits,* vol. 8, Index de Rome 1557, 1559, 1564, 57–64.

were still under investigation, for fear that such a blanket offer might give the appearance that the council was superior to the pope and the Roman Inquisition in matters of judicial appeals.[65]

For Gonzaga and Seripando, this was an opportunity to bring back to the Catholic Church Italian Protestants who had fled north during the previous generation. Already in November of 1561 Gonzaga had attempted to draw Pier Paolo Vergerio back by means of a dialogue on theological matters at Trent. In the spring of 1562, the committee that attempted to formulate a statement on the issue sought to have the council approve a safe conduct for all who wanted to return to the Church even if they were under investigation by the Spanish or Roman Inquisitions. The names of Ochino, Vergerio, and Vermigli came up in the discussion. Cardinal Borromeo encouraged Gonzaga to reconcile Vergerio in particular, if that were possible.[66] Nevertheless, the Spanish bishops at Trent who had served on the Spanish Inquisition and the representatives of the Roman Inquisition opposed any such offer of safe conduct. In the end, on account of this opposition, a less open-handed offer was approved. The council decreed safe conduct not only for Germans but individuals from any nation. However, the proposed decree offering individual Protestants reconciliation on the authority of the council was never presented in the general congregation. Therefore, the automatic offer of protection sought by Gonzaga and Seripando was eliminated. The authority of the legates to absolve heretics remained in effect, however. Gonzaga's and Seripando's desire to reconcile Protestants in 1562 may have been overly optimistic. Nevertheless, it reveals that Gonzaga wanted to leave the door open for the return of apostates. His views at Trent in 1561 and 1562 were consistent with his attitude earlier in his career toward preachers of questionable theology. As Gonzaga had advised Madruzzo in the case of Vergerio, it would be better for the council to reconcile the estranged than to create more apostates.[67]

65. On the issue of the safe conduct see Jedin, *Storia*, vol. 4/1: 157ff.

66. Carlo Borromeo to Ercole Gonzaga, May 30, 1561, in Josef Šusta, ed., *Die Römische Curie und das Concil von Trient unter Pius IV. Actenstücke zur Geschichte des Concils von Trient*, 4 vols. (Vienna: Alfred Hölder, 1904–14), 1: 28.

67. On the discussion at Trent on the issues of the safe conducts and reconcilia-

In keeping with a Habsburg preference evident since the opening sessions of the council in 1545 to address issues of discipline rather
than doctrine, the imperial representatives sought to have the council
discuss and permit the offering of the chalice to the laity in the Catholic mass. This discussion was important to the Habsburgs, who saw
the concession of the chalice as a means to shore up support for Catholicism in Germany among those who wavered in their commitment to the Church. In this matter Gonzaga was in accord with the
emperor. In relating the discussion of this matter on August 22, 1562,
Gabriele Paleotti, auditor of the Roman Rota and legal advisor to the
council, describes Cardinal Gonzaga as urging the council to act on
the issue of the chalice since it was important to the emperor, without
whose support there could not be a successful conclusion to the council. Paleotti added that many of the fathers were amazed that Gonzaga
showed such support for the proposal and thought that it reflected the
pope's views.[68] Indeed, Gonzaga rebuked Don Riccardo da Vercelli,
who opposed the concession on the grounds that he considered all the
Germans to be infected with heresy.[69] Paleotti described Gonzaga as
having angrily warned the man to cease such "foolishness." When da
Vercelli tried to continue, Gonzaga silenced him.[70] Despite the efforts
of the French and imperial representatives, as well as Gonzaga and
Seripando, there was little support for the proposal. Many bishops, especially the Italians, Simonetta among them, opposed this concession.
Some of the small number of German bishops present also opposed it,
leaving a strong impression on the council. While the superiors of the
religious orders were divided, those opposed included Diego Laínez of
the Jesuits. As it became apparent that the majority did not favor offering an indult to the Germans, Seripando then suggested that the
council merely declare that such an indult was permissible under certain conditions and leave the actual decision to the pope. The legates

tion of Protestants at Trent see Jedin, *Storia,* 4/1: 157–59, 173–75. On the continuing
prerogative of the legates to reconcile see the letter of Cardinal Francesco Gonzaga to
Ercole Gonzaga, April 1, 1562, in Drei, "La corrispondenza," 17, 222–23.

68. Gabriele Paleotti, CT 3/1: 397.

69. Pedro Gonzalez de Mendoza, CT 2: 650.

70. Paleotti, CT 3/1: 413–15.

agreed to this proposal. Nevertheless, the majority of the council was opposed, so Gonzaga offered the compromise that the entire issue of the chalice be referred to the pope without reference to an indult. At the time, Paleotti suggested that Gonzaga's willingness to support the emperor's program derived from close relationships between his family and the emperor. It also conformed, however, to the longstanding custom of Cardinal Gonzaga to seek pastoral and political compromise where it could be found.

Not long after work began in Trent in 1562, debates on reform focused on what turned out to be the most contentious issue of the entire third period of the council: the obligation of bishops to reside in their dioceses.[71] The residence of bishops had been a key element of every major plan to reform the Church in previous generations. A significant number of bishops held that this was an obligation incumbent upon a bishop *jure divino,* or by divine law. According to this view there could be no dispensation from that obligation, even one offered by the pope. Many of the supporters of this view were Spanish bishops who sought to reduce the influence of Rome in their dioceses, but they also believed that episcopal absenteeism was a root cause of many of the Church's ills and needed to be addressed. In short, in their view a thorough reform of the Church would not be possible without such a decree. On the other side were bishops who supported the prerogative of the Holy See to appoint bishops and permit them to absent themselves when necessary. They denied that residence was mandated by anything stronger than an ecclesiastical law. Further, they believed that a declaration of episcopal residence *jure divino* would weaken the authority of the pope in the Church. The legates at the council were themselves divided on this issue. Cardinals Ludovico Simonetta and Stanislaus Hosius opposed the *jure divino* formula, while Cardinals Gonzaga and Girolamo Seripando supported the stricter discipline. Indeed, Gonzaga may have viewed this as a way for the council to address the issue of papal power indirectly, as he had suggested to Bertano in 1546. Thus, episcopal residence soon be-

---

71. On the issue of episcopal residence see Jedin, *Storia,* 4/1: 187–218.

came an intensely debated issue closely related to the role of the pope. Gonzaga found himself in the undesirable position of trying to negotiate a workable settlement between the two sides.

At least part of the problem lay in the sometimes conflicting instructions that the legates received from Rome. Originally, the pope had indicated that he did not want any debate on the issue. A prohibition on discussing the basis of mandatory residence of bishops, however, would have given the impression that the council was not truly free.[72] By the end of March 1562, Pius IV permitted the debate though he did not reveal his own views on the matter until early April. He had initially indicated that he was not necessarily opposed to the view held by Gonzaga but reserved judgment. Gonzaga and Seripando then permitted open discussion of the question in the general congregations. On April 7, 1562, the leader of the Spanish bishops, Cardinal Pedro Guerrero of Granada, argued that the council should declare itself plainly in favor of a decree on residence that would recognize the obligation as a matter of divine law. Others argued that the existing legislation, including the decree of 1546 in an earlier period of the council, would suffice as long as more severe penalties were added. Heated debate continued for three days with bishops from a variety of nations and religious orders divided over the subject. At that point, in order to avoid a prolonged discussion, Gonzaga asked each bishop to submit his complaints about the problem of residence for the consideration of a commission that would examine the issue. The legates did not interfere in the free expression of differing views and Gonzaga is said to have listened benignly to Guerrero while he spoke. Seripando declared to the council fathers on April 14 that freedom to speak in the council was of paramount importance.[73] Not all thought like Seripando. Cardinals Simonetta and Hosius in particular supported the curial view that frowned on the discussion.

The variety of opinions expressed was so great that it became dif-

---

72. On the pope's resistance to the formula *"jure divino"* see Cardinal Carlo Borromeo to the Legates, March 18, 1562, in Šusta, 2: 65.

73. Paleotti, CT 3/1: 305.

ficult to determine the view of the majority without some formal ballot procedure. In order to clarify the situation, after a consultation led
by Gonzaga and Seripando on April 19 and 20, the legates decided to
put the question to the members of the council more directly. It appears that by this move Gonzaga and Seripando attempted to secure
the votes of the council fathers in such a way that a decree in favor of
residence *jure divino* would be a fait accompli and thus move reform
forward. However, some bishops withheld a direct vote because they
wished to consult the pope first. In the vote, 68 bishops were in favor
of recognizing the obligation *jure divino,* 35 against, and 35 abstained.
Afterwards, Gonzaga attempted to argue that the abstentions count-
ed as "yes" votes and that those who abstained wished to see the mo-
tion carry. The other legates refused to support this argument and he
acquiesced. This episode brought a good deal of grief to Gonzaga. After the vote on episcopal residence, the pope and the curia began to
suspect the intentions of Gonzaga and Seripando. Curial officials and
Cardinal Simonetta urged the pope to forbid discussion on the topic. Simonetta feared that with the arrival of more French bishops it
would not be possible to withstand an effort to reduce papal power
and in dispatches to the pope he raised the specter of the Council of
Basel.[74] In the view of the pope and the curia, Gonzaga and Seripando seemed to be acting in collusion with the members of the council
most resistant to papal power. They were, in fact, acting to preserve
confidence in the Holy See's willingness to carry out a comprehensive
reform.

In the aftermath of the vote on residence *jure divino,* Gonzaga sent
one of his secretaries and theologians, Federico Pendasio, to Rome to
explain his position to Pius IV. He informed the pope that the prelates
at Trent were dissatisfied with the pace of reform and spoke of nothing but a desire for a "true, sincere, and substantial reform." They held
that the lack of progress had fostered the increase of heresy. The arrival of new bishops only increased this perception. In short, the legates faced a resolute group of bishops who grew increasingly skeptical

74. Jedin, *Storia,* 4/1: 199–201.

of papal promises of reform. They sought reforms as expressed in the *Consilium de emendanda ecclesiae*. Gonzaga's instructions to Pendasio included the request to know if the pope was truly committed to a serious reform of the Church. Mandatory residence of bishops might not solve all of the problems—it might be only a beginning. It would, however, indicate the seriousness of the pope and the council about carrying out reform. In these instructions there remained evident the views Gonzaga expressed as early as 1546 that papal powers might have to be limited in part to preserve the essential integrity of papal authority and to effect reform.[75] On April 23 Gonzaga and Seripando wrote to Cardinal Borromeo and underlined the necessity of allowing the council to proceed in freedom. The difficulty in allowing some bishops to avoid voting in conscience and allowing them to defer to the pope was that this allowance in itself gave the impression that the council was not free.[76]

Pendasio's instructions were of a general sort rather than specifically focused on the issue of episcopal residence. While the pope's response included his assertion that he personally had not originally been opposed to a declaration of residence *jure divino,* he wanted more time to consider the issue, since things at the council were still unsettled. In Rome, moreover, he was impressed by arguments of those curialists and canonists who saw in such a declaration the destruction of the Roman curia. As a result, on May 8, the pope forbade further discussion of this matter.[77] In the end, he had sided with Simonetta and others who opposed Guerrero. Many in the curia came to think that Seripando and Gonzaga were part of an antipapal plot, and the pope began to consider increasing the number of legates in order to dilute the authority of those two.

Gonzaga rejected the accusations and credited much of the Roman opposition to his work to the old animosities that had existed between

75. Gonzaga's instruction to Pendasio on April 9, 1562, is in Šusta, 2: 78–82. See also Jedin, *Storia,* 4/1: 203.

76. Ercole Gonzaga and Girolamo Seripando to Carlo Borromeo, April 23, 1562, in Šusta, 2: 90–91.

77. Jedin, *Storia,* 4/1: 205.

him and the Farnese. He wrote in his own defense to Cardinal Borromeo on May 16, 1562. In particular he pointed out that the whole college of legates had favored the plan for discussing episcopal residence.
They hammered out the text of the vote over the course of two meetings. He had wanted to proceed in that way since it was otherwise impossible to see what the majority of the council fathers thought. As
for the suggestion that he showed excessive sympathy for those who
supported a declaration for residence *jure divino* by not interrupting
Guerrero during his arguments in favor of the plan, he insisted that to
have done so would have undermined the liberty of the council. He
rejected any accusations that he tried to influence the vote on the issue. Finally he took great offense at the suggestion that he be replaced
as president of the legates. Indeed, having to cede the first place in
the council to another at that point was such an affront to his honor
that his only response would be to resign his post and depart from the
council.[78] Seripando confirmed these explanations and denied that he
and Gonzaga or anyone else had been involved in some sort of plot.
He insisted that the issue of residence, including the decision to take
a vote of the council fathers, had been discussed in the presence of
all the legates, Simonetta included.[79] Despite these arguments on the
part of Seripando and Gonzaga, the pope still sought to appoint three
new legates. He was only dissuaded from doing so by both Cardinal
Borromeo and Cardinal Francesco Gonzaga. This change of heart may
have been critical in the subsequent outcome of the council. Egidio
Foscarari, bishop of Modena, said of the proposal to send new legates
and replace Gonzaga: "There is no better means, if one wants to ruin
the Church, nothing more apt to achieve this purpose." He held that
if Gonzaga were to leave Trent there was a real threat that the council itself would collapse and national councils would be held in both
France and Germany.[80]

78. Ercole Gonzaga to Carlo Borromeo, May 16, 1562, in Šusta, 2: 143ff. See also
Robert Trisco, "Carlo Borromeo and the Council of Trent: The Question of Reform,"
in Headley and Tomaro, eds., *San Carlo Borromeo,* 49–51.
79. Jedin, *Storia,* 4/1: 213.
80. For Foscarari's remarks see Šusta, 2: 161.

In the midst of these difficulties, the council itself was in a very unsettled state. In order to pacify the supporters of episcopal residence *jure divino,* the legates decided on May 23 to offer the council a written promise to take up the issue of episcopal residence in the context of discussion of holy orders. Division among the legates was now becoming clear as Simonetta, who at first agreed to this proposal, withdrew his support. Wearied by the indirect undermining of their positions by Simonetta, Gonzaga and Seripando decided to send a common statement with the signatures of all the legates to the pope, outlining all of the actions of the legates in the *jure divino* matter. Simonetta refused to sign it unless it was stated that he had approved of a discussion of residence on March 11 only if there was no specific mention of its being *jure divino.* The other legates refused to add this reservation since it was not true. It was now apparent to the other legates that Simonetta had been communicating with the curia by his own letters in addition to the common communications of the whole college of legates. It was clear that the pope did not trust Gonzaga or Seripando as he did Simonetta.[81]

The issue of episcopal residence was set aside temporarily while the legates sought to direct the council to issues such as the Eucharist and holy orders. Nevertheless, substantial bad feeling had been aroused as a result of the failed attempt to address the residence matter. Many members of the council resisted the effort to look at other issues. When the Spanish representatives in particular complained, Gonzaga and Seripando considered offering the promise in the next general congregation that they would raise the question in the context of the discussion of holy orders. Simonetta strongly opposed this offer but the Spanish found it insufficient and made a formal protest on May 18 about the way the issue had been buried. The promise of the legates on May 23 that they would attend to the issue in the context of holy orders did not satisfy the supporters of the *jure divino* formula and a protest was lodged on May 26.[82]

81. Jedin, *Storia,* 4/1: 212–14.
82. Ibid., 234.

On June 6 when the council began to discuss whether the chalice should be offered to the laity at the Eucharist, the issue of episcopal residence came up again. The pope had made it clear that the council was to discuss issues that had been left undone in 1552 as a demonstration that the council was a continuation of the earlier periods. As one who had been present in 1552, Guerrero asserted that holy orders was one of the issues that the fathers had been prepared to take up. Therefore, he asked that room be made in the agenda for a discussion of episcopal residence. Either it should be dealt with in that session, he argued, or as a part of the sessions in July on doctrinal matters. Not surprisingly, this argument met with opposition from those against the *jure divino* formulation. When Sigismondo Saraceni, the bishop of Matera, said that insistence on that discussion inappropriately took control of things that rightfully belonged to the legates, Bartolomé dos Martires, the archbishop of Braga, asked pointedly if the bishops did not have the right to make their desires known in the council. He insisted that it was up to the council to respond to these issues, and at this point Gonzaga intervened in a manner that was to cost him dearly. First, he confirmed the claim of the archbishop of Braga that the bishops were free to make proposals and that it was the responsibility of the council to decide on matters. Second, he reiterated the promise that the legates had made earlier to the leaders of the group seeking to discuss episcopal residence, namely, that the council would take up the issue in the context of the debates on holy orders. By this public and formal promise in a general congregation, Gonzaga bound the legates to address the issue at a later date but in a way that did not entirely satisfy the Spanish. He hoped to move the council away from that issue at least temporarily to allow space for the discussion of the Eucharist. Moreover, he did so knowing that Rome would not approve.[83]

By this time it was clear that Simonetta, not Gonzaga, was receiving the most important correspondence from Rome. In the curia, new accusations were made against Gonzaga.[84] In a confidential commu-

83. Ibid., 243.
84. Ibid., 246.

nication to Rome Cardinal Gonzaga had indicated that he felt bound to act in conscience in order to bring the council to a successful conclusion. This statement was interpreted in Rome as an indication of his lack of trustworthiness. In response, Gonzaga decided to make a formal request that the pope relieve him of his duties as legate, sending the request by means of his secretary, Francesco Arrivabene. Gonzaga held that he could not serve when he was not trusted and that it seemed that all of the criticisms of him heard in Rome were believed while his own defense was discounted. Moreover, he feared that if he continued in his post, all blame for what went wrong would fall on him. He also found it an indignity that Simonetta was the real leader of the council while he was relegated to being, in the words of Tommaso Caselli, bishop of Cava, *"il vecchio pro forma."*[85] In a written statement to the pope Gonzaga complained that although he had tried to do all that Cardinal Borromeo had asked of him, particularly on continuance of the council and the residence of bishops, he still left the pope unsatisfied. Gonzaga took pains to explain that his desire to act in conscience was not to be understood as disregard for the pope's views but rather that he needed to use his own discretion in some things since he was the one present at the council. As he put it rather sharply to Arrivabene: "I would rather govern myself according to my conscience than according to his [the pope's] who has the assistance of the Holy Spirit."[86] The issue of obedience had also arisen in a letter to his nephew Cardinal Francesco Gonzaga a week earlier in which he insisted that his desire to act according to his own conscience was not because he thought his own superior to the pope's, but that being at the council he was aware of factors that did not appear to be clear in Rome.[87] While the pope and others in Rome may have had concerns about Gonzaga's loyalty they saw clearly that his departure could have a serious impact on the council. The pope, therefore, refused to accept the resignation and tried to reassure Gonzaga of his

85. For Gonzaga's orders to Arrivabene dated June 22, 1562 see Drei, "La corrispondenza," 18 (1918), 71–72.
86. Ibid., 72.
87. Ibid., Ercole Gonzaga to Francesco Gonzaga, June 15, 1562, 63.

support in a brief of June 29, 1562. Gonzaga seems to have henceforth viewed his work as a matter of fulfilling an obligation. He expressed to the emperor in a letter of July 14 his hope that the pope would punish his accusers and no longer listen to them without giving Gonzaga a hearing.[88] For the moment, the conflict among the legates was set aside and the work of the council proceeded. Gonzaga, however, never regained the trust of the pope that he had enjoyed when he first went to Trent.

When the council finally approached the issue of holy orders, the matter of episcopal residence arose again as an element in defining the nature of the episcopacy. Though the pope may have wanted discussion of it suppressed, the legates insisted that such a course of action was not only difficult, but impossible. The legates, in their communication with Pius IV, insisted that so many bishops favored action on episcopal residency that the most he should hope for was a decision of the council to leave the issue to the pope, who might then issue a bull mandating residence.[89] The pope by that time was hoping to conclude the council as soon as possible for political reasons: the imminent outbreak of religious war in France, the likelihood that England and the Protestant princes of the continent would assist the Huguenots, and the upcoming Diet of Frankfurt, where the emperor's son Maximilian was to be crowned king of the Romans. The arrival of the cardinal of Lorraine at the head of a significant body of French bishops would, moreover, make it even more difficult to avoid the issue of episcopal residence. Gonzaga, in contrast, did not regard a hurried end to the council as a viable solution. Leaving Trent without carrying out a real reform risked encouraging the French and the Spanish to remain at Trent and establish a schismatic council or to convoke various national councils.[90] Gonzaga's more deliberate pace reinforced doubts

88. Ercole Gonzaga to Ferdinand von Habsburg, July 14, 1562. See Jedin, *Storia,* 4/1: 247.

89. The Legates to Cardinal Borromeo, July 20, 1562, in Šusta, 2: 259. See also Jedin, *Storia,* 4/1: 274.

90. Ercole Gonzaga to Cardinal Francesco Gonzaga, August 31, 1562, in Drei, "La corrispondenza," 18 (1918): 101.

among the pope and others in Rome about his leadership at Trent. Once again the pope considered sending new legates, although they would not have replaced Gonzaga as president.[91]

While earlier discussions had dealt with the specific issue of residence, the distinction now was based on the nature of the episcopacy. How was the council to describe the difference between bishops and priests? Were bishops superior to priests only by administrative order? Or were they different by reason of divine law? The decree under debate at the session held in 1552 did, in fact, use that phrase to make the distinction. Thus, when the council arrived at the point of addressing these issues in the fall of 1562 the stage was set for another confrontation. The arrival of the cardinal of Lorraine and other French bishops in mid-November heightened the tension. Acrimonious debate continued into January of 1563. On January 24 the French ambassadors met with the legates and indicated that they would not restrain the Gallicans among them and that they considered the council superior to the pope, citing the Council of Constance as an authority. Gonzaga and Seripando responded by insisting that the pope was superior to the council and rejected the example of the conciliarist argument.[92]

As early as December 27, the legates had sent Carlo Visconti, bishop of Ventimiglia and a friend of the pope, to Rome to explain the situation. Essentially, they argued, the council was now so large and international that it could not really be compared with the earlier periods when the legates were held in great respect and when the animosity between the French and the imperials was such as to leave the pope room to maneuver. By the end of 1562 the French and the imperial representatives were united in their desire for a thoroughgoing reform. This background was part of the legates' defense of their actions. They denied that they had been too lenient in the council. Had they forbidden any discussion of the *jure divino* formula they would have strengthened the Protestants and those Catholics who believed that in the council there was no real freedom of discussion. The legates add-

91. See Jedin, *Storia*, 4/1: 277–78.
92. Ibid., 380.

ed that the real problem was the activity of the zealots who, they said, were always vaunting their connections in Rome and producing letters both genuine and spurious that threw the council into confusion. The legates wanted a clear indication from Rome of what to do in order to eliminate this confusion, in particular, the matter of episcopal residence.[93] These instructions reflect the views of Gonzaga and Seripando, who had grown weary of Simonetta's duplicity. Gonzaga asked yet again to be relieved of his duties as of April, since the work of the council and the *"travagli d'animo"* that he experienced had tested his health. Perhaps knowledge that Federico Gonzaga, younger brother of Duke Guglielmo, was to be appointed to the college of cardinals on January 6 allowed Ercole Gonzaga to concede some public responsibility to younger members of the family. Nevertheless, the pope's instructions to the legates rejected the request to leave the council.[94]

After Visconti's return to Trent the legates seemed to think they had some room to move with regard to the Gallicans since the pope said that the succession of the decrees should not change. Even these slim hopes were dashed, however, when another instruction arrived from Rome dated January 27 insisting that in no case was the pope's title of "pastor of the universal church" to be omitted from the canon. This title included everything that the popes wanted, especially their superiority over the council. The Gallicans resisted it and the council reached an impasse. Before any further progress could be made, Gonzaga sought a postponement of the next session of the council until April 22. This postponement was approved but Gonzaga and Seripando did not live to see the council reconvene.

Conclusion

Gonzaga's attitude toward the Council of Trent developed during a lengthy career as a resident bishop and sometime-opponent of Pope

---

93. The instructions to Visconti are in Šusta, 3: 121ff. See also Jedin, *Storia,* 4/1: 380–82.
94. Šusta, 3: 188ff.

Paul III. His previous experience as pastor and ruler had led him to emphasize prudence in preaching and ruling. His tendency to negotiate with those who preached questionable doctrine rather than prosecute them echoed in his support of general safe conducts for Protestants to appear at the council. During the earliest sessions of the council, Gonzaga had suggested that some reduction in papal authority might be necessary in order to salvage those powers that the church held to be divinely established. As a resident bishop and supporter of Habsburg interests he did not automatically support curial definitions of papal power, but he was not simply pursuing an imperial agenda, either. His agenda developed from his pastoral and theological experience and his involvement in the debates over episcopal residence reflected that experience.

Gonzaga has been criticized for his work at Trent on the basis of two interrelated issues. First, it was claimed that he was not sufficiently well trained in theology to manage the debates that raged around him. As a result of this lack of training, it was argued, he grew excessively dependent on Cardinal Seripando and the cardinal of Lorraine and therefore was unable to act independently. Second, it was argued that the combination of these two factors impeded the progress of the council and nearly brought it to collapse. Closer analysis of his previous training and experience as well as the sources of criticism at Trent, however, reveals a more complex image of Gonzaga. His theological training was surely not as strong as that of many who were present at Trent, a fact that provided the basis for Tommaso Caselli's reference to him as *"il vecchio pro forma."*[95] This same case could be made against most bishops who had not been professional theologians earlier in their careers. Further, the effort that Gonzaga expended in the study of scripture and in the collection of a large library demonstrates that he was not merely a humanistically trained aristocrat. His ongoing interest in the work of the council, even before he arrived in Trent, had also exposed him to the matters discussed there. Finally, given the dependence of the council on professional theologians who hammered

95. Drei, "La corrispondenza," 18 (1918): 71.

out the proposed decrees that all of the bishops later voted on, Gonza-- ga's lack of professional training does not appear all that remarkable.

As for Gonzaga's dependence upon Seripando and others, it does seem that many in the council perceived him as dependent. Among the pasquinades preserved from the council, one tells of Gonzaga's arrival at the river Styx after his death. As Gonzaga was crossing the river, Charon asked him what he really thought about episcopal residence. Gonzaga replied, "Wait a bit as Seripando will be here soon. He knows."[96] Clearly, Seripando was theologically superior to Gonzaga and would have exerted significant influence on him. Nevertheless, other evidence provides reason not to overemphasize this relationship. Jedin suggested that in the summer of 1562 Gonzaga and Cardinal Simonetta attempted to patch up their differences in order to move the council forward. As a part of this rapprochement they agreed to lay blame for conflict over the vote on residence in April on the shoulders of Seripando. This displacement of blame would have effectively but inaccurately made Seripando appear to be the dominant of the two cardinals. That Gonzaga was not entirely dependent on Seripando can be seen most clearly in his rejection of Augustinian theological views in favor of a Thomistic position, their differences over the nature of concupiscence being the most noteworthy. The remark of Tommaso Caselli that after the arrival of the French the real head of the council was the cardinal of Lorraine must also be taken with a grain of salt. Caselli was extremely zealous for the rights of the Holy See and fiercely opposed the doctrine of episcopal residence *jure divino.*

The characterization of Gonzaga and Seripando as the source of many of the council's difficulties must also be reexamined. In Jedin's view, Gonzaga and Seripando were responsible for much of the difficulty that Cardinal Morone faced after his arrival at the council. He interprets Morone as implicitly blaming the dead legates for the political alliance of the French, Spanish, and imperial powers. Morone did indicate that the alliance of those powers might have been avoided six or eight months earlier. Jedin reads this indication as an implicit

96. CT 2: 679.

criticism of the two legates, but Morone did not mention Gonzaga or Seripando. It is more likely that Morone was indicating how the entire period of conflicted debate—involving many actors—created the diplomatic obstacles he faced in the spring of 1563.[97] Jedin does seem to indicate that Morone enjoyed certain advantages that Gonzaga and Seripando did not, such as the confidence of the pope, the support of all three great powers, and consequently, a great degree of flexibility on the part of those assembled at Trent. It is clear that while the pope repeatedly expressed the view that Gonzaga and Seripando should use their own prudence, whenever they exercised such independence they were reprimanded for it. By laying responsibility for the near destruction of the council over the matter of episcopal residence at the feet of Gonzaga and Seripando, Jedin could add emphasis to his portrait of Morone as a hero who saved the council and brought it to a successful conclusion. On closer inspection, however, the conduct of Gonzaga and Seripando indicates that they were required to engage in an almost impossible balancing act to preserve the unity of the council. Not until the near break-up of the council, along with the deaths of the two legates in March of 1563, did the seriousness of the situation become clear to many of the more inflexible proponents of papal, Gallican, or national views. For these reasons Morone could operate in a more workable context than his predecessors and the council found a compromise solution to the problem of episcopal residence and other issues.

Gonzaga's failure to guide the council to a successful conclusion also serves to illustrate other changes in early modern Catholicism. His conduct in the final sessions of Trent can be seen as the extension of his work as a patrician bishop who understood his own obligations of residence and good government in terms of local responsibility, obligations that were as important to him as duty toward the Holy See. But that sense of local responsibility did not necessarily place him in opposition to the interests of Rome. Therefore he did not share the fear of the curialists and Cardinal Simonetta that any suggestion of

97. Jedin, *Storia*, 4/2: 23.

episcopal residence as a matter of divine obligation was in and of itself a challenge to papal authority. His failures at Trent were due not so much to his administrative or intellectual strengths or weaknesses as to the fact that his views on his role in the Church and on the role of the Church in European society had become anachronistic. The time was past when Gonzaga's patrician way of proceeding could be effectively employed as a means to reform.

CONCLUSION

❦

Now displayed at a side altar in the Mantuan church of Sant'Egidio is a painting, *Deposition and Burial of Christ with Cardinal Ercole Gonzaga*.[1] Gonzaga commissioned the work around 1557 for his proposed funeral chapel in the cathedral of Mantua and it contains the only extant portrait of the cardinal drawn from life. The painter of the work is unknown, though it may have been produced by followers of Giulio Romano. Although intended for the cathedral, it hung for nearly three hundred years in the chapel of the Dominican convent of San Vincenzo in Mantua, home to several prominent women of the Gonzaga family, Cardinal Gonzaga's sister Ippolita and his daughter Anna among them. The image expresses much about Cardinal Gonzaga's varied responsibilities and experiences. On one level it is generally representative of Renaissance piety, showing the dead Christ laid in his tomb by Joseph of Arimathea, the apostle John, the Blessed Virgin, Mary Magdalene, Nicodemus, and others. In the painting, however, the addition of Gonzaga as patron and the models used for additional figures communicate further specific messages.

Gonzaga is shown kneeling before the sepulcher with his head turned to the viewer and his hand gesturing to the body of Christ. Behind Gonzaga and with his hand gently supporting him stands a Dominican saint, most likely Saint Dominic. The model for this figure was Gonzaga's old teacher at Bologna, Pietro Pomponazzi. The choice of Pomponazzi as the model, and a rather startling choice at that, re-

---

1. On the history of this painting and the figures in it see Maria Giustina Grassi, "La Deposizione con il cardinale Ercole Gonzaga in S. Egidio a Mantova," *Civiltà Mantovana,* 3rd series, 28, no. 8 (September 1993): 45–61.

stated the long-lasting devotion of the cardinal to *"messer Perreto."* Literally to his tomb Gonzaga carried his devotion to Pomponazzi and to his early studies. The lessons in philosophy that he learned in Bologna were to be validated in a more permanent way in this tribute to his old master. Thus, even at his intended mausoleum Cardinal Gonzaga paradoxically wished to maintain fidelity to philosophical ideas that were increasingly marginalized in Catholic Europe while at the same time presenting himself as a cardinal of the Roman Church. The figure of Christ is shown being laid in a sarcophagus that is inscribed with a Hebrew quotation. This evokes the biblical theology that Gonzaga studied, especially in the early years following his return to Mantua from Rome in 1537. On the other side of the sarcophagus from Gonzaga stands a Dominican sister who gestures to the body of Christ and holds a lily in her hand. Some have argued that this represents Blessed Osanna Andreasi, the Dominican tertiary and counselor to Cardinal Ercole's parents, Francesco and Isabella. Maria Giustina Grassi has made the convincing argument that the model for this figure was Cardinal Gonzaga's sister Ippolita. The presence of either woman in this painting underlines the role of the Gonzaga family in his life. Placing Ippolita in the frame makes a particularly strong statement about Cardinal Gonzaga's attention to the needs of his relatives. Indeed, the gestures of Cardinal Gonzaga and the Dominican sister can be interpreted not only as indicating the body of Christ but as reaching out to one another in what is a strong diagonal axis. Thus, on this canvas Ercole Gonzaga had seen to a final expression of his commitment to the world of Renaissance culture, sixteenth-century Italian piety, and family loyalty. It is a compact expression of the often conflicting ideals to which he committed himself over a lifetime.

As he approached his death, Gonzaga could look back over more than fifty years of cultural and religious change and conflict. Throughout those years he maintained an interest in scholarship. He had begun his schooling with humanistic studies in Mantua in the shadow of the famous humanist school founded by Vittorino da Feltre in the fifteenth century. At the University of Bologna, while studying at the feet of Pomponazzi, he had witnessed the philosophical debates that engaged the Italian universities of his day, in particular that concerning the immortality of the soul for which Pomponazzi had become famous. The influence of that period of study was apparent in Gonzaga's subsequent pursuit of articulate philosophers to serve as his intellectual companions during the remainder of his life. After his return to Mantua in 1537, Gonzaga collected a sizeable personal library. This collection of literature, philosophy, and theology from antiquity to the Renaissance became the center of an active intellectual circle of clergy and laity. During that period Gonzaga expanded upon his humanist and philosophical training by a noteworthy turn to theology. Evidence for this is found in the many scriptural, theological, and canonical books in his possession. Humanism, Aristotelian philosophy, and theological studies, that of scripture in particular, continued to reflect Gonzaga's intellectual interests for the remainder of his life.

During the years of his residence in Mantua, from 1537 to 1561, Gonzaga engaged in a reform of his diocese that drew from a wide variety of sources including his own family's political and cultural aspirations, the currents of reform thought discussed throughout Italy, particularly the thought of Gasparo Contarini, as well as the example of his friend and colleague Bishop Gian Matteo Giberti of Verona. Gonzaga ordered visitations of the parishes of his diocese in order to raise the standards of clerical life and work. He provided the student clerics at his cathedral school with a training in literature, liturgy, and basic theology. He had theological and liturgical books published for use in his diocese, including the catechism written by Leonardo de Marini. His own rooms at the episcopal residence of Mantua became an academy of sorts in which both clergy and prominent laymen of the diocese could gather to hear friars from the local Dominican convent and others give lectures on sacred scripture. He enacted a reform of local convents of nuns and did not hesitate to use the civil authority at his disposal during his regency of the duchy to enforce that reform. Gonzaga also sought to transform the piety of the Mantuan laity by means of more stringent norms of behavior in churches and the renewal of confraternal activity through the founding of the *Compagnia del Santissimo Sacramento*. For these activities he gained the support and admiration of his contemporaries, prelates such as Giberti, Contarini, Pole, and Morone.

Gonzaga came of age when the religious unity of Europe ended. He finished his life as the Council of Trent was providing a new clarity for the Roman Catholic Church. During his career he demonstrated an awareness of the complexities of the division between Catholics and Protestants. This awareness grew as a result of his presence at the papal court between 1527 and 1537, his acquisition of an extensive collection of Protestant theological works, his personal acquaintance with Italian Protestants, and his activity as a resident bishop for nearly a quarter of a century. Gonzaga rejected the essentials of Protestant theology. His loyalty to the Church of Rome was an element of his role as a northern Italian ruler. Nevertheless, this firmness was matched by an open-mindedness of approach to individual Protestants, as well as a notable degree of flexibility on certain matters of theology. In particular, his receptivity to the preaching of Bernardino Ochino and his unwillingness to obstruct the Capuchin's flight from Italy in 1542 bear this out. He did not fear dialogue on disputed questions, as long as it did not threaten the social order of which he was a guardian.

Notwithstanding his concern for reform in Mantua and his adherence to Catholic orthodoxy, Ercole Gonzaga was not what a later generation would call a model prelate. Throughout his career he engaged in pluralism and absenteeism, central abuses of the Church of his day. For many years he engaged in a bitter dispute with Cardinal Alessandro Farnese over possession of the abbey of Lucedio. Nevertheless, he grew increasingly uncomfortable with this problematic involvement in ecclesiastical wealth. In the 1540s, therefore, he renounced possession of the Aragonese diocese of Tarazona. He had come to appreciate the value of episcopal residence and recognized that he would never even visit Spain. He did not fail to maintain a pension from the diocese in order to reward family members and servants, however. Thus, he struggled to reconcile the demands of reform, as friends such as Contarini and Pole were then formulating them, with his role as a patron and ruler in northern Italy. He simultaneously attempted to maintain a clean conscience and to provide incomes for his family and friends in a manner consistent with what he viewed as his role as an honorable gentleman and patrician. In this regard he showed himself to be more than just a wealthy and self-aggrandizing Renaissance prelate and less than an ideal reformer in the mode of Contarini's *De officio episcopi.*

This paradoxical combination of values is reflected in Gonzaga's involvement in the Council of Trent. When he assumed his duties there in 1561 he continued to demonstrate the combination of reform sentiment and patrician style that was the hallmark of his entire career. He presided with great social authority in the midst of fierce debates by bishops and theologians. He approached the debates there from the perspective of one trained in both humanism and Aristotelian philosophy, and knowledgeable in sacred scripture. He examined the questions raised at the council in the light of his own experience as a diocesan reformer who had personal knowledge of Protestant theology and long-standing relationships with colleagues who had become Protestants. The political realties of Gonzaga power also impressed upon him the need to find pragmatic solutions to conciliar issues. Consequently, he demonstrated a flexible conservatism that sought to maintain the institution of the Roman Church while still responding to what he considered the most reasonable calls for reform. For example, he did not hesitate to distance himself from Pier Paolo Vergerio in 1546 when the Istrian bishop threatened to upset the social and religious balance of Mantua by discussing Protestant theology with ordinary priests. Yet, in that same year Gonzaga suggested that the Council of Trent remove the apocrypha from the Bible. His humanist and scriptural training made him particularly sensitive to the theological problems involving those books. His pragmatism on reform also manifested itself in a willingness, as late as 1562, to offer the Eucharist to the laity under both species.[2] Indeed, it was this pragmatic approach to the problems of the Church that eventually undermined his authority in the council. He alarmed the pope and curialists at the council when, in order to determine the stance of the majority of the

2. Jedin, *Storia,* 4/1: 256.

members of the council, he called for a provisional vote on whether the obligation of episcopal residence was *jure divino.*

The course of these events, from Gonzaga's studies in Mantua through to his work at the Council of Trent, forms a horizontal axis that charts his life in chronological terms. Nevertheless, studying his life along this axis alone does not remove all of the difficulty in understanding him. Ercole Gonzaga's life was filled with contradictions. He was a reformer of his clergy and the father of five children; a friend of heretics and the papal legate at the Council of Trent; a devoted pupil of Pomponazzi and a cardinal of the Roman Church. His life, with all of its contradictions, escapes complete explanation.

As paradoxical as these inconsistencies are, a partial explanation can be found in the matrix of many of Gonzaga's attitudes and actions: his elevated position in Italian society. Gonzaga's career can also be evaluated in terms of a vertical axis that is based upon his position in society and his relationship to others in Mantua and throughout Italy. While the horizontal axis emphasizes the changes his generation experienced and, consequently, the inconsistencies in his life, the vertical axis highlights that element of his career that remained constant: Cardinal Ercole Gonzaga was a prince-bishop who represented the interests and the ideals of a northern Italian ruling family. It is necessary to examine Gonzaga from this perspective if one is adequately to judge his career. Gonzaga did not look upon himself as hypocritical or as unusually inconsistent. He believed that his duties required a combination of values and commitments that arose from the various roles he played. He conscientiously carried out his duties as the spiritual ruler of the diocese of Mantua. He also upheld his responsibilities to the Gonzaga family, especially when, for many years, he was its leading representative. The mixture of obligations deriving from his spiritual and dynastic roles largely determined the range of choices available to him as bishop and ducal regent. However narrow this world view and however limited those choices may have been, Gonzaga did seek to fulfill his responsibilities as he understood them.

When Duke Federico Gonzaga died in 1540 and Ercole became the regent, Cardinal Gasparo Contarini wrote to him with encouragement. He told Gonzaga that he had the opportunity to teach other rulers, by means of his actions, about the true meaning of the office of the prince. Too many, according to Contarini, had learned that the office was for the benefit of the prince and not the people.[3] Gonzaga seems to have taken his role as prince seriously. It was his custom, during the years of his regency, to hold weekly audiences along with his co-regent, Duchess Margherita Paleologa, in the ducal palace of Mantua where any of their subjects could approach them. Gonzaga dispensed justice and favors in a manner fitting his role as a territorial ruler in northern Italy. Gonzaga presented an imposing figure of noble eminence. The Venetian ambassador Bernardo Navagero described Gonzaga to the Venetian Senate at the time he began his regency in 1540 as:

well built, tall, having a complexion that is between white and red. In his face there is a certain sweetness joined to an infinite and wonderful gravity such that anyone who sees him immediately has affection for him, but at the same time, together with that affection recognizes that he is worthy of reverence. The movements of his eyes and his other gestures are very grave and all are those of a prince; and finally every part of him, as regards the body, shows that he was born to greatness.[4]

At the heart of this idealized description is one thought: Ercole Gonzaga was a prince. Fortune had smiled upon him. He was rich, handsome, and powerful. Having received these gifts, he was intent on defending and preserving his honor and the honor of his family.

I have characterized Ercole Gonzaga as a patrician reformer. That is, I understand him to be one who, as the ecclesiastical representative of a ruling elite, saw himself as responsible for the reform of the local Church and used his influential place in society as a means to that

---

3. Gasparo Contarini to Ercole Gonzaga, July 13, 1540, Friedensburg, 53–54.
4. Albèri, *Relazioni,* 14. "Di proporzionatissimo corpo, grande di statura, di colore tra bianco ed il rosso; ha nella faccia una certa dolcezza congiunta con una infinita e mirabile gravità, dal che nasce che al primo aspetto ognuno se gli affezia, ma però talmente che insieme con quella affezione lo conosce degno di esser riverito. Ha movimenti d'occhi e di tutto il resto molto gravi, e tutti da principe; e finalmente ogni sua parte, quanto al corpo, mostra esser nato alla grandezza."

reform. This was particularly true after 1540, when he held the reins of both spiritual and temporal authority in the Mantovano. He employed temporal instruments such as civil proclamations to announce and enforce alterations in religious practice. His reform of the liturgical life of the diocese of Mantua, with a new focus on feast days that celebrated the Gonzaga family, further exalted the ruling house of the duchy. The years of Cardinal Gonzaga's regency saw an unprecedented interpenetration of religious authority and civil power.

Patrician reform is not a concept that has been used by scholars describing attempts to reform the Church in Italy in the sixteenth century. Rather, historians have focused on the role of humanism, a return to the theology of the patristic era, a generally evangelical call for reform, a renewed and reorganized spiritual life among both clergy and laity, and the activities of the Holy Office. While these areas hold great significance, an investigation that excludes other influences will overlook a reform that was as "worldly" as that of Ercole Gonzaga. Wealth and power oftentimes served to further Gonzaga's reform program. For this reason, his career presents a genuine model of reform that eludes more customary criteria and gives evidence of values distinct from either the highly humanistic and evangelical reform of individuals such as Gasparo Contarini and Reginald Pole or the sterner ways of Gian Pietro Carafa. Indeed, if there is a type of European reform that most resembles that of Gonzaga, it is that of the territorial princes of Germany. Those princes pressed reform as a part of a more general program for the administration of their own states.[5] That could also be said of Mantua under the rule of Ercole Gonzaga. This study broadens the concept of reform to include this worldly variety of patrician reform.

5. On the Reformation in the principalities of Germany see Euan Cameron, *The European Reformation* (Oxford: Oxford University Press, 1991), 267–72.

APPENDIX

The table below identifies the books of Cardinal Gonzaga that appear in the records of the *Mensa Vescovile* in the Archivio Storico Diocesano di Mantova, listed in the order in which Gonzaga either purchased them or had them bound. The titles given are transcriptions of the titles or descriptions as they appear in the original documents, with original spelling and capitalization. Bibliographical information is included where available. All archival references are from ASDM, MV.

Title	Author	Place and/ or publisher	Source	Date of purchase	Date of binding	Archival reference
uno offiti de la madonna	—	—	Mantua, Bartolomeo dei Crocii	9/27/1535	—	b. 3, f. 20r
uno offiti de la madonna	—	—	Mantua, Bartolomeo dei Crocii	1/29/1536	—	b. 3, f. 20r
uno tullio dofiziss	Cicero	—	Andrea Ragno	5/5/1536– 7/3/1537	—	b. 3, f. 18r
dui breviarii	—	—	Andrea Ragno	5/5/1536– 7/3/1537	—	b. 3, f. 18r
uno libro da imparar aschrivar	—	—	Andrea Ragno	5/5/1536– 7/3/1537	—	b. 3, f. 18r
una istituta	—	—	Andrea Ragno	5/5/1536– 7/3/1537	—	b. 3, f. 18r
la bibia, 5 vols.	—	Lyon	—	—	5/17/1537	b. 1, f. 61r
uno officio dala regina	—	—	—	—	5/19/1537	b. 1, f. 61r
cinque opere del Leutor	Martin Luther	—	—	—	5/23/1537	b. 1, f. 61r
de Armonia mundi	Francesco Zorzi	—	—	—	6/1/1537	b. 1, f. 61r
La notomia del corpo	—	—	—	—	6/1/1537	b. 1, f. 61r

(table continues)

Title	Author	Place and/or publisher	Source	Date of purchase	Date of binding	Archival reference
opusculo di sto. agostino	Augustine	—	—	—	6/2/1537	b. 1, f. 61r
libretto de comunione	—	—	—	—	6/2/1537	b. 1, f. 61r
de la observazione de la lingua latina	Mario Nizoli	—	—	—	6/19/1537	b. 1, f. 61v
dui volumi de Testi Canonici	—	—	—	—	6/21/1537	b. 1, f. 61v
de divinis nominibus et de celesti hierarchia	Dionysius the Areopagite	Venice, Benedetto Agnello —		1537	6/27/1537	b. 1, f. 61v
16 testamenti novi picoli	—	—	—	—	6/15/1537	b. 1, f. 61v
il decretale	—	—	—	—	7/14/1537	b. 1, f. 61v
Nicolo di Lira super bibia, 3 vols.	Nicholas of Lyra	—	—	—	7/17/1537	b. 1, f. 61v
Nicolo di Lira, 2 vols.	Nicholas of Lyra	—	—	—	7/21/1537	b. 1, f. 61v
uno morali di sto. gregorio	Gregory the Great	—	—	—	7/21/1537	b. 1, f. 61v
uno testamento novo picolo	—	—	—	—	7/21/1537	b. 1, f. 61v
tri libri . . . francisci georgi	Francesco Zorzi	—	—	—	7/21/1537	b. 1, f. 61v
uno Epistoli di S.to Paulo greche et latine	Paul	—	—	—	7/27/1537	b. 1, f. 62r
uno Eusebio	Eusebius of Caesarea	—	—	—	7/27/1537	b. 1, f. 62v
Baisio	Guido de Baisio	—	Brescia, Ippolito Capilupi	8/23/1537	—	b. 1, f. 44r
uno apiano alexandrino	Appianus Alexandrinus	—	Brescia, Ippolito Capilupi	8/23/1537	8/30/1537	b. 1, f. 44r; b. 1, f. 77r
Chrisostimo sopra le Epistole di San Paolo et gli atti degli Apostoli	John Chrysostom	—	Brescia, Ippolito Capilupi	8/23/1537	8/30/1537	b. 1, f. 44r; b. 1, f. 77r
Comentari di Cesare Legati	Caesar	—	Brescia, Ippolito Capilupi	8/23/1537	—	b. 1, f. 44r

Title	Author	Place and/ or publisher	Source	Date of purchase	Date of binding	Archival reference
Annotationi d'Horatio	Horace	—	Brescia, Ippolito Capiupi	8/23/1537	—	b. 1, f. 44r
Hireneo	Irenaeus of Lyon	—	Brescia, Ippolito Capilupi	8/23/1537	—	b. 1, f. 44r
Iustino	Justin Martyr	—	Brescia, Ippolito Capilupi	8/23/1537	—	b. 1, f. 44r
Pindaro tradotto	Pindar	—	Brescia, Ippolito Capilupi	8/23/1537	—	b. 1, f. 44r
Thucidide	Thucydides	—	Brescia, Ippolito Capilupi	8/23/1537	—	b. 1, f. 44r
Epithome Vadiane	Joachim Vadianus	—	Brescia, Ippolito Capilupi	8/23/1537	—	b. 1, f. 44r
sopra certi libri di Cicero	—	—	Brescia, Ippolito Capilupi	8/23/1537	—	b. 1, f. 44r
I comenti dell'oratione di Cicero	—	—	Brescia, Ippolito Capilupi	8/23/1537	—	b. 1, f. 44r
Le Croniche	—	—	Brescia, Ippolito Capilupi	8/23/1537	—	b. 1, f. 44r
Le descrittione di Siria Palestina Arabia	—	—	Brescia, Ippolito Capilupi	8/23/1537	—	b. 1, f. 44r
Le Inscrittioni di tutto il mondo	—	—	Brescia, Ippolito Capilupi	8/23/1537	—	b. 1, f. 44r
Topographia di Roma	—	—	Brescia, Ippolito Capilupi	8/23/1537	—	b. 1, f. 44r
uno plinio	Caius Pliny the Younger	—	—	—	9/26/1537	b. 1, f. 77r
un libro . . . stampato in Basilea . . . le deche di Livio	Livy	Basel	—	—	9/29/1537	b. 1, f. 77r
Dyonisio supra li Evangelii	Denis the Carthusian	—	Benedetto Britannico	10/8/1537	10/14/1537	b. 1, f. 56r; b. 1, f. 77v
Dyonisio sopra i Re	Denis the Carthusian	—	Benedetto Britannico	10/8/1537	10/14/1537 b. 1, f. 77v	b. 1, f. 56r;
Dyonisio sopra li salmi	Denis the Carthusian	—	Benedetto Britannico	10/8/1537 b. 1, f. 77v	10/14/1537	b. 1, f. 56r;
Dyonisio in Iosua	Denis the Carthusian	—	Benedetto Britannico	—	10/14/1537	b. 1, f. 77v

(table continues)

Title	Author	Place and/ or publisher	Source	Date of purchase	Date of binding	Archival reference
Quintiliano con li annotationi declamationi, 2 vols.	Quintilian	—	Benedetto Britannico	10/8/1537	10/19/1537	b. 1, f. 56r; b. 1, f. 77v
Opera de Grisostimo, 6 vols.	John Chrysostom	—	Benedetto Brtannico	10/8/1537	10/19/1537	b. 1, f. 56r; b. 1, f. 77v
Opera de Cipriano, 2 vols.	Cyprian of Carthage	—	Bendetto Britannico	10/8/1537	10/19/1537	b. 1, f. 56r; b. 1, f. 77v
uno Zacharia de concordantia evangelorum	Zacharias of Chrysopolis	—	Benedetto Britannico	10/10/1537	10/10/1537	b. 1, f. 57r; b. 1, f. 77r
Aimo della Consonantia Evangelorum	Haimo of Auxerre	—	Benedetto Britannico	10/10/1537	10/10/1537	b. 1, f. 57r; b. 1, f. 77r
uno Budeo, 2 vols.	Guillaume Budé	—	—	—	10/10/1537	b. 1, f. 77r
uno campense in Salmis	Jan van Campen	—	—	—	10/10/1537	b. 1, f. 77r
paraphrases campenses	Jan van Campen	—	Bendetto Britannico	10/10/1537	10/14/1537	b. 1, f. 57r; b. 1, f. 77r
Marullo super evangelium	Marco Marulo	—	Benedetto Britannico	10/10/1537	10/14/1537	b. 1, f. 57r; b. 1, f. 77v
Federici Nauseae	Fredericus Nausea	—	Bendetto Britannico	10/10/1537	10/14/1537	b. 1, f. 57r; b. 1, f. 77v
Expositiones in Epistola paulo	—	—	Benedetto Britannico	10/10/1537	10/14/1537	b. 1, f. 57r; b. 1, f. 77v
fasciculi conciliorum	—	—	Benedetto Britannico	10/10/1537	10/14/1537	b. 1, f. 57r; b. 1, f. 61v
omnium gentes mores	Johannes Boemus	—	Benedetto Britannico	10/10/1537	10/19/1537	b. 1, f. 57r; b. 1, f. 77v
de nativitate domini	Gregory of Nyssa	—	Benedetto Britannico	10/10/1537	10/19/1537	b. 1, f. 57r; b. 1, f. 77v
Opera Remigii	Remigius of Auxerre	—	Benedetto Britannico	10/10/1537	10/19/1537	b. 1, f. 57r; b. 1, f. 77v
Catalogi Erasmi	—	—	Bendetto Britannico	10/10/1537	10/19/1537	b. 1, f. 57r; b. 1, f. 77v
Arnobii in psalmos	Arnobius	—	Benedetto Britannico	10/10/1537	10/20/1537	b. 1, f. 57r; b. 1, f. 77v
Vallae Lucubrationes	Lorenzo Valla	—	Benedetto Britannico	10/10/1537	10/20/1537	b. 1, f. 57r; b. 1, f. 77v

Title	Author	Place and/ or publisher	Source	Date of purchase	Date of binding	Archival reference
bibia	—	—	Benedetto Britannico	10/10/1537	—	b. 1, f. 57r
Apothegmata erasmi	Erasmus	—	Bendetto Britannico	10/10/1537	—	b. 1, f. 57r
de mensibus	Theodore of Gaza	—	Benedetto Britannico	10/10/1537	—	b. 1, f. 57r
de Inventione oratoria	Cicero	—	Benedetto Britannico	10/10/1537	—	b. 1, f. 57r
Sadoletto in psalmum	Jacopo Sadoletto	—	Benedetto Britannico	10/10/1537	—	b. 1, f. 57r
de re rustica	Marcus Terentius Varro	—	—	—	10/10/1537	b. 1, f. 78r
di re cochinaria	Coelius Apicius	—	—	—	10/10/1537	b. 1, f. 78r
Agostino de civitate dei	Augustine	—	Benedetto Britannico	10/15/1537	10/19/1537	b. 1, f. 60r; b. 1, f. 77v
uno grisostimo in Epistola Paulo	John Chrysostom	—	Benedetto Britannico	10/19/1537 —	b. 1, f. 77v	
Vigilio contra Heresea	Vigilius	—	Benedetto Britannico	10/15/1537	10/20/1537	b. 1, f. 60r; b. 1, f. 77v
Antidoto contra Heresea	—	—	Benedetto Britannico	10/15/1537	10/20/1537	b. 1, f. 60r; b. 1, f. 77v
Ethica Aristotelis col comento del Fabro	Aristotle, Jacques Lefèvre d'Étaples	—	Benedetto Britannico	10/15/1537	10/20/1537	b. 1, f. 60r; b. 1, f. 77v
Bibia di 70 Interpreti	—	—	—	—	10/20/1537	b. 1, f. 57r
uno apoftecmata diogenes laertio	Diogenes Laertius	—	—	—	10/20/1537	b. 1, f. 77v
uno achelini Ciromantia	Alexander Achillinus	—	—	—	11/7/1537	b. 1, f. 78r
due dionisii opuscula minore, 2 vols.	Denis the Carthusian	—	—	—	11/7/1537	b. 1, f. 78r
uno Sto. Tomas super Epistola Paulo	Thomas Aquinas	—	—	—	11/10/1537	b. 1, f. 78r

(table continues)

Title	Author	Place and/ or publisher	Source	Date of purchase	Date of binding	Archival reference
Innocentio sopra al decretale	Innocent IV	—	Venice, Pietro Maria Carissimo	1537	11/10/1537	b. 3, f. 36r; b. 1, f. 78r
uno Albumasar	Albumasar	—	—	—	11/17/1537	b. 1, f. 78r
un ugo supra aforismi Ipocrati	Ugo Benzi	—	—	—	11/17/1537	b. 1, f. 78r
ugo super libros tegni galeni	Ugo Benzi	—	—	—	11/17/1537	b. 1, f. 78r
una opera sto agostino	Augustine	—	—	—	12/10/1537	b. 1, f. 169r
San Thomaso sopra le epistole di San Paolo	Thomas Aquinas	Johann Schotte	Benedetto Britannico	12/4/1537	12/12/1537	b. 1, f. 88r; b. 1, f. 169r
summa angelica	Angelo Carletti da Chiavasso	—	Venice, Benedetto Agnello	12/4/1537	12/12/1537	b. 1, f. 88r; b. 1, f. 169r
durantus super magister sent entiarum	Durand of St. Pourçain	—	—	—	12/23/1537	b. 1, f. 169r
Philoni Judeai	Philo	—	—	—	12/29/1537	b. 1, f. 83r
Beda in regum	Bede	—	—	—	12/29/1537	b. 1, f. 169r
Beda opuscula	Bede	—	—	—	12/29/1537	b. 1, f. 169r
Cornelii Celsi	Cornelius Celsus	—	Benedetto Britannico	1537	12/29/1537	b. 1, f. 83r; b. 1, f. 169r
Philippo pbr. Super Job	Philip the Presbyter	—	Benedetto Britannico	1537	12/29/1537	b. 1, f. 83r; b. 1, f. 169r
Catena aurea super psalmos	—	—	Benedetto Britannico	1537	12/29/1537	b. 1, f. 83r; b. 1, f. 169r
Jacobus Faber super epistolas canonicas	Jacques Lefèvre d'Étaples	—	Benedetto Britannico	1537	12/29/1537	b. 1, f. 83r; b. 1, f. 169r
Epitome sancti Augustini	Augustine	—	Benedetto Britannico	1537	—	b. 1, f. 83r
beda in testamento Veteri	Bede	—	Bendetto Britannico	1537	—	b. 1, f. 83r
beda de natura rerum	Bede	—	Bendetto Britannico	1537	—	b. 1, f. 83r
Polibio tradotto dal Lascari . . . de castramentatione romanorum	Polybius, Janus Lascaris, tr.	—	Venice, Benedetto Agnello	1537	—	b. 1, f. 32r

Title	Author	Place and/ or publisher	Source	Date of purchase	Date of binding	Archival reference
santo Thomaso sopra Santo Paolo	Thomas Aquinas	—	Pietro Maria Carissimo	1537	—	b. 3, f. 36r
de rebus turcharum	—	—	Benedetto Britannico	1537	—	b. 1, f. 83r
Summario della Scrittura Santa, 7 vols.	—	—	Mantua, Andrea, Libraro	1/5/1538	—	b. 1, f. 169v
tri Ugoni	Mattia Ugoni	—	—	—	1/23/1538	b. 1, f. 169r
uno di camerone	Giovanni Boccaccio	—	—	—	1/30/1538	b. 1, f. 169v
Opuscula dionisii	Denis the Carthusian	—	Venice, Alessandro di Bonacorsi	3/8/1538	—	b. 1, f. 164r
Glossa Ordinaria			Venice, Alessandro di Bonacorsi	3/8/1538	—	b. 1, f. 164r
opera Gregorii	Gregory	Paris	Venice, Alessandro di Bonacorsi	3/8/1538	—	b. 1, f. 164r
uno avicenna	Avicenna	—	—	—	3/22/1538	b. 1, f. 169v
uno Epistola Sto. Paolo del Lutero	Martin Luther	—	—	—	3/22/1538	b. 1, f. 169v
uno polidori	Polydore Vergil	—	—	—	3/22/1538	b. 1, f. 169v
uno officio Colibu	Jacquet of Mantua (Jacques Colebault)	—	—	—	3/23/1538	b. 1, f. 169v
uno alberto da carpo	Alberto Pio da Carpi	—	—	—	3/23/1538	b. 1, f. 169v
de rerum inventoribus	Polydore Vergil	—	—	—	4/3/1538	b. 1, f. 169v
epistoli di tulio	Cicero	—	—	—	4/13/1538	b. 1, f. 169v
filosofia cicerone cum de officiis	Cicero	—	—	—	4/13/1538	b. 1, f. 169v
uno didino in odisia grecho	Didymus Alexandrinua	—	—	—	4/13/1538	b. 1, f. 169v

(table continues)

Title	Author	Place and/ or publisher	Source	Date of purchase	Date of binding	Archival reference
uno marcantoni flaminio in salmos	Marcantonio Flaminio	—	—	—	4/13/1538	b. 1, f. 169v
omero [Greek], 2 vols.	Homer	—	—	—	4/13/1538	b. 1, f. 169v
mario nizola	Mario Nizoli	—	—	—	4/13/1538	b. 1, f. 169v
uno quintiliano	Quintilian	—	—	—	4/13/1538	b. 1, f. 169v
pietro victorio	Pietro Vettori	—	—	—	4/13/1538	b. 1, f. 169v
opera sup. Iliada et odisia omero	—	—	—	—	4/13/1538	b. 1, f. 169v
uno dictionario [Greek]	—	—	—	—	4/13/1538	b. 1, f. 169v
un libro franzeso	—	—	—	—	4/13/1538	b. 1, f. 169v
comentari Cesare	Caesar	—	—	—	4/15/1538	b. 1, f. 169v
Horatio	Horace	—	—	—	4/15/1538	b. 1, f. 169v
Terentio	Terence	—	—	—	4/15/1538	b. 1, f. 169v
Vergilio	Virgil	—	—	—	4/15/1538	b. 1, f. 169v
Vocabulario Greco et Latino	—	—	Alessandro, libraro Mantovano	6/1/1538	—	b. 1, f. 179r
summa tabiena	Giovanni Cagnazzo da Taggia	—	—	—	6/14/1538	b. 1, f. 229r
uno isolario	Benedetto Bordoni	—	—	—	6/15/1538	b. 1, f. 229r
Bibia in stampa de lion	—	Lyon	Bartolomeo Vicino	7/2/1538		b. 1, f. 181r
uno Campensis super salmis	Jan van Campen	—	—	—	7/16/1538	b. 1, f. 229r
uno missalo	—	—	—	—	8/5/1538	b. 1, f. 229r
uno salmista	—	—	—	—	8/5/1538	b. 1, f. 229r
suma ostiensa	Henry of Susa	—	—	—	8/7/1538	b. 1, f. 229r
uno duello con il vallo	—	—	—	—	8/7/1538	b. 1, f. 229r
uno vocabularium Iuris	—	—	—	—	8/7/1538	b. 1, f. 229r

Title	Author	Place and/ or publisher	Source	Date of purchase	Date of binding	Archival reference
uno libro spagnolo	—	—	—	—	8/7/1538	b. 1, f. 229r
libri da batezare, 6	—	—	Venice	9/4/1538	9/6/1538	b. 1, f. 258v; b. 1, f. 229r
uno Tulio de off.	Cicero	—	—	—	9/7/1538	b. 1, f. 229v
contra supersticiones	—	—	—	—	9/20/1538	b. 1, f. 229v
uno Cornelio Tacito	Tacitus	—	—	—	9/20/1538	b. 1, f. 229v
Dionisii in prophetas maiores	Denis the Carthusian	—	Benedetto Britannico	9/23/1538	—	b. 1, f. 201r
uno Exempla sacra scritura	—	—	—	—	9/23/1538	b. 1, f. 229v
Lutheri postilli	Martin Luther	—	Benedetto Britannico	9/23/1538	9/24/1538	b. 1, f. 201v; b. 1, f. 229v
Epitome santo Augustini	Augustine	—	Benedetto Britannico	9/23/1538	9/26/1538	b. 1, f. 201v; b. 1, f. 229v
Cesaria comentaria	Caesar	—	Benedetto Britannico	9/23/1538	9/26/1538	b. 1, f. 201v; b. 1, f. 229v
Exempla sacre Scritture	—	—	Benedetto Britannico	9/23/1538	9/27/1538	b. 1, f. 201r; b. 1, f. 229v
Erasmi in Leges pontificias	Erasmus	—	Benedetto Britannico	9/23/1538	9/27/1538	b. 1, f. 201r; b. 1, f. 229r
Pomeranii ad Romanos	Johann Bugenhagen	—	Benedetto Britannico	9/23/1538	9/27/1538	b. 1, f. 201r; b. 1, f. 229v
Melacthoni Loci comunis	Philip Melanchthon	—	Benedetto Britannico	9/23/1538	9/27/1538	b. 1, f. 201r; b. 1, f. 229v
Melacthon ad Romanos	Philip Melanchthon	—	Benedetto Britannico	9/23/1538	9/27/1538	b. 1, f. 201r; b. 1, f. 229v
Raineri in psalterium paraphrasis	Rayner Snoy	—	Benedetto Britannico	9/23/1538	9/27/1538	b. 1, f. 201v; b. 1, f. 229v
Varro de Lingua Latina	Marcus Terentius Varro	—	—	9/23/1538	9/27/1538	b. 1, f. 201v; b. 1, f. 229v
pomeranii in deuteronomio	Johann Bugenhagen	—	Benedetto Britannico	9/23/1538	—	b. 1, f. 201r
pomeranii in Job	Johann Bugenhagen	—	Benedetto Britannico	9/23/1538	—	b. 1, f. 201r

(table continues)

Title	Author	Place and/ or publisher	Source	Date of purchase	Date of binding	Archival reference
Germanus in Apocalipsis	—	—	Benedetto Britannico	9/23/1538	—	b. 1, f. 201r
uno tomo aquinatis	Thomas Aquinas	—	—	—	9/28/1538	b. 1, f. 229v
uno comentarii de la lingua latina	—	—	—	—	9/28/1538	b. 1, f. 229v
uno Columpadi suinguli Epistola	Johannes — Oecolampadius		Benedetto Britannico	9/23/1538	10/5/1538	b. 1, f. 201v; b. 1, f. 230r
Theofilacti in prophetas	Theophilact —		Benedetto Britannico	9/23/1538	10/5/1538	b. 1, f. 201r; b. 1, f. 229v
Zovingulli articoli	Ulrich Zwingli	—	Benedetto Britannico	9/23/1538	10/5/1538	b. 1, f. 201v; b. 1, f. 229r
Zovingulli epistulae	Ulrich Zwingli	—	Benedetto Britannico	9/23/1538	10/5/1538	b. 1, f. 201v; b. 1, f. 229v
Zovingulli super Exodum	Ulrich Zwingli	—	Benedetto Britannico	9/23/1538	10/5/1538	b. 1, f. 201v
Zovingulli super genesim	Ulrich Zwingli	—	Benedetto Britannico	9/23/1538	10/5/1538	b. 1, f. 201v; b. 1, f. 229v
Zovingulli super Heremiam	Ulrich Zwinguli	—	Benedetto Britannico	9/23/1538	10/5/1538	b. 1, f. 201v; b. 1, f. 229v
Zovingulli super Esaiam	Ulrich Zwingli	—	Benedetto Britannico	9/23/1538	—	b. 1, f. 201v
Zovingulli de providentia dei	Ulrich Zwingli	—	Benedetto Britannico	9/23/1538	—	b. 1, f. 201v
Cassianii de Incarnatione Domini	John Cassian	—	Benedetto Britannico	9/23/1538	10/12/1538	b. 1, f. 201r; b. 1, f. 229v
Dionisi in prophetas minores	Denis the Carthusian	—	Benedetto Britannico	9/23/1538	10/12/1538	b. 1, f. 201r; b. 1, f. 230r
Fulgentii	Fulgentius of Ruspe	—	Benedetto Britannico	9/23/1538	10/12/1538	b. 1, f. 201r; b. 1, f. 230r
Pellicani super evangelia	Konrad Pellikan	—	Benedetto Britannico	9/23/1538	10/12/1538	b. 1, f. 201r; b. 1, f. 230r
Catena aurea sancti tho.	Thomas Aquinas	—	Benedetto Britannico	9/23/1538	—	b. 1, f. 201r
Stefani Doleti	Etienne Dolet	—	Benedetto Britannico	9/23/1538	—	b. 1, f. 201r
uno comentari in Epistola paulo ad romanos	—	—	—	—	9/27/1538	b. 1, f. 229v

Title	Author	Place and/ or publisher	Source	Date of purchase	Date of binding	Archival reference
uno apocalipsis	—	—	—	—	10/12/1538	b. 1, f. 230r
uno euripida, 2 vols.	Euripides	—	—	—	10/12/1538	b. 1, f. 230r
de la opera di cicerona, 2 vols.	Cicero	—	—	—	10/12/1538	b. 1, f. 230r
uno Erodoto grecho	Herodotus	—	—	—	10/12/1538	b. 1, f. 230r
uno iustino	Justin Martyr	—	—	—	10/12/1538	b. 1, f. 230r
uno catasismo del Leuter	Martin Luther	—	—	—	10/12/1538	b. 1, f. 230r
catasisma cristiana	—	—	—	—	10/12/1538	b. 1, f. 230r
uno plutarcho grecho	Plutarch	—	—	—	10/12/1538	b. 1, f. 230r
uno Rodulfus in Leviticum	Rudolphus	—	—	—	10/12/1538	b. 1, f. 230r
uno sofochle	Sophocles	—	—	—	10/12/1538	b. 1, f. 230r
uno suida grecho	Suidas	—	—	—	10/12/1538	b. 1, f. 230r
uno tucidita grecho	Thucydides	—	—	—	10/12/1538	b. 1, f. 230r
uno cornucopia grecho	—	—	—	—	10/12/1538	b. 1, f. 230r
de la opera di cicerona, 3 vols.	Cicero	—	—	—	10/19/1538	b. 1, f. 230r
uno adciolo in Ethica aristotile	Donato Acciaiuoli	—	—	—	10/26/1538	b. 1, f. 230r
de la opera di cicerona	Cicero	—	—	—	10/26/1538	b. 1, f. 230r
uno sabelico	Marco Antonio Sabelico	—	—	—	10/26/1538	b. 1, f. 230r
Libretti no. 6 del Sanazaro de partu virginibus	Jacopo Sanazaro	—	—	Venice, Monsignore Aprutino	12/14/1538	b. 1, f. 243r
doi tomi di concilii stampati novamente	—	—	—	Venice, Monsignore Aprutino	12/14/1538	b. 1, f. 243r
un mappamondo	—	—	—	Hierolimo Suzarino	4/30/1544	b. 3, f. 113v

(table continues)

Title	Author	Place and/ or publisher	Source	Date of purchase	Date of binding	Archival reference
uno istrutione del principe Christiano	—	—	—	—	12/7/1546	b. 1, f. 331r
bocca de ferro . . . sopra la fisica	Ludovico Boccadiferro	—	—	—	12/18/1546	b. 1, f. 331r
suma de santo tomaso cioe la seconda parte et la seconda seconde, 2 vols.	Thomas Aquinas	—	—	—	12/19/1546	b. 1, f. 331r
lotavo libro della fisica	Aristotle	—	—	—	12/24/1546	b. 1, f. 331r
sessa super fisica	Agostino Nifo	—	—	—	12/24/1546	b. 1, f. 331r
suma de santo tomaso, 2 vols.	Thomas Aquinas	—	—	—	1/21/1547	b. 1, f. 331r
suma di santo thomaso	Thomas Aquinas	—	Venice, Henrico Hollonio	1/31/1547	—	b. 1, f. 278r
uno testamento novo latino	—	—	—	—	2/5/1547	b. 1, f. 331r
uno virgilio in 8o Griffo	Virgil	Sebastianus Griphius, Lyon	—	—	2/5/1547	b. 1, f. 331r
Libri Lutherani no. venti e doi	—	—	Germany, Camillo Capilupi	2/8/1547	—	b. 1, f. 277r
uno volume . . . del bocca de ferro	Ludovico Boccadiferro	—	—	—	2/25/1547	b. 1, f. 331r
tre alfabeti greci	—	—	—	—	2/26/1547	b. 1, f. 331r
uno officio dal capello	—	—	—	—	3/8/1547	b. 1, f. 331r
Santo Thomaso sopra lo evangelio di santo ioanne	Thomas Aquinas	—	Mantua, Francisco de Lanara	4/1/1547	—	b. 1, f. 278r
uno meditacione di sto. Agustino con li soi coloquii	Augustine	—	—	—	4/7/1547	b. 1, f. 331v
doi libri della justificatione tridentina	—	—	Henrico Hollonia	4/1547	4/13/1547	b. 1, f. 322r; b. 1, f. 331v

Title	Author	Place and/ or publisher	Source	Date of purchase	Date of binding	Archival reference
un libro che insegna ascrivere	—	Rome	—	—	4/19/1547	b. 1, f. 331v
doi terenti picoli	Terence	—	—	—	5/4/1547	b. 1, f. 331v
una catena Lippomani in Genesim	Luigi Lippomani	—	—	—	6/18/1547	b. 1, f. 331v
li madrigali a misura di breve libro	—	—	—	—	6/18/1547	b. 1, f. 331r
due erotimata grisolora	Manuel Chrysoloras	—	—	—	7/21/1547	b. 1, f. 415r
cento novelle stampato per il gioletto	Boccaccio	Venice, Gabriel Giolito de' Ferrari	—	9/23/1547	7/21/1547	b. 1, f. 371r; b. 1, f. 415r
Epistole Cicerone	Cicero	—	—	—	9/10/1547	b. 1, f. 415r
Costano Lascaro	Constantine Lascaris	Venice, Scoto	—	—	9/10/1547	b. 1, f. 415r
Costantino Lascaro, gregho	Constantine Lascaris	—	—	—	9/10/1547	b. 1, f. 415r
Oraciones de Ipocrate	Hippocrates	—	—	—	9/10/1547	b. 1, f. 415r
de fastis	Ovid	—	—	—	9/10/1547	b. 1, f. 415r
de fastis [bis]	Ovid	—	—	—	9/10/1547	b. 1, f. 415r
uno Terenti	Terence	—	—	—	9/10/1547	b. 1, f. 415r
uno Vergili	Virgil	—	—	—	9/10/1547	b. 1, f. 415r
Esenofonte grecho	Xenophon	—	—	—	9/10/1547	b. 1, f. 415r
Esenofonte grecho [bis]	Xenphon	—	—	—	9/10/1547	b. 1, f. 415r
uno Missal dala Stella	—	Venice, Stella	—	—	9/10/1547	b. 1, f. 415r
uno Salustio	Sallust	—	—	—	10/16/1547	b. 1, f. 415r
una filosofia morale de M. Grisostemo	John Chrysostom	—	—	—	11/3/1547	b. 1, f. 415r
una vitta de Ezelino	Rolandino da Padova	—	—	—	11/3/1547	b. 1, f. 415r

(table continues)

Title	Author	Place and/ or publisher	Source	Date of purchase	Date of binding	Archival reference
il graduale	—	—	Venice, J ulio dalla Valle	11/30/1547	—	b. 3, f. 196r
uno offiti	—	—	—	—	12/6/1547	b. 1, f. 415r
uno sessa de animalibus	Agostino Nifo	—	—	—	12/8/1547	b. 1, f. 415r
un Plauto di stampa di Basilea con le annotationi del Ioachino	Plautus, Joachim Camerarii, ed.	Basel	Padua, Giulio Gabrielli	4/20/1561	—	b. 3, f. 427r

BIBLIOGRAPHY

Primary Sources

ARCHIVAL

Archivio Segreto Vaticano, Acta Camerarii and Acta Vicecancellarii
Archivio di Stato, Mantova, Archivio Gonzaga
Archivio di Stato, Mantova, Archivio Notarile
Archivio di Stato, Mantova, Archivio Portioli
Archivio di Stato, Modena
Archivio Storico Diocesano di Mantova, *Mensa Vescovile*
Biblioteca Apostolica Vaticana, Barberiniana Latina. Codices 5788–93 contain
    correspondence of Cardinal Gonzaga for the period September 19, 1534, to
    December 4, 1546
Biblioteca Palatina di Parma, Ms. Affò 1207, ff. 183–257, *Vita del Cardinale Ercole*
    Gonzaga, by Ireneo Affò

PUBLISHED

Albèri, Eugenio. *Relazioni degli ambasciatori veneti al Senato.* Vol. 2. *Relazioni*
    di Mantova dall'anno 1540. Series 2. Florence: Tipographia e Calcographia
    all'insegna di Clio, 1841.
Aquinas, Thomas. *Libro del debito del Sacerdaote di San Thomaso d'Aquino.* Man-
    tua: Ruffinelli, 1560.
————. *Summa Theologiae* (IIa IIae). In *The Pastoral and Religious Lives,* edited
    by Jordan Aumann, O.P., vol. 47, 183–89. London: Blackfriars, 1973.
Aretino, Pietro. *Un Pronostico satirico di Pietro Aretino (MDXXXIIII).* Edited by
    Alessandro Luzio. Bergamo: Istituto italiano d'arti grafiche, 1900.
————. *Lettere di Pietro Aretino.* 3 vols. Edited by Fausto Nicolini. Bari: Laterza,
    1916.
Augustine, Saint. *Sancti Aurelii Augustini Hipponensis episcopi Opera omnia,*
    vol. 2, edited by J. P. Migne. Vol. 33 of *Patrologiae cursus completus sive biblio-*
    theca universalis, integra, uniformis, commoda, oeconomica omnium ss. patrum,
    doctorum scriptorumque ecclesiasticorum qui ab aevo apostolico ad Innocentii III
    tempora floruerunt. Paris: Garnier Fratres et Migne Successores, 1902.

————. *St. Augustine's Confessions*. 2 vols. Cambridge, MA: Harvard University Press, 1912.

Bembo, Pietro. *Opere del cardinale Pietro Bembo*. 4 vols. Venice: Hertzhauser, 1729. Anastatic reproduction, Ridgewood, NJ: Gregg Press, 1965.

Calini, Muzio. *Lettere conciliari (1561–1563)*. Edited by Alberto Marani. Brescia: Fratelli Geroldi, 1963.

Canisius, Peter. *Beati Petri Canisii, Societatis Jesu, Epistolae et Acta*. Edited by Otto Braunsberger. 6 vols. Frieburg: Herder, 1896–1923.

Cassirer, Ernst, Paul Oskar Kristeller, and John Herman Randall Jr., eds. *The Renaissance Philosophy of Man*. Chicago: University of Chicago Press, 1948.

Castellani, Giulio. *Vita di Monsignore Hercole Gonzaga Cardinale di Mantova*. Republished in *Opuscoli volgari di Mes. Giulio Castellani, editi e inediti*. Faenza: Conti, 1847, 3–26.

Castellani, Giuseppe. "La vocazione alla compagnia di Gesù del P. Antonio Possevino da una relazione inedita del medesimo." *Archivum historicum Societatis Iesu* 14 (1945): 102–24.

Castiglione, Baldesar. *The Book of the Courtier*. Translated by George Bull. New York: Viking Penguin, 1967.

Contarini, Gasparo. *Gasparis Contareni Cardinalis Opera*. Paris: Sebastianum Nivellium, 1571.

————. *The Office of a Bishop*. Translated and edited by John Patrick Donnelly, S.J. Milwaukee: Marquette University Press, 2002.

Croli da Colpetrazzo, Bernardinus A., O.F.M. Cap. *Historia ordinis fratrum minorum capuccinorum (1525–1593). Liber primus praecipui nascentis ordinis eventus*. Edited by Melchior A. Pobladura, O.F.M. Cap. Vol. 2 of *Monumenta historica ordinis minorum capuccinorum*. Assisi: Collegio San Lorenzo da Brindisi, 1939.

Dittrich, Franz, ed. *Regesten und Briefe des Kardinals Gasparo Contarini (1483–1542)*. Braunsberg: Huye, 1881.

Drei, Giovanni. "Per la Storia del Concilio di Trento: lettere inedite del secretario Camillo Olivo." *Archivio storico italiano* 74 (1916): 246–87.

————. "La corrispondenza del cardinale Ercole Gonzaga presidente del Concilio di Trento." *Archivio per le Provincie Parmensi* 17 (1917): 185–242; 18 (1918): 29–143.

————. "La politica di Pio IV e del cardinale Ercole Gonzaga (1559–1560)." *Archivio della Reale Società di Storia Patria* 40 (1917): 65–115.

————. "Il cardinale Ercole Gonzaga alla presidenza del Concilio di Trento." *Archivio della Reale Società di Storia Patria* 40 (1917): 205–45; 41 (1918): 171–222.

Duckworth, George E., ed. *The Complete Roman Drama. All the Extant Comedies of Plautus and Terence, and the Tragedies of Seneca, in a Variety of Translations*. 2 vols. New York: Random House, 1942.

Firpo, Massimo, and Dario Marcatto. *Il Processo inquisitoriale del cardinale Giovanni Morone*. 6 vols. Rome: Istituto storico italiano per l'età moderna e contemporanea, 1981–95.

―――. *I Processi inquisitoriali di Pietro Carnesecchi (1557–1567)*. 3 vols. Vatican City: Archivio Segreto Vaticano, 1998–2000.

Fontanini, Benedetto. *Il Beneficio di Cristo con le versioni del secolo XVI. Documenti e testimonianze*. Edited by Salvatore Caponetto. DeKalb: Northern Illinois University Press; Chicago: Newberry Library; and Florence: Sansoni, 1972.

Friedensburg, Walter, ed. "Der Briefweschsel Gasparo Contarini's mit Ercole Gonzaga." *Quellen und Forschungen aus italienischen Archiven und Bibliotheken* 2 (1899): 3–64.

―――, ed. "Vergeriana 1534–1550: ein Nachlass." *Archiv für Reformationsgeschichte* 10 (1912–13): 70–100.

Giberti, Gian Matteo. *Iohanni Mathei Giberti Opera, nunc primum collecta, et ineditis ejusdem opusculis aucta*. Edited by Pietro Ballerini and Girolamo Ballerini. Verona: Berni, 1773.

Gonzaga, Ercole. *Constitutioni per la Chiesa Cathedrale di Mantova*. Mantua: Ruffinelli, 1558.

―――. *Ordo baptizandi secundum ritum Romane Ecclesiae ad usum civitatis Mantue*. Mantua: Ruffinelli, 1558.

―――. *Breve ricordo di Monsignor illustrissimo et Reverendissimo Monsignor Hercole Gonzaga Cardinale di Mantova delle cose spettanti alla vita dei chierici, al governo delle chiese, et alla cura delle Anime di questo suo Vescovato di Mantova*. Mantua: Ruffinelli, 1561.

―――. *Avvertimenti del Cardinale Ercole Gonzaga al nipote per l'andata in corte a Roma*. Edited by Florido Zamponi. Florence: Tipografia del Vocabolario, 1872.

Gonzaga, Scipione. *Commentariorum rerum suarum libri tres*. Rome: Salomonium, 1791.

Guicciardini, Francesco. *Maxims and Reflections of a Renaissance Statesman (Ricordi)*. Translated by Mario Domandi. Introduction by Nicolai Rubinstein. New York: Harper, 1965.

Hewett, A. Edith. "An Assessment of Italian Benefices Held by the Cardinals for the Turkish War of 1571." *English Historical Review* 30 (1915): 488–501.

Loaisa, García de. *Documentos ineditos para la historia de Espana*. Vol. 14, *Correspondencia del Cardinal de Osma con Carlos V y con su secretario Don Francisco de los Cobos, Comendador Mayor de Leon*. Edited by Miguel Salvá and Pedro Sainz de Baranda. Madrid: Imprenta de la viuda de Calero, 1849.

Madruzzo, Cristoforo. *La Corrispondenza del Cardinale Cristoforo Madruzzo*. Edited by A. Galante. Innsbruck: Wagneriana, 1911.

Marini, Leonardo. *Catecismo overo istruttione delle cose pertinenti alla salute delle anime, di commissione del Rmo. et Illmo. S. Cardinale di Mantova composto et publicato per la città e Diocesi sua da Monsignore Leonardo de Marini Vescovo di Laodicea suo Soffraganeo*. Mantua: Ruffinelli, 1555.

Neuner, J., S.J., and J. Depuis, S.J. *The Christian Faith in the Doctrinal Docu-*

ments of the Catholic Church. Bangalore: Theological Publications in India, 1973.

Pagano, Sergio. *Il Processo di Endimio Calandra e L'Inquisizione a Mantova nel 1567–1568.* Studi e testi, no. 339. Vatican City: Biblioteca Apostolica Vaticana, 1991.

Pole, Regnald. *De Concilio liber.* Rome: Paolo Manuzio, 1562.

———. *Epistolarum Reginaldi Poli S.R.E. Cardinalis et aliorum ad ipsum Pars III. Scilicet ab exitu Legationis suae Hispanicae usque ad mortem Card. Contareni Praemittuntur Apologetica Praefatio bisarium divisa, Diatriba, et plura Monumenta ad Epistolas huius Voluminis spectantia.* Brescia: Rizzardi, 1748.

———. *The Correspondence of Cardinal Pole.* Edited by Thomas F. Mayer. St. Andrews Studies in Reformation History. 2 vols. to date. Aldershot, England; and Burlington, VT: Ashgate, 2002–.

Pomponazzi, Pietro. *Lettere inedite di Pietro Pomponazzi.* Edited by Stefano Davari. Mantua: Segna, 1877.

Putelli, Romolo. *Vita, storia, e arte mantovana nel Cinquecento.* Vol. 1, *Prime visite pastorali alla città e diocesi.* Mantua: Peroni, 1934.

Segre, Arturo. *Un registro di lettere del cardinale Ercole Gonzaga (1535–1536), con un'appendice di documenti inedite (1520–1548).* Extract from *Miscellanea di storia italiana.* 3rd ser., vol. 16, 275–458. Turin: Fratelli Bocca, 1912.

Societas Goerresiana, ed. *Concilium Tridentinum. Diariorum, actorum, epistolarum, tractatuum, nova collectio.* 13 vols. Freiburg im Breisgau: Societas Goerresiana, 1901–2001.

Solmi, Edmondo. "Lettere inedite del cardinale Gasparo Contarini nel carteggio del cardinale Ercole Gonzaga (1535–1536)." *Nuovo archivio veneto,* n.s., 4 (1904): 245–74.

Tanner, Norman, S.J., ed. *Decrees of the Ecumenical Councils.* 2 vols. Washington, DC: Georgetown University Press, 1990.

Valdés, Juan de. *Cartas inéditas de Juan de Valdés al cardinal Gonzaga.* Edited by Jose Fernandez Montesinos. Madrid: Aguirre, 1931.

Vasari, Giorgio. *The Lives of the Artists.* Translated by Gaston C. de Vere. 10 vols. London: Macmillan, 1912–15.

Viterbo, Egidio da. "Egidio da Viterbo's Address to the Fifth Lateran Council." In *The Catholic Reformation,* edited by John C. Olin. New York: Fordham University Press, 1969.

Zagni, G. "Le visite pastorali e inquisitoriali alla diocesi di Mantova (1534–1560)." 2 vols. Laurea thesis, Università di Bologna, 1976–77.

Secondary Sources

Alberigo, Giuseppe. *I vescovi italiani al Concilio di Trento (1545–1547).* Florence: Sansoni, 1959.

Amadei, Federigo. *Cronaca Universale della Città di Mantova*. Edizione Integrale. 5 vols. Mantua: C.I.T.E.M., 1955.

Antonovics, A. V. "Counter-Reformation Cardinals: 1534–1590." *European Studies Review* 2 (1972): 301–27.

Ascarelli, Fernanda. *La Tipografia cinquecentina italiana*. Florence: Sansoni, 1953.

Battistini, Mario. *Fra Andrea Ghetti da Volterra, O.S.A., teologo, oratore, pedagogista*. Florence: Libreria editrice fiorentina, 1928.

Belfante, Carlo Marco. "Il Dono dell'abito: lusso e consuetudini sociali a Mantova nel Cinquecento." In *Per Mantova una vita. Studi in memoria di Rita Castagna*. Mantua: Publi-Paolini, 1991.

Bendiscioli, Mario. "Finalità tradizionali e motivi nuovi in una confraternita a Mantova nel terzo decennio del Cinquecento." In *Problemi di vita religiosa in Italia, Atti del Convegno di Storia della Chiesa in Italia*, Italia Sacra: Studi e documenti di storia ecclesiastica, no. 2. Padua: Antenore, 1960.

Bertazzi Nizzola, Laura. "Infiltrazioni protestanti nel ducato di Mantova (1530–1563)." *Bollettino storico mantovano* 2 (1956): 102–30; 4 (1956): 258–86; 7 (1957): 205–28.

Bietenholz, Peter G., and Thomas B. Deutscher, eds. *Contemporaries of Erasmus: A Biographical Register of the Renaissance and Reformation*. 3 vols. Toronto: University of Toronto Press, 1985–87.

Black, Christopher F. *Italian Confraternities in the Sixteenth Century*. Cambridge: Cambridge University Press, 1989.

Blaisdell, Charmarie Jenkins. "Politics and Heresy in Ferrara, 1534–1559." *Sixteenth Century Journal* 6 (1975): 67–93.

Boer, Wietse de. *The Conquest of the Soul: Confession, Discipline, and Public Order in Counter-Reformation Milan*. Leiden: Brill, 2001.

Borromeo, Agostino. "Archbishop Carlo Borromeo and the Ecclesiastical Policy of Philip II in the State of Milan." In *San Carlo Borromeo: Catholic Reform and Ecclesiastical Politics in the Second Half of the Sixteenth Century*, edited by John M. Headley and John B. Tomaro. Washington, DC: Folger Books, 1988.

Bossy, John. *Christianity in the West, 1400–1700*. Oxford: Oxford University Press, 1985.

Boyle, Leonard E., O.P. "Summae confessorum." In *Les genres littéraires dans les sources théologiques et philosophiques médiévales*. Louvain-la-Neuve: L'Institut d'Etudes Médiévales, 1982.

Brecht, Martin. *Martin Luther*. Vol. 2, *Shaping and Defining the Reformation*. Translated by James L. Schaaf. Minneapolis: Fortress Press, 1990.

Brown, Clifford. *Isabella d'Este and Lorenzo da Pavia: Documents for the History of Art and Culture in Renaissance Mantua*, Travaux d'humanisme et Renaissance, no. 189. Geneva: Droz, 1982.

Brown, Clifford Malcolm. "Paintings in the Collection of Cardinal Ercole Gonzaga: after Michelangelo's Vittoria Colonna Drawings and by Bronzino, Giulio Romano, Fermo Ghisoni, Parmigianino, Sofonisba Anguissola, Titian and Tintoretto." In *Atti del convegno internazionale di studi su "Giulio Romano e l'espanzione europea del rinascimento,"* October 1–8, 1989. Mantua: Publi-Paolini, 1991, 206–7.

Brunelli, Roberto. *Diocesi di Mantova*. Vol. 8 of *Storia religiosa della Lombardia*. Brescia: Editrice La Scuola, 1986.

Bujanda, J. M. de. *Index de Rome 1557, 1559. Les premiers index romains et l'index du Concile de Trente*. Vol. 8 of *Index des livres interdits*. Sherbrooke: Centres d'Études de la Renaissance; and Geneva: Librairie Droz, 1990.

Buschbell, Gottfried. *Reformation und Inquisition in Italien um die Mitte des XVI. Jahrhunderts*. Quellen und Forschungen aus dem Gebiete der Geschichte, no. 13. Paderborn: Ferdinand Schoningh, 1910.

Cameron, Euan. *The European Reformation*. Oxford: Oxford University Press, 1991.

Cantimori, Delio. *Eretici italiani del Cinquecento. Ricerche storiche*. Florence: Sansoni, 1939.

———. *Prospettive di storia ereticale italiana del Cinquecento*. Bari: Laterza, 1960.

Capasso, Carlo. *La politica di Paolo III e l'Italia*. Bologna: Zanichelli, 1902.

Caponetto, Salvatore. *La Riforma protestante nell'Italia del Cinquecento*. Turin: Claudiana editrice, 1992.

Cartwright, Julia. *Isabella d'Este, Marchioness of Mantua, 1474–1539, a Study of the Renaissance*. 2 vols. London: Murray, 1903.

Cashman, Anthony B., III. "Performance Anxiety: Federico Gonzaga at the Court of Francis I and the Uncertainty of Ritual Action." *Sixteenth Century Journal* 33, no. 2 (2002): 333–52.

———. "The Problem of Audience in Mantua: Understanding Ritual Efficacy in an Italian Renaissance Princely State." *Renaissance Quarterly* 16, no. 3 (2002): 355–65.

Castiglione, Giambattista. *Istoria delle scuole della dottrina cristiana*. Milan: Cesare Orena, 1800.

Cavana, Angelo. *La Biblioteca del Cardinale Ercole Gonzaga: testimonianza per una nuova sensibilità teologica*. Licentiate thesis, Pontificium Athenaeum Antonianum, Facultas Theologicae. Venice: Insititutum de Studiis Oecumenicis, 1995.

Cesareo, Francesco C. *Humanism and Catholic Reform: the Life and Work of Gregorio Cortese (1483–1548)*. Renaissance and Baroque Studies and Texts, vol. 2, Eckhard Bernstein, general editor. New York: Peter Lang, 1990.

———. *A Shepherd in their Midst: The Episcopacy of Girolamo Seripando (1554–1563)*. Villanova, PA: Augustinian Press, 1999.

Chambers, D. S. "The Economic Predicament of Renaissance Cardinals." In *Studies in Medieval and Renaissance History*, vol. 3. Lincoln: University of Nebraska Press, 1966.

Church, Frederic C. *The Italian Reformers 1534–1564*. 1932. Reprint. New York: Octagon Books, 1974.

Cian, Vittorio. "Pietro Bembo e Isabella d'Este Gonzaga." *Giornale storico della letteratura italiana* 9 (1887): 81–136.

Cione, Edmondo. *Juan de Valdés: la sua vita e il suo pensiero religioso.* 2nd ed. Naples: Fausto Fiorentino, 1963.

Cocconcelli, Angelo. *Le Rivaltà dei Gonzaga coi Farnese e la riconciliazione voluta da Pio IV a mezzo di San Carlo Borromeo e del Cardinale di Mantova.* Reggio Emilia: Tipografia Mario Corsi, 1937.

Coggiola, Giulio. "I Farnesi ed il ducato di Parma e Piacenza durante il pontificato di Paolo IV." *Archivio storico per le provincie parmensi* 3 (1903): 1–23.

Collett, Barry. *Italian Benedictine Scholars and the Reformation: The Congregation of Santa Giustina of Padua.* Oxford: Oxford University Press, 1985.

Comerford, Kathleen M. "Clerical Education, Catechesis, and Catholic Confessionalism: Teaching Religion in the Sixteenth and Seventeenth Centuries." In *Early Modern Catholicism: Essays in Honor of John W. O'Malley, S.J.,* edited by Kathleen M. Comerford and Hilmar Pabel. Toronto: University of Toronto Press, 2001.

Coniglio, Giuseppe. *I Gonzaga.* Milan: Dall'Oglio, 1967.

Creytens, Raimondo. "La riforma dei monasteri femminili dopo i Decreti Tridentini." In *Il Concilio di Trento e la riforma tridentina, atti del convegno storico.* Rome: Herder, 1965, 45–84.

D'Amico, John F. *Renaissance Humanism in Papal Rome: Humanists and Churchmen on the Eve of the Reformation.* Baltimore: Johns Hopkins University Press, 1983.

Davari, Stefano. *Notizie storiche intorno allo studio pubblico ed ai maestri del secolo XV e XVI che tennero scuola in Mantova tratte dall'Archivio Storico Gonzaga di Mantova.* Mantua: Segna, 1876.

———. "Cenni storici intorno al Tribunale dell'Inquisizione in Mantova." *Archivio storico lombardo* 6 (1879): 547–65, 773–800.

Deutscher, Thomas Brian. "Carlo Bascapè and Tridentine Reform in the Diocese of Novara (1593–1615)." Ph.D. diss., University of Toronto, 1978.

Dizionario biografico degli italiani. Rome: Istituto della enciclopedia italiana, 1960–.

Dizionario degli istituti di perfezione. Rome: Edizioni paoline, 1974–.

Donesmondi, Ippolito. *Dell'Istoria ecclesiastica di Mantova.* 2 vols. Mantua: Aurelio & Lodovico Osanna Fratelli, 1612–16. Reprint, Bologna: Forni, 1977.

Dorez, Léon. *La cour du pape Paul III d'après les registres de la trésorerie secrète (collection F. DeNavenne).* 2 vols. Paris: Ernest Leroux, 1932.

Drei, Giovanni. "Il cardinale Ercole Gonzaga alla presidenza del Concilio di Trento." *Archivio della Reale Società Romana di Storia Patria* 40 (1917): 205–45.

———. "La politica di Pio IV e del cardinale Ercole Gonzaga (1559–1560)." *Archivio della Reale Società Romana di Storia Patria* 40 (1917): 65–115.

Dreyfus, John, et al., eds. *Printing and the Mind of Man: An Exhibition of Fine Printing in the King's Library of the British Museum.* London: British Museum, 1963.

Enciclopedia Cattolica. Vatican City: Ente per l'Enciclopedia Cattolica e per il Libro Cattolico, 1949–54.

Eubel, Conrad. *Hierarchia catholica medii et recentioris aevi.* Vol. 3. *Saeculum XVI ab anno 1503 complectens.* Regensburg: Schmitz-Kallenberg, 1923.

Evennett, H. Outram. *The Spirit of the Counter-Reformation.* Edited by John Bossy. Notre Dame, IN: University of Notre Dame Press, 1968.

Faccioli, Emilio, ed. *Mantova. Le Lettere.* Vol. 2. Mantua: Istituto Carlo d'Arco per la Storia di Mantova, 1962.

Fantuzzi, Giovanni. *Notizie degli scrittori bolognesi.* 9 vols. Bologna: Stamperia di S. Tommaso d' Aquino, 1781–94.

Fenlon, Dermot. *Heresy and Obedience in Tridentine Italy: Cardinal Pole and the Counter Reformation.* Cambridge: Cambridge University Press, 1972.

Fenlon, Iain. *Music and Patronage in Sixteenth-Century Mantua.* Cambridge: Cambridge University Press, 1980.

Firpo, Massimo. "Filippo II, Paolo IV e il processo inquisitoriale del cardinal Giovanni Morone." *Rivista storica italiana* 95 (1983): 5–62.

———. *Tra alumbrados e "spirituali." Studi su Juan de Valdés e il valdesianesimo nella crisi religiosa del '500 italiano.* Florence: Olschki, 1990.

———. *Inquisizione romana e controriforma: studi sul cardinal Giovanni Morone e il suo processo d'eresia.* Bologna: Il Mulino, 1992.

———. *Riforma protestante ed eresie nell'Italia del Cinquecento.* Bari: Laterza, 1993.

Fletcher, Harry George. *New Aldine Studies: Documentary Essays on the Life and Work of Aldus Manutius.* San Francisco: Rosenthal, 1988.

Fontaine, Michelle M. "For the Good of the City: The Bishop and the Ruling Elite in Sixteenth-Century Modena." *Sixteenth Century Journal* 27 (1997): 27–41.

Fragnito, Gigliola. "Gli 'spirituali' e la fuga di Bernardino Ochino." *Rivista storica italiana* 84 (1972): 777–813.

———. *Il Cardinale Gregorio Cortese (1483?–1548) nella crisi religiosa del cinquecento.* Rome: Abbazia di S. Paolo, 1983.

———. "Ercole Gonzaga, Reginald Pole e il monastero di San Benedetto Polirone. Nuovi documenti su Luciano Degli Ottoni e Benedetto Fontanini (1549–1551)." *Benedictina* 34 (1987): 253–71.

———. "Evangelismo e intransigenti nei difficili equilibri del pontificato farnesiano." *Rivista di storia e letteratura religiosa* 24 (1988): 20–47.

Ginzburg, Carlo, and Adriano Prosperi. "Le due redazioni del 'Beneficio di Cristo.'" In *Eresia e riforma nell'Italia del Cinquecento.* Florence: Sansoni; and Chicago: Newberry Library, 1974, 135–204.

Gionta, Stefano. *Il Fioretto delle cronache di Mantova.* Mantua: Negretti, 1844.

Gleason, Elisabeth G. "Sixteenth-Century Italian Interpretations of Luther." *Archiv für Reformationsgeschichte* 60 (1969): 160–73.

———. "On the Nature of Sixteenth-Century Italian Evangelism: Scholarship, 1953–1978." *Sixteenth Century Journal* 9 (1978): 3–25.

———. "Italy and the Reformation." In *Reformation Europe: A Guide to Research II*, edited by William S. Maltby. Vol. 3 of *Reformation Guides to Research*. St. Louis: Center for Reformation Research, 1992, 281–306.

———. *Gasparo Contarini: Venice, Rome, and Reform*. Berkeley: University of California Press, 1993.

Graiff, Franco. "I prodigi e l'astrologia nei commenti di Pietro Pomponazzi al *De Caelo*, alla *Meteora*, e al *De Generatione*." *Medioevo* 2 (1976): 331–61.

Grassi, Maria Giustina. "La Deposizione con il cardinale Ercole Gonzaga in S. Egidio a Mantova." *Civiltà Mantovana*, 3rd series, 28, no. 8 (September 1993): 45–61.

Gregorovius, Ferdinand. *History of the City of Rome in the Middle Ages*. Translated by Annie Hamilton. 8 vols. London: George Bell and Sons, 1902.

Grendler, Paul F. *The Roman Inquisition and the Venetian Press, 1540–1605*. Princeton, NJ: Princeton University Press, 1977.

———. *Schooling in Renaissance Italy: Literacy and Learning, 1300–1600*. Baltimore: Johns Hopkins University Press, 1989.

———. *The Universities of the Italian Renaissance*. Baltimore: Johns Hopkins University Press, 2002.

Hallman, Barbara McClung. *Italian Cardinals, Reform, and the Church as Property*. Berkeley: University of California Press, 1985.

Hartt, Frederick. *Giulio Romano*. New York: Hacher Art Books, 1981.

Headley, John M., and John B. Tomaro, eds. *San Carlo Borromeo: Catholic Reform and Ecclesiastical Politics in the Second Half of the Sixteenth Century*. Washington, DC: Folger Books, 1988.

Hudon, William V. *Marcello Cervini and Ecclesiastical Government in Tridentine Italy*. DeKalb: Northern Illinois University Press, 1992.

———. "Religion and Society in Early Modern Italy: Old Questions, New Insights." *American Historical Review* 101, no. 3 (June 1996): 783–804.

Imbart de la Tour, Pierre. *Les origines de la Réforme*. Vol. 3, *L'évangélisme*. Paris: Hachette, 1914.

Intra, G. B. "L'Antica Cattedrale di Mantova e le tombe dei primi Gonzaga." *Archivio storico lombardo* 11 (1884): 486–98.

———. "Di Ippolito Capilupi e del suo tempo." *Archivio storico lombardo* 20 (1893): 76–142.

Jedin, Hubert. *Papal Legate at the Council of Trent: Cardinal Seripando*. Translated by Frederic C. Eckhoff. St. Louis and London: Herder, 1947.

———. *A History of the Council of Trent*. Vols. 1 and 2. Translated by Dom Ernest Graf, O.S.B. London: Nelson and Sons, 1949.

———. *Il tipo ideale di vescovo secondo la riforma cattolica*. Brescia: Morcelliana, 1950.

———. *Storia del Concilio di Trento*. Vols. 2, 3, and 4. Translated by Giulietta Basso. Revised by Igino Rogger. Brescia: Morcelliana, 1962.

———. *Crisis and Closure of the Council of Trent: A Retrospective View from the*

Second Vatican Council. Translated by N. D. Smith. London: Sheed and Ward, 1967.

————. *Riforma cattolica o controriforma? Tentativo di chiaramento dei concetti con riflessioni sul concilio di Trento.* 2nd ed. Translated by Marola Guarducci. Brescia: Morcelliana, 1967.

————. "Il cardinal Pole e Vittoria Colonna." In *Chiesa della fede, Chiesa della storia: Saggi scelti.* Brescia: Morcelliana, 1972, 513–31.

————. "Il figlio di Isabella d'Este: il cardinale Ercole Gonzaga." In *Chiesa della fede, Chiesa della storia: Saggi scelti.* Brescia: Morcelliana, 1972, 499–512.

Jung, Eva-Maria. "On the Nature of Italian Evangelism in Sixteenth-Century Italy." *Journal of the History of Ideas* 14 (1953): 511–27.

Kelly, J. N. D. *The Oxford Dictionary of Popes.* Oxford: Oxford University Press, 1986.

La Rocca, Guido. "Il contributo di B. Castiglione alla formazione della politica esterna gonzaghesca negli ultimi anni del papato di Leone X: 1519–1521." In *Mantova e i Gonzaga nella civiltà del Rinascimento.* Mantua: Mondadori, 1974.

Luzio, Alessandro. "Vittoria Colonna." *Rivista storica mantovana* 1 (1885): 1–52.

————. "Ercole Gonzaga allo Studio di Bologna." *Giornale storico della letteratura italiana* 8 (1886): 374–86.

————. *Michelangelo e i Gonzaga.* Mantua: Segna, 1887.

————. *Pietro Aretino nei suoi primi anni a Venezia e a la corte dei Gonzaga.* Turin: Loescher, 1888.

————. *Mantova e Urbino: Isabella d'Este ed Elisabetta Gonzaga.* Turin: Roux, 1893.

————. "Isabella d'Este e il sacco di Roma." *Archivio storico lombardo,* series 4, 10 (1908): 5–107, 361–425.

————. "La Prammatica di Ercole Gonzaga contro il lusso (1551)." In *Scritti in onore di Rodolfo Renier.* Turin: Loescher, 1912.

————. "I carteggi dell'Archivio Gonzaga riflettenti l'Inghilterra. *Nota 1* del Socio corrispondente Alessandro Luzio." *Atti della Reale Accademia delle Scienze di Torino* 53 (1917): 167–82; *Nota 2,* 53 (1918): 209–22.

————, ed. *L'Archivio Gonzaga di Mantova.* 2 vols. Verona: Mondadori, 1922.

Luzio, Alessandro, and Rodolfo Renier. "La coltura e le relazioni letterarie di Isabella d'Este Gonzaga." *Giornale storico della letteratura italiana* 35 (1900): 193–257.

Marcatto, Dario. *"Questo passo dell'heresia." Pietrantonio di Capua tra Valdesiani, "Spirituali," e Inquisizione.* Naples: Bibliopolis, 2003.

Mayer, Thomas F. *Reginald Pole: Prince and Prophet.* Cambridge: Cambridge University Press, 2000.

Mayer, Thomas F., and Peter E. Starenko. "An Unknown Diary of Julius III's Conclave by Bartolomeo Stella, a Servant of Cardinal Pole." *Annuarium Historiae Conciliorum* 24, no. 2 (1992): 345–75.

Mazzocchi, Matilde. "Aspetti di vita religiosa a Mantova nel carteggio fra il cardinale Ercole Gonzaga e il vescovo ausiliare (1561–1563)." *Aevum* 33 (1959): 382–403.

Mazzoldi, Leonardo, Renato Giusti, and Rinaldo Salvadori, eds. *Mantova: La Storia.* Vol. 2. *Da Ludovico Secondo Marchese a Francesco Secondo Duca.* Mantua: Istituto Carlo D'Arco per la storia di mantovana, 1963.

Meersseman, Gerard. "La riforma delle confraternite laicali in Italia prima del Concilio di Trento." In *Problemi di vita religiosa in Italia nel Cinquecento: atti del convegno di storia della Chiesa in Italia.* Padua: Antenore, 1960.

McGuinness, Frederick J. "The Counter Reformation in Italy." In *Reformation Europe: A Guide to Research II,* edited by William S. Maltby. Vol. 3 of *Reformation Guides to Research.* St. Louis: Center for Reformation Research, 1992.

McNair, Philip. *Peter Martyr in Italy: An Anatomy of Apostasy.* Oxford: Oxford University Press, 1967.

Michaud-Quantin, Pierre. *Sommes de casuistique et manuels de confession au moyen âge (XII–XVI siècles).* Louvain: Nauwelaerts, 1962.

Mozzarelli, Cesare. *Mantova e i Gonzaga dal 1382 al 1707.* Turin: UTET Libreria, 1987.

Nardi, Bruno. *Saggi sull'aristotelismo padovano dal secolo XIV al XVI.* Florence: Sansoni, 1958.

———. *Studi su Pietro Pomponazzi.* Florence: Le Monnier, 1965.

Nicolini, Benedetto. *Bernardino Ochino e la Riforma in Italia.* Naples: Ricciardi, 1935.

Norberg, Kathryn. "The Counter Reformation and Women: Religious and Lay." In *Catholicism in Early Modern Europe: A Guide to Research,* edited by John W. O'Malley. St. Louis: Center for Reformation Research, 1988.

Nugent, George Edward. *The Jacquet Motets and Their Authors.* Ann Arbor, MI: University Microfilms, 1973.

———. "Jacquet of Mantua." In *The New Grove Dictionary of Music and Musicians.* London: Macmillan, 1980.

O'Malley, John W. "Saint Charles Borromeo and the *Praecipuum Episcoporum Munus:* His Place in the History of Preaching." In *San Carlo Borromeo: Catholic Reform and Ecclesiastical Politics in the Second Half of the Sixteenth Century,* edited by John M. Headley and John B. Tomaro. Washington, DC: Folger Books, 1988.

———. *The First Jesuits.* Cambridge, MA: Harvard University Press, 1993.

———. *Trent and All That: Renaming Catholicism in the Early Modern Era.* Cambridge, MA: Harvard University Press, 2000.

Parker Mattozzi, Louisa. "The Feminine Art of Politics and Diplomacy: Duchesses in Early Modern Italy." Ph.D. diss., University of Virginia, 2003.

Paschini, Pio. *Pier Paolo Vergerio il giovane e la sua apostasia: un episodio delle lotte religiose nel Cinquecento.* Rome: Scuola tipografica Pio X, 1925.

———. "I monasteri femminili in Italia nel '500." In *Problemi di vita religiosa in Italia nel Cinquecento. Atti del convegno di storia della Chiesa in Italia.* Padua: Antenore, 1960.

Pastor, Ludwig von. *The History of the Popes from the Close of the Middle Ages.* Vols. 7–15. Translated by Ralph Francis Kerr. London: Kegan, Paul, Trench, Trubner, 1908–28.

Pastore, Giuse, and Giancarlo Manzoli. *Il Messale di Barbara.* Mantua: Editrice Sintesi, 1991.

Pescasio, Luigi. *Cardinale Ercole Gonzaga: presidente del Concilio di Trento (1505–1563).* Suzzara: Edizioni Bottazzi, 1999.

Pierce, Robert A. *Pier Paolo Vergerio the Propagandist.* Rome: Edizioni di storia e letteratura, 2003.

Pine, Martin. *Pietro Pomponazzi: Radical Philosopher of the Renaissance.* Padua: Antenore, 1986.

Piva, Paolo. *L'"Altro" Giulio Romano. Il Duomo di Mantova, la chiesa di Polirone, e la dialettica col medioevo.* Quistello: Officina Grafica CESCHI, 1988.

Polizzotto, Lorenzo. "The Medici and the Youth Confraternity of the Purification of the Virgin, 1434–1506." In *The Politics of Ritual Kinship: Confraternities and Social Order in Early Modern Italy,* edited by Nicholas Terpstra. Cambridge: Cambridge University Press, 2000.

Portioli, Attilio. "I sigilli del cardinale Ercole Gonzaga." *Archivio storico lombardo* 8 (1881): 64–67.

Prosperi, Adriano. *Tra evangelismo e controriforma: G. M. Giberti (1495–1543).* Rome: Edizioni di storia e letteratura, 1969.

———. "Clerics and Laymen in the Work of Carlo Borromeo." In *San Carlo Borromeo: Catholic Reform and Ecclesiastical Politics in the Second Half of the Sixteenth Century,* edited by John M. Headley and John B. Tomaro. Washington, DC: Folger Books, 1988.

Quetif, Jacobus, and Jacobus Echard. *Scriptores ordinis praedicatorum recensiti, notisque, historicis et criticis illustrati. . . .* 2 vols. Paris: Ballard, 1719–23. Reprint, New York: Burt Franklin, 1959–61.

Rebecchini, Guido. "Libri e letture eterodosse del cardinale Ercole Gonzaga e della sua 'familia.'" *Schifanoia* 22–23 (2002): 199–208.

Renier, Rodolfo. "Vergeriana: notizie sul Vergerio e due lettere inedite indirizzatte al medesimo cardinale Ercole Gonzaga." *Giornale storico della letteratura italiana* 24 (1894): 452–56.

Renouard, Antoine Augustin. *Annali delle edizioni aldine. Con notizie sulla famiglia dei Giusti e repertorio delle loro edizioni fino al 1550.* 1834. Reprint, Bologna: Fiammenghi, 1953.

Rezzaghi, Roberto. *Il "Catecismo" di Leonardo de Marini nel contesto della riforma pastorale del Cardinale Ercole Gonzaga.* Biblioteca di Scienze Religiose, no. 73. Rome: Libreria Ateneo Salesiano, 1986.

———. "Cronaca di un conclave: l'elezione di Pio IV (1559)." *Salesianum* 48 (1986): 549–81.

———. "L'Origine del seminario a Mantova ed il Capitolo XVIII della XIII sessione del Concilio di Trento." In *L'Impegno dell'educare. Studi in onore di Piet-*

ro Braido. Rome: Facoltà di Scienze dell'Educazione dell'Università Pontificia Salesiana, 1991.

Rodocanachi, Emmanuel. *Une protectrice de la Réforme en Italie et en France. Renée de France, duchesse de Ferrare.* 1896. Reprint. Geneva: Slatkine Reprints, 1970.

Rodríguez-Salgado, M. J. *The Changing Face of Empire: Charles V, Philip II, and Habsburg Authority, 1551–1559.* Cambridge: Cambridge University Press, 1988.

————. "Terracotta and Iron." In *La Corte di Mantova nell'età di Andrea Mantegna: 1450–1550/The Court of the Gonzaga in the Age of Mantegna: 1450–1550, Atti del convegno (Londra, 6–8 marzo 1992/Mantova, 28 marzo 1992),* edited by Cesare Mozzarelli, Roberto Oresko, and Leandro Ventura. Rome: Bulzoni, 1997.

Romani, Marzio A. "Finanze, istituzioni, corte. I Gonzaga da padroni a Principi (XIV–XVII sec.)." In *La Corte di Mantova nell'età di Andrea Mantegna: 1450–1550/The Court of the Gonzaga in the Age of Mantegna: 1450–1550, Atti del convegno (Londra, 6–8 marzo 1992/Mantova, 28 marzo 1992),* edited by Cesare Mozzarelli, Roberto Oresko, and Leandro Ventura. Rome: Bulzoni, 1997.

Rurale, Flavio. "Chiesa e Corte." In *La Corte di Mantova di Andrea Mantegna: 1450–1550/The Court of the Gonzaga in the Age of Mantegna: 1450–1550, Atti del convegno (Londra, 6–8 marzo 1992/Mantova, 28 marzo 1992),* edited by Cesare Mozzarelli, Roberto Oresko, and Leandro Ventura. Rome: Bulzoni, 1997.

Russell, Camilla. *Giulia Gonzaga and the Religious Controversies of Sixteenth-Century Italy.* Late Medieval and Early Modern Studies 8. Turnhout: Brepols, 2006.

Saccani, Anna. "Ercole Gonzaga e la riforma pretridentina della diocesi di Mantova." Laurea thesis, Università Cattolica di Milano, 1953–54.

Sainte-Marthe, Denis, and Paul Piolin, eds. *Gallia christiana in provincias ecclesiasticas distributa qua series et historia archiepiscoporum, episcoporum et abbatum Franciae vicinorumque ditionum.* Paris: Victor Palmé, 1865–70.

Scaduto, Mario. *Storia della Compagnia di Gesù in Italia.* Vol. 3. *L'Epoca di Giacomo Lainez. Il Governo.* Rome: Civiltà Cattolica, 1963.

————. *Storia della Compagnia di Gesù in Italia.* Vol. 4. *L'Epoca di Giacomo Lainez. L'Azione.* Rome: Civiltà Cattolica, 1974.

Schmitt, Charles B. *Aristotle and the Renaissance.* Cambridge, MA: Harvard University Press, 1983.

————. "Aristotle's Ethics in the Sixteenth Century: Some Preliminary Considerations." In *Ethik im Humanismus,* edited by W. Ruegg and D. Wuttke. Beitrage zur Humanismusforschung 5. Boppard: Harald Boldt, 1979, 87–112. Reprinted in Charles B. Schmitt, *The Aristotelian Tradition and Renaissance Universities.* London: Variorum Reprints, 1984.

Schmitt, Charles B., et al., eds. *The Cambridge History of Renaissance Philosophy.* Cambridge: Cambridge University Press, 1988.

Schutte, Anne Jacobson. *Pier Paolo Vergerio: The Making of an Italian Reformer.* Geneva: Droz, 1977.

————. "Periodization of Sixteenth-Century Italian Religious History: The Post-Cantimori Paradigm Shift." *Journal of Modern History* 61 (1989): 269–84.

Seidel-Menchi, Silvana. "Le discussioni su Erasmo nell'Italia del Rinascimento: Ambrogio Flandino vescovo a Mantova, Ambrogio Quistelli teologo padovano e Alberto Pio principe di Carpi." In *Società, politica, e cultura a Carpi ai tempi di Alberto III Pio.* 2 vols. Padua: Antenore, 1978, vol. 1, 291–382.

————. "Inquisizione come repressione o inquisizione come mediazione? Una proposta di periodizzazione." *Annuario dell'istituto storico italiano per l'età moderna e contemporanea* 35–36 (1983–84): 53–77.

————. *Erasmo in Italia: 1520–1580.* Turin: Boringhieri, 1987.

Sensi, Mario. "Sinodi e visite pastorali in Umbria nel '200, '300 e '400." In *Vescovi e diocesi in Italia dal XIV alla metà del XVI secolo.* Italia Sacra, no. 43. Rome: Herder, 1990.

Short Title Catalogue of Books Printed in German-Speaking Countries and German Books Printed in Other Countries from 1455 to 1600, now in the British Museum. London: Trustees of the British Museum, 1962.

Short Title Catalogue of Books Printed in Italy and of Italian Books Printed in Other Countries from 1465 to 1600, now in the British Museum. London: Trustees of the British Museum, 1958.

Simoncelli, Paolo. *Il caso Reginald Pole. Eresia e santità nelle polemiche religiose del Cinquecento.* Rome: Edizioni di storia e letteratura, 1977.

————. *Evangelismo italiano del Cinquecento. Questione religiosa e nicodemismo politico.* Rome: Istituto storico italiano per l'età moderna e contemporanea, 1979.

————. "Inquisizione romana e riforma in Italia." *Rivista storica italiana* 100 (1988): 5–125.

Simonsohn, Shlomo. *History of the Jews in the Duchy of Mantua.* Publications of the Diaspora Research Institute, no. 17. Jerusalem: Kiryath Sepher, 1977.

Smalley, Beryl. *The Study of the Bible in the Middle Ages.* Notre Dame, IN: University of Notre Dame Press, 1964.

Smith, William, ed. *A Dictionary of Christian Biography.* 4 vols. London: J. Murray, 1900.

Solmi, Edmondo. "La fuga di Bernardino Ochino secondo i documenti dell'Archivio Gonzaga di Mantova." *Bullettino senese di storia patria* 15 (1908): 23–98.

Sperling, Jutta Gisela. *Convents and the Body Politic in Late Renaissance Venice.* Chicago: University of Chicago Press, 1999.

Stella, Aldo. "La lettera del Cardinale Contarini sulla predestinazione." *Rivista di storia della Chiesa in Italia* 15 (1961): 411–41.

Šusta, Josef, ed. *Die Römische Curie und das Concil von Trient unter Pius IV. Actenstücke zur Geschichte des Concils von Trient.* 4 vols. Vienna: Alfred Hölder, 1904–14.

Tacchi Venturi, Pietro. *Storia della Compagnia di Gesù in Italia.* Vol. 2, part 1:

Dalla nascita del fondatore alla solenne approvazione dell'Ordine (1491–1540).
Rome: Civiltà Cattolica, 1951.

———. *Storia della Compagnia di Gesù in Italia.* Vol. 2, part 2: *Dalla solenne approvazione dell'Ordine alla morte del fondatore (1540–1556).* Rome: Civiltà Cattolica, 1951.

Tamalio, Raffaele. *Ferrante Gonzaga alla corte spagnola di Carlo V.* Mantua: Gianluigi Arcari Editore, 1991.

———. *Federico Gonzaga alla corte di Francesco I di Francia: nel carteggio privato con Mantova (1515–1517).* Paris: Champion, 1994.

Tiraboschi, Girolamo. *Biblioteca modenese; o Notizie della vita e delle opere degli scrittori nati negli stati del serenissimo signor duca di Modena.* 6 vols. Modena: Società tipografica, 1781–86.

———. *Storia della letteratura italiana.* 9 vols. First published 1782–85. Florence: Molini, Landi, 1824.

Torelli, Pietro. *L'Archivio Gonzaga di Mantova.* Vol. 1. Ostiglia: Reale Accademia Virgiliana di Mantova, 1920.

Trisco, Robert. "Carlo Borromeo and the Council of Trent: The Question of Reform." In *San Carlo Borromeo: Catholic Reform and Ecclesiastical Politics in the Second Half of the Sixteenth Century,* edited by John M. Headley and John B. Tomaro. Washington, DC: Folger Books, 1988.

Vaini, Mario. "Gli statuti di Francesco Gonzaga IV Capitano. Prime ricerche." *Atti e memorie dell'Accademia Virgiliana di Mantova,* n.s., 56 (1988): 187–214.

Veneziani, Paolo. *La Tipografia a Brescia nel XV secolo. Biblioteca di bibliografia italiana.* Florence: Olschki, 1986.

Wilson, Nigel Guy. *From Byzantium to Italy: Greek Studies in the Italian Renaissance.* Baltimore: Johns Hopkins University Press, 1992.

Wood, Jeryldene M. *Women, Art, and Spirituality: The Poor Clares in Early Modern Italy.* Cambridge: Cambridge University Press, 1996.

INDEX

Caesar, Julius, 31, 254, 260, 261
Cagnazzo da Taggia, Giovanni, 27, 83, 260
Calandra, Endimio, 20n, 23–24, 88, 91, 127–28, 131, 142–44, 145, 148, 156, 210n29
Calandra, Giovanni Giacomo, 142
Calandra, Sabino, 142
Calvin, John, 137
Camerarii, Joachin, 266
Campen, Jan van, 22, 23, 256, 260
Campeggi, Camillo, 143
Campeggi family, 7
Capilupi, Camillo, 29, 38–39, 57, 66, 220–21
Capilupi, Ippolito, 53, 63, 135, 180, 206, 223, 254, 255
Capodistria, 36, 132–33, 135
Capuchin Franciscans, 67, 127–32
Carafa, Carlo (cardinal), 191, 192, 194
Carafa, Gian Pietro (cardinal). *See* Paul IV
Carafa family, 191, 193
Carletti da Chiavasso, Angelo, 26, 83, 258
Carmelites, xiv, 67
Casale, 82, 174, 176
Caselli, Tommaso, xv, 21n57, 42, 237, 241, 242
Cassian, John, 21, 26, 262
Castellani, Giulio, 46, 75
Castiglione, Baldassare, 14, 159
Catarino Politi, Ambrogio, O.P., 145
Cateau-Cambresis, Peace of, 190
Catherine of Austria, 174, 184
Cellini, Benvenuto, 41
Cerea, 89
Cerutti, Antonio, 79, 81, 90, 91, 113
Cervini, Marcello (cardinal). *See* Marcellus II
Charles V (emperor), 2, 52, 55–58, 61, 66, 141, 159, 160, 161, 162, 166, 169, 170, 172–76, 177, 181, 182, 183, 184, 185–91, 200, 201, 204, 207, 212, 222, 223, 226
Chierigati, Francesco, 30n80
Chrysoloras, Manuel, 265
Chrysostom, John, 21, 25, 151, 254, 256, 257, 265
Cicero, Marcus Tullius, 9, 10, 31n83, 32, 78, 253, 255, 257, 259, 261, 263, 265
Cipada, Giulio, 136
Clement VII (pope), 11, 12n31, 15, 16, 17, 161, 178, 197
Cobos, Francisco de los, 177
Colonna, Prospero, 171
Colonna, Vittoria, 72, 123, 128
Colonna family, 15
Conciliarism, 201–3, 239
Constance, Council of, 203, 239
Contarini, Gasparo (cardinal), xvii, 17, 23, 25, 29, 30, 39, 40, 42, 47–49, 50, 51, 54, 57n44, 62, 66, 70, 72, 75, 86, 89, 92, 118–27, 144, 146, 151, 155, 157, 164, 199, 202, 206, 247–52
Cornelius Celsus, 32, 258
Cortese, Gregorio, cardinal, 40, 46, 47, 164–65
Cortesi, Paolo, 53
Costantino da Carrara, 147–50
Cratander, Andreas, 26
Cremona, 147, 175
Croli da Colpetrazzo, Bernardino, 130, 131
Cueva, Cardinal Bartolomé, 193
Cyprian of Carthage, 25, 256

Da Faenza, Angelo, O.P., 109
Dalle Arme, Francesco, 33, 37–39
D'Aragona, Tulia, 64
D'Armagnac, Georges (cardinal), 205
D'Avalos, Alfonso, 173, 174, 175, 177
Da Vicenza, Francesco, 120
Degli Ottoni, Luciano, 151–55
Delfino, Antonio, 167
Della Rovere, Francesco Maria (duke of Urbino), 3
Della Rovere, Virgina, 225
Del Monte, Giovanni Maria (cardinal). *See* Julius III
Del Vasto, marquis. *See* D'Avalos, Alfonso
Denis the Carthusian, 21, 42, 255, 257, 259, 261, 262
De Plotis, Bernardino, 30n80, 180
D'Este, Ercole (duke of Ferrara), 30, 60–61, 129, 148–49, 182, 201, 203–6, 210, 212n33, 222
D'Este, Ippolito (cardinal), 133, 191, 192
D'Este, Isabella (marquise of Mantua), 2, 3–4, 7, 8, 9, 10, 12, 14–15, 54, 110, 160, 191, 246
D'Hostillia, Pietro, 79
Di Capua, Isabella, 141

Ruling Peacefully: Cardinal Ercole Gonzaga and Patrician Reform in Sixteenth-Century Italy was designed and typeset in Garamond by Kachergis Book Design of Pittsboro, North Carolina. It was printed on 60-pound Natures Natural and bound by Thomson-Shore of Dexter, Michigan.